Beyond the Secular

SUNY series in Contemporary Continental Philosophy

Dennis J. Schmidt, editor

Beyond the Secular

Jacques Derrida and the
Theological-Political Complex

ANDREA CASSATELLA

Cover image: Ayed M. K. Arafah, *The Secret*, 2017. Used with permission.

Published by State University of New York Press

© 2023 State University of New York

All rights reserved

Printed in the United States of America

No part of this book may be used or reproduced in any manner whatsoever without written permission. No part of this book may be stored in a retrieval system or transmitted in any form or by any means including electronic, electrostatic, magnetic tape, mechanical, photocopying, recording, or otherwise without the prior permission in writing of the publisher.

For information, contact State University of New York Press, Albany, NY
www.sunypress.edu

Library of Congress Cataloging-in-Publication Data

Name: Cassatella, Andrea, author.
Title: Beyond the secular : Jacques Derrida and the theological-political complex / Andrea Cassatella.
Description: Albany : State University of New York Press, [2023]. | Series: SUNY series in contemporary continental philosophy | Includes bibliographical references and index.
Identifiers: LCCN 2022049719 | ISBN 9781438493879 (hardcover : alk. paper) | ISBN 9781438493893 (ebook) | ISBN 9781438493886 (pbk. : alk. paper)
Subjects: LCSH: Derrida, Jacques. | Race.
Classification: LCC B2430.D484 C3727 2023 | DDC 194—dc23/eng/20230510
LC record available at https://lccn.loc.gov/2022049719

10 9 8 7 6 5 4 3 2 1

To my families

Contents

Acknowledgments	ix
List of Abbreviations	xiii
Introduction	1
Chapter 1 The Politics of Language and Translation	17
Chapter 2 The Time of Political Thought	61
Chapter 3 The Secular as Theological-Political	111
Chapter 4 Democracy beyond Secularism?	151
Chapter 5 Islam, Religion, and Democracy	191
Notes	217
Bibliography	259
Index	279

Acknowledgments

This book has multiple and distant origins that found their way in a relentless urge to interrogate the cultural and intellectual sources of modern exclusions of difference, of which currently and formerly colonized people and refugees are perhaps among the most dramatic examples. The accidental encounter with the work of Jacques Derrida during my doctoral studies provided critical and vertiginous sources for this pursuit.

Various engagements and critiques from a number of people over the years, and in different contexts, have significantly contributed to the final form of this book. In Canada, my thanks go to Willi Goetschel, Rebecca Comay, Simone Chambers, and Ruth Marshall. Willi has set an example of creative and critical thinking and offered invaluable mentorship over time. Rebecca's ruthless criticisms of my early understanding of Derrida have pushed me to align philosophical rigor with analytical depth. Simone's unremitting demands for clarity have left a mark that has become a conscious habit. Ruth's combination of critical spirit and attention for concrete situations has offered an inspirational model of intellectual engagement beyond the academy. Thanks are also owed to Catherine Kellogg, who enthusiastically encouraged the transformation of my PhD dissertation into a book, and to David Dorenbaum, who stood by me during the most difficult phases of my doctoral studies. In Palestine, I greatly benefited from numerous discussions relevant to this project during seminars, long commuting through Israeli check-points, and food gatherings with Shaira Vadasaria, Athina Tesfa, Sobhi Samour, Jens Haendeler, Gary English, Emilio Distretti, Haneen Maikey, Dominique Day, Rana Barakat, Omar Hamidat, Rahaf Salahat, Baha Budeir, Zeina Melhem, and Bashir Bashir. To my students at Al-Quds University, I want express the deepest gratitude for the lessons about embodied thinking, kindness, and steadfastness that they offered me as gifts. Without them, this book would have not been possible in its current form. In South Africa, I would like to thank Abdulkhader Tayob for his generous and penetrating criticism of my work; Mamadou Diawara for being a *grand frère* of Sahelic wisdom in our numerous discussions there and over the years, and above all, Uhuru Phalafala, for providing creative feedback and sustaining me unconditionally. To the unique community of the Makerere Institute of Social Research in Uganda, I want to express my gratitude for the rigorous engagement and criticism of some key ideas articulated in this book and also for the enthusiastic support and welcome to my new home.

Thanks go also to the University of Toronto's Center for Ethics, Al-Quds University, Columbia Global Centers Amman, the University of Cape Town's Center for Contemporary Islam, the University of Ghana's Institute of African Studies, Stellenbosch Institute for Advance Study, the University of Edinburgh's Race.ed Network and Divinity School, and Makerere Institute of Social Research for offering me the opportunity to present various chapters and engage in extremely productive discussions.

Generous support for the preparation of this manuscript came from a number of institutions. The Columbia Global Centers Amman in Jordan offered a Visiting Fellowship when I needed it the most, particularly after unsettling years spent in Palestine. To its director, Safwan Masri, as well as Hanya Salah and Ahmad Al-Mousa, sincere thanks for having provided me with the space and support to think deeply about, and articulate, the core argument of this book. The writing of the last chapter was financially supported by a National Research Foundation Fellowship at the University of Cape Town. I want to express my gratitude to the research group on Islam and African Publics for the critical, rich, and generous feedback it provided. A Research Fellowship at Stellenbosch Institute for Advance Study allowed for a beautiful, interdisciplinary, and stimulating environment where I could complete the manuscript. A special thanks goes to the director, Edward Kirumira, who encouraged me during my residence and importantly contributed to the decision to continue my work in Africa. Various parts of the manuscript appeared earlier.

Portions of chapter 1 were first published in "Secularism and the Politics of Translation," *Contemporary Political Theory* 18 (2019): 65–87; and in "Secular Translation: Shaping the Sense of African Social Realities" in Mamadou Diawara, Elisio Macamo and Jean-Bernard Ouedraogo (eds.), *Translation Revisited: Contesting the Sense of African Social Realities* (Cambridge: Cambridge University Press, 2018). A section of chapter 2 was previously published as "Normativity without Telos: The Messianic in the Thought of Jacques Derrida," *Bamidbar: Journal of Jewish Thought and Philosophy, Passagen Verlag* 4, no. 2 (2012): 24–43. chapter 3 is a revisitation of "Jacques Derrida on the Secular as Theologico-Political," *Philosophy and Social Criticism* 42 (2016): 1059–81.

Among the colleagues and friends who have enriched, challenged, debated, and supported the ideas of this book at different stages of its development, I want to thank especially Gil Anidjar, Miriam Abu Samra, Adrian Atanasescu, Laila Atshan, Silvana Carotenuto, Azar Dakwar, Igor Drljaca, Frieda Ekotto, Rodolphe Gasché, Margaret Haderer, Ivana Ilicic, Xunming Huang, Marthe Djilo Kamga, Ayman Khalifa, Sharry Lapp, Elisio Makamo, Mahmood Mamdani, Jaby Mathew, Chika Mba, Kim Nakjung, Michael Naas, Salman Sayyid, Igor Shoikhedbrod, Kirsty Wright, and Shirabe Yamada.

Thanks are also owed to Michael Rinella, an editor at SUNY Press, who has been particularly attentive, understanding, and helpful throughout the publication process, the press's two reviewers for their constructive and generous criticisms, and Tim Morris, who helped with the editing.

I dedicate this book to my immediate family, who has supported me over the years, and the "family" I left in Palestine. Giuseppe Cassatella and Rosana Dukić: my first and deepest gratitude goes to you. Thanks go also to my brother, Simone, who shares with me the dissipating force of our backgrounds, and to my beloved ones in Palestine. My work brought me far from you for many years now, but perhaps never so close to some of the traces and struggles that so intimately connect us.

August 2022

Abbreviations of Works by Derrida

AANJ   "Above All, No Journalists!" Trans. Samuel Weber. In *Religion and Media*, ed. de Vries, Hent, and Samuel Webe. Stanford CA: Stanford University Press. 200, 56–93.

ATTIA   *The Animal That Therefore I Am*. Ed. Marie-Luise Mallet and trans. David Wills. New York: Fordham University Press, 2008. Translation of *L'animal que donc je suis*. Paris: Galilée, 2006.

ANY   "A Number of Yes." In *Psyche: Invention of the Other Volume II*, ed. Peggy Kamuf and Elizabeth Rottenberg. Stanford, CA: Stanford University Press, 2008, 231–40. Translation of "Nombre de oui." *Psyche: Inventions de l'autre*, Paris: Galilée, 1987.

AP   *Aporias: Dying—Awaiting (One Another at) the "Limits of Truth."* Trans. Thomas Dutoit. Stanford, CA: Stanford University Press, 1993. Translation of *Apories*, Paris: Galilée, 1996.

AF   *Archive Fever: A Freudian Impression*. Trans. Eric Prenowitz. Chicago: University of Chicago Press, 1996. Translation of *Mal d'archive*. Paris: Galilée, 1995.

ATI   "Avowing the Impossible. Returns, Repentance and Reconciliation." Trans Gil Anidjar. In *Living Together: Jacques Derrida's Communities of Violence and Peace*, ed. Elizabeth Weber. New York, Fordham University Press, 2013, 18–44.

AWP   "As If It Were Possible 'within Such Limits.'" Trans. Rachel Bowlby. In *Paper Machine*, trans. Rachel Bowlby. Stanford, CA: Stanford University Press. 2005, 3–99. Translation of "Commes si c'était possible, 'within such limits.'" In *Papier machine*. Paris: Galilée, 2001.

AI "Autoimmunity: Real and Symbolic Suicides—A Dialogue with Jacques Derrida." Trans. Pascale-Ann Braukt and Miachael Naas. In *Philosophy in a Time of Terror. Dialogues with Jürgen Habermas and Jacques Derrida*, ed. Giovanna Borradori. Chicago: University of Chicago Press, 2003, 85–36. Translation of "Auto-immunités, suicides reels et symboliques: Un dialogue avec Jacques Derrida." In Jacques Derrida and Jürgen Habermas, *Le "concept" du 11 septembre: Dialogues à New York avec Giovanna Borradori*. Paris: Galilée, 2003, 133–96.

AL *Adieu to Emmanuel Levinas*. Trans. Pascale Ann-Brault and Michael Naas. Stanford, CA: Stanford University Press, 1999. Translation of *Adieu à Emmanuel Levinas*, Paris: Galilée, 1997.

BS 1 *The Beast and The Sovereign Vol. I*. Ed. Michael Lisse, Marie-Luise Mallet, and Ginette Michaud, trans. Geoffrey Bennington. Chicago: University of Chicago Press, 2008. Translation of *Séminaire. Le bête et le souverain. Volume I (2001–2002)*, Paris: Galilée, 2008.

BB "But, beyond . . . (Open Letter to Anne McClintock and Rob Nixon)." Trans. Peggy Kamuf. *Critical Inquiry* 13, no. 1 (1986): 155–70.

BL "Before the Law." In *Acts of Literature*, ed. Derek Attridge. New York: Routledge, 1992, 181–220. Translation of "Devant la loi. Préjugés." In *La Faculté de juger*. Paris: Minuit, 1985.

CF *On Cosmopolitanism and Forgiveness*. Trans. Mark Dooly and Michael Hughes. London/New York: Routledge. 2001. Translation of "Cosmopolites de tous les pays encore un effort!" Paris: Galilée, 1997; "Le siècle et le pardon." In *Le Monde des Débats*, 1999.

C "Circumfession." In *Jacques Derrida*, trans. Geoffrey Bennington. University of Chicago Press, 1993, 3–315. Translation of *Jacques Derrida*. Paris: Editions du Seuil, 1991.

CHO "Choreography: Interview." In *Feminist Interpretations of Jacques Derrida*, ed. Nancy Holland. University Park: Pennsylvania State University Press, 1997, 23–42.

CO With Catherine Malabou and David Wills. *Counterpath*. Stanford, CA: Stanford University Press, 2004.

Abbreviations of Works by Derrida / xv

DOI "Declarations of Independence." Trans. Tom Keenan and Tom Pepper. *New Political Science* 7 (1986): 1–15. Translation of "Declarations d'Independance." In *Otobiographies: L'enseignement de Nietzsche et la politique du nom proper*. Paris: Galilee, 1984.

D "Différance." In *Margins of Philosophy*. Trans. Alan Bass. Chicago: University of Chicago Press, 1982, 1–27. Translation of "Différance." In *Marges de la philosophie*. Paris: Minuit, 1972.

DIS *Dissemination*. Trans. Barbara Johnson. Chicago: University of Chicago Press, 1981. Translation of *La dissemination*. Paris: Seuil, 1972.

EC with Bernard Stielger. *Echographies of Television: Filmed Interviews*. Cambridge: Polity Press, 2002. Translation of *Échographie de la television*. Paris: Galilée, 1996.

EF "*Epoché* and Faith: An Interview with Jacques Derrida." In *Derrida on Religion: Other Testaments*, ed. Yvonne Sherwood and Kevin Hart. New York: Routledge, 2005, 27–50.

EL "The Eyes of Language: The Abyss and the Volcano." In *Acts of Religion*, ed. Gil Anidjar. New York: Routledge, 2002, 189–227.

EO *The Ear of The Other*. Trans. Peggy Kamuf. New York: Schocken Books, 1985. Translation of *L'Oreille de l'autre: otobiographies, transferts, traductions. Textes et débats avec Jacques Derrida*. Montreal: VLB, 1982.

FAPU "Fidélité à plus d'un." In *Idiomes, nationalités, déconstructions: rencontre de Rabat avec Jacques Derrida*, en collaboration avec Jean-Jacques Forté. Casablanca: Les Editions Toubkal, 1998, 1–28.

FK "Faith and Knowledge: Two Sources of 'Religion' at the Limits of Reason Alone." In *Acts of Religion*, ed. Gil Anidjar. New York: Routledge, 2002, 41–101. Translation of "Foi et savoir." In *Foi et savoir: Suivi de le siècle et le pardon*. Paris: Seuil, 2001.

FL "Force of Law: The Mystical Foundation of Authority." In *Acts of Religion*, ed. Gil Anidjar. New York: Routledge, 2002, 230–98. Translation of *Force de loi: Le "Fondement mystique de l'autorité."* Paris: Galilée, 1994.

FWT	*For What Tomorrow*, trans. J. Fort. Stanford, CA: Stanford University Press, 2004. Translation of *De quoi demain*. Paris: Fayard and Galilée, 2001.
G	"Geopsychoanalysis: . . . 'and the rest of the world.'" *American Imago* 48, no. 2 (1991): 199–231.
GES I	"*Geschlecht*: Sexual Difference, Ontological Difference." Trans. Johm I. Leavey and Elizabeth Rottenberg. In *Psyche: Invention of the Other Volume II*, ed. Peggy Kamuf and Elizabeth Rottenberg. Stanford, CA: Stanford University Press, 2008, 27–62. Translation of *Psyche: Inventions de l'autre*, Paris: Galilée, 1987.
GES II	"*Geschlecht* II: Heidegger's Hand." In *Deconstruction and Philosophy. The Texts of Jacques Derrida*, ed. John Sallis. Chicago: University of Chicago Press, 1989, 161–96.
GES III	*Geschlecht III: Sex, Race Nation, Humanité*. Ed. Geoffrey Bennignton, Katie Chenoweth, and Rodrigo Therezo, Paris: Seuil, 2018.
GD	*The Gift of Death*, trans. David Wills. Chicago: University of Chicago Press, 1995. Translation of "Donner la mort." In *L'éthique du don*, ed. J.-M. Rabaté and M. Wetzel. Paris: Transition, 1992.
GT	*Given Time: 1. Counterfeit Money*, trans. Peggy Kamuf. Chicago: University of Chicago Press, 1992. Translation of *Donner le temps I. La fausse monnaie*. Paris: Galilée, 1991.
HAS	"How to Avoid Speaking: Denials." In *Derrida and Negative Theology*, ed. Harold Coward and Toby Foshay. Albany: State University of New York Press, 1992, 143–95. Translation of "Comment ne pas parler: Denegations." In *Psyché: Inventions de l'autre*. Paris: Galilée, 1987.
IPJD	"An interview with Professor Jacques Derrida," Michal Ben-Naftali, trans. Moshe Ron. Yad Vashem, *Shoah Research Center*, 1998.
IW	*Islam and the West. A Conversation with Jacques Derrida*. Trans. Teresa Lavender Fagan. Chicago: University of Chicago Press, 2008. Translation of Mustapha Chérif, *L'Islam et l'Occident: Recontre avec Jacques Derrida*. Paris: Odile Jacob, 2006.
IW	"Interpretations at War: Kant, the Jew, the German." Trans. Moshe Ron. In *Acts of Religion*, ed. Gil Anidjar. New York: Routledge,

2002, 135–88. Translation of *"Interpretations at war: Kant, le Juif, l'Allemand."* In *Psyche: Inventions de l'autre II*, Paris: Galilée, 1987.

LI *Limited Inc.* Evanston, IL: Northwestern University Press, 1988.

LJ "Letter to a Japanese Friend." In *Psyche: Invention of the Other Volume II*, ed. Peggy Kamuf and Elizabeth Rottenberg. Stanford, CA: Stanford University Press, 2008, 1–7. Translation of "Lettre a un ami japonais." In *Le Promeneur*, N. 42, *1985*.

LR "The Laws of Reflections: Nelson Mandela, in Admiration." Trans. Mary Ann Caws and Isabelle Lorenz. In *Psyche: Invention of the Other Volume II*, ed. Peggy Kamuf and Elizabeth Rottenberg. Stanford, CA: Stanford University Press, 2008, 63–86. Translation of "Admiration de Nelson Mandela, ou Les lois de la réflexion." In *Psyche: Inventions de l'autre II*, Paris: Galilée, 1987.

MP "Me-Psychoanalysis." Trans. Richard Klein. In *Psyche: Invention of the Other Volume 1*, ed. Peggy Kamuf and Elizabeth Rottenberg. Stanford, CA: Stanford University Press, 2007, 129–42. Translation of "Moi—la psychanalyse." In *Psyche: Inventions de l'autre*, Paris: Galilée, 1987.

MP *Margins of Philosophy*. Trans. Allan Bass. Chicago: University of Chicago Press, 1982. Translation of *Marges de la philosophie*. Paris: Minuit, 1972.

MO *Monolingualism of the Other, or The Prosthesis of Origin*. Trans. Patrick Mensah. Stanford, CA: Stanford University Press 1996. Translation of *Le monolinguisme de l'autre: Ou la prothèse d'origine*. Paris: Galilée, 1996.

MS "Marx & Sons." In *Ghostly Demarcation: A Symposium on Jacques Derrida's Specters of Marx*, ed. Michael Sprinker. London: Verso, 1999, 213–62. Translation of *Marx & Son*s. Paris: Presses Universitaires de France/ Galilée, 2002.

N *Negotiations: Interventions and Interviews 1971–2001*. Ed. and trans. Elizabeth Rottenberg. Stanford, CA: Stanford University Press, 2002.

NM "Nietzsche and the Machine." Trans. Richard Beardsworth. In *Negotiations: Interventions and Interviews 1971–2001*, ed. and trans.

Elizabeth Rottenberg. Stanford, CA: Stanford University Press, 2002, 215–56.

OG *Of Grammatology*. Trans. Gayatri Chakravorty Spivak. Baltimore: Johns Hopkins University Press, 1974. Translation of *De la grammatologie*. Paris: Minuit, 1967.

OG "*Ousia* and *Grammē*: Note on a Note from *Being and Time*." In *Margins of Philosophy*, trans. Alan Bass. Chicago: University of Chicago Press, 1982, 31–67. Translation of "*Ousia* and *Grammē*: note sur un note de Sein un Zeit." In *Marges de la philosophie*. Paris: Minuit, 1972.

OFH *Of Hospitality*. Trans. Rachel Bowlby. Stanford, CA: Stanford University Press, 2000. Translation of *De l'hospitalité*. Paris: Calmann-Lévy, 1997.

OH *The Other Heading: Reflections on Today's Europe*. Trans. Pascale-Anne Brault and Michael Naas. Bloomington: Indiana University Press, 1992. Translation of *L'autre cap*. Paris: Minuit, 1991.

OB "Otobiographies. The Teaching of Nietzsche and the Politics of the Proper Name." In *The Ear of the Other*, trans. Peggy Kamuf. New York: Schocken Books, 1985, 1–38. Translation of *L'Oreille de l'autre: otobiographies, transferts, traductions. Textes et débats avec Jacques Derrida*. Montreal: VLB, 1982.

OS *Of Spirit. Heidegger and the Question*. Trans. Geoffrey Bennington and Rachel Bowlby. Chicago: University of Chicago Press, 1989. Translation of *De l'esprit*, Paris: Galilée, 1987.

OT "The Onto-Theology of National Humanism (Prolegomena to a Hypothesis)." *Oxford Literary Review* 14, nos. 1–2 (1992): 3–23.

PF *Politics of Friendship*. Trans. George Collins. London: Verso, 1997. Translation of *Politiques de l'amitié*. Paris: Galilée, 1994.

PM *Paper Machine*. Trans. Rachel Bowlby. Stanford, CA: Stanford University Press. 2005. Translation of *Papier Machine*, Paris: Galilée, 2001.

POS *Positions*. Trans. Alan Bass. Chicago: University of Chicago Press, 1981. Translation of *Positions*. Paris: Minuit, 1972.

PSY 1   *Psyche: Invention of the Other Volume 1*. Ed. Peggy Kamuf and Elizabeth Rottenberg. Stanford, CA: Stanford University Press, 2007. Translation of *Psyche: Inventions de l'autre*, Paris: Galilée, 1987.

PSY 2   *Psyche: Invention of the Other Volume II*. Ed. Peggy Kamuf and Elizabeth Rottenberg. Stanford, CA: Stanford University Press, 2008. Translation of *Psyche: Inventions de l'autre*, Paris: Galilée, 1987.

R   *Rogues: Two Essays on Reason*. Trans. Pascale-Anne Brault and Michael Naas. Stanford, CA: Stanford University Press, 2005. Translation of *Voyous: Deux essais sur la raison*. Paris: Galilée, 2003.

RLW   "Racism's Last Word." Trans. Peggy Kamuf. *Critical Inquiry* 12 (1985): 290–99. Translation of "Le dernier mot du racism." In *Psyche: Inventions de l'autre*, Paris: Galilée, 1987.

RT   "Roundtable on Translation." In *The Ear of the Other*, trans. Peggy Kamuf. New York: Schocken Books, 1985, 91–162. Translation of *L'Oreille de l'autre: otobiographies, transferts, traductions. Textes et débats avec Jacques Derrida*. Montreal: VLB, 1982.

TS   *A Taste for the Secret*. With Maurizio Ferraris, trans. Giacomo Donis. Cambridge: Polity, 2001.

SEC   "Signature Event Context." In *Margins of Philosophy*, trans. Alan Bass. Chicago: University of Chicago Press, 1982, 307–30. Translation of "Signature Événement Contexte." In *Marges de la philosophie*. Paris: Minuit, 1972.

SG   "Semiology and Grammatology." In *Positions*, trans. Alan Bass. Chicago: University of Chicago Press, 1981, 15–36. Translation of "Sémiologie et grammatologie: entretien avec Julia Kristeva." In *Positions*. Paris: Minuit, 1972.

SM   *Specters of Marx: The State of the Debt, the Work of Mourning and the New International*. Trans. Peggy Kamuf, New York: Routledge, 1994. Translation of *Spectres de Marx*. Paris: Galilée, 1993.

S   *Spurs: Nietzsche's Styles*. Trans. Barbara Harlow. Chicago: University of Chicago Press, 1978.

SQ *Sovereignties in Question: The Poetics of Paul Celan*. Ed. Thomas Dutoitand Outi Pasanen. New York: Fordham University Press, 2005.

TB "Des Tours de Babel." Trans. Joseph Graham. In *Acts of Religion*, ed. Gil Anidjar. New York: Routledge, 2002, 102–34. Translation of "De Tours de Babel." In *Psyche: Inventions de l'autre*, Paris: Galilée, 1987.

TSA "Taking a Stand for Algeria." Trans. Boris Belay. In *Acts of Religion*, ed. Gil Anidjar. New York: Routledge, 2002, 299–308.

VR "The Villanova Roundtable: A Conversation with Jacques Derrida." In John Caputo, *Deconstruction in a Nutshell. A Conversation with Jacques Derrida*. New York: Fordham University Press, 1997, 3–30.

WA *Without Alibi*. Ed., trans., and introd. Peggy Kamuf. Stanford, CA: Stanford University Press, 2002.

WAP *Who Is Afraid of Philosophy? Right to Philosophy I*. Trans. Jan Plug. Stanford, CA: Stanford University Press, 2002. Translation of *Du droit à la philosophie*. Paris: Galilée, 1990.

WD *Writing and Difference*. Trans. Alan Bass. Chicago: University of Chicago Press, 1978. Translation of *L'écriture et la différence*. Paris: Seuil, 1967.

WM "White Mythology: Metaphor in the Text of Philosophy." In *Margins of Philosophy*, trans. Alan Bass. Chicago: University of Chicago Press, 1982, 207–72. Translation of "La Mythlogie blanche: La Metaphore dans le texte philosophique." In *Marges de la philosophie*. Paris: Minuit, 1972.

WRT "What Is a 'Relevant' Translation?" Trans. Lawrence Venuti. *Critical Inquiry* 27 (2001): 174–200.

Throughout the text, page references to Derrida's works refer to the English translation first, followed by the original in French.

Introduction

In the last three decades, religion has been at the center of political discourse and life.[1] Reference to religion and, in many cases, to its violent manifestations and the urgent necessity of responding to it, has often been associated with political events, situations, and contexts. These have included ethno-religious conflicts in the Balkans; the attack of September 11th in the United States; bombings in Madrid and London, the assassination of Theo Van Gogh in the Netherlands; the Danish cartoon controversy in the early 2000s; Islamophobic legislation and policies, especially in France and in the United States, justified in the name of security and secularism against 'terrorism'; decades of wars against Muslim majority countries the Middle East, North Africa and Central Asia waged in the name of secular freedom and democracy; the continued strength of Evangelical politics in North America and of Pentecostalism in Latin America and Africa; the ongoing Israeli settler colonialism justified by ethno-religious nationalism against Palestinians; and, most recently the Arab Spring in North Africa, the affirmation of the Islamic State in Iraq and Syria, terrorist actions of Islamist groups in Pakistan, Nigeria, Somalia and France, and also a variety of anti-Muslim violence perpetrated by a mix of terrorism and state policies in India, Myanmar, and China. This situation raises a series of questions about how to now respond to what is widely considered the problematic relationship between the theological and the political.

But, first of all, what exactly is the problem associated with this nexus? And what is distinctive about it in the current situation? While it is difficult to provide a precise definition, due to the changing forms and conditions in which the relationship between the theological and the political has taken and continues to take place, some definition can, nevertheless, be provided. This problem can be taken as referring to how the dynamic connection between religion and politics is implicated in the foundation of political authority, community, and knowledge. In spite of its generality, this definition is precise enough to emphasize two of its persisting features: the encircling of central philosophical questions about politics and the sources that structure institutions, practices, and ethical orientations of communal life.

Yet, to capture what is distinctive about the theological-political today, a closer look at the contemporary predicament is required. The renewed public significance of religious movements across the globe has led many to talk about the "return of religion," a formulation that points to the theoretical and political problems connected to the global hegemony of modern secular discourse. While recent events signal that religion is not in decline in modern society, they do not by themselves indicate that a "return of religion" has really occurred. Indeed, in its recurrent use and abuse in secular discourse, the expression "return of religion" appears problematic for at least two reasons.[2] First, it presupposes the epistemic horizon of modern theories of secularization and secularism it challenges, both of which are informed by a *separatist* and *hierarchizing logic* that represents the "secular" domain as severed from and epistemically superior to the "religious," especially with regard to the sources regulating public life.[3] As Talal Asad has argued, the modern category of the "secular," naming an epistemic space allegedly "free of religion" and traditionally represented as opposed to the "religious," is not the result of a rational process of maturation and progressive emancipation of reason from religion that is to be seen as both universally valid and necessary to human freedom. If considered through a genealogy of its historical formation as a modern concept, the "secular" so conceived appears intrinsic to the formation of the epistemological regime of the modern discourse of the West, as well as the development of the modern nation-state and its colonial expansion.[4] Thus, it is only because religion was thought to have disappeared from the public sphere, as modern theories of secularism and secularization informed by the "secular" have argued, that it can "return," which is another way to say the historicization of these categories allows for the visibility of separation and hierarchization as effects of modern discourse.

Second, as scholars of religion have pointed out, the term "religion" has a Christian origin and its definition is inscribed in Christian history, whose mark has been globally extended through the world-wide spread of processes of secularization connected with colonialism.[5] Thus, the general applicability of "religion" to a variety of non-Christian religious traditions—for example, Buddhism, Hinduism, Confucianism, or Islam—raises questions about geopolitics, classification, and ordering of human life that regard the formation of epistemological and political orders informed by Orientalism, whose colonial and racial formations can be traced back to the fifteenth century.[6]

Despite the epistemic problems that give rise to the so-called "return of religion," scholars have nevertheless attempted to grasp what is peculiar about the contemporary religious phenomena to which this formula refers. For example, in a recent volume entitled *Political Theologies: Public Religions in a Post-Secular World*, Hent de Vries suggests that contemporary religious movements do not simply point to the central role played by religions in contemporary politics. For religions often inform the responses and resistance to the global spread of Western modernization and secularization. Such movements also signal that religions are active participants into the modern processes of globalization, which tends to radicalize the importance of local identities by multiplying the links of religious belongings, thereby displacing the center of communitarian bonds. As a result, de Vries notes, it becomes extremely difficult to grasp the elusive and disparate role religions play in contemporary politics.[7] At the very least, this suggests that contemporary religious phenomena are not susceptible to universally valid systematizations.

Acknowledging the limits of the current theoretical grammar, this book examines the contemporary nexus between religion and politics and redescribes it as "theological-political complex." The choice of this composite term is not accidental: the notion of "theological-political," first used by Spinoza, and explored by Derrida in one of his seminars on philosophical nationalism in the 1980s, indicates right from the start a certain cautiousness about the possibility of a simple separation of religion and politics, as both the hyphenation and the persistence of religion in politics suggest; [8] "complex" emphasizes the complexity of the modern predicament as overdetermined by the separatist schema, one that, in its epistemological and political dimensions, somewhat *already* precedes and thus informs modern reflection and institutions, and yet does not offer adequate resources to account for the social realities it addresses, but forces them under its theoretical grid.[9] As such, the "theological-political complex" is a conceptual device that performs three important functions: first, it acknowledges the world-wide persistence of public religions and the difficulty of providing universally valid explanations about the nature and political significance of religious phenomena; second, it manifests a self-critical awareness of the need and difficulties connected to transcending the modern schema, given its ubiquitous and somehow prereflective reality; third, it highlights that attending to the peculiarity of the current predicament requires rethinking not simply the relationship between the theological and the political, but also *how, whence*, and from *which* cultural tradition that relationship, and more generally the question of difference, is approached. Attentive to the interconnected genealogies of colonialism, religion, and race, such a rethinking is mindful of the hegemonic role played by the Western Christian inflected horizon that informs the modern discourse of religion and of the epistemological and political implications such a hegemony has had and still has for other traditions. As such, it is a rethinking that is attentive to the crisis of the modern paradigm and the need of moving past Western-centric modes of inquiry in order to more adequately respond to the complexity of the current predicament.

Viewed this way, the "theological-political complex" appears in all its philosophical relevance and political urgency. The persistence of religion in politics is then not a return to a premodern religious order. It is a contemporary global phenomenon that challenges conventional modern convictions and the political forms that embody them and that calls for new ways of understanding and responding to cultural and religious pluralism. Indeed, that religions are operative both on the side of modernity and on the side of its critics does more than complicate the traditional division between religion and politics. It questions the fundamental philosophical and cultural assumptions underlying secular reason and normativity that have allowed that stark separation to be conceived as possible and desirable in the first place on the basis of an allegedly universal standpoint.

From what geopolitical site is the current discourse about religion and politics articulated? What are the linguistic, epistemological, and ontological presuppositions, securing the normative center from which to effect the opposition and separation of the theological and the political, reason and faith? What cultural values inform them? And how are these presuppositions implicated in the powers instituting and justifying political arrangements informed by a binary schema that produces spiritual, ethical, racial, sexual, and cultural hierarchies and exclusions?

This book is a study of the contemporary "theological-political complex" through the lens of Jacques Derrida's political thought, which is used to critically reflect on the foundations of modern secular discourse. It aims to offer a theoretically critically informed response to the empirical significance of public religions and to the challenge they pose to modern conceptions and institutions, while also offering a systematic account of Derrida's thought on the theological-political predicament. To expand the understanding of the matter investigated, this book examines the complex interaction between religion and politics as it relates to the formations of epistemic and political orders. It does so by paying particular attention to the role that questions of language and epistemology play in political thinking, as well as the ways in which their conceptualizations affect the normative and institutional responses to cultural and religious diversity.[10]

The book's central claim is that Derrida's thought offers powerful resources to critically rethink the theological-political nexus beyond the secular paradigm. On the one hand, Derrida questions the oppositional modern logic that separates religion and politics by exposing its Western Christian, racialized, and sexualized presuppositions and the role they play in generating discriminatory hierarchies and practices. On the other hand, he points to the complex interconnection between reason and religious sources and to the democratic potential of thinking about them as interrelated. By articulating a relational approach that challenges the binary and racialized features of modern Western epistemology and politics, and one that resists the translation of the theological into a secularized political, his perspective clears an analytical space for new political grammars to emerge. In pursuing this argument, I do not aim to either suggest that Derrida engaged consistently, equally, or thoroughly with the racial, sexual, and religious character of modern secular discourse's key presuppositions or to spare him from criticism on his treatment of some of these issues. For example, while my later chapters emphasize Derrida's attention for the exclusion of sexual difference in several of his works (*PF*; GES I; *GES III*; CHO), I also endorse criticisms pointing to his lack of substantive engagements with authors other than white European males.[11] Similarly, while I highlight and develop his, not always explicit, remarks on the connection between the theological-political and race (FK; *PF*; *R*; RLW; WRT), I raise questions about why he did not develop such an important topic further and more explicitly, especially in connection to colonialism and religion, which he nevertheless addressed (FK; BB; WRT), or to capitalism.[12]

Instead, my argument seeks to highlight that his thought displays a critical awareness of the structural role that racialized, sexualized, and religious presuppositions play in modern secular discourse's discriminatory and hierarchical schema. As such, his intervention points to the epistemic salience of addressing such presuppositions not simply thematically, but at the level of the epistemological grid from which, and through which, sociopolitical life is approached. It is this critical awareness, and decolonizing potential, that I thus seek to mobilize in terms of resources for rethinking the "theological-political complex," and I do so with and beyond what

Derrida did or did not do with it. Specifically, I aim to contribute to an understanding of race in relation to the "theological-political complex" and seek to do so by addressing questions race, and its derivatives, in the general and yet restricted sense of race as an historical construct that refers to a structure of power used to ordering public life through epistemic and political exclusionary hierarchies.[13] While there is much more complexity to the nature and history of race than what this definition can capture, and much has been written about it, my hope is to show that this understanding helps illuminate the political and philosophical unconscious of racial thinking that I seek to bring to the fore; that is, mentalities and practices that consider it epistemically possible and politically desirable to set up hierarchies and divisions on the basis of pure thinking, as well as secularized and sexualized political teleologies to be deployed through assimilative translation practices.[14]

Central to the proposed reading is an appreciation of the lived experience of margins as significant to the formation of Derrida's thought, sensibility, and interests, as well as insights and philosophical practice.[15] There is no doubt that his philosophy remains in many ways linked to the Western tradition, given the European focus of his work and the special, yet not-Eurocentric, place he accords to Europe (AI; OH; R),[16] as well as his limited engagement with traditions (Islamic or Kabyle)[17] and places (Algeria)[18] that nevertheless had an impact on his writings. Yet such a philosophy also defies categorizations into such boxes as Western or non-Western. Indeed, Derrida also draws from places, experiences, traditions, and heritages that cannot be located within Europe, as testified, for example, by his understanding of "religion" through the figure of, and *as*, an Arab Jew and also through Islam, in addition to Christianity and Judaism, as part of the "religions called 'Abrahamic'" (ATI, 21; FK, 44/13), which he experienced in French Algeria.[19] Attesting to his fidelity to more than one identity (FAPU, 221), and describing himself by using an interweaving of racial, ethnic, and religious features as "a little black and very Arab Jew" (C, 58/57) and an explicit reference to "Africa" and to his retaining of "that heritage" (G, 204), Derrida recognizes, especially in his later writings, his cultural debt to Algeria, highlighting the profound impact his lived experience in such a complex context had on his thought. As it emerges from these writings, Derrida was both a colonized and a minority subject, who was exposed but excluded from Berber, Arab-Muslim, Arab-Jewish and, to a certain extent, French culture. As a Jew, he temporarily benefited from citizenship status granted to Algerian Jews, but not to Arabs and Berbers, by the 1870 Crémieux decree—a status that was violently revoked and replaced with anti-Semitic legislation by the Vichy regime in the 1940s (*MO*, 14/ 31–32; *IW*, 34–35/53).

> Of all the cultural wealth that I have received, that I have inherited, my Algerian culture has sustained me the most . . . The cultural heritage I received from Algeria is something that probably inspired my philosophical work. *All* the work I have pursued, with regard to European, Western, so-called Greco-European philosophical thought, the questions I have been led to ask from some distance, a *certain exteriority* (*certaine extériorité*), would *certainly not have been possible* if, in my personal history, had I not been a sort of child in the *margins* of Europe, a child of the Mediterranean, who was not simply French nor simply African, and who had passed his time traveling between one culture and the other feeding questions out of that instability—all of which cause the earthquake of my *experience* that I just mentioned. Everything that has interested me for a long time, regarding writing, the trace, the deconstruction of Western metaphysics—which, despite what has been said, I have never identified as something homogenous or defined in the singular (I have so often explicitly said the contrary)—all of that had to have come out of a reference to an elsewhere whose place and language were unknown or forbidden to me . . . A Judeo Franco-Maghrebian genealogy does not explain everything, far from it, but can I *ever* explain anything *without it*? (*mais pourrais-je rien expliquer sans elle, jamais*)." (*IW*, 30–32/55–57; my emphasis)

While the cultural heritage of Algeria might have inspired Derrida's philosophy, the latter "would certainly have not been possible . . . without" a "certain exteriority" of his particular and traumatic "experience" in "the margins of Europe." Pointing to the experiential conditions of possibility of his thought, Derrida's lived experience, I suggest, plays a decisive epistemic role in the critical and decolonizing thrust of his philosophy. This is noticeable especially in a series of ideas that expose and challenge hierarchical and separatist ordering typical of modern discourse and its undergirding racial logics. These ideas include his understanding of Western philosophy as a "White mythology" displaying a racialized mode of thinking (WM, 213/254); his resistance to the centering of Europe, and the traditional discourse of modernity, indeed his efforts to open up Europe to its internal differences but also what is "other than Europe" at its southern shores ("*l'autre que l'Europe*), while denouncing Europe for its links to neocapitalist exploitation (OH, 29–30/33, 57/56–57, 69/69–70; FAPU, 229); his critique of the racialized, and specifically Islamophobic undercurrents of modern European understandings of the political (RLW, 290–99/385–99; PF, 77/95, 89/109, 91/112–13; FAPU, 229), as well as of the racist and anti-Semitic features affecting European "spirit" and culture (OS, 39–40/65; OH, 6/13), whose philosophy and rationality have been called into question by twentieth-century totalitarianisms, and by the Holocaust (IPJD, 2); his exposure of globalization and secularization as originally "European-colonial" and then "Anglo-American" and "Christian" forms of "hyper-imperialist appropriation" of the public sphere supported by processes of massive land expropriation and extraction (FK, 79/66, 66/47; AI 122); his recognition of the links between the "European concept and history of the state," "the European discourse on race," and "the Judeo-Christian ideology" on the one hand, and South African apartheid on the other (BB, 165); and finally, his conceptualization of deconstruction as the analysis of "what remains to be thought" which has largely been excluded by the totalizing character of Western discourse (*LI*, 147). These ideas attain further significance if read in conjunction with his affirmation, in a 2003 conference on race, that "deconstruction is through and through a deconstruction of racism" because it questions racism's general conditions of possibility such as the traditional opposition between nature and culture, on which all naturalizations rely, and the idea of origin as filiation, especially when used as a ground for political projects.[20]

The important role of autobiographical elements emerges also by appreciating Derrida's emphasis on the epistemic potency of subjectivity, as he understands it, following Kierkegaard: "subjectivity, the *resistance of existence* to the concept or system—this is something I attach great importance to and feel very deeply, something I am always ready to stand up for" (*TS*, 41; my emphasis). Indeed, Derrida not only stresses that philosophy has always been "at the service of this autobiographical memory," but he enacts this idea through "exemplarity" which is not conceived as a particular example of a universal essence, but, rather, as a form of philosophical witnessing that exemplifies the "exemplarity of the unique" within which the universal inscribes itself without being exhausted by it (41; *OH*, 73/72). This witnessing consists in a mode of reflection from and through a singular lived experience that considers particularity as irreducible to thinking and that points to the conditions of possibility of theoretical articulations that have universal value, which is not the same as universal validity (*MO*, 19–20/39–40).

My point is that Derrida's lived experience plays an epistemic role in his philosophical work's ability to open up an analytical space to the possibility of pluralism, which modern secular discourse represses. By affirming the theoretical importance of autobiography in this way, I seek neither to fold philosophy into literature nor to hierarchize the sources of Derrida's thought or fix its origins. Nor do I intend to conclusively determine Derrida's identity or reduce the genesis of deconstruction to the historical conditions of French Algeria.[21] Instead, I aim to emphasize the theoretical value and critical potential of a perspective that draws *from* lived experience as *a* powerful epistemic source of "resistance" to "the system"—a lived experience that speaks resistance in the language of what is resisted without, however, speaking its language. Arguably, working through the experience of colonialism and marginality to European modernity through the predicament of the Arab-Jew put Derrida in a position of "epistemic resistance." This enabled him to expose the mirroring effect and logics of domination produced by Western epistemology and politics, without reaching an "outside" that would turn the margin into a privileged position exterior to modern discourse.[22] Such an experience is thus also central to his challenge to the possibility of developing critiques of, or alternatives to, modernity from some epistemic island that has not been affected by Western discourse, a theme consistent throughout his entire *oeuvre* since his early works (*OG*, 24/39).

Emphasizing this point is not to quickly dismiss powerful interventions such as that of Enrique Dussel, who has argued for the critical potential of cultural moments of "Chinese, Hindustani, Islamic, African Bantu, and Latin American Cultures" that not only predated but remained, as it were, "outside" European modernity and thus distinct because they were excluded by it.[23] Nor is it to deny that elements of these cultural moments might have survived Western colonialism, as Derrida's understanding of Islam as being "alien enough" to European modernity suggests (*FK*, 51/22, 81/69). Rather, it is to highlight that even if such moments can provide sources for transformations, the process involved in reclaiming them remains significantly affected, shaped, and contaminated by dominant Western epistemological and political orders. This means that there are significant limits to the possibility of articulating and grasping cultural meanings that have remained somehow exterior to such orders so as to delink from them from whichever margin, as recent propositions such as that of Walter Mignolo have advanced.[24] The predicament emphasized by Derrida aligns with Valentine Mudimbe's notion of the "colonial library" and with similar formulations made by Edward Said with regard to the impact of Orientalism on thinking and studying the Orient, particularly Islam.[25]

It is thus with reference to Derrida's positionality and to specific features of his philosophy that I seek to illuminate the decolonizing thrust of his thought, despite the fact that Derrida has hardly used the term "decolonization," and that he is more often associated with postcolonial thought.[26] Specifically, through this term, I seek to connote aspects of his philosophy that contribute to debates about decolonization broadly construed that involve epistemic, political, religious and material dimensions. Indeed, while not remaining insensible to questions of land and the logics sustaining global inequalities (*AF, AL, SM*), Derrida offers a non-Eurocentric analysis and critique of the racial foundations, formations and global hegemony of Western modernity that illuminates its entanglements with the colonial legacy. Concurrently, his reflections open the production of knowledge to non-Western and non-Western-centric traditions, including a thinking of the political beyond the horizon of secularism and nationalism. Starting from the 1960s (*OG*) and 1970s (*MP*), as my discussion will showcase, Derrida critically exposes the Latin Christian, Western-centric, sexualized and racialized character of modern knowledge and political models, as well as ethnocentric teleological conceptions of time and history (*OG*, OG). In his later works, from the early 1990s, he offers epistemic resources to open up a space beyond such conceptions (*SM, R*), as well as beyond the model of the secular nation-state and processes of globalization and secularization that also involve land expropriation (FK, EL, *PF, R*). By deconstructing the conditions of possibility of metaphysical binaries, exposing the colonial nature of "religion" and its world-wide extension and subsequent secularization through oppressive forms of translation, and by enacting a relational type of thinking, Derrida offers valuable resources to the decolonization of dominant discourses and approaches that can be used to build culturally diverse forms of knowledge and political life.

Exploring issues as different as translation, time, democracy, secularism, sovereignty, and Islam, the book addresses both the specialized literature on Derrida's later writings[27] and recent discussions on religion and politics in such diverse disciplines as philosophy, political theory, and religious studies.[28] Unlike the mainly philosophical approach to Derrida's perspective on religion, especially in the influential works of John Caputo, Martin Hägglund, and Michael Naas, my project illuminates the distinctively political aspects of his view as well as the centrality of the theological-political to Derrida's critical project as a whole.²⁹ Indeed, I aim to show how the theological-political nexus links and charges of political significance his early linguistic and epistemological concerns to his later religious and ethico-political ones, and thus represents a key aspect of his thought. This is apparent if one considers the relevance of the theological-political in Derrida's entire corpus as well as his continued interest in political questions (*R*, 39/64) and the political dimension of themes that do not appear immediately political such as language (*LI*, *MO*) or time (*SM*, *GT*, *OG*). While in his later writings he overtly focuses on theological-political themes (FK, EL, *IW*, *PF*, R, SM, TB, WRT) and political foundations (BL, DOI, FL), his early reflections on questions of origins—ontological, temporal, and linguistic—already manifested critical attention to the theological-political issues behind the metaphysical approach informing the institution of philosophical horizons and a deep historical sensibility for political founding (*OG*). As such, Derrida's early writings too can be considered as symptomatic of a larger preoccupation with the theological-political broadly conceived as a political problem about the foundation of authority, community, and knowledge—a problem that is therefore at the heart of his critical thinking as a whole, but it is not always or sufficiently recognized as such. Above all, my discussion of how Derrida's view of the theological-political relates to the formations of epistemic and political orders emphasizes his awareness of the racialized schema that underpins the philosophical presuppositions of the modern discourse of religion—something to which the significant scholarship around various aspects of the theological-political in Derrida has paid insufficient attention.³⁰

With regard to interdisciplinary debates on the so-called "return of religion," I address perspectives in political theology as well as Neo-Kantian theories of secularism. In response to scholarship in political theology, I show that by refraining from solving the theological-political nexus Derrida's perspective unsettles approaches that privilege one side of the relationship, thereby relapsing into an oppositional logic that closes the political from within or without. This applies to Carl Schmitt's attempt to save the autonomy of the political at the expenses of other spheres, ³¹ as well as to ambiguous aspects of Walter Benjamin's messianism that can be read as privileging the theological side of the theological-political relationship.³² With reference to Neo-Kantian theories of secularism, I challenge the alleged neutrality associated with the idea of secularization as a "rational" translation of theological idioms and categories into secular ones, as it appears especially in the work of Jürgen Habermas and John Rawls.³³ I show how their reliance on an insufficiently thematized view of translation, especially with regard to the role it plays in the formation and maintenance of the secular world order, signals that the traditional secular paradigm cuts deeper than it appears and maintains a link, both methodological and material, with the legacy of colonialism.

As such, the book broadly positions itself between specialized literature and broader scholarship. It integrates the interrogation of the theological features that keep reappearing, however opaquely, in the understanding of modern politics with genealogical investigation. I suggest that the critical import of Derrida's approach to the "theological-political complex" consists in combining these two modes of analysis, which are joined in his quasitranscendentalism, which refers to a historically inflected philosophical thinking that proceeds through formalizations as in the transcendental tradition since Kant, but that also maintains a genealogical focus on the irreducible historicity within which formalizations take place. Putting emphasis on this aspect of Derrida's thought is not new. Rodolphe Gasché and Geoffrey Bennington have offered seminal discussions of Derrida's quasitranscendentalism.[34] Authors such as Caputo, De Vries, Mathias Fritsch, and Hägglund have further developed the discussion, especially in relation to Derrida's notion of the messianic and time.[35] While building on these views, my analysis emphasizes the historico-political sensibility of Derrida's approach in general, and the specific antiracist drive this sensibility takes with regard to the culture-specific philosophical underpinnings and political commitments of modern secular discourse. I suggest that by investigating in this way how the theological-political nexus relates to epistemic orders and political formations, Derrida employs a relational approach that simultaneously exposes the proximity between the separatist logic of secularism and that of racialized thinking, and that puts limits to the possibility of reaching a vantage point to address, understand, and negotiate the theological-political relationship. Indeed, by placing irreducible historicity and relationality at the heart of his approach to religion and politics, but also language and time, Derrida allows us to think about the political *together* with the religious "in context," and thus to think of the theological-political as an historical relation. In particular, he shows that some theological dimension, but not theological in any traditional sense, cannot be strictly excluded from the political domain. This feature is maximally exemplified by his insistence on an elementary faith (*foi élémentaire*) (FK, 80/68) that reason and religion share and that informs a structure of promissory affirmation, or a "messianicity without messianism (*messianicité sans messianisme*)" (FK, 56/30; SM, 74/102). Central to the foundation of both politics and knowledge, this faith radicalizes and yet unsettles the quest of origins and naturalizations typical of modern secular and racial models, thereby opening up possibilities for different political imaginaries that remain critically vigilant against homogenizations and thus open to pluralism (ATI, 27/37). In this way, Derrida emphasizes the interconnection, but he reflects at the same time on the distinction, between the theological and the political, placing his thought in proximity to longstanding positions within the Islamic tradition(s). This approach not only challenges attempts that seek to solve or end up circumventing the theological-political nexus itself, [36] but it also profoundly questions the modes of thinking that share the possibility of ordering sociopolitical life through hierarchical and separatist schemas akin to racialized logics and colonial mentalities. Viewed this way, my interpretation of Derrida's perspective shows that his position on religion, and more broadly the theological-political, exceeds the "radical secularity" suggested by Naas and resists the "radical atheism" proposed by Hägglund, as well as associations to traditional religion as suggested by Caputo, who highlights the "religious passion of deconstruction."[37] It does so while reaching secular discourse's subterranean entanglements with the legacy of colonialism that these authors largely neglect. The emphasis on these overlooked connections, in turn, allows to illuminate the deeper reach of Derrida's critical vigilance against political closures that recent perspectives on the political dimension of his thought, such as those that Stella Gaon and Geoffrey Bennington have underlined. Unlike that of Derrida, though, these perspectives remain confined within secular Western horizons, whose racial features and colonial afterlives are therefore left unscrutinized.[38]

In presenting Derrida's take on the "theological-political complex," I engage in both exegetic and analytical readings that seek to expound Derrida's reflections on issues of language, time, religion, and politics as they relate to the theological-political relationship, with a view to explore the role this relation plays in the formation of epistemological and political orders. While I explain Derrida's view of these issues to illuminate the logic of relationality at the heart of his take on the theological-political, I also seek to *think with* Derrida and push this logic further. Indeed, my aim is to illuminate the significance and decolonizing potential of his approach to the "theological-political complex," especially for rethinking the relationship between religion and politics and democracy in ways that Derrida himself never thought, developed, or perhaps would have agreed with but are possibilities opened by the deconstructive gesture.[39] In pursing this, I draw particular attention to the critical sources his thought offers to maintain critical vigilance against epistemic hierarchizations, naturalized representations, and assimilative forms of translation on the one hand and to open up spaces for transformations beyond dominant knowledge forms and received interpretations on the other.[40] I also strive to keep an awareness throughout that Derrida's ideas, in this book, are articulated in English, and thus in translation with regard to the original French. While I selectively indicate the original French, the exegesis and expounding of the argument in English encounter the limits and possibilities of it being done in translation, as my discussion will illustrate. I leave it to the reader to judge whether I have succeeded on this score.

Employing this composite reading strategy, I start by setting the critical framework for rethinking the theological-political relation through a focus on conceptions of language and time informing dominant modern political thinking before moving on to more recognizably political topics. This choice is not simply organizational but seeks to connect two bodies of Derrida's work, the earlier "philosophical" writings with the late "political" works, in order to signal the deep continuity between the two in spite of the turn usually attributed to his intellectual trajectory (R, 39/64). Through an engagement with Derrida's early and later writings on linguistic context and translation, chapter 1 foregrounds his view on language. It aims to unpack the philosophical and political dimensions of translation and its problematic use in influential approaches to secularism and political theology that seek to effect a secularization of religious language by appealing to the allegedly neutral language of secular reason. After illustrating Derrida's critique of the colonial implications connected to the global spread of the language of secularism as the relevant translating language of the public sphere, the chapter explores the potential of resistance to dominant knowledge forms of Derrida's view of language as "promise."

Chapter 2 examines Derrida's view of time as it connects to political thought. Reading his famous notion of *différance* in conjunction with that of "White mythology," I analyze his critique of Western metaphysical thinking and teleology, exposing the dangerous proximity between philosophical foundations based on the grasp of pure origins and racialized schemas. Through this framework, I then offer critical reflections on the political stakes and implications of teleological responses to the theological-political nexus as they appear in the work of thinkers as diverse as Karl Marx, John Rawls, and Jürgen Habermas. Focusing on Derrida's alternative epistemological approach to time, the chapter moves then on to articulate his notion of the "messianic" as a nonteleological and antiracist form of political thought, illuminating its significance for rethinking questions of justice, reason, and the foundation of communal life, beyond the purity of ideal representations and thus the possibility of naturalizations.

In chapter 3, I present a distinctively political view of Derrida's understanding of the secular as the allegedly religion-free field of the sociopolitical that complements and expands the limited and mainly philosophically oriented literature on this topic.[41] Through an analysis of Derrida's later work on political founding and religion, I specifically focus on how the theological-political relationship factors in the institution of political authority. Engaging scholarship in political theology, the chapter pursues two lines of inquiry: first, it links the theme of racial formations to Derrida's critique of Schmitt and more generally to the patriarchal and exclusionary implications of relying on the notion of fraternity and the opposition to Islam in order to draw the boundaries of the political. Second, it highlights the irreducible nexus between the theological and the political by exploring Derrida's discussion of Benjamin. This inquiry leads to the idea that, for Derrida, the theological and the political are interrelated and yet distinct since first inception. Thus, they cannot be separated as in traditional conceptualizations of secularism, or collapsed into one another as in forms of critical messianism *à la* Benjmain, or religious fundamentalism.

In order to illuminate Derrida's view of democracy in the context of the "theological-political complex," chapter 4 explores his notion of "democracy to come" (*démocratie à venir*) in connection to issues of sovereignty, freedom, and equality. Building on the issue of racial formations addressed in previous chapters, the chapter emphasizes the racialized and masculine character of canonical understandings of democracy as sovereignty, highlighting the exclusion of sexual difference as typical of the modern paradigm. Through an exposure of Derrida's topical reliance on, and yet critical distance from, traditional political theology, I argue that his view enables thinking about democracy beyond "old" secularism. The chapter shows that Derrida's "democracy to come" does not simply offer resources to challenge unitary and undifferentiated conceptions of agency and identity informing secular understandings of sovereignty, freedom, and equality typical of most modern nation-states. By enabling a radical form of criticism that can resist the naturalization of *secular* democracy, it also opens a space to nonsecular perspectives, outside the West and within it, that offer important contributions to alternative configurations of communal life.

The last chapter concludes the book by exploring the place of Islam in Derrida's later writings. Through an investigation of his treatment of Islam in relation to the modern discourse of religion, secularism, and democracy,

I trace the complex and controversial role Islam plays in Derrida's political thought. Specifically, I focus on the sort of openings and closures his deconstructive logic enables beyond what he did or failed to do with it in his specific interventions. I argue that although Derrida's position is marked by controversial ambiguities and historical inaccuracy, his intervention opens up the future of the political and of democracy to Islamicate perspectives and contexts.[42] In this way, Derrida joins those forces within and beyond such spaces that resist closures within Islamic discourses, as well as various forms of Orientalist Islamophobia.

1

The Politics of Language and Translation

In "Faith and Knowledge: The Two Sources of 'Religion' at the Limits of Reason Alone" (henceforth "Faith and Knowledge"), Derrida reflects on the "return of religion," offering important insights about where one might begin a critical analysis of the "theological-political complex."

> Now if, today, the "question of religion" actually appears in a new and different light, if there is an unprecedented resurgence, both global and planetary, of this ageless thing, then what is at stake is language, certainly—and more precisely the idiom, literality, writing, that forms the element of all revelation and all belief, an element that ultimately is irreducible and untranslatable—but an idiom that above all is inseparable from the social nexus, from the political, familial, ethnic, communitarian nexus, from the nation and from the people: from autochthony, blood and soil, and from the ever more problematic relation of citizenship and to the state. In these times, language and nation form the historical body of all religious passion. (FK, 44/12)

Today, the "question of religion" is not simply about faith and knowledge, as the title of Derrida's essay indicates. It is also very much a question "of language and of nation" since the vehicle of religious beliefs is always an idiom that is inseparable from issues of translatability, nationality, and citizenship.

While attending to these issues appears central to religion, it also extends to what is commonly considered the secular domain of philosophy. In his essay "The Onto-Theology of National Humanism (Prolegomena to a Hypothesis (henceforth "The Onto-Theology')," Derrida affirms that although philosophy is considered "essentially universal and cosmopolitan," it "needs to pass through idioms," which are particular, and thus needs to "translate itself via or rather in the body of idioms" to exist at all. Like religion, philosophy is indissociable from a "national idiom" and translation and thus also from questions of linguistic context and politics (OT, 3–4).

Following Derrida, it would seem that an analysis of language and translation that is attentive to context and politics is key to a critical investigation of the "theological-political complex." This chapter takes such an analysis as its task. I begin with an exploration of "Onto-Theology" and Derrida's debate with John Searle in *Limited Inc.*, which provide key sources to articulate the relationship between language, national context, and idiom. In order to further highlight the political dimension of language, the remaining part of the chapter will turn to mainly *Monolingualism of the Other, or The Prosthesis of Origin* (henceforth *Monolingualism*), while also considering other works relevant to this theme. After expounding the philosophical and political character of translation, I consider the local and global implications of appealing to the language of secularism as a neutral instrument of secularization. I conclude by exploring the potential of what Derrida calls "language of promise" for rethinking how to approach the "theological-political complex." Throughout, I seek to show that by uncovering the entanglements between universalist modern models and hierarchical schemas typical of colonial mentalities, Derrida exposes the false neutrality and racial features of secular discourse's representations of language and translation, together with their ruinous political implications. Specifically, his reflections illuminate the politics of language and assimilatory translation as key instruments for the global hegemony of secularism, but they also point to theoretical resources for a politically sensible approach to language that does not renounce the universal aspirations of philosophical reflection.

Language and National Context

In Derrida's understanding of language, context plays a central role. But what is context? What are its boundaries? An insightful work from which to start clarifying the question of context, beyond the general idea of it as referring to a community of speakers, is his aforementioned "The Onto-Theology of National Humanism (Prolegomena to a Hypothesis)," which is part of a series of seminars on the relation between nationalism and philosophy.[1] In this essay, Derrida investigates the "aporias of the philosophical translation of philosophical idioms" (OT, 3), focusing on the nexus between philosophy, which is by vocation universal, and national idiom, which is always particular.[2] In what follows, I will focus only on his reading of Fichte's *Address to the German Nation* since it offers a key insight about the nexus between (philosophical) language and context within the problematics of translation that I will discuss throughout the chapter.

The upshot of Derrida's argument is that Fichte essentializes German nationality by presenting it in purely philosophical terms as "bearing the universal and philosophical as such." Derrida reads Fichte's view of German identity as a coming to self-consciousness through "a philosophy that has become clear in itself" (11). For Fichte, being German is to identify with the *telos* of developing a certain (philosophical) spirit that is not necessarily linked to the empirical reality of the German territory or its idiom (i.e., German), but to a certain relation to the language of German philosophy. As Fichte notes: "Whoever believes in the spirit and in the freedom of the spirit . . . wherever he may have been born and whatever language he speaks, is of our blood [*ist unser Geschlecht*], he belongs to us and will join us."[3] For Derrida, this view leads to the paradoxical effect that whoever shares the language of this philosophy without being of German nationality is German. In contrast, a person of German nationality, a "*de facto* German" who does not "speak" the language of German philosophy, is not German (13). More problematically, though, Fichte's philosophical nationalism remains "essentially equivocal" about whether he is anticipating "a Nazi heritage (which is biologizing, racist, etc.)" despite that fact that it "claims to be totally foreign to any naturalism, biologism, racism or even ethnocentrism" (16).

For Derrida, the determination of philosophical spirit in nationalistic terms is not peculiar to Fichte, but it is part of a wider phenomenon, that of "the structure of national consciousness," which demands that "a nation posits itself not only as a bearer of a philosophy but of an exemplary philosophy, that is, one that is both particular and potentially universal—and that is philosophical by that very fact." On this reading, nationalism is parasitical on philosophy because of its essential relation to universality. Nationalism is "a philosophy, a discourse which is, structurally, philosophical" (10). Overall, Derrida makes two points. First, that no nationalism is untainted by the philosophical drive to universality since nationalism presents itself not simply "as *a* philosophy, but as philosophy *itself*, philosophy par excellence," one characterized by the "*hierarchizing* evaluation of the best, true philosophy"

(13; my emphasis). Second, all philosophy, given its particular origin and vocation to universality "always has the potential or the yearning . . . for nationality and nationalism" (17). Thus, to take seriously this potential means maintaining a critical vigilance over the ways in which philosophical reflection is pursued.

> One can denounce, suspect, devalorise [sic], combat philosophical nationalism only by taking the risk or reducing or effacing linguistic difference or the force of the idiom, thus in making that metaphysico-technical gesture which consists in instrumentalizing language (but is there a language that is purely non-instrumental?), making it a medium which is *neutral*, indifferent and external to the philosophical act of thought. Is there a thought of the idiom that escapes this alternative? That is one of our questions. It does not belong to the past but is a question of the future. (23; my emphasis)

For Derrida, we cannot exclude, now and for the future, that the alternative to nationalism is not to be found in the shelter of a supposedly *neutral* philosophical language. This holds since even philosophy's inherent strive for emancipation from a particular idiom, and its embracing of an instrumental view of language (as a communicative tool) does not make it free from other, and more subtle, forms of nationalism. Indeed, portraying philosophical language as a neutral universal tool does not efface the particular origin embedded in it but, actually, silently obscures it. This raises the question whether employing such a type of language as *the* translating language, irrespective of the idiom in which is spoken, yields to a more dangerous form of nationalism, whose force is proportional to the nonappearance of its particularity. In other works, considered below and in subsequent chapters, Derrida discusses this possibility while referring to the world-wide imposition of a dominant "national" (Anglo-American) language. As the language of "masters, capital, and machine" (*MO*, 30/56), he sees the Anglo-American idiom connected to what is commonly considered a neutral secular language: this is not simply the language "called technical, objective, scientific, and even philosophical" (*EL*, 202) but also that of putatively nonreligious political understandings and forms that remain marked by the juridical, theological, and political tradition of Christianity (*BS 1; F; R*). For him, the problem with this type of nationalism is that its linguistic hegemony imposes the homogenization of a "multiplicity of languages, cultures, beliefs and ways of life" within which "a chance for the future is possible." Rather than being a sign of civilization, this homogenizing hegemony represents "the opposite of civilization" (*IW*, 80/123).

The connection between national idiom and philosophy helps illuminate the question of linguistic context, especially in relation to philosophical language. Derrida calls attention to the "odd logic" informing Fichte's view. For on the one hand, Fichte wants to proclaim German philosophy, which elevates life over death, as philosophy as such and non-German philosophy as philosophy of death. On the other hand, he wants to prevent "the dead," those who do not speak the language of German philosophy but may nevertheless speak German, to contaminate its purity. Derrida notes that Fichte wants to secure the link between German nationality and a "certain relation to the language" of German philosophy by preventing or limiting "the dead" to "twist its words" in order to save "the true destination of words, their living destination which is still exposed to the return of the dead one" (OT, 14–15).

What Derrida finds odd in this logic is not simply that the criteria for German nationality are not, for Fichte, really linguistic since one could "speak" the language of German philosophy as "philosophy of spirit and life" without speaking German as a "living tongue." It is also, and relevant to our purposes, the fact that Fichte has to proclaim as dead such "living" elements of German philosophy as the idiom and the geopolitical context—"geography" and "citizenship"—in which the life of German philosophy and its language concretely originated and continue to *live* on. In other words, the oddity is that Fichte ascribes death where there is life, though he seeks to protect life through a philosophy that elevates life over death. Intended to save the language of German philosophy from the corruption that "the malfeasant haunting of the foreigner" can bring to its purity, this operation requires an epistemic hierarchizing that simultaneously erases other views and the particular empirical conditions that enable *German* philosophy to be at all while being only presented as *philosophy* spoken in German (15–16).

By emphasizing the oddity of this logic, Derrida exposes a schema of concealment, hierachization, and exclusion that affects Western philosophical discourse at large and challenges the possibility that philosophical language may function as *the* neutral language of concepts. What is to be concealed, and is functional to linguistic and epistemic hierachization, is the irreducible relationship between philosophical discourse and the national context and idiom within which such a discourse is always constructed. What is to be excluded is "foreign difference," that which questions the stability and purity of dominant representations. As I will discuss more thoroughly in the next chapter, Derrida considers this schema to be a typical feature of the Western metaphysical tradition that is connected to a racialized type of thinking he names "White mythology." According to this schema, ideas presented as universal remain irreducibly linked to the context of their origins, and thus they can only be made universally valid through forced impositions and translations that hide the conditions affecting their formation, while excluding other alternatives (WM, 213/254). What emerges from this mythology, as it appears in Fichte, something on which Derrida comments in *The Other Heading*, is a distinctive combination of cultural and philosophical dimensions that have oppressive implications. On the one hand, there is a cultural "spirit" typical of European discourses that designate Europe as "capital," as a "spiritual heading" for "world civilization or human culture in general" (*OH*, 24/29, 28). Conceiving of universality as representable by a particular exemplar, this spirit articulates "the idea of an advanced point of exemplarity" as "the idea of the *European* idea" seen at once as "*arche*"—which refers to both natural and conventional origin—and "*telos*"—the end point or goal of humanity—an idea that traverses the entire "traditional discourse of modernity." Since "the time of Fichte, numerous examples might attest to this," says Derrida. In this "logic of this 'capitalistic' and cosmopolitical discourse, what is proper to a particular nation or idiom would be being a heading for Europe; and what is proper to Europe would be, analogically, to advance itself as a heading for the universal essence of humanity" (28/32, 48/49). On the other hand, there is a "logical schema" that provides the philosophical justification of this "*European* idea":

> In this struggle for control over culture, in this strategy that tries to organize cultural identity around a capital that is the more powerful for being mobile, that is, European in a hyper- or supra-national sense, national hegemony is not claimed—today no more than ever—in the name of an empirical superiority, which is to say, a simple particularity. That is why nationalism, national affirmations, as an essentially modern phenomenon, is always a philosopheme. National hegemony *presents itself*, claims itself. It claims to justify itself in the name of a privilege in responsibility and in the memory of the universal, and thus, of the transnational—indeed of the trans-European—and, finally, of the transcendental or ontological." (47/48–49)

The idea that Europe represents "an advanced point of exemplarity" is philosophically justified by the European spirit that claims responsibility for being both *arche* and *telos*, origin and end—a construction that is European, indeed idiomatic and national, but represented as universal and philosophical ("that is why nationalism" is "always a philosopheme"). It is in the encounter of European culture and philosophy, of a culture of the philosophical in which philosophy hides its cultural specificity under the exemplar as *the* sovereign representative of the universal that the erasure of difference structurally results out of the naturalization of European particularity. Seen this way, the "logical schema" of "traditional discourse is already a discourse of the modern *Western* world": a racialized universality (27/31). Indeed, as Derrida says, "there is nothing fortuitous" in the fact that this spirit of the exemplar as allegedly representing the essence humanity has mixed itself up with "xenophobia, racism, anti-Semitism, religious and national fanaticism" (6/13).

If only briefly, it is worth emphasizing at this point that Derrida's critical engagement with the theme of the European "spirit" and its connections to racism and antisemitism is a central one that culminates in a distinct work on the thought of Heidegger on the same. In *Of Spirit*, Derrida examines Heidegger's uses and yet surprising lack of thematization of "spirit" between 1927 and 1953, in respectively *Being and Time* [1927], the Rectorship Address entitled "The Self-Assertion of the German University" [1933]; *Introduction to Metaphysics* [1935], and essay on Trakl, "Language in the Poem" [1953].[4] Commenting on the theoretical strategies and political stakes of Heidegger's use and avoidance to use the term "spirit" and its derivatives (*Geist, geistig, geistlich*), Derrida raise the question whether, at work in Heidegger's writings, especially in the 1930s, there is an underlying philosophical racism and nationalism that locates in the German language, culture, and philosophical tradition a spiritual *leading* mission of the German people, which is regularly associated to "force" and "earth-and-blood" (*OS*, 34/57, 35/59). This mission would be the "destiny of the German people with its specific historical character" (34/57) and would consist in the "self-affirmation" of "its university as will to know and will to essence" (38/62). For Derrida, Heidegger's strategy of operating in the name of spirit and freedom—that is, the freedom of raising questions typical of philosophical spirit—can be read as breaking with, and perhaps denouncing, the biologism of vulgar forms of racism. Yet the "force to which Heidegger appeals, again and again in conclusion, when he speaks of the destiny of the West" in general and of Germany in particular, "spiritualizes National Socialism" giving it a sort of "spiritual legitimacy" (39/65). "Without there being anything fortuitous in this," Derrida continues, such a strategy "capitalizes on the worst that is on both evils at once: the sanctioning of nazism and the gesture that is still metaphysical" (40/66). So what Derrida finds deeply problematic in Heidegger is not simply the legitimation of Nazism. It is also, and as much as in Fichte, the philosophical grounding of a racialized universal discourse through the appeal to a "teleology" of "hierarchization and evaluation" (56/87) that affirms with force the sovereignty of European reason over and above other languages, and cultures—a sovereignty headed by German language as "the only language in which spirit comes to name itself" (71/113).[5]

Returning to the political connection between language and context: this emerges even more clearly in *Limited Inc*, a collection of essays in which Derrida discusses Searle's reading of John Austin's speech act theory. Here, I want to focus specifically on political aspects, which Derrida emphasizes in the "Afterword: Toward an Ethics of Discussion," where he links the political dimension of speech act theory and the attempt to fix a linguistic context to the politics of language as a politics of founding (*LI*, 105).[6] In response to Searle's invocation of speech act rules in questions of copyright, Derrida affirms that "there is always a police and a tribunal ready to intervene each time a rule [constitutive, regulative, vertical or not] is invoked in a case involving signature, events, or contexts" (135). This statement, he explains, emphasizes that the fixing of rules and contexts of utterances involves a policing power of "sanctioning, evaluating and selecting" a "cultural patrimony," an idiom, and rules for communication (135). The identification of that power, though, is not always straightforward since there are forms of policing that do not manifest themselves in a clearly recognizable manner. Unlike those that appear in the brutality of physical repression, "there are more sophisticated police that are more 'cultural' or 'spiritual,' more noble" and whose political dimension is "difficult to decipher" (135).

Derrida's target here is a type of theoretical discourse that, under the guise of philosophical reflection, fixes through exclusions and enforces apparently neutral and yet politically charged categories. He most cogently summarizes this by asking:

> Once it has been demonstrated, as I hope to have done, that exclusion of the parasite (of divergences, contaminations, impurities, etc.) cannot be justified by purely theoretical-methodological reasons, how can one ignore that this practice of exclusion, or

this will to purify, to re-appropriate in the manner that would be essential, internal, and ideal in respect to the subject or its objects, translates necessarily into a politics? Politics of language (which can lead, even if it does not always do so, to violences committed by the state), politics of education, politics of immigration, behaviour with regard to the "foreign" in general etc. This touches all social institutions . . . All this is political through and through, but it is not only political. (135)

For Derrida, the political dimension of less "visible" kinds of police affects different types of politics, especially the institution and preservation of language. In any given territory, this type of politics is linked to the attempt to fix linguistic context by determining rules, conventions, and uses of language. These are never severed from political interests as it appears, for example, in the imposition of a national language on minority groups or in the support of public institutions that determine what is proper to a specific national language (i.e., "good" French). For Derrida, such an attempt "always remains a performative operation and is never purely theoretical" and "cannot be apolitical or politically neutral" (132). For actually it "is always political because it implies, insofar as it involves determination, a certain type of non-"natural" relationship to others," whose ground remains without grounds (136). The instituting of a language as the official medium of communication in a given context establishes a mode for linguistic and social interactions whose nonnatural property is illuminated by their political origin. This institution cannot be separated from the type of politics, normative horizon, and fictions that are also introduced in the founding of a political community, as I shall discuss at length in chapter 3 (134).

To say that the determination of context is nonnatural and involves a fictional component does not imply collapsing certain cardinal distinctions such as that between philosophy and literature.[7] On the contrary, it implies recognizing first that no attempt at linguistic foundation can objectively claim the closure of context. What the fictional components do, in justificatory discourses, is to hide the violence and exclusions of the founding moment that threaten the stability of the newly established context and its representations of, for example, law, religion and ethics. Second, as a consequence, that fiction remains constitutive of any philosophical reflection about the ideal unity enabling the setting up of criteria for linguistic, ethico-political, and religious relevance which are central to linguistic foundations. The attempt to fix a context always occurs within an already existing and yet not fully determined context, whose heterogeneity and incompleteness need to be obscured and its reality renarrated for its claims of universal representation to have any traction at all.

> This leads me to elaborate rapidly what I suggested above concerning the question of context, of its nonclosure or, if you prefer, of its irreducible opening. I thus return to the question of apartheid. It is exemplary for the questions of responsibility and for the ethical-political stakes that underlie this discussion . . . Now, the very least that can be said of unconditionality (a word that I use not by accident to recall the character of the categorical imperative in its Kantian form) is that it is independent of every determination of a context in general. It announces itself as such only in the *opening* of context. Not that it is simply present (existent) elsewhere, outside of all context; rather, it intervenes in the determination of a context from its very inception, and from an injunction, a law, a responsibility that transcends this or that determination of a given context. Following this, what remains is to articulate this unconditionality with the determinate (Kant would say, the hypothetical) conditions of this or that context; and this is the moment of strategies, of rhetoric, of ethics, and of politics. The structure thus described supposes both that there are only contexts, that nothing *exists* outside context, as I have often said, but also the limit of the frame or the border of the context always entails a clause of nonclosure. (*LI*, 152)

The "unconditionality" of context never leaves the plane of contextuality since it is not "outside of all context." Yet this does not mean that "unconditionality" gets folded into the historical conditions of its manifestation. Indeed, that unconditionality "announces itself as such only in the *opening* of context" indicates that it remains conditioned, but not exhausted, by culture-specific historical, linguistic, and political conditions. This aspect of "nonclosure" puts limits to allegedly universally valid representations, as in the limit case of South Africa, where the white minority could not eventually maintain closed a context of apartheid based on the exclusion of the black majority, as Derrida mentions here but more amply illustrates elsewhere (LR, 67–69).[8] Viewed this way, unconditionality appears as linked to the event of political foundation and refers to a sort of structural excess of context, which in turn was determined on the basis of another context in a long series whose origin cannot be fixed and future conclusively determined.

Derrida advances here in relation to context a point analogous to the one he makes in his engagement with Plato and Nietzsche on the nature of the text. With regard to the former, he insists on the text's structural remainder that escapes conscious perception (*DIS*, 63/71). With regard to the latter, he emphasizes the "heterogeneity of the text," which eludes the possibility of recovering truth because the text is haunted by what always remains in it (*S*, 95/94). Thus, Derrida's claim in the passage above that "nothing *exists* outside context," which he previously connected to his affirmation in *Of Grammatology* that "there is nothing outside text" (*OG*, 158/227), is not trying to discredit values such as truth and objectivity, saying that linguistic context "exclude(s) the world, reality, history" nor to claim that "all referents" are suspended from the "real" world. As he clarifies, his notion of text is "neither limited to the graphic, nor to the book, nor even to discourse, and even less to the semantic, representational, symbolic, ideal, or ideological sphere." It implies instead reference to "reality" and such "real" domains as the "'economic,' 'historical,' 'socio-institutional'" (*LI*, 148). Rather, through that claim, Derrida affirms that there is no notion of truth, reference, and objectivity that is not already constituted from within a determined context and the "movement of recontextualization" and production of remainders it implies. Thus, there are limits to the possibility of *conclusively* establishing both truth and reference (136, 148). Derrida once again makes it clear that his work does not reject the value of truth or deny that language refers to an outside reality. In the context of his reflection on apartheid mentioned above, he speaks of the need "to call a thing by its name," "to be attentive to what links words to concepts and to realities," and of "the massive present reality of apartheid."[9] On the contrary, he emphasizes that "the value of truth (and all those values associated with it) is never contested or destroyed in my writings, but only re-inscribed in more powerful, larger, more stratified contexts" (146). Thus, far from questioning the value of truth and its embodied reality such as that of South African apartheid, as he has been accused of doing, Derrida's reflections point to the idea that truth and referents are inscribed in a complex web of political and economic forces mediated by discourse, including those of "South Africa and *apartheid*," forces that are therefore also part of "text," which "is always a field of forces: heterogeneous, differential, open" (BB, 168).[10] This means that while context (and text) cannot be fully transcended, any particular context remains structurally open to transformations.

To return to the issue of policing, Derrida clarifies that pointing out the implications of the police and the tribunal whenever rules are invoked is primarily a matter of structural irreducibility. Unless reference is fixed by "pragmatically determined situations," which involve also politico-institutional elements authorizing particular ways of using language, there would be no possibility of understanding and thus of meaningful communicative interaction (150). An appreciation of this point can counter the worry of those who consider Derrida a skeptic in ethico-political matters.[11] Derrida does not offer a pessimistic diagnosis or cynical analysis of modernity, which consider reason and philosophy as mere instruments for political domination. Instead, he acknowledges an undeniable feature of the practice of contextualization without surrendering to it. For him, the fundamental question for philosophical reflections on language and policing is "not whether a politics is implied (it always is), but *which* politics is implied in such a practice of contextualization" (136; my emphasis). By recognizing an irreducible but necessary policing aspect whenever rules are invoked, Derrida advocates for a certain critical vigilance so that the politics instituting and preserving language do not end up being politics as policing the type of values, ideals, and rules about which language usage and values can be part of communal life.

Summarizing the argument on language and context so far, Derrida insists that language is always conditioned by geo-political elements and communities of speakers, which delimit the context of communication and set the rules for meaning that are never severed from those which establish criteria of epistemic, linguistic, and ethico-political relevance. He shows that it is always within particular national communities that the boundaries of language, including the language of philosophy, are framed. By questioning the purely neutral character of language, Derrida challenges the idea that philosophical reflection employs linguistic categories that are shielded from political determinations. He also shows that such apparently neutral categories are always contingently grounded in the political order and normative forces that have authorized them in the first place.

The significance of these points for thinking about the "theological-political complex" must be emphasized. Derrida's exposition of the close relationship between national context and idiom on the one hand, and philosophy on the other, puts limits to a universalist type of thinking about the theological-political relationship. As dominant in the Western political tradition, this type of thinking finds its clearest contemporary expression in debates on religion and politics in the work of Jürgen Habermas and John Rawls, who appeal to an allegedly neutral universal language to address public disputes and political process of justification.[12] If philosophical language necessarily retains certain elements of the idiom it employs, and this obviously applies also to the language of public reason argued by these authors, it cannot be invoked as a neutral and universal medium for the legitimate adjudication of public disagreement with the good conscience that subtle nationalistic features are not also at work. Put otherwise, one could say that the traces and interests of political identity are irreducibly involved whenever an appeal to a putatively universal language is invoked for the impartial and neutral resolution of public disputes or justification of political arrangements. From Derrida's point of view, forgetting or refusing to see this point is both philosophically deficient and politically problematic, given the exclusionary implications connected to this blindness. It is philosophically deficient because it fails to consider the material conditions of possibility of philosophical language and the constraints these put on universalist discourses. It is politically problematic since a (philosophical) language that pretends to be universal, while retaining the mark of the particular context in which it developed, makes the exclusion of difference as a structural effect of its functioning. Indeed, elevating such a language to a universal plane and using it as a tool to regulate public life cannot but discriminate against particular perspectives that challenge the material conditions and specific values informing a so-called universal language.

As the discussion of Fichte has suggested, this view of language is marked by a schema of concealment and hierachization that is connected to racialized forms of thinking. Concrete realities that speak to this point are numerous in the Americas, Africa, and Australia. In different ways, indigenous groups in these contexts have often denounced the illegitimacy and nonuniversality of the language used in public life and justified in the name of an allegedly neutral secularism. In Canada, for example, the use of English and French as the official public languages hardly does justice to the linguistic context and diversity of its First Nations population whose values and culture are subject to the assimilating force of the idiomatic language(s) of the law and public institutions that are presented as neutral. More evident is perhaps the case of majority of states in Africa where the colonial language has been adopted as the official one to the detriment of indigenous languages.[13]

Translation and Secular Language

The linguistic human predicament constitutes another feature of Derrida's view of the political character of language. In his view, translation plays a central role and represents a core theme of his entire corpus. As he says, "the question of deconstruction is . . . through and through the question of translation" (LJ, 2/2).[14] For our purposes, though, I will concentrate primarily on *Monolingualism of the Other, Or the Prosthesis of Origin* (henceforth *Monolingualism*), which is arguably the most political text about translation and the human linguistic predicament. In the opening of this text, Derrida makes the following stunning claim: "I only have one language and that language is not mine," which for him represents "not only the very law of what is called translation" but the "law itself as translation" (*MO*, 10/13). The rest of the book can be considered an attempt to demonstrate what this statement announces. To support this claim, he uses a particular approach central to understanding his argument as well as a distinctive a mode of critical reflection. Derrida undertakes an autobiographical exercise as a way of philosophically working through his own lived experience, and not simply experience as such. This mode of inquiry is distinct from traditional philosophical demonstrations claiming universal validity by invoking rules of formal logic. Early in the text, Derrida anticipates objections such as logical inconsistency and performative contradiction.[15] He indicates that they do not apply to his way of proceeding since his is a form of demonstration in the manner of exemplar attestation or testimony.[16]

For Derrida, exemplar attestation is a way of reflecting on a general philosophical problem through lived experience and the particularly determined predicament in which thinking takes place. This occurs in the critical awareness that the articulation of a philosophical problem retains irreducibly particular features. Thus, the autobiographical narrative that informs exemplar attestation is not accidental, but it is a conscious choice to talk about what one is doing by doing what one is talking about. Rather than demonstrating "logically," testimony restages a predicament and asks for believing that what one says is true, which is not the same as speaking the truth (9/24). To this mode of reflection, the charge of performative contradiction misses the epistemic value of a witnessing that asks for trust on the basis of lived experience.[17] This witnessing acquires such a value especially when offered by subjects like Derrida, whose lived experience of *being* colonized[18] testifies to the undeniable exclusion produced by the so-called Western civilization and points to the false universalism of accounts that present and represent Western modernity and its values as inherently rational and universally acceptable.[19]

My point is that Derrida's witnessing offers an example of an embodied, self-critical positionality from which he unsettles dominant accounts of Western modernity. He does so by exposing the philosophical assumptions, logic, and oppressive implications of a reflexive type of critique that claims guardianship on enlightened thinking while obscuring the particular conditions and forces involved in its occurrence, spread, and hegemony.[20] While not always recognized as such, Derrida's understanding of deconstruction as the analysis of "what *remains* to be thought" (*LI*, 147) gives epistemic potency to this mode of reflection. Indeed, if read in conjunction with the idea of "White mythology" as an exclusionary and distinctively Western type of discourse, deconstruction so conceived opens a space to address excluded and yet "remaining" traditions together with the logic and history of the conditions—capitalism, colonialism, and secularism—that made such exclusion possible on a global scale.

Returning to our discussion: if the specific conditions in and from which philosophical investigation takes place are so central to exemplar attestation and its critical import, Derrida's particular predicament needs to be spelled out at the outset before we look in more detail at his main argument.[21] His point of departure is his experience of living in and through the French language as a "non-French" person. In spite of speaking French, the only language he says he knows, Derrida considers himself to be an "*aphasic*" self. For the language he speaks is not his, especially with regard to questions of history, memory, and identity (*MO*, 61/117). What lies in the background here is his lived experience of a colonized individual: a Franco-Maghrebian Jew from Algeria as the exemplary individual who benefited from, and yet was deprived of, French citizenship in virtue of his Jewish identity and subjected to colonial policies as an Algerian (14/31–32).[22] To this individual, the interdiction put into effect by the French government has not simply obstructed the appropriation of French language as a mother tongue but also cut him off from the possibility of accessing non-French cultures and languages (especially Arabic and Berber) spoken in his environment, thereby impeding the access to models of identifications that could resonate with his lived experience (61/118).[23]

The intricate linguistic situation affecting this monolingual individual produces paradoxical psycho-affective effects, a sense of both belonging to, and alienation from, multiple identities—variously described as African, Algerian, Black, Jewish, Arab, Arab Jew—leading to a complex and yet unrealizable desire to reconstruct an original idiom.[24] Yet this desire is unrealizable since all this self has are "target languages" (*langues d'arrivé*) that are in a relation of translation with each other. These are called "target" or, as Geoffrey Bennington has suggested, "arrival languages" not because they have arrived somewhere but because they are languages without a clearly identifiable origin or destination.²⁵ Placed in a situation of arrival and animated by a desire to recollect its own self in language, the monolingual self seeks to reconstitute a source language (*langue de départ*), to invent what Derrida calls a *"first language* that would be, rather, a *prior-to-the first language"* destined to translate the memory of a source language that was never available and whose space was occupied by the language of the colonizer (*MO*, 61/117). In the absence of a source language, a "first language" can only be invented on the basis of a desire activated by being in that very situation.

The predicament of arrival constitutes the cardinal point around which Derrida's view of the linguistic human condition is construed and thus requires further investigation. Early in the text, he introduces two apparently antinomical propositions: "We only ever speak one language—or rather one idiom only. We never speak one language only—or rather there is no pure idiom" (8/23). Central to the understanding of these apparently contradictory claims is the distinction between language *qua* medium or capacity of communication and language *qua* idiom. Regardless of whether one speaks different idioms, there can only be one language as a capacity for communication. Were this not the case (i.e., if there were two languages as medium) there would have to be another faculty to make their synthesis possible. Thus, we only speak one language because that is what we *can* do. Yet we never speak only one idiom because the latter is not identical to itself, but it is instead internally differentiated and marked by its relationship with other idioms. In English, for example, this impurity is apparent through the presence of words from French, German, Greek, and Latin, among others.

There are two important implications that follow from this view. The first regards the impossibility of metalanguage. As Derrida notes, "whatever remains insurmountable in it (language) . . . is quite simply that 'there is language,' 'there is language which does not exist,' namely that there is no metalanguage, and that *a* language shall always be called upon to speak about *the* language—*because* the latter does not exist" (69/128). By asking the question of the language in which the question of language is raised, Derrida points here to the limits of reaching a metalinguistic level. If all idioms are in a relation of translation with each other, no language can reach a metalevel from which to talk about "*the* language," without already relaying it into "*a* language" that relates to other languages as equal and not as *the* translating language.²⁶ The second implication concerns the impure and contaminated character of idioms, none of which can function as a source or original language. As Derrida shows in his early writings, origins are elusive and cannot be clearly grasped in human consciousness as distinct from the contingent conditions under which they occur (*LI*, 136). Like any origin, the origin of language—the determination of which would be essential to identify an original language—is affected by the same predicament (*FL*, 272/94). Thus, the duplicity at the heart of language as idiom, and its being-in-translation with other idioms, indicates that any such language cannot be an original language.

But what does it mean to say that the linguistic situation human beings always already find themselves in is that of translation? And what is translation, exactly? Answering these questions requires momentarily departing from Derrida's *Monolingualism* and digressing to explore other works in which he explicitly shows the question of translation to be central to the nature of language and to the theological-political relationship. Starting with the first one, Derrida considers translation as a key feature of language understood as form of writing. This view appears clearly and succinctly in "Semiology and Grammatology" where he illustrates the linguistic process of signification through his analysis of the sign and the movement of repetition that sustains that process.[27] For him, the possibility of written sings to be legible across time, and thus beyond their original context(s) and author(s), requires iterability or the possibility of repetition. Yet, since repetition occurs in different times and contexts, it involves the constitutive possibility of semantic alteration and differentiation that destabilizes the link between word, meaning, and reference (*SEC*, 315–17/ 375–77).

Here his famous notion of *différance* is key. Referring to neither a concept nor a word but to the difference *between* signs, this notion seeks to convey the double sense of difference and deferral of the French *différer* as well as a spatial and temporal connotation that affect the links between word, meaning, and reference (*POS*, 8–9/17; see also *D*, 7–8/7–8). While difference refers to the differing meaning of any sign "produced" by the traces of its relationship with other signs, deferral points to the infinite delay in the final determination of the sign's meaning. Such a determination cannot occur precisely in virtue of the constant play of signification: each sign cannot refer to or function as an ultimate referent since it is constituted only in relation to other signs that are subject to the possibility of alteration (*POS*, 20/30). Designating a dynamic and culturally mediated web of spatio-temporal differences within which reference is simultaneously described and constituted, *différance* points therefore to a structural undecidability within language and thus also to the limits of pure idealization. As a result, no word or sign can be considered as a self-identical unit that can conclusively fix reference, which is also to say that linguistic context cannot completely be closed. This impossibility illuminates, on the one hand, the limits of polysemy, namely, the calculation of all possible meanings of a sign. On the other hand, it points to what Derrida calls dissemination, namely, the possibility that chains of signification engender plurality of incalculable meanings resulting from the process of repetition across spaces and times (SEC, 316/376). This occurs since dissemination "explode[s] [*crever*] the semantic horizon" and produces "a non-finite number of semantic effects" that cannot be traced back "to a simple present origin" that would fix reference; and thus, as such, "it marks an irreducible and *generative* multiplicity" (POS, 45/61).

For Derrida, the impossibility of fixing reference, however, does not by itself impede temporary stabilizations or the intelligibility of the difference between word, meaning, and object. This proves to be essential to translation. It only impedes a model centered on a "pure, transparent and unequivocal translatability" (SG, 20/31). Indeed, it is because such distinctions and provisional stabilizations are possible that the transfer of meaning from one language to another can be practiced. As he notes, "in the limits to which it is possible, or at least *appears* possible, translation practices the difference between signifier and signified" (20/31). That is, it is only because one can differentiate between word (signifier) and meaning (signified) that it is possible to translate, that is, to carry over (from Latin *translatio* means "to carry over or across," "to transfer") meaning from one language into another.[28] Yet this transfer is not a *simple* one, and it involves a degree of modification: "But if that difference [between signifier and signified] is never pure, no more so is translation, and for the notion of translation we will have to substitute a notion of *transformation*: a regulated transformation of one language by another" (20/31; my emphasis). Rather than blocking translation, these limits to its transparent occurrence point to the paradoxical law of translation as one that is both "necessary and impossible" (TB, 109/210). Translation is necessary in order to determine the relationship between word, meaning, and reference in the context of the translating language. But it is impossible to conclusively do so given that such a nexus is affected by undecidability, which only impedes *full* translation. Indeed, undecidability reveals that translation always involves a certain degree of transformation since it modifies the links between word, reference, and meaning in order to carry over meaning from one language into another, where such links are reconstituted only at the expense of a fundamental loss (SG, 20/31).

At issue here is the problem of untranslatability, which Derrida develops especially in connection to the question of proper names and the work of Walter Benjamin. For Benjamin, translation is an "art form" that does not concern what is translatable, namely, cognitive content, but what is not translatable in language, that is, the relationship between content and language.[29] In his view, this element refers to language as naming, which, while expressing the uniqueness of things through proper names, does not communicate anything beyond communicability. Although this capacity does not appear immediately, since it is obscured by the fact that languages use names as repeatable nouns conveying information, it is nevertheless distinctive of human language. Specifically, it is connected to a putatively original process of naming, a "pure language," that respected the singularity of things by assigning proper names.[30] On Benjamin's reading, the task of the translator is thus to render this untranslatable singularity by echoing the mode of intention of the original, the ultimate model of which is divine language.[31]

While departing from Benjamin's ambiguous longing for a divine origin, Derrida develops the question of untranslatability through a reflection on the proper name. His classic example is that of Babel as it appears in Genesis, which he discusses in his essay "Des Tours de Babel." According to the dominant reading of the biblical story, God punishes human beings for their attempt to build a tower as high as the heavens and to give themselves a unique name in a tongue they could impose universally. By proclaiming his name and destroying their tower, God scatters the uniqueness of a single people and multiplies their tongues, an event that Derrida reads as the dissemination of God's proper name that now comes always in a divided form "Babel, Confusion," the confusion ensuing from the multiplication of languages (TB, 108/209). This example is paradigmatic for several reasons: first, it allows us to distinguish between transferability and translatability. The meaning of the sacred text, the proper name of God, is transferred in its singularity as "Babel" which "can only let itself be translated as untranslatable" (i.e., by remaining "Babel"). Here the unity between meaning and literality refers to Benjamin's idea of pure communicability: the proper name does not communicate anything beyond its literality (132–33/230–31). Second, it shows that the original is *already* divided and this questions Benjamin's idea of the indispensability of the concept of origin:[32] the dual form "Babel, Confusion" that has been received "in translation" shows that reference is divided and thus not stable already in the origin (109/208). Finally, the biblical example exposes the paradoxical law of translation as caught between untranslatability and translatability, necessity and impossibility: translation is necessary to determine the relationship between the word "Babel" and its unique reference, yet it is also impossible given the undecidability of whether "Babel" belongs to a proper name or a common noun.

The significance of "Babel" extends beyond the biblical story and illuminates the violence of the understanding of language presupposed by a model of transparent translation. Indeed, the example of "Babel" illuminates that semantic loss is a structural possibility of translation since the latter involves treating signs as if they were both proper names and common nouns. And this means that untranslatability cannot be fully circumvented but only covered up by an attempt to impose a unique, transparent idiom that fixes reference univocally, as the case of the Semites illustrates. As Derrida remarks, in the attempt to establish a name for themselves and thus also a universal language and unique genealogy, "the Semites, want to bring the world to reason, and this reason can signify simultaneously a *colonial* violence (since they would thus universalize their idiom) and a peaceful transparency of the human community" (*violence coloniale (puisqu'ils universaliseraient ainsi leur idiome) et une transparence pacifique de la communauté humaine*) (111/210; my emphasis). However, God's imposition of his own name as a proper name "ruptures the rational transparency but also interrupts colonial violence or linguistic imperialism." By destining the Semites to translation, which is both necessary and impossible, God opens the way to "universal reason," which "will no longer be subject to the rule of a particular nation" while at the same time limiting "its very universality: forbidden transparency, impossible univocity." In doing so, God makes it possible that translation "becomes law, duty and debt, but the debt one can no longer discharge" (111/210).

By dispossessing any particular idiom of the possibility of exhausting universal reason and language (as medium), God deprives any linguistic community of an ideal and transparent model of translation. Thus, God destines human beings to being-with-others-in-translation, that is, to a dutiful condition of indebtedness to what has been left out in the act of translation and that cannot be cleared. Derrida could be seen as offering a reformulation of the Heideggerrian *Mit-Sein*.[33] Because human beings always already find themselves in a predicament of translation, which can never be transparent and thus complete, the linguistic human condition is one in which linguistic and cultural differences are to be constantly negotiated intralinguistically and interlinguistically as best as possible. Hence the non-dischargeable character of the debt.

The understanding of translation emerging from the Babelian story is of philosophical and political significance. First, translation appears as intimately connected to the task of philosophy. The job of reason is translating meaning by respecting its integrity beyond linguistic differences. Intervening in a "Roundtable on Translation" in 1979, where he commented at length on the exemplary importance of the Babelian story for all discussions on translation, Derrida affirms that "the origin of philosophy is translation or the thesis of philosophy is translatability" to indicate that "philosophical discourse cannot simultaneously master a word meaning two things at the same time and which therefore cannot translate without an essential loss."[34] The resolution of semantic undecidability that characterizes and limits translation equally affects and limits philosophy too. Philosophy, to function at all, needs to "fix" the "univocality" of meaning or "master its plurivocality"; that is, it needs to determine the relationship between word, meaning, and reference as unequivocally and univocally as possible (RT, 120/159–60; see also WM, 247/295). Although this settles undecidable questions in one direction or another, it does not dissolve undecidability as such. Second, translation emerges as a political problem. While communal life requires translation as a way of negotiating differences, the predicament of translation indicates that a transparent translation is impossible and that responses to pluralism based on the universalization of a particular language and view of reason involve colonial violence and linguistic imperialism.[35]

But there is a further aspect of translation that exceeds its purely linguistic nature that Derrida explores in his essay "Me—Psychoanalysis." Here he addresses a form of translation that regards the relationship between the affective and linguistic registers. Specifically, he explores the notion of "anasemic translation" as a type of translation that puts into discursive terms the nonlinguistic conditions of language. Unlike interlinguistic and intralinguistic translations, this type of translation connects "heterogeneous territories" and gives linguistic access to a "pre-originary" origin of sense that is "other than sense," which is possible only through a translation that "must twist its tongue" as it were (MP, 133–34/148–49, 139/155). Typical of psychoanalytic translations of unconscious material into discursive articulations, this form of translation can only proceed "symbolically and anasemically" precisely because it gives linguistic access to what is, strictly speaking, "inaccessible" in that register and thus remains, in some important sense, untranslatable (138/154). While Derrida's treatment of "anasemic translation" has relevance for psychoanalytic theory and practice, and for understanding the nature of translation more generally, it is also decisive when religious experience is at issue.[36] This holds especially if one challenges the widespread modern idea of religion as being primarily a cognitive phenomenon about belief. This dimension of translation and untranslatability brings an additional complexity to Derrida's perspective that would require a more ample treatment than can be offered here, one that would need to be explored in the future, especially in relation to recent articulations of untranslatability in Islam.[37]

While acknowledging the limits of translation, however, Derrida does not refrain from reflecting about what makes a good translation. In "What Is a Relevant Translation?" he addresses this question through a discussion of the traditional model of translation, whose history and normative conceptualization remain indebted to Christianity (WRT, 199). According to that model, a relevant translation consists in a transfer of meaning between languages so that the translated word appears in the receiving language as the most appropriate or "relevant equivalent for an original" (177). As such, "the most relevant translation" is "that which presents itself as the transfer of an intact signified through the inconsequential vehicle of any signifier whatsoever" (195).[38] Inscribed in the European tradition of translation, this view, Derrida observes, assigns to the word a prominent role. Whether translation is considered according to the model "word-to-word," as in Cicero, or "sense-to-sense," as in Jerome, or "one word *by* one word," as in more recent theories of literal translation, the word is considered as "the indivisible unity of an acoustic form that incorporates or signifies the indivisible unity of a meaning or concept" (181).

At a less technical but deeper level, and above all central to our focus here, the traditional model of translation displays distinctively theological-political features. This appears most clearly through Derrida's reading, in the same essay, of Shakespeare's *The Merchant of Venice*, which Derrida sees as exemplifying "a problem of translation" for several reason. The contract between Shylock and Antonio, which obligates the latter to offer a pound of his flesh in case he fails to pay in time the loan received from the former, establishes both an "obligation of fidelity" and an "insolvable debt" to a "given original" as key to translation. Furthermore, calculation appears as the relevant standard of translation over an "incalculable equivalence" between flesh and money. Finally, a religious dimension appears irreducible to translation, which takes the form of conversion: the Jew Shylock and the literality of the body are forcefully converted into a Christian horizon, and the spirit or sense of the word by the Christian state represented by Portia (184).

On Derrida's account, the traditional understanding of translation is problematic in three respects: first, it naturalizes the unity of the word, thereby obscuring the "historical, institutional and conventional" forces enabling that concealment. Informed by a mechanistic view of language that considers words as atomistic units, this computational model of translation overlooks the complexity and functioning of language. Indeed, the quantitative calculation of verbal units presupposes that all-possible meanings can be deciphered, and thus it fails to account for the constitutive gap between word and thing and the ways in which the repetition or transfer of signs across times and contexts might generate unforeseen significations. Second, the traditional view of translation appears blind to the culture-specific assumptions that inform it and thus also to the powers that condition language and contribute to make particular understandings of it appear as universally valid. This feature emerges most clearly if one focuses on the notion of "relevance," a word of Latin origin (from *relevans* as the present participle of *relevare*, "to raise or lift up") that is commonly used in several European languages and that, as a concept, has acquired a universal currency as testified by its central role in twentieth-century translation theory and practice. [39] For Derrida, when "relevance" is associated to translation in the traditional view, it refers not simply to an unequivocal standard of measurement but also to the definition of the essence of translation: a translation is relevant, and thus valid and acceptable, if it renders what is equivalent to the original in a transparent and univocal way (WRT, 182). Far from being neutral and uncontested, this view, as seen, is derived from a particular cultural tradition that has become dominant. Finally, in the traditional view, translation functions as an oppressive and assimilatory instrument of secularization effected through state sovereignty. The "God-like" sovereign power of the state exemplified by the figure of Portia "the Christian or the Christian in the guise of the law," who commands Shylock to be merciful with Antonio's failure to respect their contract, forcefully translates Shylock's demand for (Jewish) justice with (Christian) mercy, thereby displaying a Christian mark on an understanding of political sovereignty that invokes the divine in support of "a theologico-political translation, of the translation of the theological into political" (188, 194). This appeal to the theological in support of the political by which the earthly king resembles and invokes a divine power to give mercy is, for Derrida, "the very site of the theologico-political, the hyphen or translation between the theological and the political; it is also what underwrites political sovereignty, the Christian incarnation of the body of God (or Christ) in the king's body, the king's two bodies." Figuratively, this site is also "what enables the authorization of every ruse and vile action" of powers operating under Christian universalism against difference: in this case the Jew (197). At a deeper level, translation as a theological-political phenomenon related to state sovereignty and forced conversion displays racial features. Indeed, it signals a religion-based ordering within the state, specifically one in which Christian understandings and values play a decisive role in organizing public life through social hierarchies that discriminate against non-Christians. As historians and scholars of race have documented, forced conversion was part of a racialized schema in which Christian religion informed the development of racial formations and processes of racialization since medieval England against Jews,[40] and more systematically in fifteenth- and sixteenth-century Iberian lands against Jews and Muslims, as well as against indigenous populations in the Americas, and Blacks in Africa.

In contrast to this perspective, Derrida understands translation as an "economy of in betweenness," an experience of oscillating "between absolute relevance, the most appropriate, adequate, univocal transparency and the most aberrant and opaque irrelevance" (179). The ambivalence between these poles is related to a different understanding of language and of how meaning is transferred across idioms. As seen, Derrida does not conceive of language as a sort of transparent tool for communicating content in which each word refers to a fix referent.[41] Questioning the clear distinction between the revelatory and communicative aspects of language, he thinks of the latter as mediated by power and history and as characterized by a constant movement of alteration and potential dissemination that keeps both meaning and translation open-ended. As a result, the calculability of words and their semantic content becomes more problematic than what it might appear. This holds in virtue of the instability to which meaning is subject in a given language and also of the fact that in the passage from one language to another, meaning undergoes a forceful modification that is related to its compliance to a new linguistic context. It is with reference to the asymmetry of power between the translating and translated language that Derrida emphasizes transformation as a central moment of translation. For him, rather than impeding translation, failure allows exposure of the politics behind models of language informed by putatively neutral values such as transparency and semantic equivalence. His claim that "nothing is translatable; everything is translatable" goes in this direction. It indicates that, beyond the aforementioned problematics of untranslatability, when a translation occurs, the meaning of what is translated might be so modified that it might become more "relevant" to context and interests of the translating language than that of the translated one. For instance, using the English word "religion"—which, as I shall discuss at length, is indebted to specifically Western Christian modernity—to speak generally about religious phenomena across cultural traditions, is an example of translation that seeks to fix the link between word (religion), meaning (*religio*) and reference ("religious" phenomena) by relying on the rules and interests of the translating language and culture.

Having explored translation in connection with the nature of language and the human condition, we can now consider its specific significance for the "theological-political complex" through an exploration of Derrida's "The Eyes of Language: The Abyss and the Volcano" first, and then to "Faith and Knowledge" and "Above All, No Journalist!" In the "The Eyes of Language: The Abyss and the Volcano," Derrida reads an exchange between Gershom Scholem and Franz Rosenzweig regarding the Zionist's attempt to secularize biblical Hebrew into a modern idiom, and he challenges the idea of secularization as translation. Commenting on the exchange between Scholem and Rosenzweig and the language they speak (German) to speak about sacred language, Derrida raises the question whether one can "speak a sacred language as a foreign language" (*EL*, 199). This question raises the fundamental point of which language one can use to speak of language in general and of sacred language in particular (190). Derrida risks the hypothesis that there could be a "third" language, a sort of neutral medium allowing the passage from sacred to profane language, translating one into the other. However, rather quickly, he questions this possibility: "What if, in fact, *there were no* third language, no language in general no neutral language within which were possible in order to take place within it [*dans la quelle serait possible, pour y avoir lieu*] the contamination of the sacred and the profane, the corruption of names (Spinoza), the opposition of the holy and the secular? . . . What if this neutralization by recourse to a third, already to a kind of metalinguistic referee, were also a positivist neutralization of the supernatural?" (200). Further, Derrida denies that this third language can be a possibility for Scholem, for whom "there is only sacred language," which for him (Scholem) means that the secularization of language "does not exist; it is but a *façon de parler*, a manner of speaking" (201).

For Derrida, the importance of Scholem's position rests on the challenge the latter poses to the secularization of language as a form of unproblematic translation of a sacred idiom into a secular one, but also to the political stakes this phenomenon exposes in general, and in the case of modern Hebrew in particular. As Derrida notes, "there is no real secularization [*il n'ya pas de secularisation effective*], is what this strange confession (Scholem's) suggests, in sum. What one lightly calls 'secularization' does not take place [*n'a pas lieu*]. This surface effect does not affect language itself, which remains sacred in its abyssal interior." Scholem's view suggests that secularized language is epiphenomenal to sacred language since the former is simply a manner of speaking and thus its apparent metalinguistic character is only a "rhetorical effect" (201). And yet, Derrida notes, "it is secularization that allows us to speak of a secularization that does not take place" since secularization has occurred "enough for one to be able to speak of it" as Scholem implicitly confirms by referring to the way Hebrew is now spoken "in the street" (216–17, 226).

For Derrida, then, the rhetorical effect of secularization is key for two reasons: first, because it reaches all languages and knowledge forms considering themselves objective and neutral, secular, in fact: "[W]e must not try to hide this from ourselves; this effect is massive enough to concern, in principle, the totality of the language called technical, objective, scientific, and even philosophical" (202). Second, and more deeply, the secularization of sacred language is not simply a complex linguistic phenomenon of translation. It is above all a political problem that requires the institutional apparatuses and violence connected to the formation of modern nation-states. Derrida addresses this problem by reflecting on the gravity of Scholem's own words:

> This is played out from the very first lines of the letter, after the figure of the volcano and the allusion to the danger more uncanny (*unheimlicher* [*inquietant*]) than the Arab people, to the "necessary consequence" of the Zionist undertaking Scholem has therefore just recognized—and recognition is the gravity of his confession [*et de reconnaitre c'est toute la gravité de sa confession*]—in front of the notorious anti-Zionism of his addressee, that the evil is worse and more uncanny than any other properly political danger [*tout autre danger proprement politique*]. This evil of language is also a political evil but it is not an infantile illness of Zionism. This "necessary consequence" is congenital to every Zionist project for a nation state. Scholem continues, "[W]hat about the 'actualization' of Hebrew? Must not this abyss of a sacred language handed down to our children break out again?" (201)

For Derrida, the "evil of language is also a political evil but is not an infantile illness of Zionism." It is instead a "necessary consequence" that is "congenital to every Zionist project for a nation state" (201).[42] Reaffirming his earlier statement about "Zionism [as] an *evil*, an inner evil, an evil that is anything but accidental [*un mal qui n'a rien d'accidentel*]," Derrida points here to the violence and injustice against the Palestinians as a conscious and structural ("not . . . infantile"; "congenital") consequence of Zionism as a political project that secularizes Judaism, a consequence that will have occurred with the foundation of the state of Israel (194).

Yet, Derrida does not name here, at least not explicitly, the nature of this process and of the political entities that resulted from it, though he addresses the stakes and implications of the nexus between Judaism, Zionism, and the state of Israel elsewhere, sometimes using the language of colonialism, but not across the board (*AF* 77/101, 94/148; *AL* 81–82/147–48; FAPU, 259).[43] In this way, he also stops short from developing a line of inquiry into the relationship between secularization and settler colonialism that his earlier writings on South Africa appeared to call for, albeit not directly.[44]

Derrida thus seems to agree with Scholem in maintaining that "there is no metalanguage. Secular language as metalanguage, therefore, does not exist in itself; it has neither presence nor consistency of its own" (202). His questioning of the possibility of metalanguage is linked to that of a neutral medium in which one can talk of language from a position of noncontamination and nontranslation between sacred and secular language. Concurrently, Derrida shares Scholem's insights that the secularization of sacred language as a form of translation of sacred idiom into a secular one is more than a linguistic phenomenon. Yet, by highlighting the "gravity" of Scholem's affirmations on the political dimension of "actualizing Hebrew," that is of secularizing Judaism through political Zionism in a land characterized by the "presence of Arab people," Derrida offers the resources to expose the settler colonial form secularization as translation can take when put at the service of a political project of nation-state formation that structurally and consciously involves massive displacement and dispossession of long-settled populations.

So conceived, Derrida's view has significant implications also for contemporary perspectives on the "theological-political complex" as diverse as those of thinkers like Carl Schmitt and Jürgen Habermas. In *Political Theology*, Schmitt advances the thesis that modern political categories are a secularized version of a theological heritage and conceives of sovereignty as the secular analogue of the miracle in theology.[45] This view employs a rather ambiguous notion of secularization according to which it is possible to translate Christian theological idiom and categories into the secular language of legal theory. This would occur by retaining *simply* theology's systematic structure while operating outside it in order to guarantee the autonomy of the political. In his recent writings on secularism and religion, Habermas subscribes to a form of secularization as translation.[46] He advocates for the need to translate religious language into the secular one of public reason, a language that is universally accessible to all citizens and that is to be employed in public life whenever fundamental political questions require legitimation.[47] As such, his view relies on the possibility of a neutral secular language that lies, freestanding, in a condition of noncontamination and translation because it is accessible to all citizens independently of the language they speak, natural or religious.

Derrida's view opposes all these positions. By acknowledging translation as the inaugural linguistic human condition affecting also the relationship between sacred and secular languages, his view puts limits on the possibility of philosophical (secular) reductionism in the form of secularization *à la* Schmitt.[48] Actually, Derrida believes that the modern concept of secularization remains religious, that is, tied to the Christian tradition and thus particular.[49] In this way, his perspective equally puts limits on the viability of a neutral language that could remain unaffected by the predicament of translation so that it can be invoked to *impartially* settle public disputes, as in Habermas. Indeed, if the predicament of translation points to the impossibility of metalanguage and the complexity surrounding interlinguistic translation, the notion of secularization as implying a "simple" translation appears as highly problematic with respect to both theoretical concerns and practical questions of political legitimacy, especially in state formation. At the very least, Derrida's view calls for a substantial rethinking of secularization so conceived.

But the question of "simple" translation is not the only issue that Derrida's reflections on secularization as translation bring to the fore. His reflections also expose the politics of translation that has characterized the spread of globalization of which secularization is a central element. Indeed, Derrida considers that secularization as translation involves more than translating a sacred idiom and categories into secular ones. It also involves translating various sacred idioms into the idiom of Christian "religion." In "Faith and Knowledge," Derrida recognizes the Latin and Christian origins of the term "religion" (*religio*) and the problems involved in using it to designate religious phenomena in general.[50] This emerges already from the opening of the essay: "How 'to talk religion'? Of religion? Singularly of religion, today? How dare we speak it in the singular without fear and trembling, this very day? And so briefly and so quickly? Who would be so imprudent as to claim that the issue is both identifiable and new?" (FK, 42/9). Derrida is particularly interested in the language in which the question of religion is posed. As with the question raised above with regard to language (in what language is the question of language raised?), the question of the language of religion concerns the translatability and iterability of (proper) names. "Here we are confronted by the overwhelming question of the name and everything done 'in the name of': questions of the name or noun 'religion,' of the names of God, of whether the proper name belongs to the system of language or not hence its untranslatability but also iterability" (46/15). For Derrida, this situation suggests that whenever we talk about religion in the language of *religio*, "we are already speaking Latin" (66/47).[51] This means, as a consequence, that perhaps we do not know what religion is. For as long as the question is posed in these terms, our knowledge would seem to be always already mediated by a specific name, "religion," which is used as a generic noun to translate a variety of religious phenomena. But, Derrida asks, "[W]hat if religion remained untranslatable?" (67/48).

Before considering how this possibility has been circumvented in the modern discourse of religion, it is useful to briefly clarify how Derrida understands the process of globalization within which such discourse and its translating practices have occurred. Instead of using the term "globalization," Derrida uses the French term *mondialatinisation* commonly translated as globalatinization.[52] With this term he seeks to emphasize the nature, stakes, and significance of what is too often made to pass as the worldwide extension of universal principles and the political forms that embody them. As he says, "we are not speaking here of universality; even of an idea of universality, only of a process of universalization that is infinite and enigmatic" (66/47). For him, what is made worldwide is not some universal principle but the "juridical-theological-political culture" of Christianity and its Latin language through the use of media and through the imperialist imposition of secular understandings and institutions (such, for example, international law, sovereignty and citizenship) that have inherited a specific "religious substratum" (FK, 76/49; 64/43), as well as via a massive process of appropriation of resources and dispossession made by, and benefiting, "wealthy, northern countries" (AI, 122). While Derrida recognizes that Latin is no longer spoken, he contends that its Christianizing function initially performed by European colonialism continues today through Anglo-American, the language that dominates international institutions and politics and presents itself as neutral and secular; rational in fact (66–67/47). The stakes behind this imposition concern the access to the means through which knowledge about reality is produced through which one gives sense to the "world" *(monde* in French, hence the preference for *mondialatinisation* to globalatinization), which, Derrida notes, remains "a Christian concept" (AANJ, 66) with a Christian history.[53] And since technology and means of telecommunication are central in determining the sense of what "world" means and what its spatial-temporal limits are, the relevant stakes here regard the struggle to access and control them (FK, 79/66). The significance of this determination is not simply conceptual or virtual, but it is connected to the legitimation of current international juridico-political norms and institutions, in short, the secular world order. Because this order cannot work independently of a Christian horizon for understanding, classifying and ordering religious phenomena and more generally public life, it is both not neutral and racial. Although Derrida does not use the term "racial," his reflections point to some key issues it refers to. Indeed, by naming "colonial" the logic of universalizing an idiom, as the example of the Semites illustrates, by emphasizing translation as a conversion enforced by the state, and by highlighting the nexus between European colonialism and Christian religion in the spread of globalization, he exposes a logical schema and historical processes in which the Christian religion functions as a normative standard for globally ordering human life through hierarchies that discriminate between human groups: that is, the universalization of a racial model.

It is in this context that translation plays a central role. As Derrida clarifies in "Above All, No Journalists!" translation is key in processes that define the semantic and politico-legal space of modern secular discourse. Translation is the operation through which culture-specific understandings and institutions have been exported world-wide. This has been possible not simply by first colonial and then imperialist political impositions and land appropriation, but also by the use of media and telecommunication, which has propagated and used "religion" as a sort of metalinguistic name for translation. He notes that "media function as the mediatisation between *religions*, in the name of *religion*, but above all in the name of what in Christianity is called *religion*" (AANJ, 89). For him, the unprecedented use of media and television that characterizes contemporary religions is a form of translation as Christianization and of Christianization as translation. It is a phenomenon in which specific understandings about the nature and functioning of what is called "religion" are translated in the mediatic language of Christianity.

But if translation is the means through which Christianity has actively traveled and still travels by globally shaping the language for naming and interpreting religious phenomena, it is also the one through which it has passively done and continues to do so. Translation, Derrida claims, is the medium through which a non-Christian religion names or presents itself on the international stage as a "religion" in order to gain universal visibility and legitimacy (47).[54] This phenomenon does not suggest that non-Christian so-called religions such as Islam, Judaism, or Buddhism do not have "a universal vocation" of their own. It only suggests that when any so-called religion presents itself internationally as "religion," it inscribes itself in a political and semantic space that is already under the hegemony of Christianity and its conception of universality, which "today dominates both philosophy and international law" (74).

Taken together, Derrida's reflections expose the politics of translation at work in modern discourses of religion and secularization. These reflections show that this politics is essential to control the language, interpretative schemas, and institutions of the international space by imposing a universalism marked by specific (Western) Christian traits. Yet, this politics is also a decisive vehicle for gaining visibility, agency, and legitimacy within such a space at the price of becoming, in some sense, Christian. In this way, Derrida's reflections have a double function. On the one hand, they illuminate the massive political stakes of global secularization as a form of translation. As an historico-politically charged medium employed in the response to difference, translation represents the process through which a determinate, unifying horizon for conceptualizing public life as secular is established, nationally and internationally, on the basis of a specific conception of religion presented as generic and of a logic of universality through a particular exemplar that do *in fact* assimilate difference. As such, in the Western tradition, translation has functioned very much as a key instrument for the hegemonic and sovereign control of the production and distribution of knowledge relevant to politics based on a model of racialized universality. And if we consider that, for Derrida, an underlying trait of such tradition is "White mythology," what travels worldwide through translation is, at some basic level, the racialization of knowledge and institutions. On the other hand, Derrida's reflections clear an analytic space for thinking about religion and politics at some distance from the Western Christian tradition. Indeed, while Derrida admits that deconstruction too operates within the Abrahamic archive and that is "more closely related to Christianity than to Judaism and Islam," (EF, 33)[55] his critique creates a distance from such a tradition that opens up a way beyond Christianity, as testified also by the use of his thought made by recent studies focusing on non-Christian contexts.[56]

The Politics of Language, or Sovereignty as Translation

Having analyzed Derrida's view of linguistic context and translation, I want to return to the question of the politics of language as way to connect these issues together. Illuminating why such a politics is called for by the linguistic human predicament, I emphasize that the politics of language displays translation as a matter of sovereignty and this, in turn, exposes linguistic foundations as central to rethinking the theological-political nexus.

I have suggested that, for Derrida, the linguistic human condition is one of arrival where the medium we call language is always already occupied by a multiplicity of natural languages, which are in a relation of translation that is irreducible. The nonoriginality of the arrival implies that none of these languages can serve as a source language and that recourse to a metalevel is not available for an objective determination of meaning, even if a forceful politics of translation makes it appear to be the case. This is particularly evident in questions of religion and secularization. To be in a position of arrival, then, does not mean that one can translate two languages by recurring to a "third," neutral, secular metalanguage that would allow for the transparent transfer of meaning from one language to another. Doing so would still presuppose all the assumptions (the possibilities of an original language that fully occupies language as medium, of metalanguage or the possibility of transparent translation) that have been rejected so far. All one can do is to acknowledge substitution, namely, attesting that an operation of transplanting has taken place within language as medium: the language one speaks is "a substitute for a mother tongue" (*MO*, 42/74).

In *Monolingualism*, in a long note on Arendt, Derrida expands on this point by remarking that the mother tongue refers both to the place of language or language as medium and the unique and singular experience of the relation to one's own language (85–89/100–8). Like any mother, the mother tongue is unique and irreplaceable, and thus it can only be substituted, but her place cannot be appropriated. Yet because of substitution, the mother tongue as linguistic medium cannot be anymore "mother" to what has been put in her place. Once substitution occurs, the relation to one's own language is not that of being home or of belonging but of being "hostage" to one's own language. Therefore, reflecting on the linguistic human condition requires seeing oneself as being, a host in language in both of its senses: a guest and a host prisoner of language.

For Derrida, the impossibility of appropriating language stems from its constitutive features, specifically a structure of alienation that defines its peculiarity. In his view, this is "a type of originary "alienation" that institutes every language as the language of the other" and thus indicates "the impossible property of language" (63/121). Here, "originary alienation" does not signal an ontological lack at the origin. As Derrida notes, this "alienation appears like a lack" but "lacks nothing that precedes or follows it" (25/47). Alienation represents, instead, the condition of possibility for the play of substitutions ongoing within the medium we call language, a play that can be seen from a position of arrival (in the case of Derrida, the play of substitution could refer to French substituting Arabic, Berber, or Hebrew). From that position, the institution of language makes it appear *as if* a source or original language has been alienated by a target one. But this is not possible since, in that situation, there are only target languages.

Besides pointing beyond ontological concerns, the structure of alienation indicates that language cannot be owned. As demonstrated above, Derrida's reflections on language as medium point towards the impossibility of metalanguage. Because language as medium always manifests itself in a plurality of languages, which are already in a relation of translation, there is no particular language that can claim a vantage meta-point or natural access to that medium so as to legitimately have claim to its full possession. This impossibility shows that language as medium cannot be naturally owned, and thus it is always "of the other." As Derrida notes, "the *of* signifies not so much property as provenance"; it indicates that the only language one speaks is coming from the "other," where "other" refers to a source that escapes the full possession of an individual speaker or community (68/127).

By emphasizing that language comes from the "other," Derrida illuminates the conventional nature of language as well as the political features associated with its institution and with any attempt to exhaust language as medium. Thus, viewed from the perspective of the human condition as a predicament of translation, language appears as political from first inception. Indeed, if language can never be naturally possessed, the attempt to fully appropriate it involves a degree of force that signals the presence of a politics of mastery inscribed within language (and culture).

> Because the master does not possess exclusively, and *naturally*, what he calls his language, because whatever he wants or does, he cannot maintain any relation of property or identity that are natural, national, congenital, or ontological, with it, because he can give substance to and articulate [*dire*] this appropriation only in the course of an unnatural process of politico-phantasmatic

> constructions, because language is not his natural possession, he can, thanks to that very fact, pretend historically, through the rape of a cultural usurpation, which means always essentially *colonial*, to appropriate it in order to impose it as "his own." That is his belief; he wishes to make others share it through the use of force or cunning; he wants to make others believe it, as they do a miracle, through rhetoric, the school, or the army. It suffices for him, through whatever means there is, to make himself understood, to have his "speech act" work, to create conditions for that, in order that he may be "happy" ("felicitous," which means in this code, efficacious, productive, efficient, generative of the expected event, but sometimes anything but "happy") and the trick is played, a first trick will have, at any rate been played. (23/45; my emphasis)

Since the other as master cannot possess language naturally, he can only appropriate it provisionally and artificially.[57] He can do so only through fictional constructions creating the conditions for drawing relevant distinctions (such as "felicitous" and "nonfelicitous" speech acts) but has to pretend that these are not conventional, hence the need for cunning and force. Yet his "pretending" reveals the colonial nature of the entire enterprise. The more complete the appropriation of language is sought to be in view of being naturalized, the stronger is the need for "cultural usurpation," and consequently also the need to show that what has been appropriated is one's own exactly because it cannot be.

A central role in this appropriation is played by what Derrida calls the politics of language. He notes that "every culture institutes itself through the unilateral imposition of some politics of language" (39/68). This is a politics because it concerns the institution of the law and the definition of political community, both of which are connected to the fixing of linguistic context.[58] As shown above, such a determination involves establishing the rules, conventions, and uses of language, which are never severed from political interests. While, as Derrida recognizes, these rules and conventions authorize particular ways of using language, thereby establishing a mode for linguistic and cultural identification without which there would be no meaningful interaction, they enforce linguistic and cultural hegemony, a "monolingualism of the other." That is, they enforce a dominant language imposed through a politics of language that fixes linguistic context by reducing "language to the One, that is to the hegemony of the homogenous"

(40/69). Derrida's overarching point is that the political determinations operating in the fixing of linguistic context are a matter of sovereign impositions and involve drawing linguistic, semantic, and political borders as firmly as possible, through the establishment of stable criteria for linguistic, epistemic, and political relevance. Far from being neutral, these criteria are culture specific and made effective through violence and forced translations that exclude other alternatives—human, cultural, religious, and linguistic. Indeed, these political determinations attempt to reduce to the minimum, if not eliminate, the differences regarding the relationships between word, meaning, and thing so that reference is fixed and language is made into a clearly identifiable unit, *a* language, a *given*, a homogenous one. This occurs in two distinct phases, the first of which is forcible establishment of an entire educational apparatus. As he notes, "every culture institutes itself through the unilateral imposition of some politics of language. Mastery begins, as we know, through the power of naming, of imposing and legitimating appellations."[59] This imposition displays colonial features within language and culture that regard the controlling of the means and terms for self-interpretation. It is in this sense that Derrida's statement that "all culture is originarily colonial" gains critical significance. In the second stage, as exemplified by the model of "revolutionary France," this colonial dimension is "disguised," through "cunning," as a " 'universal' humanism" deployed as "the most generous hospitality." Then, the new established language and culture are internalized and made one's own so that they appear to be the only heritage available and valuable. Embracing them would look like an "ostensibly *autonomous*" experience, whose tragic irony needs no further comments (*MO*, 39/68). But this, for Derrida, is mad. It is an instance of an appropriative madness typical of language. The madness consists in the attempt to appropriate language as medium, that site of language uniquely and irreplaceably occupied by the mother tongue since the mother tongue as the place of language is, like one's mother, irreplaceable, and thus it can only be replaced. The language of the master gives rise to an appropriative madness that is jealous of the place it seeks to conquer and needs to show that replacement has occurred.

Viewed this way, the politics of language informing the monolingualism of the other is not one among others. It is the first politics, like the politics of founding the law. As Derrida affirms, "the monolingualism of the other would be that sovereignty, that law originating from elsewhere, certainly, but also primarily the very language of the Law" (39/40). It would be, in other words, a form of sovereign imposition that marks the moment when political identity is framed through the identification, classification, and unification of cultural items that define membership. This is a moment in which the law is instituted through a particular language that admits no others and no internal dissenters and whose identity is forcefully kept stable in spite of a constitutive impossibility. An exemplary case is that of the United States, especially if viewed through the lenses of its foundation. The adoption of American English as the official language of the state not only institutionalized the Founding Fathers' view that the American Declaration of Independence, in the words of John Jay, referred to "one united people [. . .] descended from the same ancestors, speaking the same language" (Hamilton et al., 6). Above all, it sanctioned the exclusion of indigenous and non-Anglophone minority languages and cultures (French, Spanish, and Dutch) that were present in the American territory at that time, an exclusion whose effects continue in the present.[60] Of course, the United States is not the only relevant geopolitical context of this type of imposition. Numerous and perhaps more complicated examples can be found in contexts heavily marked by European colonialism, especially in Africa and the Americas.

As such, the politics of language informing the "monolingualism of the other" points to the intrinsic connection between translation and sovereignty, which the discussion of Shakespeare has showed to be linked to a theological-political dimension: the determination of linguistic context involves a God-like sovereign power that validates and enforces specific standards of knowledge, communication, religion, and politics by also imposing the relevant model of translation. Since this is an operation that establishes a stable semantic and juridical-political space in which differences are interpreted and reframed in the homogenizing language of the law, translation appears an indispensable tool to enforce and maintain that very space through assimilation. Hence Derrida's idea of the "law itself as translation" introduced earlier, whose understanding is indissociable from its Christian and secularizing connotation as "translation of the theological into political" (MO, 10/13; WTR, 184). While this phenomenon applies to the political domain, it actually cuts even deeper, reaching all the way to the distinctive mode of Western thought. Connecting, his early reflections on metaphysical thinking to sovereignty and translation, Derrida goes so far as to affirm that "forced hegemony" designates, in the Western tradition, an operation that gathers the biblical and philosophical traditions to impose an epistemic order made globally relevant through force. In this operation, *logos* appears at "the center of everything" in a position "of sovereign hegemony, organizing everything on the basis of its forced translations" (*BS 1*, 343/455).

The politics of language is therefore of paramount importance to Derrida. Its understanding is an urgent task for political thinking in general and the "theological-political complex" in particular since the stakes behind it are those of linguistic nationalism and colonialism disguised as philosophical universalism.[61] For him, investigating the politics of language is not simply essential to understand such events as colonial Algeria or revolutionary France but is of general significance today as "everywhere the homo-hegemonic tendency of language remains at work in culture" (*MO*, 40/69). Today many people are at risk of having to yield to the homo-hegemony (in particular the Anglo-American) of dominant languages and "learn the language of the masters, of capitals and machines" (30/56) and, as seen, of secularism. Indeed, this risk is already a reality in national and international institutions, legislation, and decrees that regulate the public sphere, particularly on questions of religion. The diverse range of cases includes the historic *Employment vs Smith* in the United States—where the Supreme Court judged the legitimacy of religious freedom arguments rooted in indigenous values and practices. Furthermore, there are various instances in which European national and supranational courts were called on to regulate the public admissibility of religious symbols, especially with reference to Islam. At the international level, rules protecting the rights of religious minorities, a politics of language, and translation that appeal to apparently neutral terms actually operate on the basis of culture-specific understandings that have homogenizing and hegemonic effects.[62]

By emphasizing the risk of homo-hegemony, Derrida is not putting forward a simplistic critique of modernity and the political arrangements that have accompanied it, such as democracy, the rule of law, and human rights. Instead, he exposes the colonial logic, linguistic assumptions, and mechanism (transparent translations) of naturalization characterizing the politics of language and secularization at work in dominant modern understandings. As such, Derrida's view of the politics of language shows that questions of linguistic foundation have a central significance for thinking about the "theological-political complex," especially about how theological-political nexus relates to the foundation of political authority, community, and knowledge. His view is particularly relevant to approaches that employ a neutral language to universally justify political authority of national and international institutions and the linguistic rules and uses associated with it. Together with his view on linguistic context and idiomaticity, Derrida's perspective on the politics of language challenges the idea that philosophical reflection can employ linguistic categories that can be removed from political conditioning through critical self-reflexivity so as to provide universally valid justifications in the name of secularism and reason.[63] He shows that to the extent that homogenizing schemas inform the type of translation at work in language, apparently neutral linguistic categories characterizing secular models are *in fact* contingently grounded in the geopolitical site that has authorized them in the first place. By locating the site of secular models of language in the West—especially in European and Anglo-American contexts (FK, 66–67/47)—and by exposing their entanglements with imperialism and the legacy of colonialism, Derrida illuminates the persistence of colonial mentalities in modern secular discourse and uncovers the alleged universal validity of its (linguistic) model as an effect of its hegemony.

A Language of Promise

Besides offering a critique of secular language, Derrida develops an alternative view of language that he calls "language of promise." More than a language, this is a way of thinking about language that is connected to the only one language we ever speak, the universal language as medium that the first proposition previously analyzed talks about. The promise refers, in a first sense, to the performative dimension at work in all language. "Each time I open my mouth, each time I speak or write, I *promise*. Whether I like it or not . . . The performative of the promise is not one speech act among others. It is implied by any other performative, and this promise heralds the uniqueness of a language to come" (67/126). This passage introduces a key philosophical point of Derrida's view of language that is also crucial to his political thought: the idea of a performative promise informing a structure of promissory affirmation, or what he calls in his later works "the messianic" or "messianicity without messianism" to which the "to come" of the quote explicitly refers (FK, 56/30; *SM*, 74/102). While a more detailed treatment of this issue will be presented in chapters 2 and 3, it is important to introduce its central features in order to offer a preliminary clarification of the notion of promise.

For Derrida, any time there is a linguistic act, a performative act of promise, a sort of elementary faith, is also at work. It is one that engages others through a believing that exceeds conscious intentionality and is internal to the very act of address (*MO*, 67/126). But why is this a unique speech act and in what sense? An essay that is particularly helpful to clarify these questions is "A Number of Yes." Here Derrida illustrates the logic of this promise through the structure of repetition inherent in language, a structure of double yes referring to both response and affirmation. Every time one opens one's mouth, he notes, a first "yes" is affirmed and immediately followed by another "yes": "Let us suppose a first *yes,* the archi-originary *yes* that engages, promises and acquiesce before all else. On the one hand, it is originarily, in its very structure, a response. It is *first second*, coming after a demand, a question, or another yes. On the other hand, as engagement or promise, it must *at least* and in advance be tied to a confirmation in another [*prochain*] *yes*" (ANY, 239/648–49). The first "yes" responds to a preceding predicament posed by the already being-there-with other speakers, to use Heideggerian terminology, and thus also of language. [64] The second one affirms the promise of confirming the first "yes" in the future. That is why Derrida claims that this unique performative is one of both promise and memory (240/649). Its uniqueness consists in being an act of believing deprived of content, an act that affirms an engagement to others in language as medium of communication but that does "not describe or state anything" and that therefore relates to other statements "silently" (238/636). This silence indicates that although it can be exposed through philosophical analysis, this performative cannot be made an object of knowledge. For doing so would require both some transparency of language and the unlikely possibility of suspending language while in fact using it (239/637).

Viewed through this understanding of the promise affecting all language, Derrida's "language of promise" presents a universal value. It connects all singular idioms through a promissory structure that affects all language, and yet it resists translating them according to a universal standard since the promise lacks a determinate content. As such, a "language of promise" constitutes another monoligualism "but entirely other than the language of the other as the language of the master or colonist, even though, between them, the two may sometimes show so many unsettling resemblances maintained secret or held in reserve" (*MO*, 62/118–19). Unlike the language of the master, Derrida's language of promise "neither yields nor delivers any messianic or eschatological *content*" or promise of emancipation. This monolingualism would be the *first language* one seeks to invent from the position of arrival in the absence of a given one. It is a language that "resembles" that of the colonist since it is characterized by the structure of alienation discussed above, and thus it is subject to the oppressive potential of all language. However, by recognizing the impossible appropriation of language as medium as well as its being marked by the predicament of translation, a "language of promise" can resist the homo-hegemony typical of the master's language. It *can* do so to the extent that it conceives of the promise deprived of any messianic content and is able to reduce, at least in principle, the risk involved "in becoming or wanting to become another language of the master," a risk that the structure of promise seeking to deliver a teleological content implies (62/118–19). The challenge, here, consists in how to have *"uniqueness without unity,"* how to respect the singularity of idioms and identities and yet to resist a full translation that would yield linguistic nationalism and colonial appropriations (68/127).

> Where neither natural property nor the law of property in general exist, where this de-propriation is recognized, it is possible and it becomes more necessary than ever occasionally to identify, in order to combat them, impulses, phantasm, "ideologies," "fetishizations," and symbolics of appropriation. Such a reminder permits at once to analyze the historical phenomena of appropriation and treat them *politically* by avoiding, above all, the reconstitution of what these phantasms managed to motivate: "nationalist" aggressions (which are always more or less "naturalist") or monoculturalist homo-hegemony. (64/121–22)

The articulation of a "language of promise" constitutes a politicization of language since it springs from the self-critical recognition of the historico-political character of language and thus of the remainders at work in any linguistic foundation. Associated with an awareness of structural remainders, the notion of promise indicates the ever-present possibility of reconstituting of language, which follows from the recognition of its political dimension as well as from the universal vocation of the promise itself.

As a quasitranscendental trope, Derrida's "language of promise" reconfigures the relationship between particularity and universality since it conceives of them as correlated but irreducible. As such, it resists a type of universalism that is oblivious of its mastery-like features, of its past, and of the particular conditions in which it originated. Whereas the universal (transcendental) structures the process in which the particular can seek a more general reach, the particular constitutes the empirical and ineffaceable conditions of possibility of the universal, thereby impeding pure formalizations. In this way, Derrida's "language of promise" resists a type of homo-hegemonizing universalism that, in pretending to be neutral, hides its material conditioning and culture-specific values informing hierarchical standards of interpretation that block the potential of alternatives. Instead of sanctioning the end of universalism *per se*, this resistance opens the way to a vigilant universalism, which is dynamic and aware of both its contingency and political features. We will return to Derrida's reconfiguration of universalism in the next chapter.

So conceived, a "language of promise" maintains a "critical intimacy" with both promise and hegemony, the demarcation of which needs constant negotiation.[65] For Derrida, the contamination between these elements characterizes such a language but not metalinguistically. This means that contamination only impedes a clear-cut distinction between promise and hegemony. Although a "language of promise" has always a threatening colonial face, it *can* resist the attempt to exhaust the medium of language or to place itself at some objective metalevel by recognizing the structural undecidability and limits that being-in-translation entails. Rather than constituting an impasse, undecidability marks a chance that is both "poetic" and "political" (*MO*, 62/119). It is poetic because it involves a creative moment that can open up a possibility for new linguistic understandings and ways of being against a background of undecidability. It is political because it requires taking a decision about which reminders to analyze and how to interpret them.

This last point raises the important question of interpretation and its political dimension, which is, in a sense, the central question of deconstruction conceived as the analysis of "what remains to be thought" (*LI*, 147). Without entering into a topic that could be the subject of a single study in itself, let us briefly consider Derrida's position on interpretation especially as he develops it in his engagement with Nietzsche.[66] We will then connect it to his view of a "language of promise" and the "theological-political complex." Recall that Derrida sees Nietzsche's writings as pointing to the "heterogeneity of the text," one in which truth escapes the conscious control of the author (*SP*, 95/94) This feature of the text emerges especially from Nietzsche's treatment of woman and the plurality of meaning associated with her (mother, daughter, sister, old maid, wife, prostitute, and so on) and points to an undecidability about what the true identity of woman is and, more generally, about the possibility of a conclusive determination of meaning (101, 103/101–2). For Derrida, the impossibility of fixing meaning undermines the "hermeneutic project" of recovering "a true meaning of the text," thereby keeping the activity of interpretation open-ended (107/106). This, though, does not imply abandoning the value of truth or true meaning but only taking seriously the "structural limit" of the text and pushing interpretation "to the furthest length possible" in the awareness of the likelihood that such a limit opens the text up to itself (133/132).

It is from this background that Derrida develops a view of interpretation as an active, affirmative, and open-ended operation that resists semantic closure and totalizations. Interpretation seeks to show that a given truth or interpretation is less stable than it appears to be, not only because it is subject to the differential dynamic of the signification process, but also because it arose in historical contingent conditions. Viewed this way, Derrida's active interpretation emerges as a form of *critical* practice that exposes the limits of a text in terms of instability of meaning and thus of what can be conclusively claimed about its truth. Such limits, though, are not limitations but show that undecidability is the starting predicament of philosophical investigation and interpretation, and not the beginning of its end. The motive behind sustaining undecidability is not to downplay the importance of making rigorous distinctions, of intentionality, or to affirm the indeterminacy of meaning (*LI*, 126, 128–29, 148). Nor is it to warrant any reading (*OG*, 158/227; *POS*, 63/86) or embracing of the rhetoric of free play (*WD*, 293/428). Rather, it is to call attention to those fissure points in which distinctions break down, are called into question, and thus provide an opening at the interior of the text itself.

If interpretation is a critical practice, it is also a political one that seeks to reactivate what is left out within a given text or tradition. This aspect emerges especially in *Otobiographies: The Teaching of Nietzsche and the Politics of the Proper Name*, where Derrida employs the metaphor of the "ear" (from the Greek *otos*) to emphasize, among other things, the political role of receivers in interpretation and their ability to "perceive differences." By receiving and "hearing" the differences of and in the text in different spatio-temporal contexts, the receivers also produce it (OB, 49–50/69–71). In this way, they are also in some way responsible for the text's signature and the meaning they assign to it, a meaning which cannot therefore be immediately equated to the author's intention—hence the shift from autobiography to otobiography (29/44). Receivers have not simply a political responsibility for the reading(s) they offer of a text or tradition but also, and most importantly, for their remainders, which can be reactivated in view of generating new understandings.

But how is the reclaiming of these remainders, which are those marking the promise of (a) language (of promise), to be performed if the grasping and affirmation of *truth* is not an option? Derrida hazards the thought that the text is "an utterance-producing machine that programs the movement" and that draws together opposing forces into a set of complex relationships (29/44). The difficulty of interpretative practices lies precisely in disentangling that set from *given* linguistic and historico-political determinations. This means that the "machine" in question does not program in teleological terms in order to deliver a promised meaning as the language of the master pretends to do. Instead, it does so in a nonteleological fashion. As Derrida says: " 'The programming machine' that interests me here does not call only for a decipherment but also for transformation—that is, a practical rewriting according to a theory-practice relationship which, if possible, would no longer be part of the program" (OB, 30/45).

Viewed in this light, the type of interpretation called for by a "language of promise" appears even more clearly as a transformative activity. Rather than reinforcing, by reaffirming, a fixed meaning, interpretation calls for a critical selection, which transforms by revisiting and rewriting what lives in the text as a trace (see also *SM*, 18/40, 128/168). This selection, though, does not licence *any* decision nor does it imply blindness to the specificity of judgments. Rather, it requires decisions that need to pass "through thought," decisions that "are *actions of thought*" (NM, 215–56).

For Derrida, the deciding aspect involved in selecting and identifying the movement of the machine requires that one scrutinize especially founding events and texts of a tradition, if the relapse into dogmatism is to be avoided. Doing so is not simply a question of deciphering signs but, above all, one of political intervention and responsibility. As Derrida suggests, "our interpretations will not be readings of a hermeneutic or exegetic sort, but rather political interventions in the political rewriting of the text and its destination" (OB, 32/48). These aspects can be seen already at play in the context of interpreting and reinterpreting Nietzsche's writings and language. Derrida is very clear in emphasizing that the interpretative practices he proposes do not set out to neutralize the antidemocratic aspects of Nietzsche's texts that were appropriated, not accidentally, by the Nazi regime.[67] Rather, they seek to disconnect Nietzsche's texts from Nazi interpretations by highlighting the openness of such texts as well as the fact that Nietzschean politics might not necessarily be fascist.[68] Such practices seek, in other words, to navigate the contaminations the machine produces in the awareness of the ever present risk that transformative readings are not immune to danger or relapse into authoritarianism.

Examples of Derrida's view of rewriting interventions are visible in many of his works. Some will be explored in later chapters, especially with regard to issues of political authority and community. For the moment, suffice to mention how his interpretative interventions attempt to reinterpret the philosophical tradition by raising the stakes (*surenchère*) of what is inherited by questioning and denaturalizing well-established, received conceptions.[69] Indeed, in considering given philosophical concepts, Derrida questions some of their key sedimented understandings in order to show instability of meaning and potential for transformation. In chapter 4, I will explore at length the connection between modern democracy and secularism. Other common associations such as those of citizenship and nationality, democracy and indivisible sovereignty, secularism and religion, hospitality and citizenship are relevant examples that Derrida analyzes in order to emphasize the masculine, Christian, racialized, and thus overall exclusionary features, of key political concepts of the Western tradition (*PF, OFH, R*). My suggestion, in chapter 5, that Derrida's reflections on religion and Islam open the space to a different political grammar to think about religious and social phenomena points to the critical-political potential of his view of "language of promise," one that calls for transformative interpretations of given meanings within dominant epistemic and political orders.

The significance of Derrida's view of interpretation in connection to a "language of promise" lies in the critical potential it offers to examine the "theological-political complex." A "language of promise" reconfigures the approach to language by unsettling models that pretend to fully exhaust language as medium and provide a universal standard of translation to deal with the theological-political relation, and more generally, with pluralism. Through its receptivity to memory and founding exclusions, such a language retains a political sensibility towards its origins that enables a critical and self-critical vigilance towards naturalizations and fixed interpretations. So conceived, then, a "language of promise" is not so much an attempt to provide a new foundation but, rather, an experimental effort to critically rethink the linguistic framework through which to approach the theological-political relationship, and more generally questions of difference.

2

The Time of Political Thought

Addressing the question of time in a book about religion and politics might seem off topic. Indeed, what has time to do with politically thinking about the "theological-political complex"? I seek to show that the analysis of time in relation to political thought is central to a critical framework for rethinking the theological-political nexus. I pursue this by exploring Derrida's reflections on time and political thinking, which expose how different understandings of time are informed by culture-specific epistemological assumptions informing normative responses to pluralism. Challenging a well-established view of time as a linear succession of unitary moments, and some key political theories informed by it, Derrida illuminates how a reconceptualization of time is key to a critical understanding of the "theological-political complex" that does not close off the political space to difference. On the one hand, Derrida shows that the traditional view of time is connected to a metaphysical, foundational type of thinking informed by racialized schemas that are implicated in setting up discriminatory hierarchies. On the other, he articulates a "messianic" understanding of time that resists foundationalist logics and opens up normative political thinking to a more receptive attitude towards difference and a novel understanding of the political.[1]

I begin by examining Derrida's reflections on conventional conceptualizations of time by reading his notion of *différance* through the grid of what he calls "White mythology." I draw from this some key implications for political thinking in general and for study of the "theological-political complex" in particular. I show that his view exposes the exclusionary and oppressive features of teleological modes of thinking informed by the traditional understanding of time, modes that address the theological-political relation by seeking to establish what is most original between faith and reason. Turning mainly to *Specters of Marx*, but also *Rogues* and "Faith and Knowledge," I then analyze Derrida's notion of the "messianic" and suggest that it can be interpreted as a type of nonteleological political thinking that resists the resolution of the theological-political nexus, as well as types of separatist modes of thinking displaying a dangerous proximity to racialized logics. By illustrating that messianic thinking does not endorse the binaries reason/faith, theological/political typical of modern secularism, but conceives of them as interrelated and distinct, Derrida, I suggest, provides us with the resources for thinking critically and normatively about pluralism beyond the exclusionary logic of modern secular discourse.

Time, Teleology, and Political Thinking

Time is among Derrida's central concerns in deconstructing canonical texts of the Western philosophical tradition. It is a theme implicitly at work in almost all of his writings dealing with other philosophical topics and is explicitly explored in *Given Time*, "*Ousia* and *Grammē*," and *Specters of Marx*. For the purposes of this chapter, however, I will briefly explore his essay "Différance" before focusing on *Specters of Marx*. This choice will help illuminate the connections between time, political thinking, and the "theological-political complex." Before doing so, however, I want to connect Derrida's understanding of time to his emphasis on the racialized features of the Western metaphysical traditional and do so in order to provide the general framework within which my reflections will take place. I pursue this by following the thread of the quest of origins that traverse both discourses of time and race. Indeed, I hope to show that the link between time and race, which Derrida left undeveloped, is key to appreciate the critical potential of his contribution to the "theological-political complex."

Overall, Derrida's position on time consists in articulating a perspective that radicalizes human finitude by going beyond the quest for origins, as in the traditional metaphysical understanding of time, usually associated with Aristotle. Engaging Aristotle through Heidegger in "*Ousia* and *Grammē*," Derrida takes issue with this view, which conceives of time as the "number of movement following the before and after" of undivided temporal units that unfold in space in a linear fashion (line, from the Greek *grammē*) (OG, 58/67). He finds this understanding problematic, since time is thought of on the basis of a teleological schema. The *telos* of this schema consists in the realization of the structure of time as analogous to the *grammē* seen "as a series of points" forming a "completed" line "in act," a *telos* that can be grasped as presence (presence, from the Greek *ousia*) in the mind (59–60/69).² As such, this view subscribes to a type of metaphysical thinking informed by questionable presuppositions according to which origins, exemplified here by linearity as the essence of time, can be grasped as pure, that is as distinct from the historical conditions in which they occur, and then used to justify the general validity of a philosophical system presented as neutral (*LI*, 93). For Derrida, the problem with this type of thinking is at once philosophical, cultural, and political.

> Metaphysics—the white mythology which reassembles and reflects the culture of the West: the white man takes on his own mythology, Indo-European mythology, his own *logos*, that is, the *mythos* of his idiom, for the universal form that he must still wish to call Reason. Which does not go uncontested [. . .] White mythology—metaphysics has erased within itself the fabulous scene that has produced it, the scene that nevertheless remains active and stirring, inscribed in white ink, an invisible design covered over in the palimpsest. (WM, 213/254)

This passage is part of larger reflection about the role of metaphor in the Western philosophical tradition, particularly with regard to concepts formation. For Derrida, what distinguishes such tradition is not simply the questionable "classical opposition of metaphor and concept" that erases the irreducible metaphoricity of concepts, and of metaphysical discourse at large (WM, 263/314, 258/308). It is also the schema and process through which metaphysical discourse allegedly grasps the abstract "essence" of concepts it presents as universally valid, and does so independently of the contingent conditions in which it operates (WM, 229/273). In this way, he exposes the racialized type of thinking undergirding the Western philosophical tradition, namely a mode of thinking marked by a hierarchical framework for understanding and differentiating the epistemic and ethical value of human groups and forms of life, and for organizing public life accordingly.³ Presenting *logos* as "Reason," or allegedly grasping the essence or origin of "Reason" as *logos*, this mythology displays the philosophical conditions of possibility of racialized thinking: that is, the logic and strategies of naturalization of a specific life-form portrayed as the standard of universal rationality ("the universal form") through the hiding ("fabulous scene," "invisible design") of its contingent occurrence, forceful spread, and connections to the other human realities it excludes, despite resistance from them ("Which does not go uncontested"). As such, this mythology also points to the material, psychological, and political conditions of possibility of such a discourse: the superiority of a human group and its cultural expressions are tied to the denial of the relationality—material, cultural, and political—and plurality characterizing human experience, and thus also to the violence that comes with this. Remaining unnamed here, but not so throughout Derrida's *oeuvre*, are colonialism, capitalism, and the globalization of the Western-Christian political understanding and forms (i.e., nation-state, citizenship, sovereignty, and international law). Indeed, these are key elements of the erased "fabulous scene" at issue here that have contributed to make the "White mythology" of *logos* universal, one that, as mentioned in the previous chapter, represents "the center of everything" occupying a position "of sovereign hegemony, organizing everything on the basis of its forced translations" (*BS1*, 343/455).

Seen through the notion of "White mythology," the traditional view of time as a metaphysical thinking of origins is one that maintains a proximity to the philosophical basis of racialized thinking. Although Derrida has not given explicit thematic attention to the theme of race, his insights about "White mythology," and more generally his philosophy call for the connection between deconstruction and race is, in some sense, structural, and thus relevant to the analysis of time as a thinking of origins. As Derrida affirms in a 2003 conference on race that clarifies his "silence" on the topic, "deconstruction is through and through a deconstruction of racism" insofar as it questions racism's general conditions of possibility: that is, the traditional opposition between *physis* and *nomos* (as well as *techne* and *thesis*), on which all naturalization depends, as well as the idea of origin and filiation as a basis for political projects.[4] Indeed, while deconstruction is very much a mode of interrogating origins, the reference to pure origins and their naturalization has been central to the semantics and historical instantiations of various Western forms of racism (RLW, 292/387).[5] This is apparent, especially in early racist views developed by Christians in Andalusian Spain against Jews and Muslims, in pseudoscientific and white supremacist justifications of modern racism, including Nazi and Fascist anti-Semitism, South African apartheid, Zionism, and contemporary forms of Islamophobia across Europe, North America, and Australia.

Thus, approaching the analysis of time as a thinking of origins in connection to questions of race holds important implications for studying conventional philosophical approaches to the theological-political complex, especially with regard to theoretical approaches informed by, and philosophically justifying, epistemic hierarchies and naturalizations on the one hand, and sociopolitical separations on the other. In this framework, my emphasis on the relevance of race in Derrida's thought does not seek to suggest that Derrida was at the forefront of debates about race. Instead, it intends to signal his critical consciousness about racialized thinking as a central feature of Western discourses in general and about the theological-political in particular, a consciousness that emerges throughout his work. In *Of Grammatology*, Derrida limits himself to the distinct and yet connected semantics of ethnocentrism, which he links to logocentrism as a form of metaphysics of presence informing also theological discourse (*OG*, 3/11). In "Racism's Last Word," he challenges the theological-political nature of discourses on race and connects the rule of a white minority in South Africa to the European discourses of law, the state, and race and to the logic of spectrality he then discusses in *Specters of Marx* (RLW, 294/389, 296/391). Later on, in the *The Other Heading* and *Of Spirit*, he denounces the racism and anti-Semitism produced by the European "spirit" typical of the traditional discourse of modernity (*OH*, 6/13; *OS*), while in "Faith and Knowledge," he connects the theological-political to the modern discourse of religion and highlights European colonialism and American imperialism as key agents of the world-wide spread of a Christian juridico-political culture and institutions in which a Latin Christian understanding of "religion" is used to globally organize political life according to determined religious, epistemic, and cultural hierarchies (FK, 66–67/47). This last aspect appears also in "What Is Relevant Translation?" where Derrida connects the theological-political to processes of assimilatory translation used to order public life according to spiritual and cultural hierarchies marked by Christianity. In *Politics of Friendship*, he exposes the racial connotation of canonical Western discourses about citizenship and community based on the naturalization of origins as well as about Islamophobic views of the political, most notably Schmitt's political theology (*PF*, 91/112–13). Finally, in *Rogues*, he criticizes understandings of sovereignty connected to the Western metaphysical tradition, but also to more mundane racializing practices based on the use of the term "rogue"(*voyou*) "for a marking or branding classification that sets something apart" (which apartheid exacerbates) and informs bans or excludes those considered "deviant," including those of "mixed origins" populating the "suburbs," the "unemployed" found "loitering" but also states that resist or violate international law (*R*, 63/95, 68/101, 94/135).[6]

In what follows, it is the link between the separatist and hierarchizing logics of racialized thinking and that of conventional philosophical approaches to the theological-political that I seek to bring to the fore through Derrida's understanding of time. To appreciate this connection, it is first necessary to look at his view of time and the challenge it poses to canonical Western understandings. A decisive version of this challenge occurs in his essay "Différance," where Derrida challenges "the quest for a rightful beginning, an absolute point of departure, a principal responsibility" by "putting into question the value *arche*," which refers to origin both by nature and by law, and he does so by illustrating how time is historicized by the spatial mark of its passage, or "trace" (*MP*, 6/6).[7]

> An interval must separate the present from what is not, in order for the present to be itself, but this interval that constitutes it as present must, by the same token, divide the present in and of itself, thereby also dividing, along with the present, everything that is thought on the basis of the present, that is, in our metaphysical language, every being and every singular substance or subject. In constituting itself, in dividing itself dynamically, this interval is what might be called *spacing*, the becoming-space of time or the becoming-time of space (*temporization*). And it is this constitution of the present, as "originary" and irreducibly nonsimple, (and therefore, *stricto sensu* nonoriginary) synthesis of marks, or traces of retentions or pretensions (to reproduce analogically and provisionally a phenomenological and transcendental language that soon will reveal itself inadequate) that I propose to call arche-writing, arche-trace, or *différance*. Which (is) (simultaneously) spacing (and) temporization. (D, 13/14)

In this complex passage, Derrida gives an account of the minimal unit of time, "the present," in terms of a spatio-temporal "interval," or "spacing" that is in itself divided by its connection to past and future moments. Indicating a synthesis between space and time, "spacing," as Hägglund suggests, refers both to the spatial inscription of a temporal unit that makes the latter legible at all and to that unit being related to the flow of time, since legibility is possible only *after* inscription occurs.[8] In this way, the "trace" points to a complex understanding of time as characterized by "nonsimple," that is nonunitary, temporal units. At any moment, a present unit cannot be grasped as pure, namely, independently of its spatio-temporal relations with other units. As a consequence, also "anything that is thought" on the basis of time is affected by the division brought about by the "trace."

While an adequate exploration of Derrida's view of time would require a much larger treatment, suffice here to highlight the significance of the "trace" as exposing the limits of thinking about time as a "series" of undivided and clearly identifiable units. By emphasizing that mental contents available to human understanding at any particular moment are not so easily separable from the conditions in which they appear and always contain something from a previous experience, Derrida illustrates that any such content cannot be purely grasped. Instead, it needs to be viewed in relational terms and as mediated by historical conditions. The "trace" indicates that relationality is the predicament human beings always already find themselves in. What one can aspire to find in the search for origins is ambiguity, deferral, and impurity of mental representations: *différance*. In other words, by articulating time in relational terms through the notion of "trace," Derrida unsettles the hierarchical dualism between the transcendent and the immanent, the transcendental and the empirical, the intelligible and the sensible. The "trace" signals the limit point at which these philosophical binaries are silently related in such a way that there is no sharp line distinguishing the one from the other so that their demarcating line remains undecidable. Above all, it indicates that origins are "*strictu sensu* nonoriginary" and thus can only be discoursively produced.

The novelty and significance of this view consists in moving past the metaphysics of presence, as commentators have argued.[9] In his *Radical Atheism*, for example, Hägglund highlights how Derrida's analysis of time "challenges the philosophical logic of identity" that informs, from Aristotle to Kant, versions of the metaphysics of presence. For Hägglund, Derrida's decisive move is the deconstruction of the traditional principle of noncontraction, which grounds the possibility of identity on indivisibility.[10] By pointing to the untenability of pure origins through the divisibility of the minimal unit of time signaled by the trace, Derrida's logic opens a new horizon for thinking about, among other things, the very (im)possibility of universalizabale philosophical foundations.

While Hägglund's analysis targets some key foundations of Western philosophical thinking, my reflections seek to reach its subterranean undercurrents, bringing into sharper relief the critical-political potency of Derrida's perspective. Indeed, if viewed in conjunction with his notion of "White mythology," Derrida's deconstruction of the "logic of identity" informing the thought of pure origins does not simply challenge insufficiently questioned philosophical assumptions in the Western tradition that are involved in the production of metaphysical binaries. It also exposes the racialized features of the naturalizing logics of such modes of thinking that present themselves as universal, thereby ultimately questioning their overall value. Indeed, if origins cannot be grasped as such, but can only be discoursively produced through a process that hides the historical conditions affecting idealization, then modes of thinking claiming universal validity, which are based on the grasp of pure origins, lose their justificatory ground. Above all, they fail to maintain concealed their racialized features, thereby compromising their epistemic authority and ethical respectability. By deconstructing the possibility of grasping pure origins through a reflection on time, then, Derrida destabilizes the possibility of naturalization informing racialized thinking at its very roots.

So conceived, Derrida's view of time has crucial implications for understanding the "theological-political complex." If undecidability and relationality characterize the inaugural moment of reflection, the possibility of establishing what is most *original* between the theological and the political, faith and reason, is undermined, and with it the value of separatist and hierarchizing discourses based on either. But what is also undermined, through the exposure of the potential for exclusion involved in the resistance to constitutive relationality, is political teleology. Such a mode of thinking provides solid normative foundations on the basis of a pure *telos* whose immediate grasping would require denying the irreducible relationality between thinking and its material conditioning while at the same time producing allegedly universal representations of law, politics, and religion.

If at this point it is not already apparent what time has to do with political thought, it might be helpful to make that explicit. For Derrida, Western political thought has uncritically inherited and relied upon the same metaphysical assumptions about time, and, as such, it is subject to the same challenge he poses to philosophical discourse at large. In his political writings, Derrida shows that canonical understandings of political categories such as sovereignty, law, subjectivity, democracy but also political community, equality, friendship as well as history, state, and citizenship, have been informed by such assumptions. Among these, sovereignty is perhaps the category that best illustrates the metaphysics of presence lurking behind political thinking.[11] As I shall discuss at length in chapter 4, Derrida shows how throughout much of the history of Western political thought, the nature, extent, and justification of political authority have often been implicated in some metaphysical, atemporal dimension characterized by the quest for transcendent foundations and purity of ideas to justify the political order (*R*, 17/38, 101/144, 157/215–16). This dimension has also been accompanied by sexual, racial, and spiritual hierarchies.[12] Sovereignty is the concept that has paradigmatically performed that function since it has been conceived as indivisible and placed, exceptionally before, above, and beyond the law. In other words, sovereignty has been articulated on the possibility of grasping pure origins through clear-cut distinctions that would ground sociopolitical separations. As such, its discourse has been structurally implicated, indeed has also intersected with, the logic of racist discourse, which appeals to the rhetoric of pure origin to justify separatist discrimination.

What is significant for our discussion, in the example of sovereignty, is the emphasis Derrida puts on the connection between time and political thinking.[13] By illuminating this nexus, Derrida is able to question modes of political thought that are informed by teleological thinking and the foundational conception of reason associated with it. By teleological thinking, I refer here to a type of thinking that is guided by a *telos* to be realized or approximated and that fixes an ideal horizon of expectation. This type of thinking is associated with a foundational view of reason because the latter is considered as capable of purely grasping ideas in consciousness that are unaffected by the contingent conditions in which idealization takes place.

The modes of political thinking Derrida has in mind are the political teleologies of Kant, Hegel, and Marx.[14] Despite their differences, these teleologies retain the temporal form of a future present, of projecting into the future a "modality of the *living present*" that anticipates what is to come on the basis of a *telos* grasped in its purity (*SM*, 81/111). The problem with these modes of reflection concerns the types of normativity they produce once ideas about human nature and political community are supposedly grasped in consciousness in pure terms. They are then posited as grounds providing either the substantive standards for critically evaluating current society and bringing about a new one (as in Hegel's historicization of Spirit in the modern state or as Marx's advent of communist society) or the platform for developing procedural conditions for the justification of political arrangements (as, for example, in Kant and in Neo-Kantian political philosophy). For Derrida, these types of normativity, which we can call "substantive" and "regulative," depending on whether the *telos* in question is to be realized or approximated, display problematic features and need to be challenged.

One place where this challenge is explicitly articulated is *Specters of Marx*, which Derrida dedicates to the memory of Chris Hani, a Black communist South African leader who fought against apartheid and was assassinated in 1993—a dedication that speaks to the significance of the discourse on specters for race, beyond Marxism, as I shall discuss. Here Derrida takes issue with political teleology through the analysis of some of Marx's texts and of Francis Fukuyama's *The End of History and the Last Man*. Starting with Marx, Derrida focuses especially on the figure of the specter (*revenant*), which refers to the excluded remainder at work in representations of reference, but, most importantly, it points to concrete historical forms of exclusion and segregation that include "the ghosts of those who are not yet born or who are already dead, be they victims of wars, political or other kinds of violence, nationalist, racist, colonialist, sexist, or other kinds of exterminations, victims of the oppressions of capitalist imperialism or any of the forms of totalitarianism" (*SM*, xviii/16). For Derrida, the specter unsettles the opposition between presence and absence and enables the distinction between ontology (*ontologie*) and hauntology (*hauntonolgie*), a double bind characterizing Marx's thought (125/164, 213/269). While ontology focuses on pure ideas that reduce the spectral excess to a clearly identifiable mental representation, hauntology seeks to track down what eludes such a pure operation. Viewed this way, the figure of the specter enables Derrida to illuminate two things. The first is the untenability of maintaining clear-cut conceptual distinctions, which is due to the process of concept formation: specters stand for what concepts need to exclude in order to convey the univocal meaning of what they signify, which means that concepts are as much about what they exclude as what they represent (see also *AF*, 29/51). Second, it throws light on the type of metaphysical grounding that clear-cut distinctions require, with the exclusionary implications this has, as signaled by the notion of "White mythology."[15] At some basic level, then, the figure of the specter signals the repression of difference produced by racialized epistemological orders that pretend to produce stable representations capturing the essence of what they signify. As Derrida mentions before *Specters of Marx*, but does not systematically develop in that text or elsewhere, the question of specters is central to understanding the "European discourse on race—its scientific pseudo-concept and its religious roots, its modernity and its archaisms" (BB, 165). Indeed, "that discourse belongs to a whole system of 'phantasms,' to a certain representation of nature, life, history, religion, and law" (RLW, 294/389). That is, a discourse that naturalizes what is discursively articulated through the repression of difference.

By pointing to the double bind of Marx's thought, Derrida highlights the metaphysics of presence informing Marx's normative claims and the latter's attempt to articulate a way out from metaphysical thinking, an issue we shall consider below. While recognizing that there is "*more than one*" (xx/18) spirit of Marxism, Derrida questions the "other spirits of Marxism," those informed by ontological commitments, and points to the connection between metaphysical thinking and a "substantive" normativity on the one hand, and totalitarianism on the other (110/145). Grounding his view on his reading of Marx's *The German Ideology* and *The Communist Manifesto*, Derrida observes that Marx's critique of the Young Hegelians, and of *The German Ideology* more generally, continuously relies on "an ontology of presence" that seeks to bring human consciousness "back to the world of labour, production and exchange, so as to reduce it to its conditions" (110/145, 214/269).[16] Marx considers it possible to grasp the most basic root of mental representations through concepts such as "labor" or "mode of production," which are elevated to the status of pure origins and thus remain implicated in a questionable metaphysical thinking. Derrida's problem with Marx's ontology concerns the articulation of normative claims in the form of a "substantive" normativity grounded in putatively pure origins. For Derrida, this approach remains "radically insufficient" since it privileges "an *ontological* treatment of the spectrality of the ghost" and inscribes the movement of thinking in a teleological understanding of time and history seeking to actualize a *telos*—communism as the embodiment of human essence as species-being in a classless society (114/150, 128/168). The target of his criticism here is the dangerous normativity that the companionship between metaphysics of presence and teleological thinking puts into effect. The normativity informed by ideas supposedly grasped in their purity and posited as the ground for the realization of a political teleology can be a recipe for disastrous consequences. This aspect is attested by the totalitarianisms of the past century, with the Holocaust and the pogroms being perhaps the most disastrous racialized responses to difference (130/171).

But the totalitarianisms Derrida mentions are not the only ruinous consequences of ontological Marxism. The dangerous closure of the political space to religious beliefs and practices, and more generally to difference, is particularly relevant. Derrida's criticism of such Marxism can be taken as a platform for illuminating a distinctively modern approach to the theological-political problematics, namely, the attempt to resolve it at a philosophical level. This emerges especially by looking at Derrida's criticism of Marx's position on religion. Notoriously, Marx reduced religion to an illusion rooted in the material conditions of production, which he deemed to be more fundamental than religious consciousness.[17] Derrida's discussion of Marx's political teleology does not simply clarify that this reduction was possible in virtue of Marx's ontology. Above all, it illuminates that Marx's idea of the criticism of religion as the first of all philosophical criticism depends to a large extent on the dominant modern conviction and desire that the theological-political relationship can and needs to be solved through the affirmation of the originality and priority of reason over faith.[18] It is because reason is thought to be more basic than faith and preceding it in the foundation of knowledge (and politics) that reason is thought of as capable of unmasking the illusions that constraint consciousness and, ultimately, thought.

According to the reasoning presented so far, the tenability of this view depends to a large extent on a questionable understanding of time and teleological political thinking, as well as on the particular Western configuration of *logos* as universal reason and its exclusionary implications. In this framework, it would seem that racialized thinking is symptomatic of a conviction and desire of hierachization and separation justified by a claim to truth that structurally excludes difference. Evoking "the specter of the truth which has been repressed," as Derrida says in *Archive Fever*, this excluded difference would thus indicate that "the truth is spectral, and this is its part of truth which is irreducible by explanation," which is another way of saying that pure and stable representations of truth are possible only if discursively produced (*AF*, 87/111).

The other example Derrida uses in his reflection on political teleology is Fukuyama's *The End of History and the Last Man*. Derrida criticizes Fukuyama for celebrating a version of the "end of history," a discourse informed by a political teleology that considers *liberal* democracy, modeled on the Hegelian view of the state, as the *telos* regulating the however imperfect realization of the Christian Kingdom of God on earth (75/104). Derrida's uneasiness with Fukuyama's perspective lies in the Hegelian version of incarnation it represents but, most importantly, in the unexamined axiomatics on which such view relies and that are at work in a larger trend within influential liberal theories of secularism in which liberal democracy represents the *only* horizon of the future of democracy. The axiom at issue concerns a problematic "*ideal orientation*" informing the narrative of progress of liberal democracy and on a questionable distinction that separates and opposes "empirical reality and ideal finality" (*SM*, 71/99). Although Derrida mentions it with reference to Fukuyama, the orientation at issue is relevant to Kant's philosophy as well as the neo-Kantian theories of Rawls and Habermas, both of which reject

Fukuyama's (and Marx's) "substantive" normativity in favor of a "regulative" one informed by the Kantian model of regulative ideas.[19]

What exactly is Derrida's problem with the "*ideal* orientation"? It is that it establishes and fixes an ideal horizon of expectation on the basis of a purely grasped idea or *telos* so that whatever exceeds that horizon is excluded, sacrificed, or neglected in the name of the horizon itself. In this framework, rational judgments informed by the *telos* cannot be "disproved" or challenged by concrete situations that do not measure up with, contrast with, or differ from it. This holds since the *telos* in question takes the "form of an ideal finality" so that "everything that appears to contradict it would belong to historical empiricity, however massive and catastrophic and global and multiple and recurrent it might be" (71/99). Among the empirical evidence contradicting the "*ideal* orientation" of liberal democracy, Derrida lists socioeconomic exclusion, oppression, and inequality and, above all, international law, the genesis and functioning of which depend on a particular (European) historical culture and its dominating position (100/134 ff.). These plagues, for him, cannot be tolerated in the name of liberal democracy since "never have violence, inequality, exclusion, famine, and thus economic oppression affected as many human beings in the history of the earth and humanity . . . [N]ever have so many men, women, and children been subjugated, starved, or exterminated" (106/141).

Although neither Rawls nor Habermas would disagree with Derrida's denunciation of inequality and exclusion, their theories are, nevertheless, subject to the challenges he poses to an "*ideal* orientation" towards liberal democracy. This holds first because both Rawls and Habermas fix the horizon of liberal democracy on the basis of a regulative *telos*, which sets, more or less rigidly, the future direction and forms of democracy as *liberal* and *secular* in spite of resistance from within.[20] The already mentioned case of indigenous groups in the Americas, Asia and Africa, is a forceful example from within of questioning the present legitimacy and viability of liberal secular democracy and its future, an example that points to the failures of contemporary liberalism.

Derrida's challenge also holds if one considers Habermas's and Rawls's "*ideal* orientation" in the light of their view of modernity. The putatively necessary and natural features of such a view obscure the deep link between the development and maintenance of liberal democratic thinking and the material conditions of its existence on the one hand, and inequality, exclusions, and economic oppression on the other. Indeed, while Habermas seeks to "reconstruct . . . the normative self-understanding of modern legal orders" and sees the advent of modern, rational self-reflexivity as necessary,[21] Rawls provides a naturalizing genealogy that conceives of the reasonable pluralism characterizing liberal modernity "as the *natural* outcome of the activities of human reason under enduring free institutions (my emphasis)."[22] These views, in which liberal modernity emerges as inscribed in a framework of progress informed by an "ideal orientation," pay little attention to the realities that challenge their viability. More problematic still, their embracing of such an orientation subscribes to the metaphysical gesture denounced above, one rooted in a racialized naturalization that "has erased within itself the fabulous scene that has produced it" but "that nevertheless remains active and stirring" within the semantic horizon and institutions that sustain it (*MP*, 213/254).[23] Indeed, both authors reconstruct and justify the development of modern, "rational" understandings and political arrangements in too linear a fashion. In doing so, they leave a limited epistemological role, if at all, for the contingent realities and political forces—the colonial expansion of the modern state and of capitalism, for example—that have, to a large extent, enabled, through violence, those modern understandings and arrangements to develop and prevail by producing, at home and abroad, oppression and inequalities that have continued to occur under the regulative power of international institutions, even after the decolonization of the 1960s.[24] So while both Rawls's and Habermas's commitment to freedom and equality would put them in agreement with Derrida's condemnation, the "ideal orientation" of their theories undermines their commitment to these values. For they fail to integrate into their reflections of modernity the epistemological mirroring effects of political formations indebted to colonialism, capitalism and secularism, together with the exclusion they produced and still produce, thereby philosophically reinforcing the cultural, political, and economic forces that fuel them.[25]

So, what does Derrida's view of time do to a political teleology informed by a "regulative" normativity? Derrida shows that since that type of normativity is committed to the possibility of grasping a pure *telos* by fixing an ideal horizon of expectation, it halts, as it were, the flow of time. As such, such normativity subscribes to the traditional, synchronic understanding of time that opposes and fixes past and future, thereby concealing historical injustice. In doing so, this type of normativity not only overlooks the potential of unrealized, excluded possibilities, but also annuls the possibility that the present matters in its own right, since it is subordinated to a future that can always, and only, promise the infinite approximation of the *telos*. Derrida further demonstrates that, as a consequence, such a mode of thinking is complicit with past injustice and present sufferings that are measured against a redemptive future promising emancipation. Yet, since for both political and logical reasons there is a constant need for "more" *liberal* democracy, because such a democracy can never be achieved, "necessary" suffering can be without limits and past injustice might be well forgotten. The dangerous irony, then, is not simply that the benefits of the future are indefinitely deferred while its guiding principle, the *telos*, is placed beyond the reach of critical scrutiny or even removed from the possibility of failure. It is, above all, that which is supposed to critically enlighten normative judgments about experience is blind to the role past exclusions have played and to the specificity of particular situations in the present, especially if these situations were to differ from the articulations informed by the idealized final goal. If this holds, a political teleology informed by a "regulative" normativity appears minimally receptive to difference, of the past and of the present, and fosters exclusionary practices towards ways of thinking and being that diverge from its predetermined *telos*.

Religion is an exemplary case of excluded difference, and a relevant one for discussions about liberal teleological responses to the "theological-political complex." Indeed, it is with the global spread of secularism, and its teleological narrative of progress built upon the legacy of colonialism and novel forms of imperialism, that religious citizens have been unduly excluded from participating in public life, particularly those of non-Christian faith facing a Christian secular world that has left no epistemological and political space for their difference.[26] Although Rawls and Habermas have shown more openness towards religion in recent years, their theories do not really appear to be receptive to religious difference for reasons that are connected to their approach to the "theological-political complex." Like the "ontological" Marx, these thinkers believe that the theological and the political need to be separate and that reason has priority over faith that can be justified through philosophical arguments implicitly informed by a teleological view of time. In their work on religion, this aspect emerges especially when they condition the validity of deliberative democratic processes of legitimation on rational epistemic grounds (i.e., rationally acceptable reasoning). They further prescribe the translation of religious contributions to public life into the language of secular reason, which is elevated to the rank of the most basic and authoritative ground for solving public disputes.[27]

But what are the grounds for such a prescription and more generally for solving the theological-political nexus? According to the discussion so far, such grounds are connected to a structural feature of political teleology—whether informed by a "substantive" or "regulative" normativity. I have argued that it is a prerogative of teleological thinking, and of the foundational reason associated to it, to establish an ideal horizon of expectation on the basis of a purely grasped *telos* so that everything exceeding that horizon finds little place to be. The *immediate* grasping of the *telos*, I have suggested, is connected to the conviction that undecidability about origins, including what is most original between reason and faith, can be solved through a gesture that halts temporal flow. In this context, religion represents an exemplary case of excluded difference that challenges the viability of a foundational model of reason.

After having expounded Derrida's challenge to political teleologies, we are now in a better position to appreciate the significance of connecting time and political thought. Derrida seeks to show that the commitments to teleology and metaphysics of presence within political thought are exemplary of a modality of thinking that neutralizes the time of politics, obscures its racialized features, and undermines the possibility of pluralism. He does so at two interlinked levels. Philosophically, he shows how teleological thinking fixes time into a rigid framework, which unjustifiably discriminates against ways of thinking, understanding, and being that exceed the schemas of the Western metaphysical tradition. Politically, he illustrates how political teleologies foster practices of exclusion towards "unfitting" difference that contribute to the closure of political space.

Derrida's view of the time of political thought has therefore decisive implications for the study of the "theological-political complex" since it exposes the limits of influential teleological responses to the theological-political problematics and their connections to racialized logics. Derrida shows that the extent to which Western philosophical understandings of time as longing for origins have informed and inform normative political thinking, institutions, and practices they have promoted and still promote the universalization of a racial and exclusionary model of political life grounded on ideas allegedly, and yet unwarrantedly, grasped in their purity. Although this rather bleak picture forcefully emerges from Derrida's reflections, this is not all he is offering. His analysis of time does, in fact, point to the need and possibility of thinking about time differently, as "messianic," and the need to be open to the potential that a nonteleological approach might offer in rethinking the "theological-political complex."

The Messianic as Political Thought

How to think of time otherwise? This is the guiding question addressed by Derrida's notion of "messianic without messianism" (henceforth the "messianic") as it appears especially in *Specters of Marx*, a notion he affirms as indebted to Marx's legacy (*SM*, 73–74/102, 111/ 146–47).[28] Derrida articulates the "messianic" in these terms:

> What remains irreducible to any deconstruction, what remains as undeconstructible as the possibility itself of deconstruction is, perhaps, a certain experience of the emancipatory promise; it is perhaps even the formality of a structural messianism (*un messianisme structurel*), a messianic without religion, even a messianic without messianism (*messianique, même, sans messianisme*), an idea of justice—which we distinguish from law or right and even from human rights—and an idea of democracy—which we distinguish from its current concept and from its determined predicates today. (74/102)

There are two key dimensions to Derrida's "messianic." One is temporal, and refers to an experience of time as nonteleological or "without messianism." The other is ethico-political and is linked to justice and democracy. In what follows, I consider the temporal dimension and the issue of justice while leaving the discussion of democracy to chapter 4.

The promise Derrida mentions in this passage refers to Marx's promise of emancipation, but not to its determined content. It refers to the structure of promising, to the "being-promise of a promise" that exceeds and precedes Marx's and all other promises and maintains an indeterminate form (131/173). As Derrida notes, "whether the promise promises this or that, whether it be fulfilled or not, or whether it be unfulfillable, there is necessarily some promise and therefore some historicity as future-to-come. It is what we are nicknaming the messianic without messianism." In other words, the "messianic" designates a structure of promissory affirmation that does not promise any particular future but promises the future. It affirms that "it is necessary [that there be] the future (*il faut l'avenir*)" (91/123).

Thus, thought as "without messianism," the "messianic" or "quasi-transcendental 'messianism'" as Derrida also calls it, refers to the quasitranscendental conditions of possibility of messianisms, which all require the *necessity* of the future to be *possible* at all (212/267).[29] This structure points to an experience of time characterized by an irreducible and yet necessary historical openness to the future, one that differentiates the "messianic" from historical messianism or secular teleologies. The "messianic" proceeds by preserving an undetermined, open relationship to a future that is not preordained by the historical present. Although it apparently keeps deferring the content of what it affirms, the "messianic" is a type of "affirmative thinking" that asserts the "emancipatory promise as promise," the promise that *il faut l'avenir* (94/126). Yet, the "messianic" takes the form of waiting, a "waiting without horizon of expectation or prophetic prefiguration" as Derrida notes elsewhere (FK, 56/20), because it does not pretend to *see* events as coming, but seeks to think of them *as* events, that is, as irreducibly singular.

> It is this latter event-ness that one must think, but that best resists what is called the concept, if [*sic*] not thinking. And it will not be thought as long as one relies on the simple (ideal, mechanical, or dialectical) opposition of the real presence of the real present or of the living present to its ghostly simulacrum, the opposition of the effective or actual (*wirklich*) to the non-effective, inactual, which is also to say, as long as one relies on a general temporality or a historical temporality made up of the successive linking of presents identical to themselves and contemporary with themselves. (*SM*, 87/119)

For Derrida, to think about event-ness means to think of time nonteleologically. To illustrate a different way of thinking about time, he discusses the idea of temporal disjuncture found in *Hamlet*. Repeatedly in *Specters of Marx*, he quotes Hamlet's phrase "The time is out of joint" to account for a diachronic experience of time. Hamlet's phrase is occasioned by the appearance of his dead father as a ghost coming back (*revenant*) to the living and asking his son to avenge his death and restore justice according to law as vengeance. For Derrida, Hamlet's phrase does not imply that the temporary corruption of his political community requires rectification through the law as punishment. Rather, it interrupts the linear spirit of the inherited law and recognizes that, already in the beginning, in the founding of a law seeking to keep its linear destination, a violent force excluding "deviators" is at work. In other words, Derrida attributes to Hamlet the ability to have recognized in and through the specter of his *revenant* father an "originary wrong . . . a bottomless wound, an irreparable tragedy, the indefinite malediction that marks the history of the law or history as law." The tragedy of the originary wrong, whose origin cannot be clearly identified, designates the "spectral anteriority of the crime" whose truth cannot present itself as such but can only be reconstructed *post facto* (24/46).

For Derrida, the spectral anteriority of the crime refers to an originary trauma that is intimately linked to political foundations. Although the trauma's actual cause is often out of reach, its effects are visible through surviving marks. These are marks of *"a living on (sur-vie),"* a surviving trace of what has been excluded but that intervenes in the living present by unsettling it (xx/17). That trace takes the form of specters that, as seen, do not appear in the present as something clearly identifiable. Rather they appear as some "thing" that is difficult to capture because it exceeds knowledge, or what counts as knowledge, and thus defies "semantics as much as ontology, psychoanalysis as much as philosophy" (5/26). By interrupting allegedly stable and universal representations of the present—in law, politics, and religion—specters expose the "non-contemporaneity of present time with itself," which marks the temporal disjuncture informing the time of the "messianic" (29/52).

Derrida's interpretation of Hamlet's phrase "The time is out of joint" stands, therefore, for his response to the traditional view of time and to the metaphysics of presence and teleology undergirding it.[30] It is also a response to the racialized features of such a thinking since it signals a critical awareness of the structural exclusions effected by Western discourse's representations (RWL, 294). In the "messianic" understanding of time, specters signal the remainders haunting representations presented as universally valid, thereby exposing the impossibility of closed epistemological and political orders that various teleologies seek to secure. That is why Derrida affirms that "messianic" might represent the condition of "another concept of the political," namely, one that is not associated, among other things, to unequivocal normative standards and fixed horizons of expectations based on racialized schemas that systematically close the political space by repressing ghosts as symptoms of excluded difference (*SM*, 94/126).

Returning to the trauma of political foundation, Derrida clarifies that it refers to both the specters of the past and those of the future. In his view, the specter is as much a *revenant* coming back from the past as it is an *arrivant* coming from the future. It is a figure that comprises all those who are beyond the "living present," the dead and the unborn, toward whom we have responsibility. Doing so is a matter of justice, of the "messianic" as justice.

> It is necessary to speak *of the* ghost (*fantômes*), indeed *to the* ghost and *with it*, from the moment that no ethics, no politics, whether revolutionary or not, seems possible and thinkable and *just* that does not recognize in its principle the respect for those others who are no longer or for those others who are not yet *there*, presently living, whether they are already dead or not yet born. No justice—let us say no law and once again we are not speaking here of laws—seems possible or thinkable without the principle of some *responsibility*, beyond all living present, within that which disjoin the living present, before the ghosts of those who are not yet born or who are already dead, be they victims of wars, political or other kind of violence, nationalist, racist, colonialist, sexist, or other kind of exterminations, victims of the oppression of capitalist imperialism or any other forms of totalitarianism. (SM, xviii/14–15)

The "messianic" as justice is a discourse about ghosts and their interminable mourning, interminable also because their number cannot be conclusively determined. It is a discourse characterized by what Derrida calls a "politico-logic of trauma," namely, a politico-philosophical receptivity to the politics of founding and its predicament. This receptivity refers to the trauma and ghosts produced by the structural violence that characterizes founding moments—as it appears in the case of so-called democracies like the United States, Canada, Australia, and Israel, whose establishment as political entities is marked at their roots by settler-colonial projects characterized by exterminations and exclusions of indigenous people and national minorities, as instrumental to the construction of political community—but also that of wars, racist, sexist, and capitalist forms of oppression, as the quote indicates. Without such receptivity, without the memory of an originary loss, it seems extremely difficult to critically account for what has enabled the law in the first place and thus also for the temporal rupture founding moments mark. As Derrida claims, the violence of the "originary performativity," whose "force of rupture produces the institution or the constitution, the law itself," "interrupts time, disarticulates it, dislodges it, displaces it out of its natural lodging: it is 'out of joint'" (37/60). In short, without a "politico-logic of trauma" and politics of memory it appears extremely difficult to account for the empirical conditions (i.e., historical violence) that make politics possible at all. This account is not simply instrumental to avoid the naïve confidence of redeeming past injustice by delivering or approximating a promise of universal emancipation.

The decisive significance of the "politico-logic of trauma" and of memory cannot be missed since they speak to the possibility of perceiving and accounting for difference where semantic and political orders, or more figuratively the archive, attempt to impede it. As Derrida clarifies in *Archive Fever*, the politics of memory at work in the question of the archive is not "one political question among others. It runs through the whole field and in truth determines politics from top to bottom as *res publica*." Thus, investigating the archive becomes a matter of memory and concerns "the institution of limits *declared* to be insurmountable," that is, limits at once epistemological and political, defining, among other things, what is and counts as "reason," "human," and "religion," an operation that has traditionally been performed through the quest for origins (*AF*, 4/15).

Here, for Derrida, lies the problem of the archive ("*trouble de l'archive*"), "which troubles and muddles the vision (as they say in French), what inhibits sight and knowledge": archive fever ("*mal d'archive*"). To suffer from this fever, "is to burn with a passion. It is never to rest, interminably from searching for the archive right where it slips away." It is, in other words, "to have a compulsive, repetitive, and nostalgic desire for the archive, an irrepressible desire to return to the origin, a homesickness, a nostalgia for the return to the most archaic place of absolute commencement" (91/142). While suffering from archive fever means being "in need of archives," Derrida warns about, through a discussion involving Judaism, the risks and ruinous implications stemming from an exclusive, exclusionary, and expropriating realization of this desire through "an archive which would in sum confuse itself with the arkhe," namely of setting up legal institutions, and ultimately a state, in a place identified as natural origin (94–95/147–48, 98/151). This risk is all the more dangerous, Derrida remarks elsewhere, if sustained by the "motifs of filiation through blood, appropriation of the place, and the motif of election" (ATI, 29/39). At a broader level, this warning addresses the political unconscious of racialized thinking: the epistemic possibility of rescuing origins and the political desirability of naturalizing and institutionalizing them in a specific place, with these being aspects that not simply normalize a muddled vision but also bring about human destruction.

At issue here is the very possibility of *thinking* justice. On the one hand, forgetting the exclusions of difference involved in political foundings impedes the recognition of ghosts, and thus of temporal disjuncture. It obscures the potential of unrealized possibilities and locks the future to the close destiny of a present *telos* that predetermines the conditions for inclusion from the present and the status quo, thereby potentially instutionalizing exclusions. As Derrida says in *Archive Fever*, commenting on the historian Yosef Hayim Yerushalmi's ascription to Israel alone, as a people and a place, the duty to remember and guard the archive, its site, and content: "[I]f it is *just* to remember the future and the injunction to remember, namely the archontic injunction to guard and to gather the archive, it is not less just to remembers the others, other others and others in oneself, and that the other peoples could say the same thing—in another way. And that *tout autre est tout autre*, as we can say in French: every other is every other other, is altogether other" (*AF*, 77/101). Remembering others, and every other, is a question of responsibility that attends to the relationality of human experience before sociopolitical divisions are established and justified through separatist, indeed racialized, theoretical justifications.[31] As irreplaceably attached to the singularity of each, responsibility becomes the sense Derrida attributes to the election, thereby countering its exclusivist and exclusionary interpretations. He says: "[I]t is thus that I understand or accept the concept of election, there where being chosen, well beyond any privilege of birth, nation, people, or community, signifies that no one can replace me at the site of this decision and of this responsibility" (ATI, 37/47).

For Derrida, the forgetting of all these others is also what various messianisms and secular teleologies do by instituting all sorts of checkpoints at their borders "in order to screen the *arrivant*" and also by exercising a hermeneutic authority on the interpretation of the past (*SM*, 82/110). On the other hand, a lack of receptivity to specters jeopardizes the possibility of *thinking* justice, which is not simply a question of and for the living, of life as presence, but something due to the nonliving, to the dead as memory and the unborn as promise. *Thinking* justice, therefore, cannot seem any longer possible within transcendent or transcendental perspectives; that is, within perspectives seeking to identify the most fundamental principle representing either its ultimate content, as in the tradition of political philosophy since Plato, or the ground for articulating procedures leading to justice, as in the Neo-Kantian political thought. These perspectives still aim at identifying pure ideas, those whose immediate grasping would require the halting of temporal flow and the by-default exclusion of spectral excess. Nor does it seem possible to think justice by way of gathering or bringing-together (*Versammlung*) as Derrida sees Heidegger doing in his reflection on justice as *Dikē*, precisely because gathering implies a form of totalization that interrupts temporal flow and homogenizes difference (27–29/54–57). Rather, *thinking* justice is possible if past and future, presence and absence are thought of together through disjuncture. Here the notion of disjuncture is crucial because it fosters a sensibility to past and future exclusions and the reactivation of ghosts. Animated by an antiracist thrust that is not always recognized as such—antiracist insofar as it does not repress the specters produced by forceful naturalization of hierarchies—this view of justice prevents the halting of time. It also avoids, as much as possible, the negative implications of teleological approaches to the "theological-political complex," such as limited sensibility towards difference and blindness towards structural exclusions. It would, in other words, offer the possibility of addressing difference *as* difference and thus, to a certain extent, as incalculable.[32]

The politico-philosophical significance of reactivating ghosts must be emphasized since it marks a feature that distinguishes the "messianic" from political teleologies. This reactivation plays a central role in Derrida's notion of the "messianic" as it pertains to "redemptive" practices of thinking that mobilize, in pursuit of justice, the spectral elements involved in political foundations. This point can be appreciated by focusing on the connections Derrida establishes between inheritance, responsiveness to ghosts, and emancipatory thinking. Recalling Marx's ideas that "men make their own history" under circumstances transmitted from the past and that "the tradition of all the dead generations [*aller toten Geschlechter*] weighs [*lastet*] like a nightmare on the brain of the living," Derrida reminds us that inheritance always involves a response to ghosts in the form of "conjuring (*beschwören*)" them (134/176). The urge for conjuring does not stem from moral principles but from thinking itself.

> Thinking never has done with the conjuring impulse. It would instead be born of that impulse. To swear or to conjure, is that not the chance of thinking and its destiny, no less than its limit? The gift of its finitude? Does it ever have any other choice except among several conjurations? [. . .] Problematization itself is careful to disavow and thus to conjure away [. . .] Critical problematization continues to do battle against ghosts. It fears them as it does itself. (207/261)

Although thinking is never done with the conjuring impulse, the conjuration of ghosts can take a negative form as in the case of political teleologies. Caught by anxiety and motivated by a fear of ghosts, these modes of thinking seek to safeguard the unity and stability of political identity and can lead, in extreme cases, to devastating forms of oppression and racism. For Derrida, this is what happened with the totalitarianisms of the twentieth century, fascism and communism, which were "equally terrorized by the ghost of the other, and its own ghost as the ghost of the other" and thus can be read *also* as repressive reactions "of panic-ridden fear before the ghost in general" (130/170). Less extreme but equally problematic are the closures typical of the liberal tradition, which Derrida sees as displaying strong amnesic and inhospitable features towards ghosts and difference. Following Marx's reflection on "bourgeois" thinking, Derrida highlights how, for Marx, that thinking is content to forget specters so that history can continue towards a universal emancipatory *telos*. By valuing only life as presence, liberal ("bourgeois") thinking values "life as forgetting itself" and thus forgets ghosts and what they signify (36/180). As such, it also forgets historical violence and the constitutive limits that its own particular foundations put on the universality of the discourse it champions. The lived experiences of indigenous, religious, racial, and sexual minorities in many Western democracies, and above all subalterns from the Global South, speak to the concrete manifestations of these limits.

In contrast to repressive or forgetful conjurations, Derrida points to a possible alternative. Although he recognizes that conjuration is never free from the anxiety to repress or forget ghosts, he insists that the latter can take the form of "a positive conjuration" if it considers anxiety as a chance for calling forth the dead. As he notes, "the conjuration is anxiety from the moment it calls upon death to invent the quick and to enliven the new, to summon the presence of what is not yet there (*noch nicht Dagewesenes*). This anxiety is properly revolutionary" (135/177). By calling upon death to enliven the present, a "positive conjuration" of ghosts can release the emancipatory potential of "what is not yet," thereby point to new possibilities by "redeeming" unrealized ones. It is in this sense that calling forth the dead marks a revolutionary moment, the moment of rupture that the "messianic" view of time exemplifies. Yet, it also signals how much weight the "messianic" accords to historical injustice and to practices of thinking, seeking to throw new light on the present by reactivating its ghosts.

Emphasizing the "redemptive" practices of thinking fostered by the "messianic" does not imply condemning unconditionally the forgetting of past violence and of its ghosts. Nor does it suggest blaming the somehow oblivious moving forward of a new political community. As Derrida reckons, *some* forgetting of what has been inherited is necessary to that movement.

The point is rather to highlight the significance of remembering not "what one inherits but the pre-inheritance on the basis of which one inherits"; that is, remembering the empirical conditions of founding moments which, as mentioned in chapter 1, involve exterminations and exclusion of human, cultural, and political alternatives that leave behind ghostly traces (137/181). The remembering of such conditions and of their specters is distinctive of the messianic promise which, for that reason, *can* acknowledge its own political nature and provisionality. It is a remembering that *can* thus limit, as much as possible, closure and totalization while unlocking the power of unrealized possibilities.

If it might at this point be clear what view of time characterizes the "messianic," the same might not apply to the type of normativity such a view fosters. To address this issue, it is first of all essential to consider the understanding of reason at work in the "messianic," a topic that momentarily requires departing from *Specters of Marx*. In *Rogues*, for example, Derrida offers a series of reflections on Kant that point towards such an understanding. Derrida takes up Kant's idea of defending the "honour of reason" and suggests that what is at stake in thinking might be "saving the honour of reason" against the crisis reason has undergone, and yet provoked, especially as a result of the dominating calculative mode of scientific rationality (118/167; 130/182).[33] For Derrida, "saving the honour of reason" means attending to both reason's exigencies—unconditional incalculability and conditional calculability. Above all, it means saving reason from the dominance of calculative rationality and thus, in some sense, from itself. To this end, he suggests a critical return to Kant who, in his *Groundwork of the Metaphysics of Morals*, shows that reason is not confined to calculability but is also called to attend to the demands of the unconditional and the incalculable, as the concept of "dignity" illustrates (133/186). However, Kant also articulates a view of theoretical reason that, in spite of its subordination to practical reason and its unconditional character, tends to constitutively resist the demands of the unconditional. Derrida recalls that, in the *Critique of Pure Reason*, Kant defines reason as architectonic, namely, as a type of reason that is made foundational through a systematizing approach that privileges unity, homogeneity, and calculability over divisibility, heterogeneity, and incalculability (120/170).

Derrida's problem with Kant's view is two-fold. First, it bypasses the difficulty of translating the plural and heterogeneous manifestations of reason, which have their own "distinct historicity" and resist, "in the name of their very rationality, any architectonic organization." Kant's attempt to systematize reason manifests an "architectonic desire," which is a desire to master reason's plural rationalities by "bending their untranslatable heterogeneity" and by inscribing them in a teleological schema grounded on the unifying function of regulative ideas (121/171). Second, Kant's view of reason relies on regulative ideas, each of which functions as a *telos* that defines, in a calculative fashion, the "ideal horizon" and direction of thinking so that unforeseeable events exceeding such horizon are excluded (128/80, 143/197).

At issue, here, is the powerful modern view of teleological reason (and teleology) we have been discussing all along. This is a type of reason that, by setting in advance the terms of what is to be found, "finds what it seeks" because it *knows already*, as it were, what arrives, and thus "limits and neutralizes the event" as something that does not fit with such terms (128/180). As seen, a reason so conceived inhibits, a priori, eventfulness, as well as the future to the extent that everything that does not fall in a pre-programmed structure of expectation, is excluded as irrelevant or "unfitting."

> Whenever a *telos* or teleology comes to orient, order and make possible a historicity, it annuls that historicity by the same token and neutralizes the unforeseeable and incalculable irruption, the singular and exceptional alterity of *what* [*ce qui*] comes, or indeed of *who* [*qui*] comes, that without which, or the one without whom, nothing happens or arrives. It is not only a question of the *telos* that is being posed here that of the horizon and of any horizontal *seeing-come* in general. And it is also a question of the Enlightenment of Reason. (128/180)

For Derrida, questioning teleology and teleological reason is required by a reason that responds to the unconditional in an incalculable fashion, one in which events are no longer *seen* as coming because they are not seeable, or knowable, as such.[34] And this is for Derrida a matter required by the "Enlightenment of Reason," by a reason that seeks to throw light where its own authority seeks to prevent it doing so. This is a type of reason that goes against itself and "suspends" its defenses in order to "save" its own honour" and protect itself. Without entering extensively into a topic I will develop in chapter 4, we can, nevertheless, indicate very briefly the autoimmune character of reason articulated here.

Derrida develops the notion of autoimmunity especially in connection to how immunity is used in biology, that is, as designating the production of antibodies as a defense or protection against antigens.[35] In relation to immunity, autoimmunity designates a process affecting life or any living organism, one in which self-protection and survival require destroying or suspending one's own self-defences. As such, autoimmunity is a process in which elements of life and death intertwine (80/67, 82/70). Connected to reason, autoimmunity illuminates the movement that reason undertakes against itself to save its own honor, to protect itself by suspending its defenses. This saving is not the securing of reason's immunity but its opening to difference. Playing with the double sense of the French *salut* as both salvation and salutation, Derrida emphasizes here that saving the honor of reason demands distancing oneself from the unquestioned value of autonomy and moving towards that of autoimmunity, which exposes the vulnerability and openness of the self to the other (123/173). In short, it is by being critical of its autonomy, of its own immune authority, and by opening itself to difference, that reason can save itself from itself.

What Derrida advocates for is a radical self-criticism of reason and its teleological understandings. It is a criticism that envisions a view of reason "that is other than the classical reason of what presents itself or announces its presentation according to the *eidos*, the *idea*, the ideal, the regulative Idea, or something else that here amounts to the same, the telos" (135/189). A reason so conceived attends to the exigencies of the calculable and the incalculable, or the "rational" and the "reasonable," beyond the dominance of calculative rationality, and thus beyond the metaphysics of presence providing political teleology with fixed standards for calculation (159/217). The stakes behind thinking reason *with* the unconditional are highly significant and involve what Derrida calls "another thought of the possible" and "of an im-possible that would not be simply negative," that is, an im-possible that is not impossible as the negative or opposite of possible. Another thinking of the possible is one that thinks about the "reasonable" as "the incalculable so as to give an account of it there where this appears impossible, so as to reckon *with* it" (159/217; *PM*, 73–99/284–318). It is one that attempts to account for the incalculable without necessarily counting it, that is, to think about what remains foreign to the order of one's present possibilities, especially if these are taken as remaining within a horizon in which prediction forecloses the possibility of the new to occur.

Thinking reason otherwise involves "the possibility of suspending in an argued, deliberated, rational fashion, all conditions, hypotheses, conventions, and presuppositions, and of criticizing unconditionally all *krinein*, of the *krisis*, of the binary or dialectical decision of judgment" (*R*, 142/197). This suspension is a pre-eminently politico-philosophical task since it requires questioning the conditions of reason beyond the strictly philosophical, thereby including the political, military, and economic conditions that seek to guarantee the supremacy of calculative rationality as the dominant imaginary of reason. As such, it is a task that opens up the possibility of another thinking of the political that does not rely on a calculation of its future from the present, but that remains open to transformation because it does not foreclose the very *possibility* of possibilities.

Returning to the issue of normativity, the question arises whether the messianic has any normativity at all. Hägglund, for example, questions this possibility. For him, the undecidability connected to the unconditional, and thus openness of the future, signals the absence of "any intrinsic normativity in deconstruction."[36] The account of the "messianic" provided so far appears to be converging towards this view. I have argued that the "messianic" names a type of thinking characterized by an irreducible historical openness to the future and to the "event" conceived as a radical interruption of temporal flow. Yet, although this openness manifests itself as a form of waiting, it does not imply the paralysis of agency or that the justice sought by the "messianic" is infinitely deferred. Throughout the whole of *Specters of Marx*, Derrida's attempt to think the disjuncture of time and the event to come is characterized by a strong sense of urgency and action associated with both Marx's political injunction and the notion of *différance*, an urgency that points to a normative dimension.

> In the uncoercible différance the here and now unfurls. Without lateness, without delay, but without presence, it is the precipitation of an absolute singularity, singular because deferring, precisely [*justement*], and always other, binding itself necessarily to the form of the instant, in *imminence and urgency*: even if it moves towards what remains to come, there is the *pledge* [*gage*] (promise, engagement, injunction and response to the injunction, and so forth). The pledge is given here and now, even before, perhaps, a decision confirms it. It thus responds without delay to the demand of justice. The latter by definition is impatient, uncompromising, and unconditional. (37/60)

For Derrida, Marx's political injunction, his pledge for emancipation and changing the world, is urgent and imminent. It cannot wait a deferral, as justice demands taking a decision in the present, in the "here and now," a decision that does not, nevertheless, imply that justice has occurred, and that is why deferral and difference (*différance*), affect its happening.

By inheriting Marx's injunction this way, Derrida's "messianic" displays some form of normativity, a "normativity without *telos*."[37] The "messianic" is normative insofar as it imperatively and urgently affirms *that* one is to act and decide in the present, and thus in opposition to awaiting a future to be actualized or approximated. Yet, thought "without *telos*," the "messianic" is a nonteleological type of political thinking that resists providing prescriptions on the basis of idealized final goals or universal norms and thus is nonnormative in the traditional sense. That is, it is not informed by the force of the metaphysics of presence, its epistemological mastery, and fixed ontological foundations undergirded by racial hierarchies. Rather, it is a thinking that because it is receptive to temporal disjuncture and difference leaves open the interpretations and applications of the content informing decisions according to contexts and the culture-specific values that characterize them. This means that, strictly speaking, there is no messianic politics or action in Derrida's thought, one carried out in the name of some messianic end to be implemented. Rather, there is only political agency *out of* the "messianic," which, because disentangled from teleology, remains free," as it were. This freedom lies in the action's undecidability, in its impossibility of enacting or implementing a universal rule, and in its originality. As Derrida notes in his discussion of just decision in "Force of Law," undecidability is an experience of what, heterogeneous to the calculable and the rule, remains still dutiful but not solvable through logical determination. It is the experience of exposure to singular situations, which, because of their specificity, do not fall into the scope of established rules and yet demand a decision to be taken. Once a decision is taken, a new rule is established, one that settles the undecidable impasse in one direction or another but does not dissolve undecidability as such. For Derrida, passing through the ordeal of undecidability without being able to extinguish it represents a condition for freedom. As he argues, an action or decision that would not pass the test of undecidability would not be free but "would only be the programmable application or the continuous unfolding of a calculable process" (FL, 252/44). The suspension of the rule and not its enactment, as in Kant's moral law, is the condition for freedom within which reason proceeds. Thus, because the ordeal of undecidability can never be conclusively overcome, action out of the "messianic" is always a failure insofar as it always falls short of any ideal or rule guiding action. However, for the same reasons, it is also always original, unprecedented, and singular because it takes place in the present as if it were every time the first. It is, in sum, a free action.

Viewing deconstruction as a "normativity without telos" bears resemblance to recent interpretations of the same. In her *Lucid Vigil*, Stella Gaon suggests that Derrida's deconstruction is type of inquiry that is "normative . . . but it is still not prescriptive."[38] Deconstruction is normative insofar as it affirms the injunction of maintaining a "lucid vigilance with regard to the possibility of [reason's] own conditions"; yet, it is not prescriptive in that it also destabilizes any final ground for normative prescriptions about what is good.[39] This understanding results from "the lessons of deconstruction" as a radical self-critique that questions "the modern philosophical assumption that a rational justification of political ends is possible," thereby exposing the impossibility of conclusive epistemological foundations; "notwithstanding their impossibility" such a type of critique also insists on that an "evocation of foundations is necessary for critical theories aimed at emancipatory political ends."[40] For Gaon, this view of deconstructive critique as "lucid vigilance" emerges "*clearly* in the context of the so called 'modernism-postmodernism debate (my emphasis)";[41] what sustains its normative thrust, and this is the novelty of the interpretation offered, is a sort of "unconscious drive to honor the principle of reason," a drive that a Laplanchean psychoanalytical understanding of "the relationship between subjectivity and Enlightenment reason" brings to the fore.[42]

My perspective both agrees and departs from this view. Like Gaon, I emphasize that the non-prescriptive normativity of deconstruction—what I call "non-normative" and "without telos"—is rooted in the impossibility of ultimate foundations which emerges from a radical and irreducible interrogation of origins that is deeply connected, as I shall discuss more amply in the next chapter, to the "theological-political" problematics. It is in this sense that deconstruction resists the epistemological mastery of typical of the Enlightenment. Yet, unlike Gaon, I show that this radicalization of the critical impulse of Enlightenment does not simply and "clearly" emerge in conjunction with "modernism-postmodernism debate," which remains Eurocentric. Rather it is connected to Derrida's profound awareness of the racial undercurrents of Western modernity, and thus linked to the deconstructive critique of race and colonial logics of *secular* philosophies that emerges from his corpus. These aspects of deconstruction, I have argued, appear even more forcefully by appreciating that Derrida's philosophical practice is located in a lived experience *at* the margin of the Western tradition—at the limits of Western understandings of reason and not within it, as Gaon's historical contextualization seems to suggest. While Gaon's exploration of the desire for vigilance tackles questions of subjectivity and identity, and it manifests a clear awareness of Derrida's discussion of specters—thus a potential receptivity to both Derrida's cultural difference(s) and the differences bordering the (Western) tradition of thought she deals with—her interrogation of deconstruction remains, as in the case of many commentators, locked into a specific geopolitics of reason ascribed to deconstruction and at firm distance from questions of religion. But this geopolitics and Christian horizon deconstruction decisively challenges (*OG*, FK, *PF*, WM, *MO*, *OH*, *IW*). It is a central suggestion of this book that unless the racial dimension of Western conceptions of reason is brought to the fore, as deconstruction does in the proposed interpretation, there is a risk that the deeper roots of reason's conditions of possibility and limits remain unconcealed and unquestioned. As a result, the interrogation of reason, however critical and self-critical it might be, risk sustaining discourses that remain more or less implicitly confined to a particular cultural tradition that retains the monopoly of establishing what count as (critical) reason. This is not simply uncritical, but it is something that Derrida clearly denounces from his early writings, and perhaps most forcefully through his notion of "White mythology," thereby opening the space to determine what goes under the name of critical reason to other traditions of thought.

Returning to the discussion on deconstruction normativity: the novelty and significance of the "messianic" consists in offering an alternative approach to the "theological-political complex." This approach remains normative without, nevertheless, being informed by traditional metaphysical thinking and its hierarchical and exclusionary implications. By resisting normative ideals derived out of logical determinations, the "messianic" point to a normativity that seeks to enable responsiveness to the specificity of contexts, and thus ultimately to the demands of justice. Indeed, for Derrida, normative judgments informing action or evaluating current institutions and practices are to be assessed on their ability to foster responsibility conceived as the ability to respond to the specificity of situations and the constitutive relationality of the human condition, and not simply to rational criteria publicly justifiable. As he notes, deconstruction "depends each time on the situation, the context, above all political, of the subject, on his or her rootedness in a place and a history."[43] Therefore, normative judgments cannot be regulated in advance in pre-eminently ideal terms or before being exposed to experience and the process of negotiations it demands. Negotiation here does not stand for an ideal goal but names a predicament in which reason proceeds imaginatively, without a priori guidance or stable epistemological foundations, every time anew by potentially reconsidering the terms of its proceeding. As Derrida suggests in *Rogues*, the nonteleological model of reason at work in the "messianic" is one in which reason proceeds in a creative fashion by "inventing the maxims of transactions" for deciding between its own exigencies, between conditional calculability and unconditional incalculability (*R*, 158/217). Undoubtedly, the openness inherent in messianic thinking implies a certain degree of risk in political life as Derrida recognizes when he notes that "to be out of joint" can not only "do harm and do evil" but "it is no doubt the very possibility of evil" (*SM*, 34/178).[44] Yet, that very risk constitutes at the same time a possibility of not collapsing justice and law and thus falling into the risk of naturalizing the normative assumption informing representation of law, community, and subjectivity that retains an irreducible political dimension.

Reading Derrida's perspective as normative but not in a "traditional" sense differs from interpretations of his work—including those of Simon Critchley, John Caputo, Drucilla Cornell, Richard Beardsworth, Leonard Lawlor, and Matthias Fritsch—that suggest the presence of a normative dimension in his thought.[45] Despite their differences, these authors consider Derrida's view as informed by some normative ideal—conceived respectively as the ethical priority of the other, peace, utopia of nonviolence, or the goal of "lesser violence"—and thus leave his perspective within too traditional an understanding of normativity as shaped by some logical determination and epistemological mastery.

While sharing with these views the emphasis on some kind of normativity in Derrida's thought, my view differs significantly on the nature of that normativity. According to my reading, Derrida's "messianic" can be viewed as a nonnormative normativity that dismisses the epistemological mastery, and its undergirding metaphysics of presence, involved in the positing of ideals through some grasp of origins. As seen, this is an operation that remains implicated in philosophically and politically questionable racialized hierarchies and that bypasses the process of negotiating relevant standard of translation demanded by the historicity of contexts and the experience of encountering difference. The opposition to the metaphysics of presence involves an antiracist thrust that emerges from Derrida's emphasis on specters, as well as from his challenge to strategies of epistemic hierachization and naturalization that are resisted through the messianic affirmation of openness and the call for responsibility towards others before, and beyond, separations and divisions. While specters disallow the possibility of thinking of relying on stable, and allegedly universal, representations, the affirmation of openness impedes preordaining normative guidelines about how to act on the basis of understandings presented as universally valid: a blow to "White mythology," in short.

Ruling out the presence of a robust normativity in Derrida does not suggest that there is no normative commitment in his thought, that action and decision remain normatively unsupported, or even less that his normative sources are arbitrary. As it appears especially from his later writings, Derrida does, in fact, manifest a commitment to democracy over other regimes and, in particular, to a certain understanding of democracy that emphasizes values such as openness to criticism, perfectibility, and free speech, all of which carry a normative weight.[46] Far from being arbitrary, such a commitment is, instead, inherited from the traditions he is heir to and attests to the historical character of his reflections. In this respect, my view is closer to that of Samir Haddad, who sees the normative character of deconstruction linked to the values informing and conditioning the language (of democracy) that Derrida inherits and uses.[47] Ruling out a substantive normativity indicates that Derrida's normative push does not, by itself, translate into an ethico-political program, but remains open to articulation and rearticulation according to the specificity of situations, as well as to the possibility that inherited interpretations might not be as or relevant in the future. This argument will be furthered in discussion of democracy and secularism in chapter 4.[48] My suggestion is that Derrida commits to act "here and now" and thus to respond to, and engage with situations, contexts, and people in the historical present. His commitment is normative as it is imperatively affirmed from within a given historical context that is neither epistemically nor normatively neutral nor stable. Yet, it is nonnormative as traditionally conceived since it ultimately resists the epistemological schema of traditional models and their racialized and exclusionary implications.

Between Faith and Reason: The "Faith" of Messianic Thinking

The objection can be raised that articulating a structure of temporal experience through the notion of the "messianic *without* messianism" leaves open the question whether the messianic retains specific religious features. The objection goes to the heart of Derrida's thinking and requires a considered answer. Doing so allows us to further clarify the nature of messianic thinking and situate where the "messianic" stands in relation to reason and faith and, more generally, the "theological-political complex."

One way to start looking at the relationship between the "messianic" and the "theological-political complex" is by elucidating the relationship between the former and messianism. Derrida clarifies that the "messianic" is heir to Marxism and that Marx has an open debt to religion with regard to specters and the promise of emancipation. He notes that "if there is a spirit of Marxism which I will never be ready to renounce, it is not only the critical idea or the questioning stance . . . It is even more a certain emancipatory and *messianic* affirmation, a certain experience of the promise that one can try to liberate from any dogmatics and even from any metaphysico-religious determination and from *messianism*" (*SM*, 11/146–47). While Marx could only *try* to emancipate his view from messianism, his criticism of religion put him at a distance from institutionalized religion, and marked the unique "good" spirit of Marxism that Derrida seeks to retain (113/149).

If this short genealogy sheds some light on the origins of the emancipatory promise (in Marx and Derrida), and also why a seemingly religious language is retained, it leaves unexplained the relation between messianism and the "messianic."[49] While acknowledging the necessity of clarifying the difference between the "messianic" and messianisms—or what he calls "two messianic spaces"—Derrida remains deeply ambivalent about whether to resolve their relation in terms of priority.

> How to relate, but also how to dissociate the two messianic spaces we are talking about here under the same name? If the messianic appeal belongs properly to a universal structure, to that irreducible movement of the historical opening to the future, therefore to experience itself and to its language (expectation, promise, commitment to the event of what is coming, imminence, urgency, demand for salvation and for justice beyond the law, pledge given to the other inasmuch as he or she is not present, presently present or living, and so forth), how is one to *think* it *with* the figure of Abrahamic messianism? Does it figure abstract desertification or originary condition? Was not Abrahamic messianism but an exemplary prefiguration, the pre-name [*prénom*] given against the background of the possibility that we are attempting to name here? But then when we keep the name, or at least the adjective (we prefer to say *messianic* rather the *messianism*, so as to designate a structure of experience rather than a religion), there where no figure of the *arrivant*, even

as he or she is heralded, should be pre-determined, prefigured, or even pre-named? Of these two deserts, which one, first of all, will have signalled toward the other? Can one conceive an atheological heritage of the messianic? (210/266)

Derrida's ambivalence emerges from two viable possibilities: the "messianic" as an abstraction derivative of the historical event of "Abrahamic messianism," or as its "originary condition" of possibility. Referring to the nexus between revelation and revealability, which invokes the relationship between reason and faith, this dilemma mirrors a recurrent philosophical puzzle concerning the link between the transcendental and empirical, the universal and the particular that emerges in several of his texts (*AF*, 87/127; *PF*, 18/36; FK 48/18).[50] Derrida remains very cautious on these questions, affirming that the two possibilities "do not exclude each other" (*SM*, 211/266). He reiterates his hesitation in several other places, declaring in one intervention that "another schema has to be constructed in order to understand the two at the same time, to do justice to these two possibilities," namely, a schema that goes beyond the language of transcendental philosophy (FK, 48/19; EF, 43; VR, 23). At stake here is the trap of a binary reductionism that, by either prioritizing the historical over the philosophical, or the philosophical over the historical, remains locked between an ahistorical transcendentalism or a philosophically blind historicism.

Several commentators have focused on various iterations of this dilemma in Derrida's thought, paying attention to the nature of the "quasi-transcendental" in his view, the idea that transcendental concepts remain connected to the empirical conditions out of which they emerge.[51] Addressing these debates, I propose to read the "messianic" as a quasitranscendental concept irreducibly related to the concrete context of its emergence and to the notion of "White mythology." I do so by developing a clue to the riddle at issue offered by Derrida himself in *Specters of Marx*. There, just after the long passage quoted above, he puts limits to any "simple" universalization at work in the "messianic" that would repeat the naturalizing logic of the Western metaphysical tradition he criticizes. Derrida remarks, in fact, that "open, waiting for the event as justice" the hospitality of the "messianic" "is absolute only if it keeps *watch over its own* universality" (*cette hospitalité n'est absolue que si elle veille sur sa propre universalité*, SM, 211/267; my emphasis).

How are we to interpret this claim? What does it mean to say that the "messianic" is *really* open—it is a transcendental condition of possibility of messianism that must be indeterminate and thus open—if it "keeps watch over its own universality"? To elucidate this matter through the proposed interpretative grid, it is helpful to keep in focus Derrida's attention on questions of foundings—political, linguistic, and philosophical—and the temporal disjuncture they mark. Doing so helps emphasize the historicity of the "messianic" within the broader framework of "White mythology." Indeed, it is precisely because the "messianic" is sensible to time and to the rupture brought about by temporal disjuncture that it presents a critical awareness of its historical character and of the irreducible and only cancelable exclusions of specters produced by political foundations. To this purpose, and without deviating too much from our trajectory here, we can make two brief digressions concerning the institution of language and of the archive.

As seen in the previous chapter, Derrida rejects the possibility of metalanguage by pointing to the linguistic predicament of the human condition as one of being-with-others-in-translation. The critical awareness of this predicament requires acknowledging the colonial aspect of natural language, the contingency of its institution, and thus its historical occupation of the medium we call "language." Similarly, Derrida shows that philosophical language and its objects of investigation (especially truth and reference) are always constituted from within a specific historical context, the fixing of which is never philosophically neutral but can be traced back to an event of political foundation. Thus, taken together, the colonial aspect of natural language and the politically conditioned character of philosophy point to the fact that philosophical reflection is always already historically situated and politically conditioned, and it remains so in spite of the general forgetting of this very predicament.

The connection between the historicity of the "messianic" and the topic of foundations can also be appreciated by considering the institution of the archive. In *Archive Fever*, Derrida conceives of the archive as, among other things, the geopolitical and historical site where relevant public forms of subjectivity, understandings, and ethics are framed in the aftermath of a founding event (*AF*, 3/14). The archive constitutes the place that stands before but "contains" the originary crime, which is excluded from visibility because it has allowed the archive to be there in the first place. This crime marks the "fabulous scene" characterizing the institution of political community as it does those of wider juridico-political institutions and semantic horizons typical of the "White mythology" of *logos* as universal. As seen, the out-of-joint structure of messianic time is connected to the originary crime and its specters, a connection that places the "messianic" within an historically inherited archive. As a result, messianic thinking is always tied to historical contexts and traditions. Even as a mode of transcendental inquiry, it can never fully depart from the empirical (historical) domain.

This point is also confirmed several times by Derrida in *Specters*. He first declares that "haunting is historical" thereby indicates that messianic thinking cannot fully be removed from historical situatedness. Second, he praises Marx's and Engels's ability to indicate the "intrinsically irreducible historicity" or "aging" of their own theories. He further discusses the notion of inheritance as the reaffirming and going beyond a tradition, emphasizing that "the being of what we are is first of all inheritance." Finally, he places deconstruction in the French intellectual scene of the 1950s—shaped by the continental "classics of the end," including Hegel, Marx, Nietzsche, and Heidegger all filtered by Kojève—while bearing witness to the totalitarian terror of Stalinism in Eastern Europe (*SM*, 2/22, 14/35, 68/94, 16/37).

These brief digressions help further the understanding of the historical character of the "messianic," which always points to a specific context and its conditions, without for this reason remaining bound to it. The "messianic" is articulated in a language, idiomatic and philosophical. It draws from sources contingently grounded on historico-political determinations, which, in the aftermath of a founding event, have authorized an epistemological order, and its undergirding cultural values, but not others. Such determinations have also established the archive within which the "messianic" operates. Therefore, viewed from the angle of foundings and the temporal disjuncture they mark, the transcendental aspect of the "messianic" always contingently depends upon its historico-political conditions. This is what Derrida calls "the pre-inheritance on the basis of which one inherits," which defines the character of the "messianic" as much as it points to excluded possibilities or existing alternatives. So conceived, this view reconfigures the relationship between the transcendental and the empirical, the universal and the particular, which are conceived of as correlated but irreducible. While the formal character of the "messianic" elucidates the conditions of possibility of determinate messianism(s), the latter provides the historical context mediating the articulation of such conditions.[52] By exposing the always historical character of thinking, the correlation at issue disallows a universalism that "does not watch over" itself, a universalism that is able to pass as *universally valid* by obscuring its own particularity, which is at the same time made a universal standard for translation. As seen in the previous chapter, this is a type of universalism retaining colonial and racialized features. Thought that way, the correlation at issue also exposes a gap between the determined form the "messianic" takes as a historical messianism and the irreducible possibilities of being otherwise—possibilities that are signaled by concrete exclusions in the past and possible ones in the future, as our discussion of ghosts has shown. It is the resources for criticism offered by the acknowledgement of this gap, which a political sensibility for foundings and temporal disjuncture helps to identify, that Derrida's messianic mobilizes to rethink universalism. He does so by resisting the ways in which traditional approaches to universalism typical of the "European spirit" exemplified by Fichte and Heidegger, and more generally of "White mythology," give in to naturalizations and racialized discourses.

Viewing the historicity of the "messianic" from this angle offers a distinctively political route that while remaining closer to the language of transcendental philosophy attempts to make productive the potential of such a language without neglecting the deadlock in which the "messianic" is placed by transcendentalist schemas. Indeed, the interpretation of the relationship between messianism and messianicity in the light of the revelation/revealability problematic has been subject to much discussion, especially in the work of Caputo, De Vries, Fritsch, and Naas.[53] Unlike others, Naas takes up Derrida's claim about the need for "another schema" to think about that relationship. While he agrees with Caputo that Derrida does not eventually stand for the "messianic" as a sort of metalanguage for translating historical messianisms, he is not entirely satisfied with de Vries's idea that Derrida oscillates between two options on which one cannot decide.[54] Following Derrida's suggestion to "displace" the problematics in its current formulation, Naas argues that Derrida does in fact displace the messianism/messianic problematics by rethinking it through the notion of the name and the promise. This, on Naas's account, emerges particularly in "Faith and Knowledge" where Derrida's treatment of two "historical" names ("messianic" and *khora*) would suggest a "reinscription of the particular, determinate name *in the name* or *as the name of a promise* that marks the idiom and opens it to translation."[55] While the "messianic" is a proper name belonging to the Judeo-Christian tradition and *khora* to the Greek one, they are both common names referring, respectively, to a general structure of temporal experience and of space that extend beyond the particular.

The significance of Naas's suggestion for our discussion consists in making explicit how Derrida's notion of the "messianic" (and *khora*) is a "historical" name that names a promise, which can be used for rethinking universalism through the lenses of translation. To support this view, Naas refers to Derrida's emphasis on an irreducible gap between the "*possibility (as a universal structure)* and the *determinate necessity*" of historical formations.

On Naas's account, this gap would allow to criticize any determinate religious or nonreligious form "in the name of the most originary possibility" (FK, 93/88). What the historico-political angle of my analysis highlights, however, is that it is not simply in the name of a more originary possibility that sociopolitical forms claiming to be universal can be criticized. Valuable resources for criticism can also be drawn by looking at historical injustice and thus at the concrete alternatives that are excluded most manifestly, yet not solely, in founding moments but remain as remainders with effects that persist into the future. Examples of this kind are not difficult to find in a variety of contexts across the world—from Palestine to South Africa, Canada and the United States to Australia, to name a few—among indigenous populations, ethnic and religious groups and traditions that have, in part, survived colonization and the advent of modernity.[56] They can, more generally, be found among victims of war, colonialism, racism, sexism and economic imperialism, as Derrida himself mentions (*SM*, xviii/16). So my aim in pointing to the historical correlation discussed so far is to emphasize the pragmatic significance that Derrida's sensibility for political foundations marking his quasi-transcendentalism offers, in spite of its theoretical limits.

Highlighting the correlation between the transcendental and the empirical in Derrida's "messianic" is not a novel move. For examples, de Vries, starting from an appreciation of Derrida's use of religious language, considers the "messianic" and messianism as standing in a relation of "mutual implication and oscillation" since the openness of the former indicates that it "has no existence 'outside,' 'before,'" or without the latter.[57] Fritsch argues for a similar position via a discussion of iterability.[58] He contends that, considered from a transcendental point of view, iterability illustrates via repetition the "quasi-transcendental" aspect of the messianic promise as irreducibly historical. On his account, iterability "is inseparable from what it makes possible" and thus the rupturing of future horizons operated by the "messianic" is inseparable from the historical horizon in which the messianic promise takes place.[59]

While not disagreeing with the positions of de Vries, Fristch, or Naas, the angle of my analysis gives my interpretation a distinctively political and anti-racist thrust. Indeed, my reading emphasizes the political nature of Derrida's thinking and the historico-political bent this gives to the "messianic" as a powerful form of critical thinking. My point is not simply that his emphasis on political foundings, temporal disjuncture, and memory of ghosts illuminates the extent to which a powerful politico-philosophical and historical sensibility informs Derrida's "messianic" and, more generally, his entire philosophical intervention. This seems confirmed by Derrida himself on two occasions: first, in *Specters of Marx* when he notes the importance of political philosophy for philosophical reflection in general since the former "structures implicitly all philosophy or all thought on the subject of philosophy" (*SM*, 115/151); and second, in his reflections after 9/11 when he affirms the need to awaken philosophy from a dogmatic slumber through a new reflection "on political philosophy and its *heritage*" (my emphasis) (AI, 100). Above all, my point is that, by informing the critique and reconceptualization of traditional universalism, the politico-philosophical dimension of Derrida's offers resources to unsettle the logic and strategies informing the racialized schemas typical of "White mythology." Indeed, his reflections on a self-vigilant universalism display a politicization of knowledge production relevant to public life, one that allows for moving past the naturalizing logic that enabled the culture-specific epistemological and political models of the Western tradition to pass as rational and universally valid, while being in fact made so through political enforcements.[60]

If the emphasis on the historicity of Derrida's "messianic" helps us further clarify its nature, it can also help us respond to recent interpretations of his thought that ironically freeze this central feature while emphasizing its importance. In *Radical Atheism*, for example, Hägglund argues that a radical atheism informs Derrida's entire corpus, an atheism that denies "the existence of God and immortality" and thus questions the desirability of a condition beyond temporal finitude.[61] Hägglund grounds his whole argument on Derrida's view of time to show that its trace-character illuminates human finitude or mortality and displays an unconditional affirmation of life as survival. For Hägglund, whatever one can experience and desire requires the affirmation of a finite time of survival without which there would be no experiencing and desiring in the first place.[62] As a condition of life in general, the finite time of survival affects God himself who can only be made intelligible and desirable as mortal, hence Hägglund's thesis of Derrida's radical atheism.

Although focused on time and finitude, Hägglund's analysis retains, ironically, an atemporal flavor. By insisting that Derrida's view of time exposes the law of finitude, which is "not something that one can accept or refuse, since it precedes every decision and exceeds all mastery," Hägglund seems to find a ground in Derrida's thinking that is safe from unsettlement because it stands before, and beyond, human agency and thus also interpretation.[63] In this way, he locks such historical thinking into the fixity of a formal, atemporal outlook, a sort of reconstructed universalism not subject to the interpretative constraints of its historical context and thus at risk of neutralizing the receptivity and legibility of traces signaling historical injustice. Hägglund's interpretation remains therefore problematic since it overlooks the self-critical force and pragmatic significance of Derrida's "messianic" as I have presented them. While the "messianic" points to a necessary, and yet undecidable, future, it also always points to its historical specificity and thus the contextual constraints within which it operates. And this means that the "messianic" is never free from historical conditioning to the point of escaping *all* decision and mastery. Although in some sense it structurally "precedes" history but never purely so, the "messianic" is always also preceded and affected by the interpretative decisions of those from whom the past is inherited. Put more simply, while the nature of time exceeds humans, and might well precede their decision and mastery, its interpretation does not if it is to remain historical and thus sensitive to finitude.

What are the implications of the historicity of the "messianic" for thinking about its relationship with the "theological-political complex"? Because the "messianic" acknowledges its own historicity and irreducible link to religious sources, it does not conceive of the theological-political nexus as a relation that can be severed as do modern teleological approaches. On the contrary, it points to the interrelation between the religious (messianisms) and the nonreligious (the messianic as philosophy) and exposes that the hyphen linking the theological and the political stands for the insolvability of their relation. This is where the innovation of Derrida's perspective lies. Unlike the "ontological" Marx, Derrida does not reduce religion to an illusion rooted in the material conditions of production and then emancipate reason from every religious source. Nor does he try to posit a clear-cut distinction between reason and faith as in modern theories of secularism and their contemporary liberal revisitations. Rather, he acknowledges the irreducible nature of religious sources persisting in Marx's thought and more generally in the Enlightenment project of secularization while affirming the importance of not forgetting them by fully severing the nexus between reason and faith.

This aspect is particularly evident in his engagement with Kant in "Faith and Knowledge." Here Derrida seeks to think about religion *at* the limits of reason alone and not within its limit as Kant did, thereby maintaining a hierarchical epistemic relation between the two. Engaging Kant's *Religion within the Limits of Reason Alone*, Derrida recalls Kant's opposition between two understandings of faith. On the one hand "dogmatic faith" associated with the "religion of cult alone" that collapses knowledge into religious faith and, on the other, "reflective faith" which, independent of "any historical revelation," appeals to practical reason to distinguish faith and knowledge, thereby indicating the rational standards for "moral religion"—which appear thus satisfied only by Christian religion (FK, 49/20). Overall, what Derrida finds problematic, indeed "dizzying" in this oppositional formulation, is the underlying logic of hierachization and naturalization at work in Kant's view: Kant does "not simply classify heterogenous religions under the same name" indebted to Western Christianity. He also appears to suggest that because the Christian religion is capable of liberating faith from dogmatism, it is the "only truly 'moral' religion," the model of natural religion, which means that, for Kant, no morality is rationally possible outside of Christianity. If this holds, Kant's attempt to provide a rational justification of "moral religion" leads to the opposite result of grounding reason on Christian religion precisely because "Christian revelation teaches us something essential about the very idea of morality" (50/22).

While Derrida praises Kant's attempt to go beyond religious dogma and interpreting faith in a new way, namely, independent of historical revelation but also in association with reason, he considers his logic deeply problematic. Not only does Kant naturalize "religion" as a generic name allegedly capturing the reality of all so-called "religions," thereby embracing a logic typical of "White mythology." He also employs a foundational and oppositional logic presenting fundamentalist traits, as it were. By placing "reflective faith" above and against "dogmatic faith," Kant establishes what we might call a "logic of the more or most fundamental," where "reflective faith" and, ultimately, reason is considered more basic than the historical "dogmatic faith" of revelation; indeed, religion *within* the limits of reason. So construed, Derrida says, this oppositional and foundational logic "could also define, even for us today a place of conflict, if not war, in the Kantian sense" since it remains implicated in an "infinite spiral of outbidding, a maddening instability" among those standpoints, religious and not, that seek to occupy the most fundamental position. For Derrida, this mad spiral emerges most clearly if one acknowledges that globalization is in fact a "globalatinization" (*mondialatinisation*)": a form of an originally "European-colonial" and now Anglo-American global imposition, exported in the name of peace through the spread of secularization, the modern nation-state, capitalism and international law (79/66). In other words, through Kant, Derrida identifies in the modern philosophical mode of naming and understanding religious phenomena, and more generally framing and solving the theological-political relation, the site to find resources to understand the logic of religious and non-religious fundamentalisms.

For Derrida, the pressing question here is whether it is possible to think of a way out from this binary opposition between faith and reason. Ruling out Hegelian and Heideggerian alternatives that repeat, in different ways, the Kantian gesture of separating and the prioritizing reason over faith, Derrida explores a third way through the "messianic." This alternative becomes once more relevant as way of thinking about revelation and revealability, reason and faith, the theological and the political without severing or prioritizing their relationship. This possibility, for Derrida, must be thought *at* the limit of reason, where reason shares with religion an elementary experience of faith or trustworthiness. To speak of the "messianic," here, Derrida invokes again the figure of the desert to point to an "extreme abstraction" in which the undecidable relation between revelation and revealability, faith and reason, might represent "the chance" of "another 'reflecting faith,' of a new 'tolerance,'" one that is not solely Christian (FK, 59/36; AI, 125–30). Thought in terms of "abstract messianicity," as he calls it here, this desert is, figuratively, a place of abstraction, and thus of reason, that is connected to an experience of elementary faith which is not reducible to religious faith (FK, 56/31).

But what exactly is this elementary faith? In chapter 1, I have noted that it refers to the performative dimension of language and is connected to the promise inscribed in every social address. In "Faith and Knowledge," Derrida clarifies things further. He notes that the semantics of faith (*foi*)—which encircle a domain that includes the notions of credit (*croyance*), trustworthiness or fidelity (*fiabilité ou fidélité*), the fiduciary (*fiduciaire*), and trust (*fiance*) (66/47)—does not "belong" exclusively to religion and that elementary faith can be thought of as a quasitranscendental figure. It is a sort of minimal "fiduciary link" that is prior to "the opposition between the sacred (or the holy) and the profane" and precedes "all determinate community, all positive religion" precisely because, as their quasitranscendental condition possibility, it opens them up. This quasitranscendental figure refers to "experience of faith, of believing, of a credit that is irreducible to knowledge and a trust that 'funds' all relation to the other in testimony" (55/29). This means that every time there is an address to others or a social relation, a promising faith is at work, one that reaches beyond religious experience to include the sphere of knowledge and science, and thus also nonreligious institutions.

> "The lights" and the Enlightenment of tele-technoscientific critique and reason can only suppose trustworthiness. They are obliged to put into play an irreducible "faith," that of a "social bond" or of a "sworn faith," of a testimony ("I promise to tell you the truth beyond all proof and all theoretical demonstra-

tion, believe me, etc."), that is, of a performative of promising at work even in lying or perjury and without which no address to the other would be possible. Without the experience of this act of elementary faith (*foi élémentaire*) there would neither be "social bond" nor address to the other, nor any performativity in general: neither convention, nor institution, nor constitution, nor sovereign state, nor law, nor above all, here, the structural performativity of the productive performance that binds from its very inception the knowledge of the scientific community to doing science and technics . . . But wherever this tele-technoscientific critique develops, it brings into play and confirms the fiduciary credit of an elementary faith which is at least in its essence or calling religious (the elementary condition, the milieu of the religious if not religion itself). We speak of trust or of trustworthiness in order to underscore that this elementary act of faith also underlies the essentially economic and capitalistic rationality of the tele-technoscientific. (80/68)

For Derrida, both scientific and philosophical reason suppose trustworthiness since they are compelled in their activity to rely on a testimonial faith that promises to tell the truth and asks to be believed before any proof. The testimonial character of faith here is crucial, since it emphasizes the key role of the promise in any social relationship. Any address to others requires a background of minimal trust in order to be effective at all. That is, it requires a promise to tell the truth and a call to be believed beyond proof, even if one is lying (VR, 22). This, in turn, suggests that faith is a sort of miracle since it involves a call to be believed without demonstration. "Believe what I say as one believes in a miracle": this is what is involved, Derrida says, "in the very concept of bearing witness" (FK, 98/93).[64]

But, as Naas has highlighted, there is an additional aspect of the testimonial character of elementary faith that needs to be mentioned. For it offers critical sources to counter the racialized schemas we have been questioning all along. Even if faith is the source of social bond, it is a form of "interruption" and not of commonality, one that does not indicate a "reciprocal condition, but rather the possibility that every knot can come undone, be cut or interrupted." For Derrida, the link to the other occurring in the act of address is not based on some common knowledge or genealogy, but on the "secret of testimonial experience," and thus on one's own singularity. On this reading, what links and is shared is, paradoxically, what cannot be shared and counted, "a sort of incommensurable equality within absolute asymmetry" (FK 98–99/93–94). This suggests that as an experience of "non-relationship" providing the source of social bonds, elementary faith seeks to respect the singularity of each, and as such, it unsettles the possibility of naturalizing communal identities—be these ethnic or religious, natural or conventional. So conceived, then, elementary faith displays not simply Derrida's distrust about communitarianism, as Naas has suggested.[65] At a more basic level, it questions the conditions of possibility of closing the political as it happens in modern political orientations as diverse as Schmittian political theology, Neo-Kantian deliberative democracy, and neo-Hegelian politics of recognition, all of which remain anchored to naturalized logics haunted by racialized schemas.[66]

The significance of this aspect of elementary faith cannot be missed. While appearing to weaken the possibility of communal life, faith breaks open the grounds of modern political imaginaries. This view emerges perhaps more decisively in Derrida's 1998 paper "Avowing—The impossible: 'Returns,' Repentance and Reconciliation" presented at a conference with French-speaking Jewish thinkers. Here he connects the idea of "interruption" associated to testimonial faith and singularity to a chance for thinking about the togetherness of communal life, "living together," beyond "the *natural* as well as the *conventional* relation," even in the presence of differences that are, or appear at present, to be irreconcilable (AWI, 26/36).

> "Living together" is reducible to neither organic symbiosis, not to the juridico-political contract. Neither to "life" according to nature or birth, blood or soil, nor to life according to convention, contract or institution. "Living together," if it were possible, would mean putting to the test the insufficiency of this old couple of concepts that conditions, in the West, more or less any metaphysics, any interpretation of the social bond, any political philosophy or any sociology of being-together, the old couple *physis/nomos*, *physis/thesis*, nature/convention, biological life/law [droit]—law which I distinguish here, more than ever from the justice of "living together." One will never think the "living together" and the "living" of the "living together" and the "how" of "living together" unless one transports oneself *beyond everything* that is founded on this opposition of nature and culture. (ATI, 27/37)

For Derrida, the classical opposition between *physis* and its others (*nomos/ thesis/techne*) grounds the tradition of Western philosophy and the sources for thinking sociopolitical life. Yet, as seen at the outset with reference to his 2003 intervention in a conference on race, this opposition also grounds all forms of naturalization on which racialized thinking and racist discourses rely.[67] It is thus by interrupting the opposition of nature and culture that the antiracist potential of elementary faith comes to the fore, as a basis for a different thinking of "the *peace* of 'living together.'" It is one that resists logics of naturalization associated with overtly racist ideologies but also with the more sophisticated and yet racialized philosophical approaches typical of "White mythology" (ATI, 26/36). Derrida is aware of the difficulty involved in thinking and practicing "living together" this way, which he qualifies as "almost unthinkable, very close to impossible," and ventures to think this option through the difficult example of Israel/Palestine. Yet, he is concerned to emphasize that the elementary trust of faith connects to the "language of the heart [*coeur*], of accord and concord" but also to the possibility of protecting singularity as a condition of any "living together" vigilant against totalizations that reduce the "together [*ensemble* (adjective)]" to a "whole [*ensemble* (the noun)]" but also that use "technological resources of investigation, communication, ubiquity, and unprecedented speed" to police the "possibility of the secret, of separation, of solitude, of silence and of singularity, "under the pretext of transparency," and we could add, of security (34/44). In other words, elementary faith would be the basis from which to rethink communal life beyond racialized thinking but also against the politics of surveillance, and thus not simply communitarianism.

Returning to the nature of elementary faith, we have seen that such a faith is not confined to religion, but it affects reason too in a variety of domains, including science, philosophy, and politics. In opposition to that tradition of the Enlightenment that maintains the incompatibility of reason and religion, Derrida suggests that reason "bears, supports and supposes" religion since they share, as a common source, "the testimonial pledge (*gage*) of every performative" (66/47). More specifically, he affirms, as in the aforementioned quote, that elementary faith is "at least in its essence or calling, religious" and is "the elementary condition, the milieu of the religious, if not of religion itself" (80–81/68). The claim here is that an elementary experience of faith is necessary to both reason and religion since they both require a trust without which no social bond and knowledge would be possible. In this way, rational thinking preserves an irreducible connection to a dimension typical of, but not exclusive to, religion.

In emphasizing this connection, I do not mean to suggest that Derrida collapses reason into some form of religious faith emancipated from positive religion, thereby providing an opening to some form of irrationalism or dogmatism. On the contrary, I seek to highlight that his take on elementary faith points to the critical sources the latter offers to rethink the relationship between universality and particularity beyond transcendental schemas, especially as it emerges in the revelation *versus* revealability problematics discussed above.

> But the gap between the opening of this *possibility (as a universal structure)* and the *determinate necessity* of this or that religion will always remain irreducible; and sometimes <it operates> within each religion, between on the one hand that which keeps it closest to its "pure" and proper possibility, and on the other, its own historically determined necessities or authorities. Thus, one can always criticize, reject or combat this or that form of sacredness or belief, even of religious authority, in the name of the most originary possibility. The latter can be *universal* (faith or trustworthiness, "good faith" as the condition of testimony, of the social bond and even of the most radical questioning) or already *particular*, for example, belief in a specific originary event of revelation, of promise or of injunction, as in reference to the Tables of the Law, to early Christianity, to some fundamental word or scripture, more archaic and more pure than all clerical or theological discourse. But it seems impossible to deny the *possibility* in whose name—thanks to which—the derived *necessity* (the authority or determinate belief) would be put in question, suspended, rejected, criticized, even deconstructed. One can *not* deny it, which means the most one can do is to deny it. Any discourse that would be opposed to it would, in effect, always succumb to the figure of the logic of the denial < *dénégation* >. (93–94/88–89)

For Derrida, there is an irreducible gap between the possibility and determined necessity of historical religious forms, and one might say, any social form. Exposed by elementary faith, this gap points to the possibility of historical forms to be otherwise, or not having been at all, and thus also to the acknowledgment that universal claims originating from occurred historical forms remain irreducibly particular. Indeed, as the condition of social bond, as its minimal "basic" trust, elementary faith does not guarantee the necessity of the social form it enables. For doing so would mean collapsing the transcendental into the empirical and thus denying, as Derrida affirms in his discussion of Schmitt, the "abyss" between the two (*PF*, 86/104). It only provides the possibility for social forms to be determinate, a possibility that therefore is open to "what still remains undetermined and indeterminable" (*FK*, 38/58). As such, that faith can be considered as the possibility in "whose name" or "thanks to which" any determinate form can be criticized, and thus as informing a type of universalism that neither forgets irreducible particularity nor remains confined to occurred historical forms. And since it is possible to avoid the denial of elementary faith by recognizing its elementary character, the most one can do is to deny it but not eliminate it. For Derrida, this denial, which appears to have characterized much of Enlightenment thought, neither gives more "rationality" nor less "religiosity." It actually signals a complex psychological and political process in which repression appears as the grounding mechanism for the traditional forms of universalism of "White mythology" and their exclusionary implications. Viewed this way, then, elementary faith is far from giving in to, as Derrida puts it in *Rogues*, "the slightest hint of irrationalism, obscurantism, or extravagance." Instead, it represents "another way of *keeping within reason* [*raison garder*] however mad it might appear" (*R*, 153/211). In other words, by providing sources for criticism and for rethinking universality, elementary faith is not opposed to reason, nor is it reduced to some form of credulity without church.

Together with historicity, elementary faith helps therefore highlight the significance of the "messianic" for the "theological-political complex." Conceived as a historically sensible thinking that does not prioritize reason over and against all faith, the "messianic" allows for moving the thinking about theological-political past secular discourse. By emphasizing that reason draws from sources from which the religious cannot be strictly excluded, the "messianic" illuminates that reason and faith, the theological and the political are interrelated but distinct and need to be thought about together. Taking this interrelationship seriously elucidates that discourses claiming to proceed in the name of reason while opposing all forms of faiths fall into a dangerous logic that is not free from fundamentalist and racialized traits. Indeed, Derrida's exposure of the limits affecting what I called the "logic of the more or most fundamental" since Kant extends the scope of such traits to secular modes of teleological thinking that deny all forms of "religiosity" as well as the specters highlighting the limits of universal representations.

These modes operate, somehow atemporally, on the basis of an epistemic hierarchy that uses reason to naturalize a Western Christian understanding of "religion" to classify all religious phenomena and to solve the theological-political relation by *simply* appealing to logical determinations. In this way, Derrida's emphasis on the intertwinement of reason and religion illuminates that the stakes at issue in rethinking the "theological-political complex" today go beyond the relationship between reason and faith and require a rethink of the racial logics at work in the formation of epistemic and political orders.

3

The Secular as Theological-Political

Offering an account of Derrida's understanding of the concept of the secular is a difficult task not simply for the ambiguous nature this field designates, but also because Derrida never articulated such a perspective in straightforward terms. My aim here is to present his perspective on this issue as it relates to the theological-political complex. Drawing from some of his key late writings on political foundings and the law, I articulate his view of the secular domain as the allegedly religion-free field of the sociopolitical through a focus on how the theological-political relationship factors into the foundation of political authority and community. My suggestion is that Derrida's perspective offers powerful resources with which to think about the secular beyond the traditional modern paradigm. In pursuing this argument, I retain the notion of the secular, which has been traditionally conceived as free of religion, to put into sharper relief Derrida's contribution to moving past secular interpretations. Questioning the tradition of the Enlightenment that emphasizes "reason alone" as a way to address the relationship between religion and politics, Derrida shows how the secular domain cannot be purified of all forms of faith and is best thought of as theological-political, especially if viewed from the event of its foundation. He illuminates the secular as characterized, from first inception, by an experience of elementary faith that reason and religion share. This faith exposes the irreducible link between religion and reason and allows for thinking about the theological-political relation as such, as a relation, without the urge to solve it. By focusing on the minimal faith that reason and religion share, Derrida reconfigures the conceptualization of the secular domain in a way that both underscores, rather than severs, the interrelatedness and yet distinction between the theological and the political, and that resists the racial features of modern secular discourse, whose logic of hierachization and separation produces naturalized representations of political community and law. Before delving into the analysis and discussion of Derrida's view of the secular, I set the context of the discussion by highlighting the core points of his position on the questions of secularization and religion. I then proceed to explore his view of the event of political foundation as caught by a constative and performative dimension in order to provide the angle through which to understand his view of the secular. I suggest that Derrida's emphasis on the correlations between these two dimensions illuminates the ever-present possibility of resisting the political configurations that founding events institute, especially when these naturalize the origins of political community. Focusing on his essays "Force of Law: 'The Mystical Foundation of Authority'" (henceforth "Force of Law"), and "Before the Law," I then take up his perspective on the status of the law to elucidate the nature of authority and the model of interrelation of Derrida's secular. By exploring his argument as to why the impossibility of grasping the origin of the law points to a mystical foundation of authority and to the role an elementary faith plays in the foundation of the political, I clarify the sense in which the secular, in his philosophy, is best thought of as theological-political.

The Secular in Context: Secularization and Religion

Although he never thematized it such, Derrida's perspective on the secular can be reconstructed from a series of politico-legal essays published between the 1980s and the early 2000s in which he offers important reflections on secularization and religion. I wish to explore these in order to provide the framework within which to situate his view of the secular. It is worth noting that while the theological-political problematics constitutes the theoretical space of these reflections, the Middle East, and specifically Israel/Palestine, represents its recurrent geopolitical context of reference and of interest, charging therefore Derrida's reflections with further political significance (AI; EL; FK; *IW*; *SM*).

Starting with secularization, Derrida recognizes the importance of what he calls "the secularization of the political (*sécularisation du politique*)" for democratic life, namely, dissociating religious authority from state powers, that is, "the separation between the theocratic and the political (*separation du théocratique et le politique*)" (*IW*, 53/85). As seen in the previous chapter, Derrida believes that secularization remains a Christian concept involving a problematic translation between secular and sacred idioms that has important political implications for questions of sovereignty but also knowledge production relevant to public life. In contrast to traditional theories of secularization, Derrida rejects the hierarchization and separation between religion and politics without abandoning a "*certain* tradition" of the Enlightenment (FK, 64/45–46). In "Faith and Knowledge," for example, he acknowledges his debts to the critical spirit of the Enlightenment and sides with it in support of republican democracy against religious dogmatism, orthodoxy, and fundamentalism (47/17). Yet he also questions whether fundamentalism and violence are circumscribed to religions only and do not also affect secular understandings and politics.

> It is not certain that in addition to or in face of the most spectacular and most barbarous crimes of certain "fundamentalisms" (of the present and of the past), *other* over-armed forces are not *also* leading "wars of religion," albeit unavowed. Wars or military "interventions," led by the Judeo-Christian West in the name of the best causes (of international law, democracy, the sovereignty of the people, of nations or of states, even humanitarian imperatives), are they not also, from a certain side, wars of religion? The hypothesis would not necessarily be defamatory, nor even original, except in the eyes of those who hasten to believe that all these just causes are not only secular but *pure* of all religiosity. (63/42)

Overall, Derrida's view of secularization questions all those discourses that pretend to isolate the political domain and neatly dissociate what differentiates the religious sphere from the ethical, juridical, political, and economic (63/42–43, 100/99). Viewing Carl Schmitt as the most extreme proponent of this view, he connects the urge to separate the religious sphere to that radically antireligious tradition of the Enlightenment that goes from Voltaire and Feuerbach to Heidegger, passing through Marx, Nietzsche, and Freud (45/14, 65/46).[1] In its most radical forms of criticism, this tradition "naively" opposes reason, science, and modernity to faith and religion and does so with a force that appears to have sought the end of religion, and not simply its privatization (45/14). Yet Derrida also seeks to depart from less antireligious approaches—such as those of Kant, Hegel, and Heidegger considered in the previous chapter—that in the attempt to distinguish philosophy from theology, reason from faith, the theological from the political, rely on a logic that establishes reason as more fundamental than faith. As seen, Derrida's problem with all these approaches is both philosophical and political. Philosophically, the secular separation between reason and faith effected through the affirmation of the former as more fundamental than the latter retains racialized features. Politically, it risks fueling, rather than diffusing, fundamentalism and exclusion.

Derrida's resistance to the separatist paradigm of the Enlightenment emerges even more clearly from his position on religion, which, as mentioned, is mediated by the figure of the Arab Jew and a reference to the Islamic tradition in addition to Christianity and Judaism as key to what he calls the "Abrahamic" (ATI, 21; FK, 44/13). As Anidjar has suggested, Derrida's notion of the "Abrahamic" points to the complex interrelations between Christian, Jewish, and Muslim monotheisms and represents "the very condition of 'religion'" because it enables the possibility of comparing religious phenomena that were not easily subsumable under the name of "religion" as distinct objects of analysis before the nineteenth-century discourse of religion. Yet, because it allows these comparisons and the discernment of Christian hegemony in the formation of such a discourse at the expenses of Judaism within Europe, and of Islam outside of it, the "Abrahamic" represents the figurative sites from which Derrida rethinks "religious difference" beyond what "exceeds any recognizable religion" and thus, as a religious phenomenon, remains "unrecognizable as such."[2] It is a site in which, especially in modern times and through global secularization, translation is charged with political significance; as Derrida says, it is "as if the business of translation were first of all an Abrahamic matter between the Jew, the Christian, and the Muslim" (WRT, 184). The epistemic value of Derrida's use of the Abrahamic therefore rests in its pointing, from a specific figurative site (the Abrahamic itself and thus the religious traditions associated to it) to the possibility of religious difference beyond universalist models operating through assimilatory forms of translation, thereby opening a passage to other traditions and understandings of religious phenomena that also go beyond the Abrahamic itself.

Derrida is thus very cautious in dealing with "religion" and proceeds both with genealogical sensibility and theoretical prudence. On the one hand, he finds the concept of religion "obscure" and manifests his awareness that any discussion about it occurs more or less implicitly in relation to Christianity (*IW*, 57/92). As mentioned, Derrida is aware that the term "religion" has a Latin origin (*religio*) and that it has functioned as a metalinguistic term for translating and ordering non-Christian religious phenomena so that any recovery of the meaning of what "religion" stands for is already mediated by Christianity (FK, 64/44). On the other hand, he considers the suspension of certainties and, thus proceeding with a dose of faith, as essential when dealing with the topic of religion.[3] Given these constraints and the difficulties of providing precise definitions, Derrida puts forward two interconnected claims. He affirms that "religion is the response" and that it is characterized by two sources (64/44, 70/52). With the first claim, Derrida proposes a third meaning of "religion" in addition to the two offered by etymological analyses of *religio*. Whether as *relegere*, meaning to gather or collect, or as *religare*, meaning to link or bind, the Latin etymologies of "religion" remain, for him, inadequate to account for an experience that is typical of religion but is not confined to it: the response to the other in the form of an elementary faith (74/58–59). Derrida suggests that "religion" can also mean to respond (*respondere*), which is at issue every time there is an address to others. Conceived as a response, "religion" is thus connected to the elementary, promissory faith characterizing every linguistic act (71/53). Indeed, the witnessing so central to religious experience involves an act of promise, a commitment before others to tell the truth, and a call to be believed. As seen in the previous chapters, this is what characterizes "the testimonial pledge (*gage*) of every performative," namely, the elementary faith shared by reason and religion, one that is central to the functioning of both religion and science. For Derrida, the experience of elementary faith is one of the two sources of religion, the second one in the order of his description. The other source, the first one, is what he calls the experience of the unscathed (*indemne*), salvation (*salut*), sacredness (*sacralité*) or holiness (*santité*) (70/52). Like the second source, the experience of the unscathed is connected to the idea of promise since religion is hardly thinkable without a promise of salvation (42/9).

Of the two sources of religion, which Derrida considers as distinct but irreducible, the experience of faith is particularly relevant to our discussion. For him, some minimal faith identifies the point of connection between religion and science. It provides the basis for rejecting the strict separation between the theological and the political in the secular domain, as I shall show below. Before doing so, though, it is worth clarifying a bit more the relationship between the two sources of religion since this will help illustrate further just how deeply religion and science connect and thus how problematic is the antireligious rhetoric that speaks in the name of the Enlightenment.

Derrida believes that the experience of witnessing identifies the point of convergence between the two sources of religion (98/96). Recall that, as an act of testimony, the elementary faith conditioning any social bond and scientific endeavor is a sort of miracle since it is a call to be believed beyond proof. Yet, since elementary faith involves, as indicated in chapter 1, both promise and its repetition, its miraculous character is always already mechanical, and thus marked by a feature that is typical of science. Miracle and machine are therefore apparently incompatible elements that are as characteristic of elementary faith as they are of religion and science.[4]

For Derrida, it is by appreciating the link to something technical or mechanical in elementary faith, and more generally in religion, that we can understand how the two sources of religion connect. Derrida observes that there is a tendency in religions to protect their identity—idiom, soil, communal bond, and nation—and more generally the immunity of their first source, the unscathed. In their attempt at self-protection, religions employ the technological means that processes of globalization have only made more widely accessible, means that enable religions to live on, and even "swell" (82/70). Today, without the unparalleled use of cyberspace, there would be no propagation of religious messages and cults. This is visible, he notes, in "the multiplicity, the unprecedented speed and scope of the moves of a Pope versed in televisual rhetoric," in the "airborne pilgrimages to Mecca," and in "the international and televisual diplomacy of the Dalai Lama, etc." (62/40). Yet by employing cybertechnology religions appropriate the means of abstraction, typical of science, which they normally reject, since these means threaten the very identity of religion itself. Indeed, science and telecommunication introduce repetition and delocalization within religions, thereby threatening the safety of religion's identity that undergoes an internal differentiation. Under the risk of jeopardizing what they seek to protect, religions react against the means of their survival in order to return to the purity of their origins (81/88). Derrida uses the notion of autoimmunity to account for this paradoxical process that affects the life of religions and links them constitutively to science beyond the elementary faith that already connects them. Religion, he notes: "produces, weds, exploits the capital and knowledge of the tele-mediatization" and "reacts, immediately, *simultaneously*, declaring war against that which gives it new power only at the cost of dislodging it from all its proper places [. . .] It conducts a terrible war against that which protects it only by threatening it, according to this double and contradictory structure: immunitary and autoimmunitary" (82/71). Examples of this double process of appropriation and rejection are visible in the appropriation and use of telecommunication and military technology on the part of various religious groups across the world in order to defend, and return to, what is most original in religion. Yet they are also visible in the aggressive, mediatic campaigns against sacrificing life through abortion, artificial insemination, and genetic manipulation sustained by certain religious affiliations that oppose the intrusion of science in what is considered the most natural: life (86–88/77–80). If the protective traits of religions' autoimmunitary logic suggest a certain conservatism, Derrida warns us that they also do the opposite. Religions' reactions are attempts to return "*both* to obscurantist dogmatism *and* to hypercritical vigilance." In other words, they can be both particularistic attempts to return to the purity of nation, idiom, and community and universalist protests against the forms of modern alienation brought by technology (92/86).

The significance of Derrida's reflections lies in the exposure of the complex entanglements between religion, science, and secularization. Especially through autoimmunity, Derrida offers an account of the logic of religions' life and of the ambiguity affecting processes of secularization. While religions globalize themselves through the use of techno-science, they also react to this process and its scientific thrust by violently rejecting it, however differently in their own context of reference. In this way, they simultaneously internalize and negate a process of differentiation that splits their identity while guaranteeing its persistence. Acknowledging this double bind allows us to understand that religions' manifestations in the public sphere do not signal a return but, as Derrida suggests, a *"resurgence <déferlement>,"* namely, the rise of a more vigorous movement marked by its unprecedented use and rejection of technology as well as by its global reach (81/70). Thus, contrary to much Enlightenment thought on secularization, which refers to historical processes of differentiation and separation between religious and nonreligious outer spheres, Derrida shows that religion and science intertwine in much more complex and intimate terms than those which are usually perceived.

These brief considerations on Derrida's view of secularization and religion help further elucidate his general resistance to the separatist paradigm of the Enlightenment, a resistance that also marks his view of the secular. Perhaps this feature is best captured by his claim that "the fundamental concepts that often permit us to isolate or to *pretend* to isolate the *political*—restricting ourselves to this particular circumscription—remain religious or in any case theologico-political" (63/42–43). Here Derrida seems to fully subscribe to Schmitt's thesis about modern political categories as secularized versions of a theological heritage.[5] This convergence appears especially in Derrida's analysis of sovereignty, which he sees as inextricably linked to a political theology that moves from Greek mythology to democratic thought

(*R*, 17/38). Yet, although Derrida often uses the notion of theologico-political in Schmittian terms (AI; *R*; *BS 1*), a connection explored by Naas,[6] it is not in this sense that I wish to propose we analyze his view of the secular domain. One reason for this choice is Derrida's opposition to Schmitt's idea of secularization. As seen in chapter 1, Derrida recognizes the theological debt of many modern political concepts but believes that the modern concept of secularization cannot be severed from religious sources, especially if secularization implies a successful translation of theological idiom and categories into secular ones.

I propose that the notion of theologico-political in Derrida's understanding of the secular can be interpreted also in another way, especially if one focuses on political foundings. I suggest that it is from the angle of political foundation that we can best understand his view of the secular domain as *theological-political*, namely, as indicating the irreducible relation and yet distinction between the theological and the political. This is where my use of "theological-political" resembles Spinoza's use of it in the *Theologico-Political Treatise*: the "theological-political" indicates, through the hyphenation, the irreducible relationship between the theological and political domains, and it exemplifies a relational approach that resists the logic of hierachization and separation of both secular and racialized discourses.[7] Illustrating Derrida's view, then, requires elucidating first how he understands the founding event, to which I shall turn next.

The Event of Political Institution

The essay "Declarations of Independence" (henceforth "Declaration"), is the place in which Derrida analyzes most explicitly the question of political foundation through an analysis of the American Declaration of Independence and the Declaration of the Rights of Man. Although focusing on a particular act of political foundations, this essay refers to declarations and contains a preliminary articulation of central features that structurally characterize the foundation of a politico-legal order, especially the complex temporality, structure of contamination, and faithful character of the act of political institution. Here Derrida concentrates on the ambiguous nature of the declarative act, which simultaneously institutes and describes a new entity. This ambiguity points to the problem of identifying who *actually* signs an instituting act, but what is most important is that it raises a philosophical concern that is not simply logical but also chronological. It refers to how a people can declare themselves to be a people without being already constituted as such.

At issue here is the aporetic nature of a declarative act of independence and the problem of taking a conclusive decision on whether, *at* the event of foundation, the act of positing the law is constative or performative.[8] For Derrida, this is a matter of "necessary undecidability (*nécessaire indécidabilité*)" since he views the founding event as characterized by a structural correlation between the performative and the constative so that the declarative act is intelligible only if these two are taken as irreducible one to the other. As he notes, "one cannot decide—and that's the interesting thing, the force and the coup of force of such a declarative act—whether independence is stated or produced by this utterance." That is, one cannot decide whether the "people have already freed themselves in fact and are only stating the fact of this emancipation in [*par*] the Declaration" or rather "they free themselves at the instant of and by [*par*] the signature of this Declaration" (9/20).

One might, of course, object that Derrida disregards the historical-legal dimension of any declarative act and especially the political, economic, cultural, and legal evolution preceding what then only appears to be a sudden change. Yet, if one considers the *Federalist Papers*, things do not look so historically sensitive. Here John Jay regards the Declaration as referring to "one united people,—a people descended from the same ancestors, speaking the same language" and "attached to the same principles of government."[9] This view sanctions the exclusion of ancestry (Indigenous or of African descent), languages (indigenous, French, Dutch, German, or Spanish) and political principles (Loyalist, Democrat, or Republican) present in the thirteen American states at the time of the Declaration. In this regard, the American Declaration can be considered as an event that created a people, indeed a nation, that did not exist as such but that was invented through a decision on who and what to exclude and select.[10]

Derrida's point about undecidability is not that it impedes decision or the institution of the law. Rather, it is that it illuminates retroactive legitimation as "the sought-after effect (*l'effet recherché*)" of political foundings (DOI, 9/20).

> But this people does not exist. They do *not* exist as an entity, it does *not* exist, *before* this declaration, not *as such*. If it gives birth to itself, as free and independent subject, as possible signer, this can hold only in the act of the signature. The signature invents the signer. This signer can only authorize him- or herself to

> sign once he or she has come to the end [*parvenu au vout*], if one can say this, of his or her signature, in a sort of fabulous retroactivity (*rétroactivité fabuleuse*). (10/21–22)

In the instituting act, the signature produces the signer through a deferred effect, a "fabulous retroactivity," where "fabulous" refers to the representation of the founding event after its happening: fiction. Already recognized as structural to political foundings in the Western tradition of political thought from Plato to Machiavelli and Rousseau, fiction represents, for Derrida, the fabulous retelling of the founding event, which escapes full rational grasp and is made possible by a temporal disjuncture. The disjuncture indicates that the future anterior structures the temporal modality of the founding moment. The people have in the present the right to sign because they "will already have had" it, so they are able to authorize the declarative act (10/22).

The temporal complexity of the founding event raises the question of what its ground is. Derrida identifies two elements: faith and violence. He notes that the performative act of foundation is a "vibrant act of faith (*vibrant acte de foi*)" enacted through an appeal to "God," a "last instance" or absolute ground the declarative act needs in order to make its constative effects meaningful and lasting. By authorizing the people to sign, God makes possible the conjoining of the "two discursive modalities," performative and constative, that characterize the founding act of faith (12/27). This faith appears as religious, but, as we shall see, it is not reducible to religious faith and is enacted through a "coup de force [that] makes right, founds right or the law, gives right" (10/21). Commenting on this point elsewhere, Derrida notes that the modality of the future anterior performs a "modification of the present to describe the violence in progress," one that "always" founds political communities (FL, 269/88). This violence often involves exclusion and exterminations of human, philosophical, and political alternatives that leave behind ghostly traces. Although they are concealed by the fabulous story, these traces continue to haunt future generations and the legitimacy of the law, which, for that reason, *cannot* be universal, that is, it can only be made so discursively. The extermination and forced assimilation of indigenous people in, for example, the United States, Canada, Israel, or Australia, people who, nevertheless, continue to challenge both the universal legitimacy and language of the law under which they live, constitute a good historical illustration of Derrida's idea. This holds even though demography plays a negative role in the visibility of such popular struggles. Perhaps nowhere better than post–War World II South Africa does Derrida's point appear so clearly. As he says, "in the case of South Africa, certain 'conventions' were not respected, the violence was too great, *visibility too great*, at a moment when this visibility extended to a new international scene, and so on. The white community was *too* much in the minority." Thus, the fiction introduced by the founding violence setting up "the unity of the 'entire nation' could not correspond to the division effected by the white minority" (LR, 67, 69). Derrida's overall point is that the politico-legal order that originates the nation as the key modern model of political community is instituted by an act of faith supported by violence that seeks to establish and naturalize a fictional unity at the origin of such a community, which therefore remains marked by racialized traits and a legitimation deficit that cannot be solved.[11]

But there is another important aspect of political founding that regards the complex relationship between constative and performative: the institution of the archive, which involves both political and epistemic questions about the interconnections between land, representation, and race. *In Archive Fever*, Derrida conceives of the archive as, *inter alia*, the geopolitically and historically determined site where representations of relevant forms of, for example, knowledge, law, religion, and subjectivity are framed in the aftermath of a founding event, representations that inform and regulate access to resources and political processes (*AF*, 3/14). Above all, the archive constitutes the place of memory that stands before but "contains" the originary crime, which is excluded from visibility because it has allowed the archive to be there in the first place. This crime marks the "fabulous scene" characterizing the institution of political community through pure representations invoking origins. As seen, this is what Derrida calls "archive fever," a compulsive longing for origins where, physically and symbolically, origins remain elusive. As he says, to have such a fever means "to have a compulsive, repetitive, and nostalgic desire for the archive, an irrepressible desire to return to the origin, a homesickness, a nostalgia for the return to the most archaic place of absolute commencement" (91/142). Yet, the resolution of this fever through a political project of state formation based on the rescuing of origins can have disastrous implications. As Derrida warns through a discussion of the case of Judaism and Israel, which is structurally in line with models of settler colonialism in the United States, Canada and Australia, such political realization is connected to the naturalization of origins, "expropriation," and the racialization of knowledge forms seeking to produce homogenous representations (94/147). In all these cases, the establishment of the archive, which as Derrida emphasizes through Freud is connected to territory, marked land dispossession and the establishment of epistemic, political, and social hierarchies.

Above all, the attempt to realize politically the unity sought in memory is to constitute oneself through, and as, violence. As he says, "as soon as there is the One, there is murder, wounding, traumatism" insofar as *"L'un se fait violence"* that is "the One makes itself violence. It violates and does violence to itself but also it institutes itself as violence. It becomes what it is, the very violence—that it does to itself. Self-determination as violence" (*AF*, 78/125). This is then what is at stake, in the occlusion of the perfomative and the mobilization of the constative for the purpose of telling, while naturalizing, the story of the founding event and the "unity" of the people. In response to this situation, Derrida mobilizes a memory of specters that counters the exclusivism and longing for origins of "archive fever." Still in the context of his discussion of Judaism and the state of Israel, he not only connects justice to the duty to "remember the others, other others and others in oneself," that is, every other as a singularity as worthy of justice as oneself (*AF*, 77/101). He also urges us to remember that in what one "takes to be his own home, or indeed his own land" one can be both "guest" and "host," that is, someone who not only receives but is also received, and thus claiming land and home as exclusively ones' own has, as Anidjar emphasizes, nothing less than colonial implications (*AL*, 42/79).[12] As Derrida puts it pointedly elsewhere, "belonging excludes any absolute appropriation, even the radical right to property" (ATI, 38/48). This means for him that there is no straightforward and conclusive answer to such questions as "Who can allocate places? Who can authorize himself, while avowing it, to grant here, to refuse there, to grant to one and to refuse to the other the chances to make this place his place, to elect it or to believe himself elected to it?" (ATI, 41/51).

Moving forward: although Derrida emphasizes the role of decision in political foundations, his approach does not have a totalitarian impulse *à la* Schmitt.[13] On the contrary, it exposes and resists its oppressive configurations. In *Political Theology*, Schmitt articulates a "decisionist" theory of sovereignty that, contrary to traditional liberal constitutionalism, grounds the validity of the legal order "on a decision and not on a norm."[14] In his view, sovereignty retains a traditional theological structure that endows the sovereign with the power to "definitely" distinguish normality from exception, through a "pure decision," an "absolute decision created out of nothingness."[15] The purity of this decision finds its source in a more fundamental distinction, that between friend and enemy. Defined as "the specific political distinction" in *The Concept of the Political*, the distinction between friend and enemy is necessary for the political whenever the eventuality of war is "an ever present possibility." [16] Sovereignty lies "necessarily" in this political distinction, which must be clear-cut in view of determining a stable political identity and the "normal situation" required by the applicability of norms.[17] Thus, although Schmitt emphasizes the theological framework structuring the political, he wants the latter to be autonomous and thus separable from the economic, religious, and aesthetic spheres.

Derrida's position is in some respects similar to, and yet significantly different from, that of Schmitt.[18] While diagnostically highlighting the role of decision in political foundings, Derrida does not celebrate its goodness, but he exposes and puts limits to totalitarian outcomes and racist foundations of the political. Like Schmitt, Derrida considers the politico-legal order as grounded in a performative act that is exceptional with respect to the norm and that ruptures the temporal continuity of normal legality. Yet, since the declarative act presents a contamination between the performative and the constative, it cannot deliver a pure distinction, one that seeks to "definitely" establish the boundaries of political community, thereby closing the political space in a totalitarian fashion informed by racist orientations. This point emerges forcefully in *Politics of Friendship* where Derrida deconstructs Schmitt's pure distinction of the political as well as the schema of the friend as brother informing Schmitt's political theory. Derrida shows that Schmitt constructs the concept of the enemy determining the boundaries of the political against Islam on questionable philosophical grounds. By considering the "ever present possibility" of war as a *real* presentation of the enemy, Schmitt fills the gap between conditions of possibility and historical occurrence, thereby denying the "abyss" between the two (*PF,* 60/148–49). For Derrida, this move suggests that Schmitt identifies the presence of the enemy a priori by pretending to *know* what an enemy is, who she or he is, and whether internal or external to the political community. It is on the basis of this knowledge that the decision about who is to be waged war against is taken and considered as "preliminary." Through this "strategy of presupposition," Schmitt obliterates, and yet testifies to by denying, the spectral elements involved in making distinctions and thus embraces the problematic metaphysics of presence discussed in the previous chapter (86/104, 125–26/148–49).[19]

Further, Derrida illuminates that Schmitt subscribes to the racialized thinking associated to the White mythology of the Western philosophical tradition, a thinking that takes clear sexual connotations. By framing his discussion of the enemy within the Greek and Latin/Christian semantics of *polemios/ hostis* as well as that of the brother, Schmitt seeks to stabilize the identity of the political friend through that of the brother and thus through a "*familial, fraternalist* and thus *androcentric* configuration of politics" that is older than Schmitt's and marks the Western Christian model of politics inherited from the Greeks as much as it also affects the Jewish and Muslim traditions (viii//12, 103/126). "The concept of politics rarely announces itself without some sort of adherence of the State to the family, without what we call a schematic of filiation: stock genus or species, sex (*Geschlecth*), blood, birth, nature, nation-authocthonal or not tellurian or not. This is once again the abyssal question of the *phusis*, the question of being, the question of what appears in birth, in opening up, in nurturing or growing, in producing by being produced" (viii/12). Derrida asks: "And what about the sister? Where has she gone?" (96/118). In this modern theory of the political, he says that "what disappears in becoming indiscernible in the middle of the desert is the woman or the sister" (156/ 180). For Derrida, Schmitt does in one stroke continue and consolidate a patriarchal and racialized understanding of politics on the basis of a discourse on nature (*phusis*) that is, nevertheless, culture specific and rooted in determined political realities. "As in every racism, every ethnocentrism—more precisely, in every one of the nationalism throughout history—a discourse on birth and on nature, a *phusis* of genealogy (more precisely, a discourse and a phantasm on the genealogical *phusis*) regulates, in the final analysis, the movement of each opposition . . . This *phusis* comprises everything—language, law, politics etc." (91/112–13). Derrida's point is that, by establishing the primacy of the friend as brother, where fraternization stands for "the symbolic bond alleging the repetition of a genetic tie," and by naturalizing that relationship for political purposes, Schmitt, does not simply reinforce the masculine character traditionally attributed to politics and thus the exclusion of sexual difference (99/122).[20] By employing a robust version of the metaphysics of presence in theorizing about origins as common genealogy, and by drawing the boundaries of the political through the separatist logic of friend/ enemy, Schmitt also reinforces the ground of a racialized, and specifically anti-Muslim, configuration of political life inscribed in European history, thought, and politics (93/114).[21] After quoting Schmitt's idea that "never in the thousand year struggle between Christians and Moslems did [it] occur to a Christian to surrender rather than defend Europe of out of love toward the Saracens or Turks," Derrida affirms:

> At a determining moment of the history of Europe, it was imperative not to deliver Europe over to Islam, in the name of a universal Christianity. You are obliged, you will always have been obliged to defend Europe against its other without confusing the genres, without confusing faith and politics, enmity and hostility, friendship and alliance or confusion. However, a coherent reading of this example should go further: today more than ever such a reading should take into account the fact that all the concepts of this theory of right and of politics are European, as Schmitt himself often admits. Defending Europe against Islam, here considered as a non-European invader of Europe, is then more than a war among others, more than political war. Indeed, strictly speaking, this would not be a war but a combat with the political at stake, a struggle for politics [. . .]. It is no longer a thoroughly political front. In question would be a defensive operation destined to defend *the* political, beyond particular states or nations, beyond any geographical, ethnic or political continent. On the political side of this unusual front, the stakes would be saving the political as such, ensuring its survival in the face of another who would no longer even be a political enemy but an enemy of the political—more precisely, a being radically alien to *the* political as such, supposing at least that, in its purported purity, it is not Europeanized and shares nothing of the tradition of the juridical and the political called European. (89/108–9)

As a Catholic jurist involved in the anti-Semitic politics of the Nazi regime, Schmitt emerges also, and above all, as an anti-Muslim thinker of the political. As Derrida remarks, for Schmitt, Islam is not an enemy that can be confronted politically; it is not a political enemy. As the excluded other that has been instrumental to the political formation of Europe, and constituted as exterior and yet intimately related to it, Islam represents "an enemy of the political," one without which the Western Christian understanding of the political "would lose its political being" (77/95). [22] While Derrida shows that this articulation is specific to Schmitt's, he also points to the fact that Schmitt is part of a longer tradition. Indeed, as earlier discussions of globalization and religion should have made clear, this view refers to epistemic and political formations of the Western Christian tradition whose understandings and institutions have become dominant through global process of colonization, secularization, and assimilative translation.

Going back to the nexus between the constative and the performative, for Derrida, acknowledgment of the contamination between the two implies recognizing the philosophically dubious status, given their correlation, of attempts seeking to separate them and fix their relationship *at* the act of founding. It also implies recognizing that at the core of founding predicaments there is an opening created by the play between such dimensions. This play constitutively limits the totalizing tendency of instituting acts seeking to halt the continuous interaction of the performative and the constative in order to establish conclusive determinations, as the case of South Africa mentioned in the discussion of context illustrates.[23] It also unsettles attempts seeking to naturalize the political, thereby keeping vigilance on racial political foundations.

Viewed from the event of foundation, then, Derrida's view of the sociopolitical appears as characterized by a structure of contamination that impedes closure but also, and importantly so, by an act of faith that exceeds the legal order. It points to dimensions that need to be carefully scrutinized before self-assuredly affirming the autonomy of the political or too quickly proclaiming the nondispensability of the theological. The remaining parts of this chapter aim to clarify these issues.

The Mystical Foundation of Political Authority

The complex character of the founding event raises the question of what exactly its status is and how to interpret it. The answer to these questions demands, first of all, that we clarify the nature of political authority and the law, the analysis of which will help elucidate, in the next two sections, issues of interpretation and, most important, the non-purely political character of the secular.

Derrida investigates the nature of political authority and the law in "Force of Law."[24] Engaging Michel de Montaigne, Blaise Pascal, and Walter Benjamin, he aims here to sever the nexus between law and justice and to show that violent force is irreducible in the foundation of the law and its conservation. His reflections start from an analysis of the "force of law" or its "enforceability," which raises immediately a problem of interpretation.

If the enforceability of the law suggests, as Kant has shown, that force is implied a priori in the concept of the law and that the law is a form of authorized force, then it becomes difficult to distinguish when the force of the law is and when it is not just and legitimate (FL, 233/17).

For Derrida, this problem points to "the mystical foundation of authority," namely, the idea that the institution of politico-legal authority retains an irreducible uninterpretability (239/29). He sees Benjamin as the most recent proponent of this view since he (Benjamin) considers the foundation of the law as a violent act that is uninterpretable because it occurs in an "ungraspable revolutionary instant" that is heterogeneous to time and history (274/98). But it is Montaigne, and especially to Pascal—once he is stripped of his Christian pessimism—to whom Derrida seeks to pay tribute (241/32). Montaigne formulated the idea of a "mystical foundation of authority" when he declared that laws are respected because of the credit granted to them as laws and not in virtue of their justice.[25] Pascal, who appropriated Montaigne's formulation, combined justice as law (*droit*) with force and illuminated an essential feature of the law—that its institution and justification imply a performative and an interpretative force (241/32). Indeed, for Derrida, the law is a performative force since it rips apart the relatively homogenous horizon of signification on which it intervenes in the founding act. Yet, it is also an interpretative force since the rupture provoked by that act requires an intervention that reconstitutes a linguistic context within which the interpretation of the instituting act as legitimate can occur only *post factum*.

According to Derrida, then, there is a structural delay between the foundation and justification of the law that is connected to the temporal modality of the future anterior affecting founding moments. The intelligibility of the law depends on the future (*avenir*), on the interpretative order that will be produced after the fact (*après coup*) but that "was destined *in advance* to produce" the "proper interpretative models" of self-legitimation (270/90). This situation indicates that although the founding act establishes the validity of the politico-legal order, it remains unreadable in itself, and thus, against Schmitt but with Benjamin undecidable: neither illegal nor legal.[26]

> The operation that amounts to founding, inaugurating, justifying law, to *making law*, would consist of a *coup the force*, of a performative and therefore interpretative violence that in itself is neither just nor unjust and that no justice and no earlier and previously founding law, no preexisting foundation, could, by

> definition, guarantee or contradict or invalidate. No justificatory discourse could or should ensure the role of metalanguage in relation to the performativity of institutive language or to its dominant interpretation. Discourse here meets its limit—in itself, in its very performative power. (241–42/32–33)

The impossibility of interpreting in advance the *coup de force* disallows the appeal to metalanguage in order to justify it. This means that the violent foundation of the law is not justifiable within the semantic horizon it institutes since the temporal disjuncture between origin and justification signals an irreducible gap between the two that no metalanguage can fill.[27] For, if such an operation were possible, it would be necessary to justify the founding act independently—hence at a metalevel—from the interpretative horizon it institutes, which is the historical and semantic horizon to which justification is bound. Doing so would mean falling into the metaphysical trap of believing that the origin of the law appears as such to rational scrutiny so that it can be rationalized and naturalized. As Derrida notes, "those who say 'our time,' while thinking 'our present' in light of the future anterior present do not know very well, by definition, what they are saying. It is precisely in this nonknowledge that the eventness of the event consists, what one naively calls its presence" (269/88).

For Derrida, those who believe that the origin of the law is presentable as such, as presence in *their* present time, subscribe to the problematic metaphysical thinking investigated in the previous chapter. In contrast to this view, he thinks that the origin of the law cannot be rationalized because it does not appear as presence to human consciousness. Like any origin, the foundation of the law is affected by iterability, the movement of a differential repetition that characterizes experience and that inscribes a "differential contamination" at the heart of any foundation, thereby impeding any origin as such (272/94).

But what exactly is iterability and how is it connected to the law? Derrida introduces the notion in his discussion of meaning and context in "Signature Event Context."[28] Iterability refers to repetition as the possibility of written signs enduring in time, and thus being legible at all, beyond their original context and in the absence of their author(s) (SEC, 317/377). The possibility of traveling across time and contexts suggests that repetition contains the constitutive possibility of alteration and differentiation resulting from the mediation effected by the contexts in which meaning is produced (324/385). By standing for a differential and altering repetition, iterability represents a law that contaminates the purity of phenomena, including the law itself.[29]

To understand how iterability is connected to the law, it is necessary to briefly digress in order to address Derrida's reading of Benjamin's "Critique of Violence" occurring in the second part of "Force of Law" because it is in that context that his reflections on iterability and the law emerge most forcefully. It is not my intention to engage in a detailed discussion of this complex relationship as this is beyond the scope of this chapter. I simply wish to draw attention to the iterability of the law, the exploration of which, I hope, will also shed light on the nature of authority and the structure of contamination that is crucial to Derrida's understanding of the theological-political predicament.

In his "Critique of Violence," Benjamin sets out to articulate a critique of violence capable of illuminating the relationships among violence, law, and justice. His aim is to provide a critique of violence that differs from traditional legal philosophies such as natural and positive law theories, which see violence only as a means to an end, natural or historical respectively, and dogmatically presuppose that a justification exists between means and ends.[30] By viewing violence as a justifiable means used to institute and preserve the law, these theories can only conceive of violence as either law-making or law-preserving, but never as it relates to justice. In this way, they cannot offer a critique of violence as such, but only of how it is used as a justifiable means.

In addition to their general dogmatism, Benjamin considers natural and positive law theories deficient for three specific reasons. First, they are rationally impotent and hopeless against the "ultimate insolubility of all legal problems" since they are unable to distinguish when violence is used as means only or as an end in itself.[31] Second, these theories support a law that is "rotten" and "ambiguous" because, to remain so (i.e., to remain an instituting violence), the law needs to preserve itself and its own power and thus needs to make "power-making violence" as its own end.[32] Finally, these theories conceive of the law and its historical development according to a dialectic of "oscillation" between law-making and law-preserving violence, thereby reducing history to the historical decaying of laws.[33]

In contrast to traditional legal theories, Benjamin articulates a critique of violence as a "philosophy of history," a philosophy of the history of violence that is capable of thinking beyond a means-end model and thus of identifying violence as such, and not *in relation* to an end. For him, a proper critique of violence requires the "destruction" of law-making as power-making violence so as to move beyond an idea of the law that uses violence for its own sake.[34] It requires "a criterion of violence itself as a principle," a criterion making possible "a critical, discriminating, and decisive approach" capable of breaking the dialectic of historical change and of grounding evaluations in the justness of end.[35] Such a criterion is provided by divine violence, which is a "different kind of violence" since it is not "law-making" and "bloody," but "law-destroying" and "lethal without spilling blood."[36] As "pure manifestation," divine violence is a "pure immediate violence" situated "outside the law" that is capable of breaking through the cycle of laws by deposing (*Ersetzung*) the law and abolishing state violence (*Staatsgewalt*). Although not "recognizable as such with certainty" by human beings and exceeding the realm of the law, this type of violence, nevertheless, allows for moving past the insolubility of all legal problems by providing a firm criterion for discriminating between violence as end and as means.[37] Divine violence can do so since it deposes the law, halting any positing or law-making as power-making violence, but not violence as such. It is able to manifest, unambiguously, divine justice, thereby inaugurating a "new historical epoch" without law.[38]

For Derrida, the theme of the "annihilation of the law" is what is most problematic in Benjamin's text, which, he contends, contains a profound ambiguity about the possibility of a final solution. It thus has a disturbing affinity with the issue of "destruction," employed by both Schmitt and Heidegger, and thus ultimately about the possibility of justice (FL, 258/67, 261/73). Derrida connects the theme of destruction of the law to Benjamin's understanding of "critique" conceived as "*krinein*," the capacity of choosing, of taking a "decision in the form of judgment" that "has an essential relation, in itself to the sphere of law" and thus to violence. Similar to the Kantian understanding of critique, the concept of violence as critique allows for evaluative judgments in ethico-political and legal spheres connected to the claim to authority or the authoritative right to judge, even though this is not to be pursued through transcendental reflection, but through the appeal to a principle transcending human finitude (265/79–80). Conceived as decisive judgment involving the right to evaluate, Benjamin's view of "critique" implies a discriminating "force" that is putatively capable of separating what resists conclusive discriminations and breaking from all relations. Despite Benjamin's critical thrust and preoccupations, his understanding of critique displays features—the epistemic possibility for and desire of purity—typical of the metaphysical tradition Derrida criticizes, including elements displayed in racialized logics, such as setting things apart by breaking the constitutive relationality of the human condition and of relations to others. As such, Benjamin's view holds important implications for questions of race that appear perhaps only indirectly in Derrida's emphasis on Benjamin's use of critique's "force" in a series of "radically problematic distinctions," of which the following are only the most important examples: founding *versus* preserving violence; mythic violence founding the law *versus* divine violence annihilating the law; and justice as the principle of all divine positing of ends *versus* power as the principle of mythical positing of law (264/78–79). These distinctions are, at times, accompanied by an "essentialist" language and the theme of "decay"[39] pointing to seemingly "reactionary" and nostalgic features of Benjamin's text, which therefore remains too ambiguously connected to "Schmittian or Heideggerian schemas" (281/111).

For Derrida, however, the stability Benjamin seeks to secure for his own distinctions, especially the one between law-making and law-preserving violence, is undermined by iterability.

> The very violence of the foundation or positing of law (*Rechtsetzende Gewalt*) must envelop the violence of the preservation of law (*Rechtserhaltende Gewalt*) and cannot break with it. It belongs to the structure of fundamental violence in that it calls for a repetition of itself and founds what ought to be preserved, preservable, promised to heritage and to tradition, to partaking [*partage*]. A foundation is a promise. Every positing (*Setzung*) permits and promises, posits ahead [*permet and pro-met*]; it posits by setting and promising [*en mettant et en promettant*]. And even if a promise is not kept in fact, iterability inscribes the promise as a guard in the most irruptive instant of foundation. Thus it inscribes the possibility of repetition at the heart of the originary. Better, or worse, it is inscribed in this law [*loi*] of iterability; it stands under its law or before its law [*sous sa loi ou devant sa loi*]. Consequently [*du coup*], there is no more pure foundation or pure position of law, and so a pure founding violence, than there is a purely preserving violence. Positing is already iterability, a call for self-preserving and repetition. Preservation in turn refounds, so that it can preserve what it claims to found. Thus there is no rigorous opposition between positing and preserving, only what I call (and Benjamin does not name it) a *differential contamination* between the two, with all the paradoxes that this might lead to. (272/94)

This is a decisive passage. The "law of iterability" affects the violence founding the law and the more fundamental violence ("the structure of fundamental violence") involved in the disruption of pure origins and foundations. Characterized by a differential repetition, iterability brings differentiation and alteration to the core of the law ("differential contamination"). While "differential" points to the splitting of origins "produced" by differential repetition, "contamination" refers to the intertwinement between positing and conserving that is involved in any act of foundation seeking to preserve what has been founded. In other words, because iterability inscribes a differential repetition and alteration in every origin, including that of the law, any violence positing the law or law-making violence is always already a differentiated repetition of itself and thus also a law-preserving violence. This suggests that the origin of the law can only discursively be produced but is nowhere to be found.

This is what Derrida calls the "paradox of iterability," which "threatens the rigor" of Benjamin's distinctions. By inscribing "preservation in the essential structure of foundation," iterability impedes the radical heterogeneity between the law-making and law-preserving violence that Benjamin seeks to maintain (278/104). In this way, any attempt to overcome the "*differential contamination*" between these two types of law by appealing, as Benjamin does, to a decidable but unknowable radical exteriority identified with the divine (divine violence as "outside the law") finds a limit in the relationality of the human predicament. As Rodolphe Gasché has suggested, what the law of iterability exposes is not simply that pure "critique" as discriminating position remains implicated in the things or relations over which it decides and which contaminate its alleged purity. It is also that critical decisive judgments and decisions occur *in relation* to others. Thus, rendering justice, which animates Benjamin's text, requires a responsibility to attend the singularity of others and of situations before all separations.[40]

Although Derrida criticizes Benjamin's attempt to secure stable distinctions, he reckons that the latter somehow acknowledges the contamination at the heart of the law. For Derrida, Benjamin recognizes such a contamination in his discussion of the violence of capital punishment and of the police, which are examples in which the law is reduced to the manifestation of violence for its own sake. Indeed, Derrida notes, Benjamin claims, in discussing the death penalty, that "there is something rotten in law," which for Derrida implies that something condemns the law, "ruins it in advance" (FL, 276/101–3). Benjamin further describes the police as an institution in which law-making and law-preserving violence cannot be clearly distinguished since they both preserve the law by applying existing rules, and they make the law by legislating in all those cases in which no clear legal situation exists. The police represent a limit case in which the distinction between law-making and law-preserving violence is "suspended" and collapses into a "spectral mixture" that reveals the police's "ignominy" and renders the law they enforce "ambiguous."[41] As Derrida notes, this mixture points to a deconstructive operation at work in Benjamin's text. "Modern police force ruins" or "one could say deconstruct" the distinction between law-making and law-preserving violence, a distinction "that nevertheless structures the discourse that Benjamin calls a new critique of violence" (277/103). However, and in spite of his implicit recognition of iterability and contamination, Benjamin, for Derrida, "never gives up trying to contain in a pair of concepts and to bring back down to distinction the very thing that incessantly exceeds and overflows them" (277/103). Although Derrida does not put sufficient emphasis on Benjamin's idea that mythic violence seeks to keep the distinction alive in order to counter fascism, his point is that the logic of divine violence does not exclude the possibility of similar effects, if it can resolve "differential contamination."

Taken at face value, Derrida's interpretation of Benjamin attributes to the latter a sort of naïve essentialism—the quest for a pure, unmediated, instance external to the historical cycle of violence—and of protofascism—the attempt to return to a pure origin as a remedy to decay, which are all features Benjamin tried to oppose in "Critique of Violence" and other writings.[42] Yet it is not entirely clear that Derrida is *simply* advancing these charges, though he has been severely criticized for his view.[43] Some commentators have argued that, perhaps, Derrida's interpretation performs rhetorical strategies attempting to *defend* without apology the value of Benjamin's text.[44] Others have emphasized that his view puts further emphasis on a possible consequence arising from the rather opaque and enigmatic text of Benjamin.[45]

It is not my intention to engage in interpretative questions here, as a rich literature already exists on this topic, whose diverging views seem hard to reconcile.[46] However, I seek to underscore that independently of how one interprets Derrida's evaluation of the "Critique of Violence," Derrida offers an example of critical vigilance that limits destructive effects, however unintended they might be. Indeed, Derrida puts into sharp relief the serious stakes involved in a discourse that, sustained by an essentialist language and, at times, displaying an apocalyptic tone, seeks to push the agenda of historical materialism further by appealing to an ambiguous figure that points to the possibility of a radical exteriority, and whose manifestation is equivocally connected to the theme of destruction and a logic of separation. To the extent that such a discourse *also* animates Benjamin's text or is not excluded by it, Derrida's illumination of its possible and dangerous implications is both timely and necessary.

What does this digression on the relationship between Derrida and Benjamin add to our discussion of iterability and the law? Besides illuminating, albeit very briefly, Derrida's position on Benjamin's "Critique of Violence," this discussion on their relationship helps us highlight the significance of iterability for Derrida's position on the mystical foundation of authority. Iterability does not simply expose the connection between the violence instituting the law and the more complex violence associated with differential repetition.[47] This remains an important point. Iterability illustrates a framework of interrelation characterizing the secular, especially when seen as theological-political, as I shall indicate below. It also exposes the limits connected to interpreting and universally justifying the neutrality of the secular domain by recurring to a metalanguage. Iterability suggests that the origin of the politico-legal order, as with any origin, cannot be isolated and cognitively grasped as such since it is inscribed in a movement of differential repetition that makes origins elusive and that resists separatist schemas. If this holds, approaches seeking to justify the law by attempting to make intelligible its origin do either fill the gap between foundation and justification through fictions that conceal unrecognized metaphysical claim or, if they consciously do so, hypocritically appeal to the voice of justifiable reasons where only force can speak. Thus, *pace* universalist rhetoric, Derrida's view on iterability shows that no legitimating discourse couched in the neutral language of reason alone *can* represent the interests of human beings as such in the aftermath of political founding. At a more basic level, his view exposes the racial implications involved in discourses of legitimation in which origins get naturalized as the examples of the American Declaration of Independence and of South Africa illustrate.

However, what Derrida does not show is how to think about postfounding predicaments given the aforementioned gap and the need for justification. Does the awareness of the gap between origin and justification contribute to avoiding further violence after the founding moment? If so, in which ways and at which stage? Which type of judgment should be employed to evaluate the fabulous fiction of the founding moment? Although Derrida is lamentably silent on how to think about the immediate aftermath of political founding and on how to judge the new politico-legal order, he leaves us with two cautionary warnings that perform, nevertheless, a critical function. First, he warns us that the "rational" judgments about the myth of founding are placed in a contestable context that was enabled through exclusions. By emphasizing this point, Derrida does not advocate refusing to evaluate newly constituted institutions, blurring the distinction between fictions of totalitarian and democratic regimes or devaluating the analysis of what constitutes a legitimate regime. Rather, he points to the importance of being critically aware of the background conditions that have favored and made relevant certain normative understandings and not others, and thus to the idea that "rational" judgments are blind and potentially exclusionary if not complemented by genealogical investigation. Second, he cautions us that discourses of universal legitimation proclaiming the neutrality of the secular domain towards a plurality of worldviews conceal founding exclusions and naturalizations. They institutionalize a violence that becomes structural to the constituted political community, and that produces intergenerational oppressive effects, as the aforementioned historical examples indicate.

The temporal and differential features of the law discussed so far are particularly significant to the understanding of Derrida's view of the secular domain. These features illuminate that the law's authority does not rest *solely* on normative justifications, as in the tradition of natural law or in liberal constitutionalism, but on a historical and forceful act informed by some form of faith that authorizes, as it were, the law. To affirm this is not to discredit the relevance and necessity of normative justifications in founding predicaments. Rather, it is to point out first, that the irreducible gap between the origin and justification of a politico-legal order makes discourses of legitimation always already political because they are constitutively dependent on fictions that conceal forceful exclusions; second, that because the instituting violence inaugurates, through such exclusions, a *particular* historical horizon of interpretation, Derrida's view of the secular domain cannot retain a neutral halo as Mark Cauchi has suggested.[48] Finally, and most significantly for our purposes, an element of faith plays a significant role in political foundations.

Acknowledging this role is crucial to understanding the "mystical foundation of authority." Because the instituting faith represents also the inaugural condition of any epistemic horizon that resolves semantic undecidability through force, but not undecidability as such, no interpretative system can make sense of its instituting moment from within itself. This means not simply that any discourse finds its limit in the performative power from which it originates, despite the recognition that any new legal system relies upon already existing, and thus interpretable, legal structures and traditions (FL, 242/34). It also means that the very possibility on which a particular configuration and interpretation of political authority relies constitutes also a possibility for radical criticism and self-criticism of political authority as such. For no founding moment can close the gap between condition of possibility (elementary faith) and determined necessity of specific forms of juridico-political power, as highlighted in the previous chapter. Therefore, the foundation of the law's authority can be called mystical because its irreducible uninterpretability depends on "a silence" that "is walled up in the violent structure of the founding act." This silence indicates that the authority of the law rests on the "faith (*foi*)" granted to it, on an act that provides "no ontological or rational foundation" because it takes place in the realm of belief and not in that of reason and knowledge (240/30). While apparently leveling all political-legal systems, the claim that all systems of law rely on a mystical element does not seek to offer evaluations.[49] Rather, it seeks to expose that irreducible element of faith which the antireligious impulse of the Enlightenment has obscured to the point of removing it so decisively from the agenda of philosophical reflection that it has been rendered invisible to contemporary debates. However, because this faith plays a central role in the moment of political foundation, its appreciation seems central to understanding the nature of the secular domain.

But the appreciation of such a faith is crucial also for another reason. Besides marking the mystical nature of political authority and the limits of justificatory discourses, that faith also points to possibilities for transformation. This is another aspect missed by the Enlightenment amnesia. For Derrida, because the law rests on "a violence without ground [*sans fondement*]" that, nevertheless, founds a new political order upon preceding legal structures and traditions, it is "essentially *deconstructible*." This means that the law is susceptible to transformations and that new possibilities for emancipation might be disclosed (FL, 242/34). This eventuality is connected to the suspension (*epokhē*) of the credit accorded to the law, as if one were to perform an act of theoretical fiction through which the validity of the law is put on hold and the history of the law, of how it came into being, is investigated. As Derrida acknowledges, the act of suspension exposes us to the risk of a legal void. However, that risk constitutes also a "political chance" that might disclose new possibilities for justice by increasing our responsibility towards the past and the future, and above all towards others (242/35). On the one hand, responsibility towards the past is the "task of recalling the history, the origin, and thus the limits" of "law [*loi*] and right [*droit*], of values, norms, prescriptions that have been imposed and sedimented" in our inherited tradition and appears therefore as "less readable" or "presupposed" (247–48/44). As mentioned in the previous chapter, this responsibility requires the memory of the history of law, a memory that is not limited to the content of the received law but one that also reaches the conditions of its establishment and its remainders. As Derrida puts it in *Specters of Marx*, memory does not regard simply "what one inherits but the pre-inheritance on the basis of which one inherits." Put another way, it concerns remembering the empirical conditions of founding moments, which often involve exterminations and exclusions of human, philosophical, and political alternatives that leave behind ghostly traces (*SM*, 137/181). For him, the memory of the past fosters the awareness that any established law is provisional because of its political nature from first inception. But, above all, memory displays a normative potential since it represents the possibility of reactivating unrealized or excluded possibilities in view of transformations, as discussed in chapter 2. On the other hand, responsibility towards the future represents the task of suspending the authority of its conceptual and institutional apparatuses, together with the faith or credit accorded to the law, so as to avoid a "dogmatic slumber" (FL, 249/46). If this operation might appear to be the opposite of responsibility, it is for Derrida an "increase in responsibility" since it calls for continued vigilance of the law and its origin *without* abolishing the law while opening up the space "in which transformations, even juridico-political revolutions, take place" (248–49/45–46). The 1992 ruling of the High Court of Australia, what has become known as the Mabo decision, represents a good example of the emancipatory potential of deconstruction, as Paul Patton has noted.[50] Pressed to look at the memory of the past, the court recognized for the first time a form of ownership of land based on indigenous law that had been denied since the establishment of the first British colony in Australia in 1788. This ruling, Patton suggests, is "a striking example of a partial deconstruction of an established and historically contingent body of law" which, however imperfectly, has been ameliorated.[51]

Appreciating the mystical and faithful character of the law together with its possibilities of emancipation, one might argue, does not address crucial questions regarding the requirements of *some* justification that any political-legal order needs in order to be effective at all. If the origin of the law always escapes human reach, how should we understand the nature of political justification? What should we make of the founding faith in the absence of metalanguage?

Before the Law

Derrida's essay "Before the Law" addresses some of these questions, particularly that of the origin of law and the hermeneutic puzzle of being "before the law." Here he interprets Kafka's story bearing the same title as a way to reflect on the relations between generality and singularity through the relationship between law (general) and literature (singular), including also the question about the origin of both. The story concerns a doorkeeper standing before the gate of the law and a man from the country seeking admittance to the law. Since the doorkeeper denies access only at the present time, the man from the country waits until the end of his life to eventually hear from the doorkeeper that the door was meant uniquely for him, but it was now time to close it.

For Derrida, this story presents a series of paradoxes, the most significant of which is, for our discussion, the predicament faced by the man from the country who stands "before the law." But what does "before the law" mean? And, more specifically, what does "before" mean in "before the law"? For Derrida, "before" refers to both a spatial and temporal dimension, "before the law and prior to the law [*devant la loi et avant la loi*]" (BL, 216/134). It indicates a complicated relationship between "outside" and "inside" that can be appreciated by distinguishing man *qua* subject to the law and man *qua* creator of the law. Although the man of the country believes himself to be already under the law, inside its jurisdiction, and that the law should be universally accessible, he finds out that the law is "never immediately" accessible to him *qua* subject to the law, and thus he remains in a sense outside it, as "an outlaw" (196/114, 204/122). That man can also be considered as being outside the law because, considered as man *qua* creator of the law, he stands in a position that temporally precedes its institution (*avant la loi*), which grants him the power to provide the doorkeeper with the "entitling authority" to guard the law (201/118). This paradoxical situation raises a radical question: If the law always eludes human reach, does the "before" of "before the law" point to a transcendent origin, one that is outside law and history?

Derrida seems to reject this possibility when he emphasizes that all there is before the law is the man from the country who provides the doorkeeper with a guarding authority. Yet, the question of the law's inaccessibility is more complex. The impossibility of *immediately* accessing the law signals a structure of delay inherent in the law: the access to its origin is indefinitely deferred and kept secret, as it were. The secret is that the law "has no essence"; it has no *proper* origin, and therefore the foundation of the law "never takes place in a presence." Indeed, neither the doorkeeper who "turns his back to the law" in order to "prohibit all presentation" nor the man from the country "who faces the law" has access to the law since "neither is in the presence of the law" (206/123, 201/119).

For Derrida, that the law is not presentable and has no essence indicates that the truth of the law is its nontruth. As such, the law can only "*guard itself*"; it guards the secret that it has no *proper* origin and that its own door opens "on[to] nothing"; it stands over the abyss (206/123). This openness on the abyss constitutes the structure and "force" of the law against which human beings can employ deconstructive strategies that can bring emancipatory results without seeking to get away with the law.[52]

Significantly for our discussion, the structure of the law does not exclude that, as Derrida notes in "Force of Law," a transcendent or even theological dimension still characterizes the legal order.

> The foundation of the law remains suspended in the void or over the abyss, suspended by a pure performative act that would not have to answer to or before anyone . . . And the "being before the law" that Kafka talks about resembles this situation, both ordinary and terrible, of the man who cannot manage to see or above all to touch, to catch up with the [*loi*]: it is transcendent in the very measure that is he who must found it, as yet to come [*comme à venire*], in violence. One "touches" here without touching on this extraordinary paradox: the inaccessible transcendence of the law [*loi*], before which and prior to which "man" stands fast, only appears infinitely transcendent and thus theological to the extent that, nearest to him, it depends only on him, on the performative act by which he institutes it: the law [*loi*] is transcendent, violent and nonviolent, because it depends only on who is before it (and so prior to it), on who produces, founds it in a absolute performative whose presence always escapes him. The law [*loi*] is transcendent and theological, and so always to come, always promised, because it is immanent, finite and thus already past. Every "subject" is caught up in this aporetic structure in advance. (FL, 270/89–90)

The man from the country, *qua* subject to the law, cannot access the law because it is he who authorizes it *qua* creator of the law. Thus, the law remains transcendent and theological because it is always ahead ("to come") of him, "outside" of him and yet always already "inside" him, as part of his power to institute it. The act of authorization is an "absolute performative" not in the sense that it can be clearly separated from the constative function it also enacts. Rather, it is absolute because it is independent of, and heterogeneous to, any previous normative order and horizon of knowledge from which it could be possibly derived. It is a pure act in that it constitutes itself *in* and *as* an interruption of the previous order, in the exception, to use a Schmittian vocabulary.

But what is crucial for our discussion is that this "absolute performative" is informed by elementary faith, namely, an elementary experience of trustworthiness that is prior to, but shared by, the determinate faith of positive religion and that informs the structure of promissory affirmation or the "messianic." This point emerges clearly in "Faith and Knowledge," where Derrida, commenting on the "messianic," refers explicitly to elementary faith and connects it to political foundings and democracy.

> This abstract messianicity belongs from the very beginning to the experience of faith, of a believing, of a credit that is irreducible to knowledge and of a trust that "founds" all relation to the other in testimony (*cette messianicité abstraite appartient d'éntrée a à expérience de la foi, du croire ou d'un crédit irréductible au savoir et d'une fiabilité qui "fonde" tout rapport à l'outre dans le témoniage*). This justice, which I distinguish from right, alone allows the hope, beyond all "messianisms," of a universalizable culture of singularities, a culture in which the abstract possibility of the impossible translation could nevertheless be announced. This justice inscribes itself in advance in the promise, in the act of faith or in the appeal to faiths that inhabits every act of language and every address to the other . . . This messianicity stripped of everything, as it should, this faith without dogma, which makes its way through the risk of absolute night, cannot be contained in any traditional opposition, for example that between reason and mysticism. It is announced wherever, reflecting without flinching, a purely rational analysis brings the following paradox: that the foundation of the law—the law of the law, institution of the institution, origin of the constitution—is a "performative" event that cannot belong to the set that it founds, inaugurates or justifies. Such an event is unjustifiable within the

logic of what will have opened. It is the decision of the other in the undecidable. Henceforth reason ought to recognize what Montaigne and Pascal call an undeniable "mystical foundation of authority." The mystical thus understood allies belief or credit (*croyance ou crédit*), the fiduciary or the trustworthy (*fiduciaire or fiable*), the secret (which here signifies "mystical") to foundation, to knowledge, we will later say also to science as "doing," as theory, practice and theoretical practice . . . The chance of this desert in the desert (as of that which resembles to a fault, but without reducing itself to, that via negativa which makes its way from a Graeco-Judeo-Christian tradition) is that in uprooting the tradition that bears, in atheologizing it, this abstraction, without denying faith, liberates a universal rationality and the political democracy that cannot be dissociated from it. (FK, 56–57/31–32)

This very complex passage is significant to our discussion for several reasons. First, it illuminates elementary faith as the thread running through the three themes analyzed so far: language, time, and politics. That faith is central to Derrida's understanding of the idea of a "language of promise," of the "messianic" as justice and, as we see here, of politics. Second, it exposes the nexus between the three main essays analyzed in this chapter ("Declarations," "Force of Law," and "Faith and Knowledge") by linking together, respectively, the paradoxical temporality, mystical feature, and faithful character of the act of political founding emerging in them. Finally, it makes explicit that an elementary faith is central to the foundation of the political and of democracy, a faith that exceeds knowledge because it is placed in a dimension without guarantees or certainty as that of credit—hence the "risk of the absolute night."

This last point has decisive implications for understanding why Derrida's view of the secular breaks with modern secular discourse, especially if one concentrates on the nature of elementary faith. In the previous chapter, I have suggested that such a faith consists in a minimal structure of belief that all human interaction presupposes. It is a quasitranscendental figure that represents the condition of possibility of both reason and religion. Indeed, Derrida believes that since reason and religion have in "the testimonial pledge (*gage*) of every performative" a common source, reason "bears, supports and supposes" religion (FK, 66/46). He also believes that since elementary faith is "at least in its essence or calling, religious (the elementary condition, the milieu of the religious, if not of religion itself)" (80–81/68), rational thinking preserves an irreducible connection to a dimension typical of, but not exclusive to, religion (R, 153/211). By emphasizing the link between reason and religion through an elementary faith, Derrida allows for a view of their relationship that moves past the radical antireligious impulse of the Enlightenment that wanted them strictly separate, especially in the secular domain.

But how does all this relate to Derrida's claim in the aforementioned passage from "Force of Law" that the "law (*loi*) is transcendent and theological"? A clue to this question might be found by reflecting on the role elementary faith plays in political foundings where the absence of grounds impedes the appeal to a stable cognitive horizon. In such situations, the encounter with a mystical limit exposes trust as an act of bearing witness that is involved in the foundation of both politics and knowledge. It is one that gives the law a dimension that "appears," Derrida says, "infinitely transcendent and thus theological" (FL, 270/90). Here "appears" suggests that this dimension need not be taken in traditional terms since elementary faith is not simply placed "outside" the law, in a transcendent place proper to God or any other ultimate instance. Rather, it stands in a more complicated relation to the law, one in which the distinction between "inside" and "outside" does not firmly hold, as Derrida's reading of Kafka has shown. How exactly this distinction and the law are related is not very clear in Derrida, and it remains open to interpretation whether this unclarity is due to his shortcomings or to the limit-nature of the subject matter.[53] What is clear, however, is that "inside" and "outside" are not simply opposed to each other, as transcendence and immanence are according to traditional understandings. It is in the intertwining and play between them that Derrida's notion of transcendence (and thus of the theological), perhaps *another* notion of transcendence, is at work. The question remains, though, what the nature of this transcendence is. He notes, as in the above quote about being "before the law," that transcendence is, in some sense, horizontal since it refers to a dimension that is "ahead" (as opposed to "above") of the subject because it is still "to come." Perhaps a clue on the relationship between the outside and inside of the law can be found in a context not strictly related to the law that invokes the figure of "invagination" to point to this nexus. Commenting on the relationship between scientific discourse and deconstruction, specifically on whether the latter is inside or outside the former, Derrida affirms: "I confess I have no simple, stable answer to this question. And this is also a result of the invaginated structure of this limit, this form of frontier that, if I can put it like this, includes the outside in the inside without integrating it" (AWP, 98/317).

Given the ambiguity surrounding Derrida's reconceptualization of transcendence, one could think that he is looking for something more fundamental than reason and religious faith and this would be precisely his notion of elementary faith. Perhaps, this is the reason why some commentators have pointed out that Derrida's "faith" is somehow contradictory and delusional since it risks repeating the very foundational universalism it seeks to disturb.[54] On the one hand, this faith would be a *rational* faith in reason that seeks to provide a sort of unconditioned or neutral space from which to criticize religious and secular perspectives, which are then submitted to the ultimate judgment of reason.[55] On the other hand, it would arise from a type of enquiry which is linked, as Derrida acknowledges, to the emancipating spirit of the Enlightenment but that remains more connected to its historical context and philosophical and religious sources (Latin Christianity) than he wants to concede or acknowledge.[56] So conceived, the critique goes, elementary faith cannot provide the space for the unconditioned criticism it seeks to offer because of its historical heritage and of its a priori rational inclination. If it continues to seek such a space, Derrida's elementary faith suffers from the delusion of pretending to be different from the neutrality of the Christian Enlightenment it criticizes.

This forceful objection strikes at the core of Derrida's thinking. Yet it can be turned into an occasion for clarification. In the previous chapter, I have shown that Derrida's thinking is historical and aware of its own historicity. I have also illustrated that his receptivity to political foundings and their structural exclusions points toward the impossibility and danger of universal claims as traditionally conceived by various forms of Enlightenment universalism. I have argued that by acknowledging the particularity from which his thinking originates, Derrida does not simply manifest a critical vigilance about unwarranted generalizing gestures that spring from an amnesic attitude about the specificity of contexts from which universalist forms of Western discourses originate and to which they remain irreducibly connected. He also unsettles the hierarchical and separatist logic, and naturalizing strategies, informing such discourses. Although operating within the critical spirit of the Enlightenment, Derrida also highlights the colonial and imperial features of various versions of Enlightenment universalism sustaining global secularization. His view of elementary faith indicates that such secularization cannot be conceived as a project of full emancipation from "all faiths" and that faith in "reason alone" is what the Enlightenment did not have the courage to question. Taking this view seriously has several implications. First, it implies questioning the idea that reason regulates in advance the scope of the faith it has in itself (as in a "rational" faith in reason) since doing so would reinstitute reason as the most fundamental element between religious faith and reason. Second, it implies that if Derrida's thinking is more connected to Christianity than he is willing to recognize (EF, 33), this connection exceeds Christianity since it critically addresses the colonial and imperialistic features of modernity that have ended up contaminating both the Enlightenment and its Christian sources. Finally, while it might appear that "faith" is the most fundamental ground, and Derrida's language leads us to think so, it is, nevertheless, a ground that, as the founding moment exemplifies, stands over the abyss. While in "Faith and Knowledge" Derrida affirms that elementary faith is a sort of foundation that "steals away the grounds of what it founds," in *The Beast and the Sovereign*, he mentions that "the abyss is not the bottom, the originary ground (*Urgrund*), of course, nor the bottomless depth (*Ungrund*) of some hidden base. The abyss, if there is an abyss, is that there is more than one ground [*sol*], more than one solid, and more than one single threshold [*plus d'un seul seuil*]" (BS 1, 334/446). As a groundless ground parting company with other grounds, the ground over which Derrida's elementary faith stands is, *stricto sensu*, no ground at all.

By insisting on the centrality of elementary faith, then, Derrida does not seek to provide a sort of unconditioned, ahistorical, or neutral space from which to criticize religious and secular perspectives. Although it points to the conditions of possibility of reason and religion thereby somehow preceding them, elementary faith is a *quasi*transcendental that occurs in historical languages and therefore remains irreducibly tied to historicity. Discussing the essence of language and the pledge (*gage*) in connection to Heidegger, Derrida affirms, in a long footnote, "that the fact that it [the pledge] precedes language does not mean that it is foreign to it. The *gage* engages in language—and so always in *a* language" (*OS*, 130/148). Instead, what Derrida seeks to emphasize through elementary faith is a point of irreducibility, and yet commonality, between reason and religion, the theological and the political, one from which to think about them from within their historical relationship. And this is what the hyphen in the notion of theological-political suggests: irreducible interrelatedness, and yet distinction, between the theological and the political. Indeed, it is because of elementary faith that the theological-political problematics can be thought as such before and beyond the urge to solve it.

The Secular as Theological-Political

This discussion about elementary faith, the law, and transcendence helps illuminate the nature of the secular in Derrida's view. If the performative act of foundation reveals the law to be, in some sense, transcendent and theological, and if elementary faith retains a dimension typical of but not exclusive to religion, then the secular domain is not purely political but theological-political. It is one in which a theological dimension cannot be strictly excluded but that cannot be considered theological in any traditional sense. The irreducibility and non-dispensability of elementary faith indicates that the theological-political relationship cannot be resolved in the foundation of political authority, but marks instead its very nature.

To illustrate this point, let us connect Derrida's reflections on elementary faith, the mystical foundation of authority, and the event of political foundation. As mentioned, political authority retains a mystical character because its foundation rests on an uninterpretable act of (elementary) faith. Escaping the catch of rational justification, this act is located both "inside" and "outside" the law and plays a central role in the event of political foundation by giving credit to the conventions according to which a new political order is justified. In this way, the reality of the founding act appears as inextricably linked to some form of transcendence. While in the Declaration of Independence, transcendence is explicitly anchored to God, this need not be the case for making the claim that religious sources are involved in political foundations. The ambiguous location of elementary faith with regard to the law and its being shared by religion as much as by reason suggests the impossibility of strictly excluding such sources from the institution of the political. Rather than providing a secure anchoring, these sources, for Derrida, point to the groundless character of the founding act and thus the provisionality and openness of the political order it institutes.[57]

Appreciating this impossibility as a way to point to the groundlessness of political foundations helps also clarify the sense in which Derrida attributes a theological dimension to the secular domain and situate his thought, however briefly and nonexhaustively, within contemporary debates in political theology. As mentioned, Derrida agrees with Schmitt on the theological heritage of modern political categories but rejects his view of secularization and the implicit analogy between the political domain and theology that emerges from Schmitt's analysis of political sovereignty. In all its ambiguity, this analogy signals Schmitt's close proximity to traditional theology as a form of metaphysical discourse. As Samuel Weber has shown,

Schmitt employs a method ("the sociology of concepts") that attempts to recover the fundamental essence of political concepts out of their historical differentiation. Thus, he remains implicated in the metaphysical tradition Derrida profoundly challenges.[58]

Derrida's position needs to be distinguished from that of Benjamin too. While drawing significantly from, and mostly agreeing with, Benjamin's analysis of the law, Derrida criticizes Benjamin's understanding of divine violence as a critiquing (*krinein*) criterion that is able to clearly discriminate between different types of violence. In particular, Derrida calls into question the ability of critique to distinguish between law-founding and law-preserving violence, and thus its ability to resolve the "differential contamination" that iterability inscribes in any foundation. For this reason, Derrida sees Benjamin's equivocal treatment of divine violence as pointing to a dimension that retains a significant ambiguity as to whether the link to traditional theological themes, is, in spite of Benjamin's commitment to historical materialism, still *too* theological.

Derrida's political theology is neither a form of theological discourse under the guise of legal theory as in Schmitt nor a form of critique sustained by theological tropes as in Benjamin, even less a type of negative theology. If anything, it is a mode of interrogation and exposition of the constitutive instability and openness affecting political and epistemic orders. This is apparent from the way in which Derrida appeals to theological tropes. For him, the theological dimension associated with the secular domain does not depend on whether an explicit reference to God or to an exceptionality derived from a theological notion of sovereignty is made or any attempts to grasp an ultimate instance. Rather, it is connected to the paradoxical and exceptional character of the founding act that points to an elementary faith where the appeal to reason to recover pure origins remains trapped in a problematic metaphysical thinking marked by racial undercurrents, as the discussion of political foundings in general, and that of Schmitt in particular, has shown. So, rather than providing a guarantee of stability through God, the sovereign as God, or any other traditional theological figure, Derrida's appeal to a theological dimension shows the impossibility of closure of the secular domain, but also its constitutive entanglement with the religious.[59]

This is where Derrida's innovation lies. By rupturing, through elementary faith, that Enlightenment understanding of the secular domain as a self-enclosed epistemic and political reality, Derrida opens such understanding to an altogether different type of transcendence. His emphasis on elementary faith and its features allows him to expose the structural instability, historicity, and openness of political orders and epistemic horizons together with the possibility of their critical interrogation and transformation. These latter are features and possibilities that are not impeded or threatened by religious sources, but made possible, in some sense, by them.

Emphasizing Derrida's opening to religious sources, though, does not imply suggesting that he envisions a religious foundation of politics or that his thought is distinctively religious or theological.[60] As mentioned above, the faith at the origin of the secular displays a theological dimension that is, nevertheless, not theological in traditional terms since it is "irreducible to any and all religion or implicitly theocratic institutions" (*R*, 153/211). Rather, it is to emphasize his distance from the antireligious impulse of an influential strand of the Enlightenment, a distance that does not deter him from standing for the secularization of the political conceived as the dissociation of political and religious authority.[61] As he affirmed in his reflections in *Islam and the West*, Derrida's support for the "separation between the theocratic from the political" is opposed to neither religion, a connection between religion and politics, nor elementary faith: "Now I believe one can radicalize the secularization of the political (*secularisation du politique*) while maintaining this necessity for faith in the general sense that I have just defined and then, on the foundation of this universal faith, this faith without which there is no universal bond, one can and one must respect strictly defined religious affiliations" (*IW*, 58/93).

My understanding of Derrida's conception of the secular complements and expands the limited literature on the topic. Commentators such as Mark Cauchi and Michael Naas have also insisted on the centrality of an elementary faith to Derrida's secular.[62] Building in part on their views, my position remains distinct in two ways. First, the angle of my analysis is political and focuses on political founding, particularly how the institution of the secular as the field of the sociopolitical is marked by the theological-political relationship. This gives to my perspective more of a political edge and also puts emphasis on the political stakes and empirical significance of Derrida's position, especially in light of the common modern belief that the foundation of political life is strictly non-religious. Second, I show that it is from the point of view of the event of political foundation that we can appreciate the distinct and novel character of Derrida's secular as well as its political and epistemic relevance.

In "Derrida's *Laïcité*," Naas suggests that Derrida was strongly committed to a deconstructed version of secularism or *laïcité*, as it is understood in France, namely, one that was first submitted to a critique of "its theological-political origins exposed through a radical desacralization" leading to a view of reason that is not opposed to religion. This type of *laïcité* can be seen, for Naas, as "a radical secularity that inscribes faith (though not religion) at the very origin of the sociopolitical."[63] Through an analysis of Derrida's deconstruction of the theological origins of secularism, sovereignty, globalization, and of the political more generally, Naas points to Derrida's commitment to enlarge the understanding of *laïcité*. This, he says, "will have to be considered not in complete opposition to religion but in relation to a faith that first opens up religious experience" and that "is at the origin of both the political and religion."[64]

As should now be clear, I agree with Naas's point about the centrality of elementary faith for Derrida's secular. Yet my view differs on the emphasis I put on politics and political founding, and especially on the interrelation between some form of the theological and the political at the very origin of the sociopolitical. While Naas acknowledges that elementary faith is central to opening up the field of religion and politics, his notion of "radical secularity" seems to exclude the implication of religious sources at the origin of the sociopolitical. In contrast, my analysis shows that such sources cannot be strictly excluded from Derrida's secular. For this reason, we can read the theological-political in connection with his view of the secular *also* in non-Schmittian terms—as pointing to a structural interrelation between the political and some form of the theological that is not theological in any traditional sense, and yet not nonreligious.

My view partly differs from Cauchi too. In his "The Secular to Come: Interrogating the Derridean 'Secular,'" Cauchi sets out to articulate Derrida's conception of the secular especially through an analysis of Derrida's view of the structure of identity in general and that of European Christianity in particular. In his analysis, Cauchi combines Derrida's view of identity and translation, which he applies to Derrida's understanding of the "religious" and "the secular," and more precisely to secular Europe and religious Christianity. Emphasizing that, for Derrida, identity presents a structure of internal difference and that translation is never transparent and complete, Cauchi suggests that Derrida's secular is best understood as "secular to come," where the "to come" indicates an irreducible otherness *in* the secular (as well as in the religious) that prevents its closure as a self-identical reality.[65] Simply put, the Derridean secular is never purely so for Cauchi. As he argues, "it is precisely because the secular always involves faith that is always to come. It is precisely because the secular cannot be wholly purged of religion . . . and in fact presupposes something in religion that is not necessarily religious," that the "secular is never—not in the past, not in the present, not in the future—wholly or purely secular."⁶⁶

Clearly, my position is in line with Cauchi's idea that Derrida's secular cannot be purely nonreligious. Yet, I reach this conclusion through a different route that emphasizes more political aspects and attends to the great attention Derrida has paid to theological traces implicated in questions of political authority, force, and law and, more generally, political formations as well as the role they play in the production of knowledge relevant to public life. It is not simply in virtue of the structure of identity that the secular is not a self-enclosed political reality, as Cauchi argues. It is so because of its empirical constitution through sources from which the religious cannot be excluded. While Cauchi focuses on Derrida's works on identity and translation and privileges an understanding of the secular as a property defining culture and identity, I focus more on questions of force, authority, and the law and consider the secular primarily as designating the empirical field of the sociopolitical instituted in the act of political foundation.⁶⁷ My suggestion is that by understanding Derrida's secular in this way, that is, from the angle of its foundation, the relevance and political "force" of his view comes most decisively and fruitfully to light.

Yet, at a deeper level, my interpretation of Derrida's secular significantly differs from these approaches to the extent that they both remain bound to modern secular discourse, either through *laïcité* or a notion of the secular linked to Europe and Christianity. What my perspective emphasizes is that the significance of Derrida's perspective rests on the epistemic resources it provides to move beyond the modern secular paradigm and the racialized thinking undergirding it while opening a space to the role religion can play in public life. As such, his view cannot be assimilated to discourses of the postsecular such as those of Jürgen Habermas and Charles Taylor, which remain firmly within a secular perspective that is more open to religious views, and yet is oblivious of the interconnected genealogy between race, the secular, and the category of religion.⁶⁸ Resisting the logic of hierarchization and separation at work in both secular and racialized discourses, Derrida's view enables thinking about the theological and the political from within their constitutive and contextual relationship, and thus at distance from the modern gesture of stepping outside it through the appeal to origins. His nonfoundational insistence on the moment of foundation and on elementary faith radicalizes the question of origins without longing for them and illuminates the possibility of *thinking* the theological-political relation as such, as an irreducible relation. This is possible since such thinking does not succumb to, but instead puts limits on, modern secular discourse's drive to solve the theological-political relation, a drive connected to a compulsive and destructive search for origins that has both colonial and racial connotations. These are limits that apply to Enlightenment secularism and its logic of the most fundamental between faith and reason, to approaches in political theology seeking to maintain the autonomy of the political, and to forms of religious fundamentalism that seek to absorb the political into the theological.

What my emphasis on the theological-political as mode of relational thinking seeks to do, then, is to highlight that if the hyphen between the theological and the political is eliminated, either through purely political or religious rule, there is a risk of relapsing into the logic of separation and hierachization, which also involves deeply problematic forms of naturalization through assimilatory translation. Understood as such, the notion of theological-political in Derrida therefore clears an epistemic space beyond the modern secular paradigm and its colonial heritage, opening opportunities for imagining configurations of public life that resist racial ordering and the exclusion of religion from the foundation and shaping of communal life, as I will discuss more amply in the last chapter.

On this reading, the critical potential of Derrida's view for contemporary debates on religion and politics lies precisely in that elementary faith neither calls for a return to religion nor abandons reason or Enlightenment's critical thrust altogether. Rather, it allows for taking the "return of religion" as a chance to critically rethink the public domain beyond dominant secular imaginaries and models. In other words, it enables to rethink such domain beyond both the separation and hierachization between theological and the political, reason and faith, and the idea of secularization as the neutral translation of the theological into the political. In this way, Derrida illuminates that rethinking the secular today, and especially how the theological-political nexus relates to the foundation of politics and knowledge, requires rethinking the nature of political authority and normativity beyond the modern epistemological confidence that fundamentalism falls only in the camp of religion, or that it follows from a lack of separation between the theological and the political.[69] As such, his intervention questions the epistemic privilege of Enlightenment secularism in matters of public life[70] and opens the space to a variety of views and traditions that do not support such a separation but are not for that reason to be dismissed as inconsequential to peaceful communal life.[71]

4

Democracy beyond Secularism?

I have suggested that Derrida's perspective on the secular questions the binary and fundamentalist logic of the modern paradigm that self-assuredly prioritizes reason over faith and that radically separates the theological from the political. By exposing the metaphysical assumptions and political risks associated to this model, his political thought breaks with conventional conceptualizations and reorients discussions about the secular domain towards a more relational approach. While my interpretation has explicitly highlighted the implications of this view for a more critical understanding of the political, it has raised, but not yet investigated, its impact on issues of political community.

In this chapter, I take up this matter and explore Derrida's reflections on democracy in the context of the "theological-political complex" with a view to reflecting on the nexus between democracy and secularism that Derrida himself left somewhat undeveloped. I do so by focusing primarily on *Rogues,* where Derrida offers his most focused treatment of democracy through the notion of what he calls "democracy to come" in connection to issues of sovereignty, freedom, and equality.[1] I suggest that, without rejecting the separation between religious and state powers, his view helps denaturalizing *secular* understandings of democracy, thereby offering resources to think about political community beyond secularism. In this way, Derrida clears a space for religious and not-religious positions, in the West and beyond, that offer important contributions to democratic thinking and practices without embracing modern secularism.

Democracy, Sovereignty, and Political Theology

In *Rogues,* Derrida discusses "democracy to come." He starts from an exploration of the idea of sovereignty, which he considers with reference to a long tradition of political theology as well as international law and politics linked to Greek and European legal history (*FWT*, 146–48/235–40), idioms, and cultures (*R*, 32/56). Sovereignty, he notes elsewhere, is the indivisible and absolute "power to *give,* to *make,* but also to *suspend* the law; it is the exceptional right to place oneself above right, the right to non-right" (*BS 1,* 6/37). Located above the law, sovereignty has "the power of life and death over the subjects" and of deciding "what is proper to man" (*FWT,* 144/233, 147/239).² In his view, this definition of sovereignty characterizes European legal history, one caught between the biblical tradition that instituted the penal code after God's commandment "Thou shalt not kill," and the philosophical tradition that has hardly ever contested the legitimacy of the death penalty (*FWT,* 146–48/235–40).³

For Derrida, the link between democracy and sovereignty appears clearly if one considers the former as a form of sovereign power, as the original Greek articulation of democracy suggests. "Democracy would be precisely this, a force (*kratos*), a force in the form of sovereign authority (sovereign, that is, *kurios* or *kuros,* having the power to decide, to be decisive, to prevail, to have reason over or win out over [*avoir raison de*] and to give force of law, *kuroô*), and thus the power and *ipseity* of the people" (*dēmos*) (13/33). Democracy is defined as the power (*kratos*) of a people (*demos*) capable of deciding and enforcing law. This definition points to an idea of selfhood that is presupposed every time a sovereign authority is at stake, an idea that is best captured by what Derrida calls *ipseity.*

> Before any sovereignty of the state, of the nation-state, of the monarch, or, in democracy, of the people, ipseity names a principle of legitimate sovereignty, the accredited or recognized supremacy of a power or a force, a *kratos* or a *cracy.* That is what is implied, posed, presupposed, but also imposed in the very position, in the very self- or autopositing, of *ipseity itself,* everywhere there is some oneself, the first, ultimate, and supreme source of every "reason of the strongest" as the right [*droit*] granted to force or the force granted to law [*loi*]. (12/31–32)

In this quote, we find the two essential features of democracy as a form of sovereignty: a type of selfhood (*ipseity*) displaying the supreme source of authority and a type of reason that, supported by force, founds the law. By selecting these two features Derrida is privileging an understanding of democracy from the point of view of its foundation or functioning in exceptional cases over the regular functioning of it as the shared government of the people.[4]

Starting with the first feature, what is *ipseity* exactly? Referring, in Latin, to the idea of "self" and "same," or to what in Greek is *autos* (self, same) and in English selfhood, *ipseity* evokes the figure of the wheel and the rotating movement of the self's return to itself, which precedes the distinction between *physis* and its others (*nomos, techne, thesis*) and is implied in the notion of self-determination (10/29). In determining itself, in giving itself its own law, the self has a power to cause the unconditional and immediate return of the self to itself as its end. Understood as *ipseity*, then, sovereignty represents a force of self-constitution and self-legislation supported by a forceful reason that initiates a circular motion of relating or returning to itself as its own end. This motion exposes sovereignty's unconditional, indivisible, and unitary character since it establishes a circular and immediate identification of the cause with the end. Yet this is not the only sense Derrida attaches to the idea of the wheel. We shall explore below how rotation for him means also alternation, alteration, and return to the self in nonimmediate and autoimmunitary fashion (18/39).

For Derrida, the circularity of *ipseity* displays the theological features that Western political thinkers have, more or less, explicitly associated with sovereignty, including its democratic form. These features appear most clearly in Alex de Tocqueville's *Democracy in America*, where he affirms that "the people reign over the American political world as God rules over the universe. It is the cause and the end of all things; everything rises out of it and it is absorbed back into it" (14/34). For Derrida, Tocqueville's affirmation goes beyond rhetoric and signals deeper philosophical convictions. Besides invoking God as the figure in which the rotating wheel reaches its perfection (i.e., God is the cause and end of everything), Tocqueville connects democratic sovereignty to a version of political theology inaugurated by the Greeks. His view of democracy as God resembles the figure of the Prime Mover that Aristotle discusses in the *Metaphysics* and links to Greek mythology. In this work, Derrida recalls, Aristotle characterizes the *energia* of the Prime Mover as a pure actuality, a principle of self-sufficiency setting everything in a circular motion whose final end is the non-mediated return to itself. He defines this first principle as "God" and "as a life (*diagōgē*)" that is "at once desired, desirable (*erōmenon, to proton orekton*), and partaking in pleasure," a definition that poses autoaffection as a circular and theologically inflected model of selfhood (*ipseity*) (15/35). This model, Derrida notes in *The Beast and the Sovereign*, is also at work in the *Politics*, where Aristotle offers an "an ontological definition of sovereignty" (*BS 1*, 345–46/458). Since Aristotle considers the principle of self-sufficiency—of which the Prime Mover is the highest example—as the best for the life of the polis, he establishes the circularity implied in self-sufficiency as the model of sovereign selfhood par excellence.

Derrida's interest in the *Metaphysics* extends beyond sovereignty's circularity to reach the theological grounding Aristotle gives to his argument. Derrida emphasizes Aristotle's use of a political analogy that *seemingly* anchors the unitary character of the Prime Mover to a mythological model of indivisible sovereignty articulated by Homer in the *Iliad*. Opposing the government of many to champion that of the one, Homer refers to Zeus as he who wins over his father, Cronos, and asserts his sovereignty as the god of all kings. Derrida reads Homer's claim, to which Aristotle refers and acknowledges as having a certain authority at the end of book 12, as declaring the sovereignty of indivisibility and unity over multiplicity. By relying on the authority of Homer and on his view of sovereign authority, Aristotle, for Derrida, subscribes to what will become a long tradition of political theology.

> This theogonic mythology of sovereignty belongs, if it does not actually inaugurate, a long cycle of political theology that is at once paternalistic and patriarchal, and thus masculine, in the filiation fathers-son-brother. I would also call it ipsocentric. This political theogony or theology gets revived and taken over (despite the claims to the contrary by such experts as Bodin and Hobbes, whom I cannot treat here) by a so called modern political theology of monarchic sovereignty and even by the unavowed political theology—itself just as phallocentric, phallo-paterno-filio-fraterno-iposcentric—of the sovereignty of the people, that is, of democratic sovereignty. The attribute "ipsocentric" intersects and links with a dash all the others (those of the phallus, of the father, of the husband, son or brother). *Ipsocentric* could even be replaced by ipso*cratic*, were that not a pleonasm, for the idea of force (kratos), of power, and of mastery, that is analytically included in the concept of ipseity. (*R*, 17/38)

For Derrida, democracy and sovereignty are linked by a long tradition of political theology that connects ancient conceptualizations of sovereignty as theological, ipsocentric, and masculine to contemporary ones. What is distinctive about this view is not that democracy is a form of sovereignty, but that the source of its authority is connected to an "unavowed" theological idea of sovereign agency displaying theological features and sexual biases. As mentioned in the previous chapter in connection to Schmitt, the traditional conceptualization of democracy based on fraternization as model of friendship is characterized by the oblivion and neutralization of sexual difference that affects fundamental understandings of such key concepts to the "theological-political complex" as citizenship and sovereignty. Above all, it embraces forms of racialized thinking to conceptualize political life, including democracy, "in whose heritage one inevitably meets again the law of birth, the natural or the "national" law, the law of homophilia or of autochthony" in the form of a symbolic fraternization seen as the model of social bonding (*PF*, 104/127, 99/122).

Derrida illustrates the aforementioned claim about sovereignty by exploring some canonical figures of Western political thought.[5] Starting with Plato and Aristotle, he claims that the *Statesmen* and *Politics* are works in which a theological model of sovereignty appears through the unitary and indivisible character of God that is often invoked as an evaluative standard for the classification of regimes, including democracy. While Plato invokes God with reference to the model constitution, "a god among men" (*hoion theon ex anthrōpōn*), which democracy resembles, Aristotle uses the same formulation to address the regime of a model ruler of such a pre-eminent excellence that he would need no law as he would be himself the law.[6] Although Derrida does not sufficiently stress Aristotle's emphasis on the plurality of the state as opposed to Plato's idea of unity and that neither beast nor God-like individuals should be part of the polis, he does highlight that both Plato and Aristotle reiterate the aforementioned tradition of political theology to the extent that they either conceive of and praise (Plato), or conceive of but not unquestionably praise (Aristotle), a theological model of sovereignty as indivisible.[7]

Moving to the modern period, Derrida investigates, in addition to Tocqueville, Bodin, and Hobbes, whom he mentions in *Rogues* but discusses in *The Beast and The Sovereign*. He refers to passages from these authors' major works suggesting that their theories rely on a divine model which shapes the figure of the sovereign on the basis of God's image. Beginning with Bodin, Derrida quotes a passage from chapter 8 of *Six Books of the Republic*: "For if Justice is the end of law, law of the work of the prince, the prince the *image* of God; then by this reasoning, the law of the prince must be *modeled* on the law of God" (*BS 1*, 48/79) He argues that, by modeling the sovereign and state law on the image of God and divine law respectively, Bodin presents a view of human sovereignty that is theological and ipsocentric and that does not save the autonomy of the political, but reaffirms its dependency on the theological.

Hobbes's model of sovereignty is not clearly emancipated from political theology either. In opposition to many commentators who consider Hobbes's view of sovereignty as purely political, Derrida hypothesizes that it might instead retain "a profound and fundamental theological and religious basis." His arguments rely on two points. First, Hobbes's theory, despite its conventional outlook, is based on a divine model, as the opening pages of the *Leviathan* suggest: "'Artificial Animal' that the Leviathan is, imitates the natural art of God" (47/78). Second, Hobbes does not fully exclude God from the political covenant, thereby failing to rule out a theological foundation of politics.[8]

If modern thinkers do not fully emancipate their theories of sovereignty from traditional political theology, later ones do not fare much differently. For Derrida, Schmitt represents the paradigmatic modern thinker of sovereignty who still conceptualizes it in theological and ipsocentric terms. What interests Derrida in Schmitt's view is the link between the sovereign's decisionist exceptionality and indivisibility, which "excludes it [sovereignty] in principle from being shared, from time and from language" (*R*, 101/144). To constitute itself, the sovereign exceptionally withdraws from the dividing passing of time *in* which he, nevertheless, operates and from the shareability of the language *in* which he makes his own authority universally meaningful, justified, and effective *post facto*. This situation indicates, on the one hand, that an "unavowable silence" characterizes sovereignty since the latter can only establish itself in its retraction from language through a decision. Yet this silence cannot last long. For as soon as someone speaks about, gives meaning to, or seeks to justify sovereignty and as soon as the latter is operative (i.e., it operates *in* time or takes time in order to operate), an element of sharing (in language) or divisibility (in time) is introduced, which shows that "pure sovereignty [indivisible] does not exist" (101/104).

On the other hand, the constitution of sovereignty displays the force required in order to retract from the mediating conditions in which, and through which, it operates such as time and language. And this, for Derrida, suggests that "abuse of power is constitutive of sovereignty itself," which "can only tend towards imperial hegemony." Because it operates in time and language "sovereignty can only *tend*, for a limited time, to reign without sharing" (102/146). The process through which sovereignty protects and yet compromises its own unity is what Derrida's notion of autoimmunity, a form of both self-protection and self-destruction, tries to capture. Although sovereignty is indivisible, it needs "divisions" (time and language) in order to function, and these compromise the immunity of its indivisibility (101/144). This suggests that sovereignty is "always in the process of positing itself, by refuting itself," of positing its immunity and suspending it, hence its autoimmunity. I will come back to the autoimmunity of sovereignty in more detail below.

According to Derrida, the novelty and importance of Schmitt's understanding of sovereignty is that it displays theological and ipsocentric features through a notion of sovereignty *qua* exceptionality. It is not simply because the sovereign operates as an ipsocentric self that indivisibility is gained. Sovereignty *qua* indivisibility is made possible at all because the sovereign determines himself in the exception by immunizing himself against time, language, and more generally from anything that points to contamination, differentiation, and shareability. Viewed in the context of Derrida's critique of the metaphysics of presence discussed earlier on, and more generally of "White mythology," this exceptional immunization relies on a separatist logic supported by an ethnocentric, indeed racialized, mythology. It is grounded in the enforcement of political determinations that are informed by a fictional discourse on origins that naturalize them in order to provide the unity of representations and ultimately of political community. Put simply, Derrida's point is that whenever origins are invoked and naturalized in a political discourse about sovereignty, racism is not very far away. Indeed, reading his position on Schmitt and on sovereignty more generally in conjunction with his brief reflections on South Africa's apartheid brings to the fore a structural link between a political theology of indivisible sovereignty and the separatist logic of racism. Just as the former relies on the possibility of grasping pure origins in the form of abstract universal concepts in order to effect clear-cut determinations—friend and enemy, but also religion and politics—so too does the latter employ a rhetoric of pure distinctions in order to justify the discrimination, and not simply discernment, of difference on the basis of which the setting apart (hence *apart*heid) of human groups occurs (RLW, 292/387).

Thus, for Derrida, the forceful self-exclusion from time and language, as conditions characterizing any recognizable human predicament, is central to understanding the nature of sovereignty in Schmitt. This retraction places the sovereign, like God, beyond history and meaning. Most importantly, it exposes the paradox of sovereignty, namely, that sovereignty is incompatible with the universality of the law it establishes. Because it forcefully constitutes itself through withdrawal, sovereignty jeopardizes the universality implied in the law, that is, its meaningful applicability to all in given place, thereby indicating that "there is no sovereignty without force, without the force of the strongest, whose reason—the reason of the strongest—is to win out over [*avoir raison de*] everything" (*R*, 101/144).

It is in this context that Derrida connects his discussion of sovereign exceptionality to contemporary examples of democratic sovereignty and to the term "rogue," giving the title, in the plural, to his book *Rogues*. He draws attention to the racial connotation of "rogue" (*voyou*), which is used "for a marking or branding classification that sets something apart" and informs "a banishing or exclusion" both of those considered deviant—including those of "mixed origins" populating the "suburbs," the "unemployed," those found "loitering"—and states which resist or violate international law as the "reason of the strongest."

Derrida focuses especially on states (63/95, 68/101, 94/135). He notes that it is specifically with reference to how "rogue" has been used since the 1990s by several American governments in order to identify, condemn, and often unilaterally attack, both terrorist organizations and states that were violating international law, a law considered democratic and regulating supposedly democratic institutions such as the United Nations (99/142). Derrida recalls that, since 1993, the American government declared that it would make use of Article 51 of the Charter of the United Nations whenever it deemed it appropriate to defend vital US interests. Representing the only exception—hence the link to Schmitt—to the jurisdiction of the United Nations Security Council, Article 51 recognizes the individual or collective right of defense against an armed attack until the council has taken the necessary measures to restore international peace and security. For Derrida, it is by focusing on the exceptionality of sovereignty in the international context that the notion of "rogue state" needs to be understood. The appeal to "rogue state" to justify a unilateral, sovereign intervention in a shared international arena signals that rogue, in fact, describes the United States itself—the state among the most powerful in the UN Security Council that mostly uses the rhetoric of "rogue states" to act in violation of the international law it claims to defend (96/139). By pointing out that the states that dub other states rogue are themselves the rogues, Derrida connects the notion of "rogue" to the "logic" of what is considered legitimate sovereignty: "[T]he states that are able or are in a state to make war on rogue states are themselves, in their most *legitimate sovereignty*, rogue states abusing their power. As soon as there is sovereignty there is abuse of power and a rogue state" (my emphasis). In other words, abuse of power is the logic characterizing the legitimate sovereignty of many democratic states, one that indicates that sovereignty "can reign only by not sharing" (102/146). Examples illustrating this logic are not difficult to find, especially after September 11. The recourse to sovereign exceptionality to abuse power in order to suspend both domestic and international law on the part of the United States, along with some other states, is public knowledge.

Although focusing mainly on indivisibility, Derrida's view of democracy as sovereignty does not overlook central features of modern democracy. While Derrida acknowledges that democracy refers also to heterogeneity, multiplicity, and division, and he recognizes that modern democratic sovereignty imposes limits on the theologically justified privileges of the king, he highlights that the reference to unity, unconditionality, and indivisibility, or more simply *ipseity*, continues to mark its nature. Despite the Lockeian-Montesquieuan institutional division of powers that characterizes modern democratic regimes, democracy, for Derrida, is tied back to the people, conceived as an ipso-centric, unified agent as both his discussion of Tocqueville above, and the analysis of the American Declaration of Independence presented in chapter 3, show, especially in relation to naturalization of the nation as the modern model of political community.

Now, for Derrida, the locus of the problem with modern democracy is that the agent exercising the sovereign function retains the prerogative of withdrawal from the law that is revived in times of exception. Although modern democracy is characterized by a constitutionally divided sovereignty, its constituting power is informed by a conception of selfhood that still presents theological features. The issue here is not simply the indivisible and thus in some sense undemocratic—because annulling the multiplicity inherent to democracy—form that sovereignty must take in order to make democracy an effective political regime.[9] The issue here also concerns the undemocratic and potentially oppressive features a model of sovereignty based on theological exceptionality fosters when a supposedly shared power acts in defiance of sharing, as the example of rogue states shows. Derrida's lack of interest in thinkers of the liberal tradition—such as Montesquieu, Madison, Hamilton, and Adams, but also Constant and Mill—is surprising. He thus might appear to overlook the fact that a major thrust of modern theories of sovereignty concerns limiting the tyranny of the majority over minorities and individuals. Yet his interest in early modern theorists of sovereignty—such as Bodin and Hobbes—can be taken as furthering the same limiting, but from another angle. It is because democratic sovereignty retains the prerogative of being indivisible in virtue of its model of selfhood constituted through a divine-like exceptionality, and in spite of the constitutional division of powers, that minorities and pluralism might be at risk. The recourse to sovereign exceptionality to suspend the civil liberties of targeted minorities or individuals after September 11 in the United States or at Guantanamo Bay is a good illustration of this point.

The emphasis on force mentioned above introduces the other element characterizing sovereignty, including its democratic version, announced at the outset: the nonoppositional association of animal force and reason that Derrida discusses in *The Beast and the Sovereign*. For him, Jean de La Fontaine's fable *The Wolf and the Lamb* best exemplifies this association in its opening line: "[T]he reason of the strongest is always the best." This line refers to the story of the wolf who justifies its tyranny over the lamb with force and introduces the analogy between beast (wolf) and sovereign, one that Derrida sees as being recurrent in political philosophy, especially in the modern period. Following the tradition of political thought since Aristotle, Derrida claims that man is understood not simply as a political animal but as a political man, who, in his sovereignty, is both superior to the beast, which he masters, and like a beast in the manifestation of his political sovereignty (*BS 1*, 26/50).

To support this claim, he refers again to canonical (Western) political thinkers, including Machiavelli, Hobbes, and Rousseau. For example, in the *Prince*, Machiavelli appeals to the figure of the beast to paradigmatically speak about political sovereignty. He shows that since princes are forced by necessity to fight not only according to law, which is proper to man, but also according to force, which is appropriate to beasts, "it *is necessary* for a prince to know how to use *as appropriate the beast and the man*" (84/124–25). Similarly, Derrida observes that Hobbes appeals to the allegory of a monstrous animal in the *Leviathan* and presents state sovereignty as an indivisible force that supposes the right of man over the animal and that is stronger than man in order to protect him (29/53). Finally, Derrida notes that Rousseau makes creditable (*accrédite*) the analogy between the political sovereign and the beast used by Caligula, whom he mentions in book 1 of the *Social Contract*. By doing so, Rousseau too appropriates the analogy between the beast and the sovereign, despite the fact that this view violates his concern for equality.

Besides illustrating the connection between beast and sovereign, Derrida's brief discussion of Rousseau, Hobbes, and Machiavelli provides the occasion to explain why that association has been so powerful and recurrent in (modern) political thought. The sovereign, like the beast, is "outside the law" where "outside" can mean "at distance from," "above," or refer to a place where the law "does not appear, or is not respected, or gets violated" (17/38). That discussion also illustrates that the sovereign is like the beast because he uses force to affirm (his) reason. For Derrida, this is the problem of sovereignty, the problem of a force that "because it is indispensable to the exercise of right, because it is implied in the very concept of right, would give right or found right, and would give reason *in advance* to force" (my emphasis) (207/ 278–79). This problem runs through the Western tradition of political thought, especially in those discussions that associate justice with the right to force.[10]

The question arises, then, what type of reason is the reason given by the sovereign in general, and by the democratic sovereign in particular? Is it reason itself? Is it "the reason of the strongest" which "is always the best" as La Fontaine says? And, does "best" here refer to right or force? Derrida addresses these questions by discussing how the Western tradition has conceived of knowledge and reason, and, more precisely, of the authority of *logos*. On his reading, both reason and knowledge have been traditionally represented as sovereign, forceful powers that set indivisible limits. These representations involve the question of limit, of knowing what a limit is, whether it is divisible or indivisible, and what its origin is. They imply, in other words, the "question of the *arkhē*," which means "both commencement and commandment" and is thus a "figure of the sovereign himself" (312/416). While briefly mentioning the biblical traditions and only in passing Plato's definition of reason as the "reason given" by a sovereign power, Derrida focuses mostly on Aristotle's discussion of *logos* and *zōē* in the *Politics* and on the problematic type of Greek logos his view gives rise to (208/279).[11] He observes that Aristotle's definition of man as a rational animal (*zōon logon ekhon*) capable of reason (*logos*) and who is "by nature a political living being" links *logos* to the political by following a method that goes back to the origin and thus to the *arkhē* (344/456). In a single stroke, both man and the political are defined in terms of *logos*: "[M]an as political animal is indissociable from the definition of man as having the *logos, logon ekhon*" (347/460).

For Derrida, the problem with Aristotle's perspective rests on the operation effected by the conceptualization of *logos* as reason and as a power to establish the limits of the human, the animal, and the political. Following Heidegger, Derrida emphasizes that Aristotle's view ignores the contestable meaning of *logos*[12] and life (*zōē*),[13] and, in doing so, it "overcomes [*a raison de*] another interpretation or several other interpretations or ways of hearing *logos*," thereby showing that reason operates through imposed translations. Derrida does not save Heidegger from this accusation either, noting that his claim about reason as gathering to be more originary than reason as *logos* is but another example of forced translation. In both cases, the issue at stake in the definition of *logos* as reason and as a power that sets limits is one of forced translations that become dominant after "a conflict of forces in which reason wins by force" has occurred (318/424). It is in this sense of "forced hegemony" that Derrida has talked of European logocentrism as designating an operation that, in gathering together the biblical and philosophical traditions, represents *logos* at "the center of everything," in a position "of sovereign hegemony, organizing everything on the basis of its forced translations": a key feature of "White mythology" (343/455).

The American Declaration of Independence constitutes a good illustration of Derrida's point about the idea of democratic sovereignty as implying forced translation supported by reason. As mentioned in chapter 3, the Declaration was regarded by the founding fathers as referring to *one* united people, descending from the *same* ancestors, speaking the *same* language, and committed to the *same* political principles. Yet a closer look at the context in which it occurred reveals that the Declaration sanctioned the exclusions of groups, languages, and understandings present in the original thirteen US states. Viewed from this angle, the Declaration can be considered as an event in which the creation of *one* people was made possible by a naturalization based on forced translations of political values, and understandings according to a univocal language that was then enforced and made hegemonic in the American territory.

Derrida's point about the sovereign hegemony of reason marks the culmination of the analogy between the beast and the sovereign and illuminates why sovereignty has been conceptualized as a power of self-determination that combined force and reason. The sovereign, like the beast, uses force to affirm himself. Yet, unlike the beast, he "gives reason to force in advance" in order to *force* translations that become hegemonic. This operation is not successful when reason and force oppose each other but when "force is on the side of reason and wins out, a bit like 'the reason of the strongest'" of La Fontaine's fable (319/425). In this way, the "reason" of sovereignty does not only designate the "reason given" but also the right the sovereign has to judge as just, legitimate, and prevailing "the reason he gives because he is the strongest" (208/280).

Drawing together Derrida's reflections on sovereignty, we can now recapitulate his view of democracy as a sovereign power. Connected to a long tradition in the West that conceives of it as theological, ipsocentric, and masculine but not always self-consciously so, democracy is a power of self-determination that forces translations about the relevant epistemic and ethico-political values of a given place. Situated above the law, this power not only makes and suspends the law, but it also retains the exclusive prerogative to decide on questions of life and death, on what life is and on what is proper to political life. This means, Derrida notes in *Rogues*, that for democracy to be effective and prevail over other regimes, a sovereign power of a unitary agent, the people, is required, namely, "a force that is stronger than all other forces in the world" (R, 100/143). This power refers to "the reason of the strongest" that determines with theological features and animal force the conceptual architecture and political boundaries that establish the frame—military, political, linguistic, economic, and philosophical—in which democratic life takes place. As seen in the discussion of political foundings, and more broadly with reference to Derrida's notion of "White mythology," this frame is constituted on the basis of violent exclusions of human, philosophical, and political alternatives of which indigenous, sexual, ethnic, racial, and religious groups are relevant examples. These exclusions are instrumental in establishing political arrangements and relations of force that determine a unified political identity by securing, legalizing, and legitimating *après coup* the justificatory discourse about relevant representations and criteria for membership. While the sovereign force constituting democracy is supposed to protect democracy itself and its universal aspirations, it threatens democracy from within since an indivisible force constitutes its core, one on which the constitutional division of powers relies and ends up protecting.

Yet, since democracy points also to divisibility, multiplicity, and heterogeneity, all of which counter sovereign *ipseity*, it can be considered as interrupting that very model. For Derrida, one influential source for this view is Rousseau's idea that a genuine democracy—which has never existed and will never exist because it is contrary to the natural order—would be possible only if there were gods. By introducing an element of plurality and division in the word "gods," Rousseau challenges the unity and indivisibility of sovereignty and "announces democracy or at least some democracy beyond government and democratic sovereignty" even though his own discourse remains anchored to the political theology of indivisible sovereignty (75/110).

But it is in connection to his discussion of democracy as "democracy to come" that Derrida's view of sovereignty beyond indivisibility takes a more incisive form. In *Rogues*, he calls for a conceptualization of democracy beyond sovereignty's indivisibility through the notion of autoimmunity. As seen above, when associated with sovereignty, autoimmunity illustrates that sovereignty's effectiveness is constitutively linked to the impossibility of its indivisibility. This holds insofar as autoimmunity refers to the suicidal feature of the life of the self, whose immunity and unity are threatened from within. As Derrida notes, autoimmunity "consists not only in destroying one's own protections" and "in compromising oneself [*s'auto-entamer*] but in compromising the self, the *autos*—and thus ipseity" (45/71). In this framework, Derrida suggests that today's politico-philosophical task is to distinguish "sovereignty (which is in principle indivisible) from 'unconditionality'" without giving in to relativism or to a blind battle against sovereignty as such (xiv/13).[14] This means, on the one hand, preserving sovereignty contextually and with increased response-ability according to the specificity of situations. As he notes, "one cannot combat, *head-on*, *all* sovereignty, sovereignty *in general*" without threatening at the same time "the classical principles of freedom and self-determination" typical of the nation-state which, in some cases, acts as an essential protection against international and hegemonic powers, whether these are of political, linguistic, philosophical, economic, or religious nature (158/216). On the other hand, it means unconditionally calling into question and limiting the logic of political sovereignty and with it the ideas of indivisibility, exceptionality, and unity.

But what does this mean concretely? For Derrida, it means mobilizing theoretical sources that seek to democratize the indivisible sovereignty of democratic nation-states, international institutions, and law by challenging a foundational thinking of sovereignty as a pure idea and thus its potential of for producing racial, sexual, cultural, and religious hierarchies. Informed by this type of thinking, these institutions have ended up supporting, however surreptitiously, "the reason of the strongest" in both domestic and international affairs. This challenge requires decentering the geopolitical and philosophical grounding of sovereignty within the West and its cultural representations. As Derrida pointedly says in *The Other Heading*: "It is necessary to recall ourselves not only of the *other heading*, and especially to the *heading of the other*, but also perhaps to the *other of the heading*, that is to say, to a relation of identity with the other that no longer obeys the form, the sign, or the logic of the heading, nor even of the *anti-heading*—of beheading, of decapitation" (*OH*, 15/21). In other words, when rethinking sovereignty, as a figure of the heading, it is necessary to consider divisions within it that illuminate not simply what has been other to Western modernity in its formation ("the other heading"), which our discussion of Schmitt has identified pre-eminently in Islam. It is also necessary to consider conceptualizations of sovereignty rooted in other traditions ("the heading of the other") but also differences internal to identity ("the other of the heading") that the logic of the heading typical of Western philosophy tends to repress, without however renouncing all sovereignty ("anti-heading"). With a gesture similar to his discourse of a New International in *Specters of Marx*, Derrida advocates for, as he puts it in *Rogues*, "the creation of an international juridico-political space that, without doing away with every reference to sovereignty, never stops innovating and inventing new distributions and forms of sharing, new divisions of sovereignty" (*R*, 87/127).[15] Note here the emphasis Derrida puts on invention, which he conceives of as the task of a nonteleological reason that strives to open space for novelty to occur and be received.[16] Connected to the democratization of the international political order, invention becomes a matter of destabilizing traditional discourses about sovereignty and of questioning sovereign institutions (especially the nation-states and international law) so as to open the way for conceiving of new forms of power sharing that limit indivisible sovereignty and unilateral impositions.

What Derrida tries to do is move away from thinking about sovereignty as a pure idea that remains too close to a theological model geopolitically fixed in the West and marked by sexualized and racialized features. He focuses, instead, on issues of translation and division that expose indivisibility to sharing, division, and difference. This shift is to be understood in the context of his understanding of language and critique of metaphysical thinking, both of which, as seen, put limits on foundationalism and racialized thinking while pointing towards experiences of translation and relationality. It is also to be understood in the context of his view of autoimmunity, which undermines the political theology of indivisible sovereignty. While this shift might appear to be purely theoretical, it is related to the practical manifestation of autoimmunitary processes affecting the life of political institutions. Here, Derrida has in mind situations in which the universality of human rights is used to put limits to, and to challenge, the sovereignty of the nation-state, as in the case of crimes against humanity or war crimes (87/127–28). Unlike liberal humanitarianism, however, his view does not attempt to go beyond nation-state sovereignty in the name of some principle of humanity as invoked in human rights discourses. While Derrida insists on their crucial importance and supports them, he emphasizes that human rights are informed by a principle of humanity and, as such, still presuppose a political theology of sovereign selfhood that might be dangerously used, if one follows Schmitt's sharp criticism of it, as an ideological instrument of imperialism (87–88/128).[17]

What should we make, then, of Derrida's proposal about how to rethink democratic sovereignty? It is clear that Derrida advocates for a view of democratic sovereignty as an internally divided form of power, one that is shared beyond the simple division of powers, divided in its selfhood. Yet, it remains unclear what exactly such sovereignty would look like, how it would work in national and international contexts, and with which implications. Further, the willingness to retain current sovereignty contextually raises questions about the extent to which Derrida's view breaks, or seeks to break with, the political theology he criticizes. Granted that these are outstanding issues of his view of sovereignty, we can, nevertheless, emphasize that his perspective opens a path for thinking differently about sovereignty and thus also about a concept of the political that is both theological and racial. Derrida's point is that by paying more attention to time and language as media displaying the relationality of the human predicament, we can gain a more complex understanding of sovereignty's exposure to division, shareability, and difference. Because of its existence *in* time and language, sovereignty can only *be* "by refuting itself," namely, by refuting its own indivisibility, unity, and nondifferentiation in its very selfhood: it can only be autoimmune (101/144). This is what dominant modern theories of sovereignty have obscured by protecting the inner core of sovereignty through a division of powers "external" to the sovereign selfhood of the people, indeed of the nation as *the* relevant political identity of the modern state, powers that remain themselves sovereign and thus indivisible.

So conceived, Derrida's view has important consequences for expanding the horizon of theoretical debates but also for the practical effects of calling for (more) power sharing in critical questions concerning domestic and international law and politics as well as economics. Indeed, far from being a battle against the will of the people as the "will of God," his view helps illuminate that the "higher sovereignty" of multinational international corporations operates precisely according to some form of theological exceptionality that allows them to escape the sovereign control of states and to maintain unequal and nonshared international relations of power.

The significance of Derrida's view of democratic sovereignty for the "theological-political complex" lies especially in its critical potential. His perspective points to the limits of thinking about democracy as a form of sovereignty of the people conceived as an ipsocentric agent. Derrida not only exposes the persistence of theological tropes in the political discourse and practice of democracy, in spite of the purely secular, namely, nonreligious, terms in which political life is often portrayed. He also indicates that as much as the indivisibility of sovereignty is untenable, so are the indivisible limits between the theological and the political that traditional secular understandings of democracy have sought to establish by paradoxically appealing to theological sources. Indeed, by thinking together reason and force as nonopposed features of sovereignty, and by distinguishing unconditionality from sovereign indivisibility—that is, by thinking about sovereignty through autoimmunity—Derrida exposes the contestability of philosophical distinctions seeking to establish indivisible (i.e., sovereign) limits between human beings, humans and animals, life and death, what is political and what is not political, limits that remain fragile because they are grounded in force. In this way, he clears an analytical space for thinking about sovereignty beyond traditional political theology without, nevertheless, fully doing away with it.

Rethinking Democratic Freedom and Equality

Freedom and equality constitute the other relevant features of Derrida's discussion of democracy.[18] At the beginning of *Rogues*, Derrida states that the notion of "democracy to come" presents an ambiguity that is related to the variations historically associated with democracy. Since its conception in Ancient Greece, democracy does not refer to a word with a stable, univocal meaning, but to one whose meaning freely changes. This observation leads him to claim that there is a "freedom of play, an opening indetermination and undecidability *in the very concept* of democracy" (*R*, 25/47).

For Derrida, the possibility of historically molding the meaning of democracy suggests that democracy does not designate a traditional concept. Instead, it refers to "a concept without a concept," to a conceptual empty space that can be filled with different and historically determined understandings of what democracy means.[19] Indeed, although it is linked to the Greek and then European idioms and cultures that imported the Greek *dēmokratia* into the Latin *democratia*, it is not obvious that "there exist in Greek a stable, and univocal meaning of the democratic itself" (32/56). On his reading, it is Plato who anticipates this view when, in the *Republic*, he describes democracy as a multicolored regime. For Derrida, it is more than a regime since it is like "a supermarket of constitutions" where anyone interested in founding a state can go in order to pick the desired model. By articulating democracy as neither a regime nor a constitution, Plato already announces the freedom and semantic indeterminacy typical of democracy that also informs "democracy to come."[20]

But what interests Derrida in the Greek tradition is that it offers the resources to think of democratic freedom and equality differently, particularly through the idea of autoimmunity. To recall it, autoimmunity refers to a process of self-protection through the destruction of one's own defenses that affects life.[21] Associated with democracy, it designates a trait of a political community that cultivates as a principle of self-protection the possibility of self-sacrifice, a sort of Freudian death-drive that enables protection through self-destruction (157/215). For Derrida, the autoimmunity of the Greek understanding of democracy appears if one reflects on the aporia generated by the freedom at play in the concept of democracy, one that impedes a final configuration of the relationship between freedom and equality. He recalls that for both Plato and Aristotle, democracy is marked by freedom and by equality according to number (for both) and according to worth (for Aristotle only). This view allows for a paradoxical outcome: in order to preserve its freedom, democracy leaves free and in a position to exercise power those who, once in majority, could attack democracy's freedom and put an end to it, in the name of democracy itself. This paradox reflects the difficulty of negotiating the freedom of the *demos* as a collective and the freedom of each of its members, namely, of reconciling freedom and equality. For Derrida, this is "one of the many perverse and autoimmune effects of the axiomatic developed already in Plato and Aristotle"; "in the name of one couple, the couple made up of freedom and equality, one agrees to a law of number or the laws of numbers (equality according to number) that ends up destroying both couples" (34/58). Although Derrida does not mention it explicitly, we can say that this is the aporia later thinkers of democracy also grappled with. Whether by ensuring democratic equality over individual freedom as in Rousseau, or by protecting liberty against the tyranny of the majority and its leveling equality as in Tocqueville and Mill, modern thinkers of democracy too responded to the problem of balancing freedom and equality in order to limit the dangerous potential of either.

On Derrida's reading, then, there is something suicidal about democracy: in order to preserve itself as such, democracy allows for the possibility of its own destruction, hence its autoimmune character. In ancient times, Aristotle limited this suicidal aspect by restricting democratic freedom through the democratic equality guaranteed by alternation in ruling. Although modern understandings of democracy have enriched and developed this view of alternation, the risk of self-destruction has not faded away. As Derrida notes, "the great question of modern parliamentary and representative democracy, perhaps of all democracy, in this logic of the turn or round of the other time and thus of the other, of the *alter* in general, is that the *alternative* to democracy can always be *represented* as a democratic *alternation*" (31/54). Without engaging more recent and complex scholarship on liberal democracy, Derrida seeks to highlight here that the autoimmunity of democracy has played, and still plays, a central role in political life, one of "autoimmune pervertibility" (34/59).[22] He supports this point by mentioning several examples throughout history: colonization and decolonization that both promised democracy but ended up leading to civil wars; the fascist and Nazi totalitarianism that ascended to power democratically; and finally, recent cases of "suspension of democracy" in in the United States where security concerns justified the curtailing of democratic freedoms in the battle against terrorism after September 11 but also and in his native Algeria where the 1992 democratic elections were interrupted to avoid the risk of an antidemocratic majoritarian government. While his example of Algeria is questionable, not least for the oppressive and ongoing consequences it led to, by the time Derrida was writing *Rogues*,[23] it was part of a larger reflection on the logic of autoimmunity applied to political community that has a broader scope, as I shall address in the next chapter.

For Derrida, Aristotle's idea that democratic freedom and equality informed by the idea of taking turns in government exposes the autoimmune process of democracy as a movement of sending off [*renvoi*] the moment and place in which democracy will take a conclusive form. This movement occurs in the complex relationship between space and time that, as seen in chapter 2, Derrida calls "spacing." It is a movement that consists in the local differentiation of the shape democracy will take and the temporal deferral of the final determination of its meaning and, as such, is connected to the notion of *différance*. By operating within this spatio-temporal schema, the sending off connected to the autoimmunity of democracy illuminates further why democracy is neither a static concept nor a fixed political form. As Derrida notes, democracy "is never properly what it is, never itself" because it defines itself "by this lack of the proper and the self-same," which destines it to be defined, in theory and practice, only "by turns" (37/61). Because it operates in space, the *renvoi* of democracy can represent both a "sending off *of* the other through exclusion" and a "sending off *to* the other" through inclusion and respect for difference. The variations on the scope of inclusion and exclusion to citizenship, on the more or less restrictive regulations on freedom of expression or other civil liberties that have historically marked different democratic regimes, are some examples of this type of *renvoi*. They indicate that it is hard to prove what *proper* democracy is or requires in terms of freedom and equality. Because it operates in time, the same *renvoi* calls for a "putting off [*renvoyer*]" until later the moment when a particular regime, whether nondemocratic or where democracy is at risk, will be ready for the advent or return of democracy. The deferral of elections in Iraq or Afghanistan after Western interventions in the 2000s or the suspension of elections in the already mentioned Algerian case are recent examples of the temporal side of democracy's *renvoi* (36/61).

By pointing to the suicidal logic of democracy and to instances that oppose it, Derrida does not celebrate antidemocratic elements. When discussing the case of Islam, he takes the side of democracy but also of configurations of religion and politics that are not foreign to Islamic history and experiences. In particular, he advocates for the hermeneutic task of pluralizing the interpretation of the Koranic heritage and its possible references to democracy as well as for joining forces with those who fight for the secularization of the political, that is, the separation between religious and state powers (31–33/55–57; see also, *IW*, 53/85). Nor does he suggest fundamentally altering the sovereign juridico-political framework (rule of law, border controls, restriction on the rights of citizenship, and so on) establishing those essential limits that guarantee the existence of any democratic political community.[24] Instead, his emphasis on the autoimmunity of democracy represents an attempt to think differently about freedom and equality in democracy.

Derrida believes that taking seriously the autoimmune logic of democracy opens up a space for thinking experimentally about democratic freedom and equality beyond the power or mastery of a sovereign subject and of reason reduced to calculability. While this constitutes a chance for novelty to occur, it also poses a threat to the very autonomy of the self. This aspect emerges particularly in his reflections on Nancy's *The Experience of Freedom*. In this work, Nancy attempts to think about freedom beyond autonomous mastery within an implicit but unrecognized autoimmunitary logic (52/79). Nancy claims that what is lacking today is a philosophy of democracy capable of thinking about freedom as sharing and not as the mastery or power (*kratos*) of a unitary subject. Taking as a premise the idea of sharing as spacing, Nancy seeks to identify a presubjective and precratic freedom that is unconditional and incommensurable but, nevertheless, equally shared, and calls this sharing fraternity. Although Derrida confesses that he lacks the tenacity of Nancy to question the entire ontology of freedom of the Western philosophical tradition, he claims that "in political philosophy the dominant discourse about democracy presupposes this freedom of power, faculty, or the ability to act, the force or strength, in short to do as one pleases, the energy of an intentional and deciding will" (44/69). While Derrida also emphasizes the difficulty of envisaging another experience of freedom that could be effective for democratic life, he seems, however, sympathetic to Nancy's project, particularly with respect to the logic of autoimmunity Nancy's view sustains. For Derrida, this logic is central to a novel understanding of freedom since it points beyond the view of a powerful, sovereign self and the image of the wheel and of the immediate, undifferentiated return of the self to itself. As seen, autoimmunity consists in compromising the self in its very selfhood (*ipseity*) and not simply in destroying one's own protections. It consists in a return to the self that is not immediate but, instead, characterized by a decisive alteration that brings, in some sense, death to the self (45/70). Viewed this way, the notion of autoimmunity opens up the possibility of thinking about democratic freedom beyond its understanding as power and mastery that has characterized many of its classical representations since the Greeks. Quoting relevant passages from the *Republic* and from the *Politics*, Derrida emphasizes that Plato and Aristotle generally treat democracy in terms of freedom and of freedom in terms of mastery or power. For example, while Plato portrays democratic man as one who has freedom conceived of as the "licence to do as he likes," Aristotle sees freedom as "the fundamental principle of the democratic form." Both views are informed by the idea that freedom (*eleutheria*) is associated with licence (*exousia*) or "the power to do as one pleases," a sovereign power connected to mastery as the capacity one has to do so (23/45, 43/69).

Although Derrida does not mention any other philosopher of the politico-philosophical tradition he invokes, we might, nevertheless, think that his claim about the "dominant discourse" about democracy and freedom in political philosophy refers to such thinkers as Rousseau and Kant and the republican idea of freedom as free will or autonomy as well as to Mill and the idea of liberal freedom as freedom to pursue ones' desires, to do as one pleases. Without overlooking the important differences among these thinkers and their various conceptions of freedom, we can take Derrida's point to mean that classical representations of freedom have all supposed freedom to involve a power of a sovereign subject, whether pursing the dictates of reason or desires.[25]

Clearly Derrida's claim about the "dominant discourse" needs more elaboration and engagement with key political thinkers. Nonetheless, we can highlight the potential offered by his view of autoimmunity. While recognizing that the task of uncoupling freedom as power or mastery from sovereignty is a difficult one, especially for both the theory and practice of democracy, Derrida sharpens some of the questions potentially needed to start thinking about democratic freedom beyond a political theology of sovereignty. As he affirms in *The Beast and the Sovereign*, attempting to overcome sovereignty would deny that "liberty and sovereignty are in many respects indissociable concepts" and "would also threaten the value of liberty" in the name of which and through which the idea of sovereignty is questioned. To start thinking about liberty differently would require acknowledging, on the one hand, the indissociable nexus between sovereignty and liberty and on the other, "putting up with" the idea that the question of sovereignty does not require making a decision between "indivisible sovereignty and divisible non-sovereignty, but between several divisions" of it (*BS 1*, 301–2/401–2). In this context, the notion of autoimmunity plays a crucial role since, together with language and time, it thematizes the logic that threatens indivisible sovereignty and thus the supposed integrity of selfhood typical of traditional understandings of freedom as the power of an individual or community as well as of modern (liberal) democracy. At the same time, autoimmunity exposes the chance to move past such understandings.

But how exactly does autoimmunity help us think about freedom differently? In *Rogues*, Derrida suggests that autoimmunity points to an experience of freedom that is relational before being masterful since it is open to the event conceived as the unforeseeable encounter with the other or difference that "divides" the self.

> If an event worthy of this name is to arrive or happen, it must, beyond all mastery, affect a passivity. It must touch an exposed vulnerability, one without absolute immunity, without indemnity; it must touch vulnerability in its finitude and in a nonhorizontal fashion, there where it is not yet or is already no longer possible to face or face up to the unforseeability of the other. In this regard, autoimmunity is not an absolute ill or evil. It enables an exposure to the other, to what and to who comes—which means that it must remain incalculable. Without autoimmunity, with the absolute immunity, nothing would ever happen or arrive; we would no longer wait, await, or expect, no longer expect one another, or expect any event. What must be thought here, then, is this inconceivable and unknowable thing, a freedom that

> would no longer be the power of a subject, a freedom without autonomy, a heteronomy without servitude, in short, something like a passive decision. (*R*, 152/210)

Autoimmunity points to an understanding of freedom that challenges the sovereign power of a subject or community. Informed by a theological model of selfhood that remains immune to differentiation, this sovereign power is what autoimmunity divides. Autoimmunity points to another experience of freedom, that of a "passive decision" conceived as the possibility of letting oneself be affected or "divided," as it were, by what comes unexpectedly. Here the terms "experience" and "passivity" are crucial. The former emphasizes a way of thinking about freedom that starts from experience, and not from ideal theory. The latter illuminates the possibility of encountering difference before actively subsuming it under the familiar as the same, and thus taking into account vulnerability as a form of nonviolent or disarmed exposition of the other.[26] This exposition is meant to resist the force of appropriation and forceful translation involved in a model of sovereign freedom that projects a normative gaze onto the other, independently of the experience and the specificity of the encounter. That is why Derrida affirms that for such a novel experience of freedom to occur, "a certain unconditional renunciation of sovereignty is required" (xiv/13).

This type of freedom is heteronomous not because it is under the jurisdiction of authorities external to the will (such as those of the senses, of the church, or of political leaders) but because, not bound to actual knowledge or the pretense of accessing the singularity of the other, it is receptive to difference before appropriating it through the sort of forced translation discussed throughout this work. That is, starting *from* the experience of social encounter, this novel understanding of freedom allows for being dialogical *before* being normative so as to take into account and respect difference as something that exceeds mastery and that keeps freedom free, as much as possible, from predeterminations.[27] As Derrida notes, "no politics, no ethics, and no law can be, as it were, deduced from this thought" (xv/14). There is no wonder why Derrida insists so much on the political significance of elementary faith as the one that informs his view of the "messianic." The suspension of certainties, calculation, and knowledge that characterizes such a faith, together with the sense of interruption and inaccessibility to the other it emphasizes, are central to a nonmasterful experience of freedom. Indeed, to the extent that elementary faith constitutes not simply the condition of possibility of knowledge and sociality but also their interruption, it makes room for receptivity and potential dialogue, which deliberative models end up jeopardizing through their insistence on normative predeterminations.

To put this more pointedly: instead of focusing on a normative schema that neutralizes the specificity of the other before the social encounter, Derrida's understanding of freedom operates differently. It concentrates on the experience of letting oneself be affected by the other and allows for the transformation of ones' own assumptions as a result of the encounter. In this way, it enables thinking about freedom in terms of interruption and invention, and not only in terms of the application of idealized norms. As such, this type of freedom is connected to the difficult thinking of the incalculable *with* the calculable, and of a subject whose mastery is "liberated" by autoimmunity from a theological phantasy. By immunizing the self against time, language, and difference more generally, this fantasy normalizes the space of freedom with exclusionary effects for any of the specific elements (cultural, religious, and political) of the self that fall outside pre-established normative schemas.

But if autoimmunity is key to a different understanding of freedom, it is also central to a different thinking of equality. Derrida notes that, in his reflections on freedom, Nancy resists the opposition between equality and freedom, and thinks about the equality of individuals in the incommensurability of their freedom, that is, about equality *in* freedom. Thus, he sees Nancy as grappling with the aporia between freedom and equality, which Derrida redescribes as the antinomy between equality as measure or calculation and freedom as what is unconditional and heterogeneous to measure (48/75). Commenting on Aristotle's famous insight that the origin of democracy is linked to the problematic belief that equality in one respect means absolute equality, Derrida emphasizes that equality is not always opposed to freedom. Indeed, if people are equal in their incommensurable freedom, namely, "they are equally free," then "equality becomes an integral part of freedom and is no longer calculable." This means that, grouped under legal equality, are "several unequal kinds of equality" such as calculable equality according to number and worth, but also incalculable equality in freedom (48–49/75–76). For Derrida, this indicates not simply that the meaning of equality is not univocal, but also that equality represents both "chance and threat," hence the link to autoimmunity.

> Like the search for a calculable unit of measure, equality is not simply some necessary evil or stopgap measure; it is also the chance to neutralize all sort of difference of force, of properties

(natural or otherwise) and hegemonies, so as to gain access precisely to the *whoever* or the *no matter who* of singularity in its very immeasurability. Calculable measure also gives access to the incalculable and the incommensurable, an access that remains itself necessarily undecided between the calculable and the incalculable—and that is the aporia of the political and of democracy. But, by the same token, by effacing the difference of singularity through calculation, by no longer counting on it, measure risks putting an end to singularity itself, to its equality or its nonquantifiable intensity. (52/80)

As a calculable unit of measure, equality represents the chance to address the protection of the singularity of each individual in her or his own incommensurable freedom. Yet, the same equality also constitutes a threat since calculation risks, in its very measurement, obliterating singularity, especially in anything that is not quantifiable. For Derrida, the equivocal meaning of equality suggests that there is no given rule about how to measure incommensurable freedom and no obvious reason why this measuring should be limited to politics and citizenship. For Derrida, the equivocal meaning of equality suggests that there is no given rule about how to measure incommensurable freedom and no obvious reason why this measuring should be limited to politics and citizenship. For, if freedom is no longer a calculable property of a subject (as Nancy maintains), which raises the question whether the legal identity of the citizen is the minimal unit for calculating equality, it remains open whether democratic equality as a measure (equality) of the immeasurable (freedom as singularity) remains confined to the nation-state or must be extended to a larger set of singularities including non-human living beings (52–54/80–81).

By illustrating the autoimmune character of equality, Derrida calls into question understandings of democratic equality informed by criteria of commonality as likeness or sameness exemplified by the political friend as brother. Indeed, if the model for establishing, through calculation, political membership is neither given nor univocal and thus stable, the symbolization of social bonds through the appeal to origins, natural or conventional, loses its authority. As Derrida affirms in *Politics of Friendship*, the "deconstructive self-limitation" of democracy, its autoimmune character, "keeps the power of universalizing beyond the State and the nation, the account taken of anonymous and irreducible singularities, infinitely different and thereby indifferent to particular difference, to the raging quest of identity corrupting the most indestructible desires of the idiom" (*PF*, 106/129). Illuminating the dissymmetry and singularity of identity, individual or communal, democracy's autoimmunity questions the model of political community based on naturalizations and ordering of difference, thereby opening a space for thinking the political beyond hierarchies typical of racialized schemas that find today their most forceful expression in the nation-state.

> It would now be a matter of suggesting that a democracy to come—still not given, not thought, indeed repressed—not only would not contradict this dissymmetrical curving and this infinite heterogeneity, but would in truth demanded by them. Such a dissymmetry and infinite alterity would have no relation to what Aristotle would have called inequality or superiority. They would indeed be incompatible with all sociopolitical hierarchy *as such*. It would be therefore a matter of thinking an alterity without a hierarchical difference at the root of democracy . . . This democracy would free a certain interpretation of *equality* by removing it from the phallogocentric schema of *fraternity*. (232/259)

The difficulty at the core of this antiracialized thinking of democracy consists in determining the sense in which one may "still speak of equality—indeed, of symmetry—in the dissymmetry and boundless of infinite alterity" (233/260). As I hope the discussion so far has made clear, this determination is a task of "'political' translation" and of "responsibility" towards others and "assigned to us by the other" (232/258–59). "There is no 'how'" that "could take the form of precepts rules, of norms or previous criteria available to a knowledge," which means that the "'how' must be invented by each at each moment." This is a task that resists and challenges the epistemic possibility and ethico-political desirability of hierarchies and separations, but also of guaranteeing equality through a calculative rationality conceiving of difference in numerical terms, as typical of modern secular models indebted to scientific rationality (ATI 34/44).

As with his position on sovereignty, Derrida's view on democratic freedom and equality has significant implications for the "theological-political complex." By uncoupling democratic freedom from power and mastery, and equality from filiation and calculable commonality as likeness by birth or convention, Derrida exposes the exclusionary potential of ways of thinking about freedom and equality from within a paradigm of sovereign self-hood that remain tied to a theological and genealogical schema of filiation, one that institutes hierarchies at the root of the political and of democracy. Although he does not suggest what a democracy without freedom as mastery or equal singularity would look like, Derrida opens space to expand the political imaginary beyond the secular and the nation-state as model political community marked by racial traits. He does so by illuminating a path for thinking about democratic freedom and equality that is radically critical of its sedimented convictions and of oppressive implications. Since these are salient features of the democratic spirit, Derrida's perspective can be seen as pushing the agenda of democracy further by considering the implications of tightening, through uncritical inheritance, the nexus between democracy, and especially modern forms of *sovereign* freedom and equality.

"Democracy to Come": Political Community beyond Secularism

So far, we have kept in the background, and without explicitly analyzing it, the notion of "democracy to come" as the relevant object of Derrida's reflections on democracy. But what does that notion actually mean? And how is it related to the "theological-political complex"? As mentioned at the outset, the notion of "democracy to come" escapes straightforward explanation, partly because of its odd propositional outlook, partly because Derrida does not offer a precise definition, and partly because of the complex matter this notion addresses. Although Derrida does not consider "democracy to come" to belong exclusively to the juridico-political sphere, it is in the context of an international political order that "democracy to come" can be understood as referring to modern democracy. As Derrida notes in *Rogues*, post-Kantian modernity and its focus on the possibility of a universal, international, and interstate political order "is one of the possible horizons of the expression 'democracy to come'" (81/118). Derrida's preference for modern democracy also appears from his already noted support of secularization, criticizability, perfectibility, and free speech.[28] For Derrida, a more precise understanding of "democracy to come" requires clarifying, first of all, how not to read it before appreciating its "positive" potential. By making clear that his "negative strategy" is not a sort of negative theology, he claims that "democracy to come" cannot be reduced to an idea or ideal given its aporetic character and the freedom at work in its concept (8/27, 82/120). This view rules out the association of his position with that of classical thinkers, including Plato's constitutive idea of democracy, Aristotle's democratic ideal of "ruling in turns," and the Rousseauian idea of a perfect but impossible democracy (37–38/71). For more complex reasons, "democracy to come" cannot be reduced to a regulative idea of the Kantian sort either. These reasons have something to do with the apparent proximity between Derrida and Kant.[29] Derrida considers Kant's regulative idea "a last resort" that retains a "certain dignity" for interpreting "democracy to come." Derrida does also not exclude that "will not one day give into it" and acknowledges that "democracy to come" resembles a regulative idea (83/122). Like Kant's regulative idea, "democracy to come" cannot be experienced as such, though for different reasons—in virtue of its différantial character and not because it is beyond the realm of experience.

Despite this proximity, Derrida manifests some reservations with regard to Kant's regulative idea and affirms that "'democracy to come' should, above all, not mean a regulative Idea in the Kantian sense." First, unlike the regulative idea that is impossible because beyond experience, Derrida's "democracy to come" is "*im-possible*" (82/120). Here, *im-possible* does not refer to the negative of possible, to impossible, but to another thought of the possible. More precisely, it refers to what remains foreign to the order of one's present possibilities, especially if these are taken as remaining within the horizon of a sovereign self that is able to predict what is to come and thereby forecloses novelty. Although it exceeds calculability, "democracy to come" cannot be indefinitely deferred in the name of a regulative idea because the "to come," as we shall shortly see, points also to a sense of urgency and to the finite time of politics that requires making decisions in the present. Further, since im-possibility does not imply beyond experience but simply beyond any *particular* experience, "democracy to come" is, as Derrida affirms, "what is most undeniably *real*," and thus not quite like Kant's regulative idea (84/123). The second reservation regards the idea of responsibility as related to what goes beyond the calculated application of a rule. While Kant links responsibility with the capacity of responding to the universal demands of morality through the application of a dutiful, self-legislated rule, Derrida views it differently. He conceives of responsibility as response-ability, the capacity to respond to the specificity of contexts through negotiation and invention, and not only through the application of a dutiful rule informed by an idealized regulative schema. Finally, Derrida's last reservation concerns his unwillingness to subscribe to the entire Kantian architectonic in order to appropriate the regulative idea model, as our discussion of teleological reason in chapter 2 has shown (85/124).

These reflections bring us to the "positive" elements of "democracy to come," which are particularly relevant to the "theological-political complex." One feature of "democracy to come" is that it enables us to think about democracy beyond the political theology at work in some influential understandings of sovereignty and freedom. As seen, Derrida deconstructs the idea of democratic sovereignty as both indivisible *and* unconditional by putting emphasis on the mediating conditions of its existence, which expose its autoimmunitary character. Similarly, he distances himself from a theologically inflected model of democratic freedom and equality through the idea of autoimmunity. In the attempt to move past the political theology that has informed many secular understandings of democratic sovereignty, these two aspects of Derrida's view, I have suggested, push the thinking of democracy beyond secularism and racialized models of political community, most notably the nation-state.

The break with secularism is further emphasized by the second "positive" feature of "democracy to come," its connection to the "messianic." Derrida recalls how already in *The Other Heading*, he made that association by stating that "['democracy to come' is] not something that is certain to happen tomorrow, not the democracy (national or international, state or trans-state) of the *future*, but a democracy that must have the structure of a promise—*and thus the memory of that which carries the future, the to-come, here and now*" (85/124). In *Rogues*, he reiterates the same point by claiming that "'democracy to come' is inextricably linked to justice," to the "messianic" and to another thinking of the event (87/127). Without collapsing "democracy to come," which designates primarily a thinking about democracy as a political regime, into the "messianic," which refers to a modality of thinking about time and justice, the association between them illuminates several issues. Derrida's thinking about democracy does not separate the theological from the political, thereby indicating that democracy does not operate within a strictly secular horizon. Indeed, while chapter 2 has shown that the "messianic" temporality structuring the future of democracy impedes the solution of the theological-political nexus, chapter 3 has emphasized that some theological dimension cannot be excluded from the foundation of democracy as a politico-legal order.

On this reading, Derrida's view of "democracy to come" does not *simply* take secularization as a condition of possibility for democracy, as Fritsch suggests.[30] Though Derrida recognizes that the process of secularization allows for the breaking of hermeneutic authority that is decisive to an open-ended inheritance, to the right to question, and thus to deconstruction itself, he also affirms that secularization remains religious.[31] Above all, his thinking illuminates the problems connected to the radical separation of the theological from the political that is envisaged by traditional secularization theories. This elucidation emerges, as I have shown, from his reflections on language, time, and political authority. It also emerges, perhaps less explicitly, from his critical view of the political theology which continues to inform democratic sovereignty. Taken together, all these reflections expose the theological threads woven into political concepts, discourses, and practices, in spite of the rigorously nonreligious terms in which modern political life is often described and understood. Secularization cannot be taken *merely* as a condition of possibility for democracy in Derrida since this view contrasts with his emphasis on the public role of religion(s), as well as with the irreducible theological-political relation that marks his view of the "messianic" and of the sociopolitical field in which modern democracy as a regime operates and cannot be disconnected from.

Furthermore, Derrida's thinking about democracy allows for a more receptive attitude towards difference that appears especially if one concentrates on the meaning of the "to come." Playing around with the French *avenir* (future) and *à venir* (to come), Derrida emphasizes two connected elements. On the one hand, the "to come" indicates an open disposition towards the event conceived as the unmasterable coming of the future that challenges the type of sovereign self-hood informing the agency of individuals and of democratic nation-states. On the other hand, it refers to a sense of urgency, taking the form of an active waiting, a sort of passive decision that refrains from imposing on others normative projections before the experience of the encounter. As Derrida notes, "the 'to' of the 'to come' wavers between an 'imperative injunction (call or performative) and the patient *perhaps* of messianicity (nonperformative exposure to what comes, to what can always not come or has already come)" (*R*, 91/132). This wavering represents the radical possibility of what we have characterized above as an experience of nonmasterful freedom. While not targeting religious views and individuals in particular, these features of "democracy *to come*" inscribe the thinking of political community within a perspective that does not structurally exclude them from public life.

Finally, the connection between "democracy to come" and the "messianic" links the former to justice. This has consequences for rethinking the relationship between religion and politics. Similar to Derrida's view of justice, whose nonteleological features impede the fixation of its true essence, "democracy to come" is characterized by an open relationship with the future. Indeed, the "to come" does not announce that democracy *is* to come or that "democracy to come" is the democracy *of* the future. It only affirms democracy's historicity, which opposes the fixation of its meanings and forms from the present and "grounds" the possibility of infinite political critique.

> The expression "democracy to come" does indeed translate or call for a militant and interminable political critique. A weapon aimed at the enemies of democracies, it protests against all naïveté and every political abuse, rhetoric that would present as a present or existing democracy, as a de facto democracy, what remains inadequate to the democratic demand, whether nearby or far away, at home or somewhere else in the world, anywhere that a discourse on human rights and democracy remains little more than an obscene alibi so long as it tolerates the terrible plight of so many millions of human beings suffering from malnutrition, disease, and humiliation, grossly deprived not only of bread and water but of equality or freedom, dispossessed of the rights of all, of everyone, of anyone. (86–7/126–27)

The notion "democracy to come" allows for a political critique of those views that identifies the outlook democracy takes at any given time as incarnating the true democratic spirit and as responding to its demands while tolerating the injustice of massive plagues. That is, it provides us with powerful resources for judging and criticizing the present of democracy in its own historicity without recurring to any specific normativity, which is not to say that this criticism is devoid of any normative power. These resources help challenge anyone seeking to assume the exclusive right to establish what democracy's appropriate demands are and what forms it should take, locally and transnationally. Because this right can be extended to the question whether *secular* understandings and forms of democracy are adequate to the demands of the democratic spirit, the possibility of criticism provided by "democracy to come" affects all those secular perspectives that consider a strict separation between religion and politics as required by the democratic demands of respect for pluralism. After all, this is an intrinsic possibility offered by democracy as a historical regime, whose autoimmunitary character fosters a radical self-criticizability.

> "Democracy to come" takes into account the absolute and intrinsic historicity of the only system that welcomes in itself, in its very concept, that expression of autoimmunity called the right to self-critique and perfectibility. Democracy is the only system, the only constitutional paradigm, in which, in principle, one has or assumes the right to criticize everything publicly, including the idea of democracy, its concept, its history, and its name. Including the idea of the constitutional paradigm and the absolute authority of the law. It is thus the only paradigm that is universalizable, whence its chance and its fragility. But in order for this historicity—unique among all political systems—to complete, it must be freed not only from the Idea in the Kantian sense but from all teleology, all ontho-theo-teleology. (86–7–127)

The historicity of democracy emphasized by "democracy to come" allows for a radical criticism through an act of theoretical suspension of democracy, as it were. That is, it allows for the possibility of suspending, "in the name of democracy" itself, the certainty of the necessary association between democracy and the features that are commonly linked to it (89/129). This possibility is not without risks since it opens democracy to the possibility of its own destruction.[32] Indeed, the promise informing "democracy to come" affirms that "there be the future," but this does exclude that such a future might not be one in which democracy will be the relevant political category or at least a category defined by indivisible sovereignty, autonomous freedom, and secularism as we "know" it today. After all, as Derrida reminds us, "the time of politics and thus of democracy" is "necessarily finite" (29). While reflecting on the possibility of another view of the political in his *Politics of Friendship*, Derrida points implicitly to this possibility through the following question: "Would it still make sense to speak of democracy when it would no longer be a question (no longer in question as to what is essential or constitutive) of country, nation, even of State and citizen—in other words, if at least one keeps to the accepted use of these words, when it would no longer be a political question?" (*PF*, 104/127). According to the thrust of my argument, what is at issue here are not simply traditional models of community based on nationality and sovereignty, but the modality of thinking that grounds their validity and guarantees their currency. It is, in other words, the political theology and "White mythology" sustaining secular political thinking.

So affirming that the future of democracy might not be *secular* is not to suggest that Derrida fully opposes secularism or democracy. Derrida does not reject secularism as a political doctrine implying the separation of religious authority from state powers and the institutionally guaranteed freedom of religion. As he says,

> I believe that democracy to come . . . assumes secularism (*laïcité*), that is, both the detachment of the political from the theocratic and the theological (*affranchissement du politique par rapport au théocratique et théologique*), thus entailing a certain secularism (*sécularité*) of the political, while at the same time, encompassing freedom of worship in a completely consistent, coherent way, and absolute religious freedom guaranteed by the State, on the condition, obviously, that the secular space of the political and the religious space are not confused. . . . I believe that the secular (*laïcité*) today must be more rigorous with itself, more tolerant toward religious cultures and toward the possibility for religious practices to exist freely, unequivocally, and without confusion. (*IW*, 50–51/81)

What I am suggesting about his view of "democracy to come" is, instead, the possibility of conceiving of democracy beyond the political theology informing secularism, and thus also beyond the metaphysical thinking ("White mythology") and its multiple exclusionary implications that mark modern *secular* discourse. As I have argued throughout, this type of discourse is characterized by a separatist logic that relies on racialized forms of philosophical naturalization that inscribe hierarchy at the core of the political, with these being features remaining connected to, indeed renewing, the legacy of colonial mentalities.

This double bind of chance and threat reflects what we have indicated earlier on as the autoimmunitary character of democracy, that is, a trait designating a sort of death drive that enables the possibility of self-destruction in view of self-protection. While the possibility of a different future of democracy might look frightening at first sight since it disjoins democracy from well-established features of its makeup, it might also be liberating to the extent that it denaturalizes what seems an inevitable connection. Holding this perspective is not to downplay the value of democracy and the type of viable and desirable safeguards it offers, in its current form, against authoritarian regimes. Nor is it to reject the significance of the separation between religious and state powers for the future of democracy in general, and of that envisaged by Derrida in particular. Rather, it is to push political thinking to critically question its sedimented convictions by following the critical and self-critical drive of the democratic spirit. It is this spirit of democracy, the possibility of questioning the equation between democracy and any of its historical forms that have occurred or are at present, especially in the West, that renders democracy a "universalizable paradigm." This would be a paradigm that is in principle open to a variety of positions belonging to different geopolitical contexts and cultural traditions that, without necessarily embracing modern secularism and its heritage, can, nonetheless, offer contributions to "democratic" thinking and practices.[33] Although Derrida is well aware of the semantic specificity of "democracy" and that the possibility of its translation into non-Greek or non-European idioms and traditions is not obvious (R, 32/56), this very possibility acquires particular significance as an epistemological and political task.

Note here that Derrida's support for the right to self-critique and perfectibility, together with the freedom of expression this presupposes, might make it appear that he embraces key features of liberal understandings of democracy from Mill to Neo-Kantian political thinkers such as Rawls and Habermas. While his support for these features clearly indicates Derrida's preference for modern democracy as a regime in which the right of free speech is institutionally guaranteed, his perspective cannot be simply reduced to a version of liberal deliberative democracy. Indeed, besides Derrida's resistance to individual freedom as autonomy, the right to self-critique generated by autoimmunity is not grounded on a normative standard that sets what democracy *requires* but, rather, on the radical historicity of democracy and its perfectibility. That is why Derrida refuses to specify in advance which understanding of equality and freedom democracy demands, as Mill and Rawls do, or what rules of communication are to regulate public deliberation as in Habermas or, as just suggested, whether democracy means necessarily *secular* democracy, as in liberal political theory.[34]

These "positive" features of "democracy to come" (the thought of unconditionality without sovereignty and the connection to the "messianic") help us clarify further why Derrida has opted for this notion to talk about democracy. Lacking the modal verb "to be" in order to remain ontologically and semantically free from final determinations, "democracy to come" refers more to a way of thinking about democracy and the future than to a strictly political concept. This lack does not deprive this notion of political connotations but makes it hyper-political by exposing the political agency behind the meanings that are historically ascribed to democracy. The intrinsic historico-political variations of democracy that "democracy to come" takes into account lead Derrida to hazard the thought that such a notion "would be like a khora of the political," namely, a sort of receptacle or opening space that precedes particular determinations because it makes them possible without at the same time being reducible to a transcendental trope (xiv/14, 82/120).[35] An important implication of this very difficult and controversial claim is that "democracy to come" presents a unique flexibility. It allows, says Derrida to "endlessly oscillate" between, on the one hand, "a constative analysis of a concept" that is determinate and historical, and, on the other hand, a performative call "to believe in it" and have faith in its promise (91/32).[36] This is possible because of the irreducible gap between the very possibility of democracy sustained by the faith in its promise and its historical determinations, a gap that our discussions of elementary faith in relation to the "messianic" and the foundation of the secular domain in the previous chapters have already highlighted.

In other words, "democracy to come" provides, figuratively, the theoretical space from which to criticize and reconfigure every time the understanding of democracy in the name of democracy's promise or faith in it and according to the specificity of contexts.[37] As such, its articulation constitutes an intervention that unsettles all those views that claim a privileged right to *know* what democracy is and should be. Thus, instead of establishing another model of democracy, "democracy to come" represents a political intervention that provides the theoretical sources and space to think through, criticize, and politicize claims about the truth of democracy—what the promise of democracy consists in, what its demands are—in theory and practice.[38]

Connecting "democracy to come" to the "messianic" and the thought of unconditionality without sovereignty has important implications for understanding how Derrida rethinks the question of political community in the context of the "theological-political complex." While both connections illuminate, in different ways, a mode of thinking about communal life that breaks with a secular horizon, the second in particular points to a form of hospitality that affects, among others, religious views and citizens. This feature appears especially if one reflects on Derrida's claim that hospitality represents an exemplary figure of the unconditionality without sovereignty characterizing "democracy to come" that is clearly distinct from the conditional hospitality mediated by a juridico-political framework in which the scope of openness is regulated in advance by normative criteria or by claims about origins. I want to suggest that the openness implied by the hospitality of "democracy to come" illuminates further the possibility of rethinking democracy beyond secularism, since it points to a thinking about communal life that undermines, and does not simply expose, the separation between the theological and the political.

But, first of all, what does Derrida mean by hospitality? It is not my intention to delve deeply into his complex and multifaceted philosophical view of hospitality, which I have already and briefly touched on, albeit indirectly, in the previous chapters. Instead, I want to focus specifically on its political aspects.[39] With reference to the political, Derrida understands hospitality as a way of thinking about the possibility of "determining citizenship, democracy and international law, etc. in another way" in the context of "unprecedented historical situations" (*OFH*, 149/131). The crisis of secular understandings and political arrangements informed by a however secularized political theology of sovereignty is one of the "unprecedented" historical situations that the thought of unconditional hospitality addresses in order to proceed "in another way." Along with recurrent phenomena of global migration, structural racism, humanitarian wars, land expropriation, poverty and economic recessions, and environmental degradation, this crisis signals the extreme difficulties of dominant liberal democratic theories and politics to respond to the challenges posed by the contemporary predicament, partly because some of these phenomena are structural to the formation of liberal ideologies and societies. In contrast to these theories, Derrida's view of hospitality seeks to think about the present of democracy beyond outlooks that are informed by racialized teleological schemas, indivisible sovereignty, and traditional political theology, that is, beyond "old" secularism.[40]

My point is that the hospitality inherent in "democracy to come" illuminates why Derrida's view of political community opposes the sovereign solution of the theological-political nexus that has marked traditional approaches to secularism and thus also keeps a critical vigilance over the oppressive implications associated with that operation. This holds since "democracy to come" breaks with the metaphysical and racialized approach ("White mythology") of the masculine political theology informing democratic discourse. It does so by affirming a type of relationality that is aware of the historicity and interconnectedness of the human predicament, and thus "divides" sovereignty through the openness to, and responsibility towards, difference and the future. In this way, Derrida's thinking about political community is in line with his positions on language, time, and religion discussed so far.

As seen in the introduction, the separation between the theological and the political has been a central feature of modern secular discourse. Guided by the conviction that reason can provide its own foundation and do without faith, and that reason should have primacy with regard to the foundation of political authority, knowledge, and community, many modern secular understandings have put into effect the solution of the theological-political relation. They have done so by inverting, without unsettling, the foundational, indeed fundamentalist, modality of thinking they have ascribed to traditional theology: sovereign, self-sufficient foundations are possible, desirable, and to be effected through imposed translations based on a particular view of reason made universal through force. We have also seen that this type of foundation has been supported by a type of thinking informed by sexist and racialized schemas, whose destructive implications can only be denied by fictional discourses. In contrast to these models, I have argued that Derrida views the theological-political relation as irreducible, not fully translatable and as profoundly questioning the racialized quest for origins; that he considers religious sources to be involved in political foundations; and that he conceives of reason and religion as sharing an elementary faith, the recognition of which can offer a greater respect for religious freedom and difference more generally that remains vigilant about the risk of naturalizations. Exploring, in this chapter, Derrida's position on democracy, I have supplemented the arguments of the preceding chapters by presenting and discussing his critical analysis of the political theology of democratic sovereignty. This has exposed, through autoimmunity, the dangerous foundationalism of sovereign indivisibility and its racial implications and has illuminated alternative conceptualizations of freedom and equality beyond the dominant modern models typical of the secular nation-state.

It is in this context, then, that "democracy to come" can be considered as reconfiguring the thinking of democracy beyond the separation of the theological and the political typical of traditional secularism. Although Derrida does not develop this point, his "democracy to come" helps clarify that determining indivisible or sovereign limits between religion and politics, or between and within human groups, through forceful translations and normative projections, jeopardizes the respect for pluralism, thereby betraying democracy's thrust for equality and heterogeneity. To the extent that such a determination is informed by metaphysical, indeed racialized, thinking, it also leaves dangerously open the door to racial frameworks operating beneath the rhetoric of neutrality and humanism. This holds to the extent that sovereign indivisibility depends on a problematic political theology that operates through imposed translations and normative positions that disregard the irreducible relationality and pluralism of the human condition. Viewed in the context of the "theological-political complex," Derrida's "democracy to come" can, therefore, be taken as indicating that the respect of cultural and religious pluralism in democratic societies might depend more on a vigilant universalism that values translations based on terms that are contextually negotiated, than on the insistence on fixed rational standards that are supposedly required by the idea or ideal of (secular) democracy itself. In his words: "[N]aturally, the religion of the other must be recognized and respected, as well as his mother tongue, of course. But one must translate, that is, at the same time respect the language of the other and, through that respect, get his meaning across, and this presupposes [what you have called] universal democracy" (*IW*, 45/72). Is a nonsecular political future possible? Is it desirable? These are the questions that Derrida's perspective ultimately raises, thereby opening up the political imaginary to potentially different configurations of translation and of the political.

I close these reflections by addressing a powerful recent interpretation of Derrida's political thought on democracy, with which mine shares some important aspects but also seeks to maintain a certain distance from. In his *Scatter 2*, Bennington explores an impressive number of political thinkers by thinking with Derrida and through deconstruction. He advances the hypothesis that Derrida's political thought on democracy points to an understanding of politics that resists the metaphysics of presence's attempt to reduce to homogeneity what Aristotle indicated as politics' intrinsic plurality. "Scatter" is the name Bennington gives to this dispersing plurality, which undergirds the metaphysics of presence and yet has in general been "repressed in the Western tradition of political philosophy."[41] In what Bennington suggests is "a more Aristotelian spirit than Derrida recognizes" scatter "is at one and the same time the possibility of the political (the political bond always gathers a dispersion, on pain of not being political)"—namely, what allows for there *to be* politics at all—and "simultaneously, the necessary possibility of its end (the dispersion constantly unbinds the bond and scatters, other wise the political would become absorbed by the One and cease being political)"— the possibility that politics *remains* politics, and is thus not absorbed into metaphysics. His notion of "politics of politics" seeks precisely to capture the persistence of this dispersive plurality:

> Politics begins with this doubling up. As opposed to metaphysical thinking, for which the end of politics is the end of politics,

the putting down of politics in the interest of some redemptive future after the big trumpet moment of the Last Judgment, a deconstructive thinking of politics "discerns eschatology from teleology" and tries to think the future not as a horizon that both conceals and opens onto death as redemption, nor, as we shall go on to see in more detail in a moment, as more modestly guided by an Idea in the Kantian sense (the more sober and apparently secular form of redemption), but as a "to-come," an *à-venir* that does not gather up the Moment even in a Heideggerian way but projects a scatter of moments, of *eskhata* without *telos*, of *kairoi* that do not add up to any grand design of history.[42]

For Bennington, the end of politics, the concrete achievement of its guiding normative idea or ideal, is what metaphysical thinking pushes for. This movement amounts to the end or consummation of politics, that is, its termination. Yet, because metaphysics always already operates within politics, the reduction of (political) difference to sameness, as in conventional understandings of politics, finds its concrete limit. And this is what Derrida's understanding of "democracy to come" illuminates most decisively through the notion of auto-immunity, which reiterates the impossibility of identity as unitary, undifferentiated self-identity as in traditional conceptions of sovereignty.[43]

There is much to admire in Bennington's exploration. His analysis does not only show that a deconstructive reading of Western understandings of the political and of sovereignty through "democracy to come" puts into sharp relief the irreducibility of difference and of politics in all philosophical thinking. This point converges with my criticism of the alleged neutrality of secular philosophies discussed in earlier chapters, as well as with the highlighted resistance towards the closure of the political. Above all, his intervention illuminates that "democracy to come" exposes the irreducible multiplicity at the core of (political) identity, which many secular philosophies still entangled with versions of the metaphysics of presence have ended up suppressing, as I have argued throughout. Yet, by remaining within the bound of the Western tradition and not sufficiently appreciating the importance of religious sources in Derrida's thought of democracy, Bennington misses the antiracist force of Derrida's understanding of democracy as resisting the possibility of naturalization so crucial to racial models traversing the Western tradition, precisely through the appeal to elementary faith, as I discussed in chapter 2. A more perceptive appreciation of the Aristotelian spirit, as

Bennington proposes, might not be enough to keep at bay the silent modes of naturalization at work in metaphysical reductionisms, and in Aristotle's philosophy, if it confines dispersing plurality within the West. And these are modes that Derrida recognizes as being deeply connected to issues of race affecting Western metaphysical thinking, to which he responds by, *also*, rethinking the nexus between reason and religion. To address more decisively and deeply the political and theoretical issues of metaphysical reductionism and their implications, and thus attending to dispersing plurality all the way down as it were, an appreciation of Derrida's reflections on the racial nature of the metaphysics of presence and of the critical sources offered by elementary faith is in order. This appreciation, as I have demonstrated throughout, requires a reflection on the theological-political problematics and its links to "White mythology." My point is that by keeping the exploration within the bounds of the Western tradition and of (its) reason alone, as Bennington tends to do, and not *at* their limits, as Derrida does, the wider scope and deeper decolonizing force of Derrida's critical thought is missed, and so are the critical resources his discussion of elementary faith and religion offers to questions pluralism and race.[44] Is this seemingly secular neglect in any way connected to the very reductionism that is called into question?

5

Islam, Religion, and Democracy

Islam is a topic that Derrida's later writings kept returning to, dealing with it in complex and contentious ways (C; *GD*; FK; *HAS*; *IW*; *R*; TSA). In these works, references to Islam occur in a variety of contexts and forms, making it hard to circumscribe its meaning and functions. Indeed, Derrida alternatively or simultaneously associates Islam with the Abrahamic traditions, mysticism, religion, Islamism, fundamentalism, but also to forces resisting and criticizing the hegemony of Western political models, including globalization, secularism, the market, and democracy. Focusing primarily on "Faith and Knowledge" and *Rogues*, where Islam is evoked in direct relationship to questions about the modern discourse of religion, secularization and modern democracy, this concluding chapter seeks to trace the complex and controversial role Islam plays in Derrida's later writings, especially with regard to those questions.[1] My aim is not simply to illuminate Derrida's view on Islam as it pertains to the "theological-political complex." My primary focus is on the limits and possibilities his deconstructive logic offers with regard to the Islamic tradition(s) beyond what Derrida said, or did not say, in specific instances. I suggest that although his view is marked by ambiguity and at times uncritical accounts, his reflections on Islam open up the future of the political and of democracy to Islamicate perspectives and contexts. In this way, Derrida's intervention joins forces within and beyond such spaces that resist closures within Islamic discourses, as well as various forms of Orientalist appropriations.

Islam and Religion

Derrida's view of Islam is arguably shaped by his relationship to it. Despite his clear focus on the Western canon, Derrida does not neglect the cultural and experiential influences that the Islamic tradition and spaces played in his formation. Particularly in his later writings, he manifests an intellectual debt to the culture of Algeria. As he notes in one of his last interventions: "Of all the cultural wealth I have received, that I have inherited, my Algerian culture has sustained me the most" (*IW*, 30/55). Without eliding the cultural complexity of Algeria, which Derrida understands as being not solely Arab, Berber, and Muslim but also "Western" (39), and without downplaying Derrida's self-proclaimed inability to talk about the Islamic (and Jewish) tradition (HAS) or to feel confident about its history (*R*, 32/56), it is remarkable that his references to Algeria recurrently evoke Islam and the "Maghrebi Arabo-Muslim" context of his upbringing (ATI, 21; FAPU, 222, 229).[2] At some point, Derrida even affirms his readiness "to think like certain Muslims" (C, 142/135) and declares feeling quite close to ("*assez proche de*") thinkers who present themselves as "heir[s] of Islam ("*héritier de l'Islam*") (FAPU, 232). Also noteworthy is that Derrida's references to Islam in these later writings often come through Algeria's Islamism, the history of which cannot be read independently of French settler colonialism, the reactions it triggered, and the complex and long-lasting traumatic pyscho-political effects it provoked, including the use and reproduction of violence.[3]

Marking these aspects at the outset is not intended to prioritize them or aggrandize their relevance, but only to note that the Islamic tradition appears to play a certain background role in Derrida's thought, a role that is characterized by experiential and political conditions, more than cultural ones, given the limited engagement with texts directly related to Islam or his knowledge of Arabic.[4] It also helps underscore again that it is within an Arabo-Islamic context characterized by the figure of the Arab Jew that Derrida has first access to the question of religion that is central to his political thought. This access was marked by the interconnections between the so-called Abrahamic religions interacting in French Algeria, which was under the domination of a Christian juridico-political culture and institutions.[5] As mentioned in chapter 3, Derrida's notion of the "Abrahamic" points to the complex interrelations between Christian, Jewish, and Muslim traditions. It represents "the very condition of 'religion'" since it enables the possibility of comparing religious phenomena that were not easily subsumable under the name "religion" as distinct objects of analysis before the nineteenth-century discourse of religion, as well as identifying the unequal relations of power between them.

So what is Islam, for Derrida? As with any Aristotelian question of this kind, Derrida is cautious and proceeds somehow obliquely, conscious that the "is" of the question regards both ontological and ontic aspects that cannot be addressed independently of linguistic and political dimensions. Indeed, Derrida is well aware that modern discussions about Islam cannot occur independently of dominant Western discourse and emphasizes the need "to deconstruct the European intellectual construct of Islam," which is not disconnected from practical realities (*IW*, 38/65; FAPU, 230). Indeed, as discussed in chapter 3, Derrida criticizes Schmitt for identifying Islam as the external enemy of the European understanding of the political, indeed a key condition of its formation, thereby targeting a specifically anti-Muslim configuration of political life inscribed in European history and politics (*PF*, 77/95 89/108–9).[6] As such, Derrida's awareness signals the limits affecting an analysis offered from the margins of the dominant epistemological order in which he operates. This raises the broader question whether it is possible to talk meaningfully about Islam *as* Islam through a framework that essentializes, racializes, and constitutes as other the object it describes.[7] If we follow Derrida's understanding of deconstruction as "the analysis of what remains to be thought"—because excluded by the "White mythology" of modern discourse and yet remaining deeply affected by it—and also consider the implications of Islam's position of being in part exterior to European modernity's formation, then Islam appears in more than one sense to be part of "what *remains* to be thought."

Despite these difficulties, Derrida addresses these questions in "Faith and Knowledge," in the context of his reflections on religion. To recall it, Derrida critically acknowledges that, while the term "religion" is commonly used to designate religious phenomena in general, it has a Latin Christian origin and is connected to hegemonic processes of global secularization and secular translations that render its use even more problematic when addressing other religious traditions. This is particularly relevant to Islam, which became a "religion" as a result of colonial encounters, and to what is commonly considered the Arabic equivalent for religion (*dīn*), whose understanding in Islamic contexts and discourses is taken to exceed "religion."[8] Notwithstanding these constraints, it is in relation to the language of "religion" that Derrida discusses Islam, which he groups under the "religions called 'Abrahamic.'"[9] Commenting on the context of his intervention, he offers preliminary observations about larger patterns characterizing public debates on religion.

> We represent and speak four different languages, but our common "culture," let's be frank is Christian, barely even Judeo-Christian.

> No Muslim is among us, alas, even for this preliminary discussion, just at the moment when it is towards Islam, perhaps, that we ought to begin by turning our attention. No representative of other cults either. Not a single woman! We ought to take this into account: speaking on behalf of these mute witnesses without speaking for them, in a place for them, and drawing from this all sort of consequences. (FK, 45/13)

Derrida emphasizes that discussions about religion and its alleged "return" occur "just at the moment when it is towards Islam, perhaps, that we ought to begin by turning our attention." Yet at the very moment in which he denounces the typical exclusion of Muslims and women in European, "manifestly" Christian and masculine discussions on religion, and opens a space for them without "speaking for them," Derrida maintains a somehow paternalistic tone. "We should have, we ought to have begun by *allowing* them to speak" (47/17; my emphasis). Further, precisely where language and who controls it are at issue, Derrida is both perceptive and forgetful. While he pairs Abraham with "Ibrahim," when mentioning the 1994 massacre in Hebron's Tomb of Patriarch for Jews, or Sanctuary of Abraham for Muslims (a naming that Derrida does not use), he omits the Arabic name of the city, *Al Khalīl*.[10] Further, when referring to Islam as "religion" he never uses or refers to, as far as I know, the relevant Arabic terms *dīn* or *sharī'a* and their semantic fields, as a way to step into the possibilities that his critique of the epistemic regime of "religion" makes room for.[11]

In spite of these shortcomings, Derrida's sensibility for the language of "Islam" is undeniable and reaches its peak when he focuses on the name "Islam." Like "religion," the invocation of "Islam" requires paying attention to the nature of names and their usage, especially when they are invoked for political purposes.

> And among the Abrahamic religions, among the "fundamentalisms" or "integrisms" that are developing universally, for they are at work today in all religions, what, precisely of Islam? But let us not make use of this name too quickly. Everything that is hastily grouped under the reference to "Islam" seems today to retain some sort of geopolitical or global prerogative, as a result of the nature of its physical violence, of certain of its declared violations of the democratic model and international law (the Rushdie case" and many others—and the "right to literature"), as a result of both the archaic and modern forms of its crimes

"in the name of religion," as a result of its demographic dimension, of its phallogocentric and theologico-political figures. Why? Discernment is required: Islam is not Islamism and we should never forget it, but it operates *in the name* of the former, and thus emerges the grave question of the name. (45–46/14)

"Islam is not Islamism," says Derrida, after raising the question of fundamentalism in connection to the "return of religion." Although this view appears to quickly reduce Islamism to fundamentalism, thereby neglecting the complexity and diversity of Islamist projects, it brings to the fore the question of the name in relation to Islam and religion.[12] What of Islam? What does it refer to? How to distinguish Islam from what operates in its name? What use can be made of the name "Islam"? For Derrida, the discernment required by these questions passes through "the grave question of the name," the "proper name," and thus also through issues of "untranslatability" and "iterability," as seen in our discussion of language in chapter 1 (46/14). While Derrida only raises but does not develop these connections in relation to Islam, doing so has important implications for understanding what Islam might stand for and do to the modern discourse of religion, if seen from the perspective of the name.

On the one hand, if "Islam" is a proper name that is worth retaining when referring to phenomena associated to "religion," it preserves a certain singularity that designates a unique referent connected to a particular idiom, foundational texts, beliefs, and practices that are relevant to all Muslims across contexts.[13] As such, it is a name that retains a degree of untranslatability withstanding the pluralization and transformation of its meaning to the point of neutralizing its distinctiveness and the elasticity of the link word-meaning-object. The uniqueness at issue here is not simply connected to doctrinal sources and practices grounded on sacred texts but is embedded in the historical discourses and lived experiences associated with the birth, spread, and development of Islam across the world. Though occurring through different disciplines often in disagreement with each other—theology (*kalam*), jurisprudence (*fiqh*), and philosophy (*falsafe*)—and in a variety of historical contexts (clearly, the experience of Islam in Morocco or Iran, is different from Islam in Turkey, South Africa, or Indonesia) and conditions (Islam in premodern and modern times), these developments continue to refer to a unique referent that can be distinguished from non-Islamic ones and that Muslims continue to subsume, globally, under the name of "Islam."[14]

Of course, untranslatability raises important questions about the determinability and stability of reference, especially when it is invoked in controversial situations. Commenting on the untranslatability of the Qur'an, Derrida says that "it is tied to all the fundamentalisms, in particular in Islamic areas. Nowhere else is the attachment to the untranslatable letter of the Qur'an so inflexible" and "nowhere, it seems to me, the fixed literality of the original message, in its very body sanctify itself to the extent that it does in the Moslem religion" (AANJ, 88). Here Derrida addresses the dangers of appealing to untranslatability as a way to justify and theologize literal interpretations of sacred texts that would recover its univocal truth, thereby closing the gap between text and interpretation, and use it to marshal political projects. While also raising the question whether " 'fixed literalness' is an essence that helps to define 'Moslem religion,' " as Asad has argued, Derrida's claim signals larger hermeneutic and political problems concerning the scope of untranslatability and the relevant authorities and criteria involved in processes defining when and how it applies. Asad's suggestion that Derrida overlooks important distinctions in Islamic discourse—such as literal *versus* metaphorical text, and exoteric *versus* exegetical sense—that are key to "interpretation in the understanding of Quranic language," together with his (Asad's) avoidance of refuting or justifying the "doctrine of inimitability" invoked by Muslim theologians in questions about the translatability of the Qur'an, speaks both to the difficulty of the matter at issue and the relevance of untranslatability to the referents that go and can go under the name of Islam.[15]

Yet, it is perhaps with regard to the violence perpetrated in the name of Islam as "religion" that the complexity and significance surrounding the nexus between name, untranslatability, and its referent(s) emerges more forcefully. As Derrida says, "never treat as an accident the force of the name in what happens, occurs or is said in the name of religion, here in the name of Islam" (46/14). What goes under the name of Islam, of Islam as "religion," so that it *can* be done or *claimed* to be done in its name? Pointing to the modern violence from which various so-called religions seek to defend themselves and use in turn in reactionary fashion, Derrida underscores, later in the text, the "new archaic violence" and sexist connotations involved in this phenomenon with reference to Islam in general, and Algeria in particular, a phenomenon in which women are often the primary targets (85/75). As he says, "what is involved is always avowed vengeance, often declared as sexual revenge: rapes, mutilated genitals, corps exhibited, heads paraded . . . This is the case for example, but it is only an example, in Algeria today, in the name of Islam, invoked by both belligerent parties, each in its own way" (89/81). While Derrida's focus on violence singles out Islam here, raising questions about a residual Orientalism in his view, he could also have paid attention to other so-called religions in the name of which archaic violence was perpetrated at the time of his writings. For example, during the war in ex-Yugoslavia in the 1990s many Bosnian Muslim women were brutally and systematically raped by Serbian militias seeking to Christianize, as it were, their off-spring. Yet he is careful to also denounce the violence committed against Muslims in the name of secular causes.[16] He says that

> it is not certain that in addition to or in face of the most spectacular and most barbarous crimes of certain fundamentalism (of the present and of the past), other over-armed forces are not also leading "wars of religion," albeit unavowed. Wars or military intervention led by the Judaeo-Christian West in the name of the best causes (of international law, democracy, the sovereignty of the peoples, of nations or of stats and even humanitarian imperatives), are they not also, from a certain side, wars of religion. (63/42)

On the other hand, still following Derrida's reflections on language and interpretation, "Islam" requires repetition or iteration, as do all proper names that persist and are legible across time and space. Occurring in different contexts and under different historical conditions, iteration is a process that introduces the structural possibility of semantic changes. Yet, this possibility does not authorize departing altogether from the authoritative texts, beliefs, and practices of Islam when engaging in interpretation, licensing any or univocal interpretations, reducing meaning to literality or to readers' receptions, and even less by appealing to a metalanguage that would allow recovery of the truth of the text. It helps instead illuminate, as Derrida first put it in *Of Grammatology* with the formula "there is nothing outside text," the idea that meaning—and with it, truth and reference—is inseparable from the medium of its transmission and its material embodiments. This has important implications for the degree and type of transformations that affect it (*OG*, 158).[17] On this reading, "Islam" travels in, and is apprehended through, the mediation of language, and thus also through processes of translation and interpretation across places and periods with iterations that affect and expand its meaning. As such, meaning associated with "Islam" is based on sacred texts and affected by the community of its believers, their experiences, agency, and contexts of operation. Located in different geopolitical settings, periods, and situations, such believers interpret and practice Islam under conditions and constraints—cultural, epistemic, economic, and political—that constitute the mediating web through which they understand and determine what the term means and presently requires of Muslims. Developments within Islamic discourses in the early period through adaptations to pre-Islamic traditions in Asia and Africa,[18] later ones that are reflective of modern conceptualizations and conditions such as Islamic Reformism, or more recent articulations of Islam in Europe and the United States that respond to their context of reference are relevant examples that speak to this issue.[19]

Approaching Islam through the question of the name offers conceptual resources to understand what "Islam" might mean in ways that illuminate how it opposes both its essentialization, as in forms of Orientalist Islamophobia and traditionalist Islamic guardianship, as well as its de-essentialization, as displayed by views of Islam that force it into modern models.[20] Addressing the historical conditions in which Islamic discourses are produced and transformed, processes of interpretation and translation find their limit in a certain untranslatability of what Islam "is," which impedes its de-essentialization. As seen, untranslatability carries with it nonnegligible problems. Yet, it is arguably in connection to the uniqueness and distinctiveness of the referent(s) named by Islam, and thus to a certain untranslatability, that disagreements about what counts as "Islamic" occurs, which is something central to any Islamic discourse as such.

Besides helping to clarify what Islam "is," the question of the name can have a more radical potential. As a proper name associated to "religion" that retains a degree of untranslatability, as Derrida's reflections on "religion" and globalization showcase, "Islam" would be a different name and framework, other than "religion," to address religious and sociopolitical phenomena that concern a significant number of the world population today. This is an important implication of the logic of the proper name invoked by Derrida in relation to Islam as "religion" that has recently found some traction among Muslim scholars.[21] Salman Sayyid, for example, has recently developed an understanding of Islam that resonates with this logic. For him, "Islam is the name that gives Muslims a name," giving them visibility and subjectivity according to terms that are aligned to their experience *as* Muslims. Specifically, Sayyid speaks of a "singular Islam" that is subject to struggles of rival interpretations by various Islamist groups that all seek to give Islam a meaning through political projects.[22]

Read through the question of the name as proposed by Derrida, then, the importance of "Islam" as another name to name *also* what is generally referred to by "religion" is not simply quantitative. It also pertains to a distinctive language for conceptualizing religious and sociopolitical phenomena that has important implications for how to rethink the "theological-political complex." Here singularity does not imply lack of diversity. Indeed, Islam includes views that unite the religious and the political, others that highlight the differentiation between state and religion,[23] and others still that emphasize the co-existence of such perspectives as giving birth to complex and diverse social configurations.[24] Yet traversing all positions is the idea that, despite modernist developments toward individualistic models, Islam exceeds "religion."[25] Encompassing social, legal, and economic dimensions, "Islam" points to a distinct framework and values for understanding communal life in ways that, opposing the separation between religion and politics but not that between religious and political authority, are neither merely religious, nor reducible to Western secular forms. Although Orientalist mentalities have stereotyped Islam as inherently leading to authoritarian regimes, it is far from evident that rejecting the separation between religion and politics implies authoritarian forms of communal life—though these are visible in many postcolonial states—nor that all aspects of political life in Muslim societies requires religious foundations.[26] Arguably, the diversity, flexibility, and complexity of the Islamic tradition(s) has a rich potential to draw from to revisit the theological-political problematics. Emphasizing this potential, though, does not come unreservedly. Controversial questions about gender equality and pluralism that have marked, and still mark, discourses and practices connected to what is claimed to be prescribed by the *shari'a* require the utmost critical vigilance, as do uses of religion in modern Muslim politics that seek to ground theocratic or authoritarian political projects, as in the case of the Talibans in Afghanistan, the Mullah's regime in Iran, but also al-Qā'idah, Boko-Haram, and the Islamic State throughout the Middle East, Africa, and Asia—phenomena that cannot be considered independently of larger historical periods and modern political formations. Developments on questions of gender and pluralism traversing different disciplines in contemporary Islamic scholarship, on issues of piety and social justice in Islamic ethics, as well as on theological-political imaginaries in modern Islamic political thought, exemplify this vigilance and provide a critical space from where to think further about these issues without recurring to secular models.[27]

The question of the proper name is not the only grid though which Derrida approaches Islam as "religion." His reflections also focus on issues of modernization and globalization.

> Judaism and Islam would thus perhaps be the last two monotheisms to revolt against everything that, in the Christianizing of our world, signifies the death of God, death in God, two non-pagan monotheisms that do not accept death any more than multiplicity in God (The Passion, the Trinity, etc.) two monotheisms still alien enough at the heart of Graeco-Christian, Pagano-Christian Europe, alienating themselves from a Europe that signifies the death of God, by recalling at all a costs that "monotheism" signifies no less faith in the One, and in the living One, than belief in a single God. (51/22)

Islam is "still alien enough" but also "alienating" itself from the secularizing experience of an essentially Christian European Enlightenment. As such, it occupies a complex position in relation to modern epistemology and politics. On the one hand, Islam is partly the agent of its own alienation to a European model of secularization in which little space is left to religion in political life. While the source of this positioning can in some aspects be based on a reactional resistance to colonial oppression, there seem to be specific features connected to the identity of Islam, arguably its values and understandings that perhaps keeps it foreign to European secularization—features that opposes the severing of the theological-political nexus. These elements would seem to have in part survived European secularization so as to make Islam "still alien enough" to it. Seen in the context of our discussion of Derrida's critique of globalization as the world-wide extension of a Western-Christian, racialized knowledge and political forms relevant to public life, Islam would thus be a surviving tradition to European colonization that, by opposing the death of God, also resists experientially, epistemically, and politically the binary logic of modern secular discourse.

On the other hand, if Islam is only "still alien enough" to European secularization, it is not totally foreign to modern processes. Indeed, as Derrida suggests later on in the text, Islam is also an active participant in the same processes of modernization and globalization it opposes. Like other so-called religions, Islam "allies itself with tele-technoscience, to which it reacts with all its forces"; "it is [. . .] globalization (*mondialatinisation*)" (82/72). As discussed in chapter 3, this paradoxical alliance and resistance typical of religions is best illustrated by the notion of autoimmunity, a process in which self-protection and survival require destroying or suspending one's own self-defenses. With reference to religions, autoimmunity illuminates a double movement of appropriation and often violent reaction to modern global

Islam, Religion, and Democracy / 201

logics and means. While so-called religions globalize themselves through the use of techno-science, they also react to this process and its scientific thrust by violently rejecting it, however differently in their own contexts. In this way, they simultaneously internalize and negate a process of differentiation that splits their identity while guaranteeing its persistence. Thought of as "religion," Islam too "produces, weds, exploit the capital and knowledge of telemediatization" in order to survive, thereby somehow furthering its own secularization. And yet it "reacts, immediately, simultaneously, declaring war" on these elements in order to protect its own integrity as religion. For Derrida, if the becoming modern of Islam as religion is not taken into account, "the surge <*déferlement*> of Islam will be neither understood nor answered" (58/34).

According to Derrida, the reactional violence to modern processes associated with Islam is not simply reactionary, but it also shows a connection to rational elements. For him, there is "no incompatibility, in the said 'return of the religious,' between the 'fundamentalisms,' the 'integrisms' or their 'politics'" and a "rationality" that can be "hypercritical" (81/69); between "fanaticism, dogmatism or irrational obscurantism" and a "hypercritical acumen and incisive analysis of the hegemony and the models" of modern politics, including "globalatinization, religion that does not speak its name, ethnocentrism putting on, as always a show of 'universalism,' market-driven science and technology, democratic rhetoric, 'humanitarian' strategy or 'keeping peace' by means of peace-keeping forces" (89/82). This view parallels an earlier comment in a footnote in which Derrida associates Islamism with fundamentalism but also with a "hypercritical" rationality that "can sometime resemble a deconstructive radicalization of the critical gesture" (81/69):

> "Islamism" which represents today the most powerful example of such fundamentalisms as measured by the scale of global demography. The most evident characteristics are too well known to dwell on (fanaticism, obscurantism, lethal violence, terrorism, oppression of women, etc.) But it is often forgotten that, notably in its ties to the Arab world, and through all the forms of brutal immunitary and indemnificatory reactivity against a techno-economical modernity to which a long history prevents it from adapting, this "Islamism" also develops a radical critique of what ties democracy *today, in its limits, in its concept and its effective power,* to the market and to the tele-technoscientific reason that dominates it. (81/69)

It is worth noting here that Derrida puts "Islamism" in quotation marks, signaling perhaps a more complex perspective (not all Islamism is fundamentalist) than the one emerging from his distinction between Islam/Islamism seen above.[28] So what gives "Islamism" a rational-critical force, if some of its violent features suggest the opposite? Highlighting the forms of "Islamism" tied to the Arab world, Derrida refers to a long history that "prevents" "Islamism" from "adapting" key forms of European modernity. What prevents "Islamism" from doing so? A tentative response to this question can be pursued by reflecting on the sources and positioning of Islam as that in the name of which "Islamism" operates, but also as that without which it could not be "*Islam*ism." From Derrida's characterization, what prevents from adapting modern European forms would not simply be the exclusionary process of modern formations, as his discussion of Schmitt reveals. Derrida's language seems to point again here to something else, arguably the normative sources shaping an Islamic form of life, sources that will have played a key role in preventing the adaptation of such forms. It would thus be the link between these sources and Islamism that helps us understand both a certain resistance to modernity and the basis on which a radical critique of modern models of politics and reason is developed.

At issue here is the question of reason, namely, what counts as reason beyond how and what reason counts and what role "Islamism" and Islam as "religion" play in all of this. Given Derrida's critique of the teleological character of modern secular reason discussed in chapter 2, his reference to "Islamism's" opposition to the dominance of "tele-technoscientific reason" is key. It signals a normative position that, much like deconstruction, resists the reduction of reason to calculative rationality and the secular orders informed by it (globalatinization, humanitarianism, market-driven science, democracy, and economy). This is perhaps where a deeper convergence between deconstruction and "Islamism" occurs, in a space where the link between reason and religion acquires central significance. As seen in chapter 2 and 3, Derrida shows that the separation between reason and religion is not a precondition for publicly acceptable political models, as modern secular discourses based on a calculative model of reason hold. On the contrary, he sees that separation as symptomatic of a fundamentalist mode of thinking that amplifies the problems of security, legitimacy, and solidarity it seeks to solve by setting a hierarchical relation by reason and faith that is line with, and in some sense renews, the legacy of colonial logics. In his view, a minimal faith that is "in its essence or calling, religious," but that cannot be solely reduced to religion, is central to the foundation of both knowledge and community (80–81/68). Figuratively located at the limits of both reason and religion, such a faith enlivens critical thinking, since it signals the possibility of political understandings and forms to be otherwise. Also, as a source of social bonds that help expose the distinction and yet interrelation of the theological and the political, and that also interrupt the opposition of nature/culture, such a faith provides sources for a different thinking of "living together." It does so since it enables resisting the logics of naturalization associated with religious orthodoxies and racist ideologies, but also with the more sophisticated racialized secular approaches typical of "White mythology."

Read through Derrida's parallel, which invokes a larger discussion on the nexus between reason and religion, Islamism's critique of the dominance of tele-technoscientific reason signals a "hypercritical" rationality. This is a type of rationality that "can sometimes resemble" that of deconstruction since, like the latter, it targets the fundamentally secular understanding of reason—a religion-free *scientific* reason—and the exclusionary institutions and epistemic orders informed by it. Yet, precisely because Islamism's rationality can only "resemble" that of deconstruction, "Islamism" must display a distinctive rationality of its own, one rooted in the sources and life form it draws from which are connected to Islam. If this holds, then Derrida's reflections on the rationality of "Islamism" do not only recognize the epistemic and political value of a distinct understanding of reason there where secular discourse sees only "fanaticism, dogmatism or irrational obscurantism." They also neither exclude that the "critical gesture" of deconstruction is closer to an "Islamic reason," as it were, than would appear at first sight, nor that some of Derrida's Muslim interlocutors might be found among Islamists rather than those embracing secularism.[29]

The significance of Derrida's approach to Islam as "religion" rests in the exposure of Islam's critical-political potential. Islam, as perhaps another name to address the religious phenomena that are also irreducibly social and political, names people, traditions, and practices whose values, understandings, and positionality question, and testify to, the racialized and exclusionary features of Western secular models. On this reading, Islamophobia is inseparable from questions of race. Islam also names human realities that, while integrating aspects of modernity, refuse to sever the theological-political relation as a condition for public life, drawing from distinct cultural sources and ethical values. So, not simply "the question of 'Islam'" as religion illuminates "Islam *as* a question" to the modern paradigm, as Anidjar has suggested about Derrida's view.[30] Such a view also points, albeit not uncritically, to Islam as *a* framework from which to develop a different grammar to address pressing questions of public life. While Derrida does not advance this point explicitly, at least not in these terms, this possibility remains an important implication that the logic of deconstruction helps bringing to the fore, one strictly linked to the question of translation and its potential for decolonization.

To further elaborate on this aspect, this study has taken as epistemically relevant the lived experience of subjects and their tradition(s), particularly when this experience provides sources for "testing" the alleged universal validity of epistemological and political orders through the exposure of their violent formation and maintenance. This, I have argued, not only resonates with the experience of colonized subjects such as Derrida, and Muslims more generally. It is also in line with the critical and decolonizing potential of an understanding of epistemological and political formations through deconstruction, conceived as "the analysis of what remains to be thought." Viewing Islam through these lenses does not mean to suggest that there has not been thinking or developments about Islam in Muslim societies or elsewhere. Quite the contrary. Rather, it is to emphasize the importance of thinking of Islam as referring to what remains of it as "alien" to European colonialism and modernity, as well as what has been transformed by its encounter with it. This distinction is as important as unstable, given the force and scope of Western hegemony in processes of knowledge production and circulation.[31] To *think* Islam and *from* Islam this way is a task of translation that responds to modern conditions and resonates with Islamic history, the spread of Islam across the world and its adoption of and adaptation to pre-Islamic traditions in Asia and Africa,[32] to the development of Islamic thought between the eighth and tenth centuries through the encounters and confrontations with a variety of intellectual and cultural traditions in the so-called "Graeco-Arabic translation movement,"[33] to the evolution and renewal of Islamic discourses under modern conditions,[34] it appears difficult to think of Islam without translation.[35] One key challenge for projects of decolonization today rests very much on the possibility of liberating translation from assimilatory models that would reverse and replicate its modern forms as instruments of domination. In this regard, Derrida's analysis of language and his emphasis on dissemination, and not simply assimilation, offers resources to approach translation as a critical and transformative praxis of meaning making and remaking through which to reclaiming the epistemic and political value of cultural sources and experiences of subaltern groups, while remaining at a distance from colonial schemas and drives. Ethnography, in this regard, is an indispensable companion of philosophical reflection that can illuminate how nonassimilatory forms of translation are negotiated and effected in daily practices, but is a pursuit that is beyond the scope of this work.

Islam and Democracy

Democracy represents another theme in relation to which Derrida develops his reflections on Islam, especially in *Rogues*. For him, the relationship between Islam and democracy is an urgent political issue.

> If one thus takes into account the link between the democratic and the demographic, if one counts, if one calculates and does the accounts, if one wants rationally to give an account, an explanation or a reason [*render raison*], and if one takes into account the fact that this Islam today accounts for a large number of people in the world, then this is perhaps, in the end, the greatest, if not the only, political issue of the future, the most urgent question of what remains to come for what is still called the political. The political, which is to say, in the free play and extension, in the determined indetermination, of its meaning, in the opening up of its meaning, the democratic. (*R*, 29/52)

For Derrida, the nexus between Islam and democracy is perhaps the "most urgent" question of the "political," which in modern times has become "coextensive" with the democratic (28/51). The urgency of this nexus stems from both the demographic relevance of Muslims in the world and the relevance of demography to democracy: the global population of Muslims is not negligible for the weight it can have in democratic life. Yet, since the political is commonly considered co-extensive with the democratic, and the future of democracy is far from being certain and secular—given the plasticity of its concept but also the antidemocratic tendencies displayed by many Western democracies in their exercise of sovereignty and support of neocolonial projects justified in the name of secularism. Thus, it cannot be excluded that the future of the political, and of democracy, will not intertwine with Islam in deeper ways, beyond calculative considerations. This is perhaps what it means "rationally to give an account" while counting.

Before looking at how Derrida understands the relationship between Islam and democracy, it is worth noting the difficulties connected to that very task. First, the identification of the objects of analysis is far from straightforward. Which "democracy" and "Islam"? Whose "democracy" and "Islam"? As seen earlier on, Derrida is aware of the epistemic difficulty of talking about Islam. This stems not simply from the European hegemony on the production of knowledge and the Orientalist force it has exercised on the representation and constitution of Islam, a situation that affects both Muslim and non-Muslims alike. It also depends on the coherence amid multiple features characterizing Islam, including a variety of groups that speak and claim to speak in its name. Similarly, while democracy would appear to be a more easily definable object, as testified by the identifiable and yet diverse forms it has taken since the Greeks, these very elements—democracy's historicity and plasticity—hinder more substantive conceptualizations and translations, as highlighted in chapter 4. Furthermore, discussions about Islam and democracy do not occur in the abstract, but under determinable and determined normative and political conditions. In this regard, Derrida's reflections occur within a nonneutral framework that favors the secularization of the political seen as the dissociation of religious and political authority: this entails separation between the theocratic and the political (*IW*, 53/85, 57/87), the protection of religious freedom (*IW*, 50/81), the right to free expression and public critique (*R*, 87/127), but also the political potential and possibility of denaturalizing present democracy, and more broadly the political, which (as seen above) is something that is also importantly connected to Islamic critiques of Western secular models.

So how does Derrida understand the link between Islam and democracy? The title of the chapter in *Rogues* in which he explores this matter presents an ambiguity: Islam would be "The Other of Democracy" (28/51). According to Anne Norton, this formulation signals that Derrida's position is "not open to solidarity with Islam or Muslims." In her view, Derrida "names Islam the enemy of democracy, philosophy and reason."[36] Yet things might be more complex. While in Derrida's syntactical formulation, Islam and democracy can be seen as opposing each other, the "of" could also indicate possession and thus a possibility that might be internal to democracy, and to Islam, as I will discuss below. Indeed, Derrida has consistently rejected binary conceptualizations and, especially in the Algerian case, has insisted on the idea that different parties there only "oppose different models of democracy, representation and citizenship" (*N*, 116; *IW*, 39/66). Further, as seen in the discussion of Islamism, there are reasons to doubt that Derrida sees Islam as the enemy of reason, and there also are opportunities to see connections between Islam and democracy in *Rogues*, which is what I intend to show below.

Derrida's tentative hypothesis about the relationship between democracy and Islam, a hypothesis that he names as "Arabic *and* Islamic" to "refer to the Arabic literality of the language of the Koran" reads as follows: "Islam, or a certain Islam, would thus be the only religious or theocratic culture that can still in fact or in principle, inspire and declare any resistance to democracy. If it does not actually resist what might be more or less contested, it can at least resist the democratic principle, claim, or allegation, the legacy of the old name 'democracy'" (*R*, 29/52). While Derrida ambiguously oscillates between "Islam" and a "certain Islam" using a disjunctive formulation, in a passage preceding this quote, he anticipates what gets qualified here as a "certain Islam" but also as democracy.

> What is this hypothesis or hypothec? Today in what is called the European tradition (at the same time Graeco-Christian and globalatinazing) that dominates the worldwide concept of the political, where the democratic becomes coextensive with the political, where the democratic realm becomes constitutive of the political realm precisely because of the indetermination and "freedom," the "free play," of its concept, and where the democratic, having become consubstantially political in this Graeco-Christian globalatinizing tradition, appears inseparable in the modernity following the Enlightenment from an ambiguous secularization (and secularization is always ambiguous in that it frees itself of the religious, all the while remaining marked in its very concepts by it, by the theological, indeed, the ontotheological), the only and very few regimes, in the supposed modernity of this situation, that *do not present themselves* as democratic are those with a theocratic Muslim government. Not of all of them, to be sure, but, let me underscore this, the only regimes that *do not fashion themselves* to be democratic, the only ones that *do not present themselves* to be democratic, unless I am mistaken, are statutorily linked to the Muslim faith or creed. (28/51)

Although Derrida is excessively economic in considering Islam as the only religious culture resisting democracy in its modern secularized form—indeed indigenous populations in the Americas, Asia, and Africa could also be mentioned here—he is concerned with specifically theocratic Muslim regimes that oppose not any democracy, but modern *secular* democracy.

While he mentions Saudi Arabia, his main focus is Algeria, where the 1992 elections were interrupted in virtue of the perceived risk that a "likely majority that presented itself as essentially Islamic and Islamist," the *Front Islamist de Salut*, would halt democracy, as it was attributed to its intentions (31/54). Derrida reads this event as appearing "particularly symptomatic" of the relationship between "Islam and democracy" and as displaying an autoimmune logic, one in which the provisional death of democracy is brought about for its longer-term survival. As he put it, "the Algerian government and a large part, although not a majority of the Algerian people (as well as people outside Algeria)" decided "in a sovereign fashion to suspend, at least provisionally, democracy *for its own good*" (30/53, 33/57).

To recall the discussion of democracy in the previous chapter, Derrida addresses here one of its key problems since the Greeks. Arguably, this problem finds its most evident modern examples in the advent of Nazism and Fascism out of democratic regimes: the paradoxical relationship between freedom and equality. This paradox consists in the fact that protecting the freedom of the demos as a collective does not exclude the possibility that once in majority, such a collective could attack individual freedom putting an end to it, precisely in the name of democracy itself. While Aristotle limited this suicidal aspect of democracy by restricting democratic freedom through the democratic equality guaranteed by alternation in ruling, and modern thinkers from Rousseau, Tocqueville up to Rawls and Habermas have struggled to balance freedom and equality in order to limit the dangerous potential of either, the Algerian case indicates that the problem remains. As Derrida says, "the great question of modern parliamentary and representative democracy, perhaps of all democracy, in this logic of the turn or round of the other time and thus of the other, of the *alter* in general, is that the *alternative* to democracy can always be *represented* as a democratic *alternation*" (31/54).

Derrida's characterization of these events in Algeria has been subject to some criticism, with commentators raising objections on a number of issues. Norton, for example, mentions his questionable and somewhat inaccurate reconstruction of the 1992 events as well as his uncritical attitude toward the military, which he portrays as saving democracy.[37] Echoing her critique, Arthur Bradley points to Derrida's one-sidedness in considering the military coup from a governmental perspective that ends up reinforcing a decisionist model of sovereignty at the expenses of the self-determining will of the voters.[38] While these criticisms reveal problems with Derrida's characterization of the Algerian event, a deeper and, for our purposes, more significant question concerns what exactly, of this event, would be "particularly symptomatic" of the relationship between Islam and democracy. In this regard, Derrida affirms that

> one might see this "Algerian" event (the rise of an Islamism considered to be antidemocratic that will have prompted the suspension of a democratic electoral process) to illustrate the hypothesis of at least a certain Islam. And this Islam, this particular one and not Islam in general (if such a thing exists), would represent the only religious culture that would have resisted up until now a European (that is, Greco-Christian and globalatinazing) process of secularization, and thus of democratization, and thus, in the strict sense of politicization. (31/54)

There is a puzzling ambiguity marking this passage. On the one hand, Derrida talks of a "particular Islam" and "not of Islam in general," clarifying what exactly it resists to in what goes under the "old name of democracy." Whereas in *Politics of Friendship*, "old" referred explicitly to the masculine and ethno-nationalist understandings of community and citizenship and only implicitly to political theology, in *Rogues*, "old" refers explicitly to the latter, targeting the question of *European* secularization, which does not, however, exclude other forms of differentiation between religion and politics. In this context, "this Islam," a theocratic one, would thus be opposed to the modern, European, and Christian understanding of the political as characterized by an ambiguous process of secularization—and thus of translation of the theological-political—considered to be central to modern democracy. On the other hand, his formulation does not exclude the Algerian event being exemplary of a hypothesis that encompasses Islam more generally, confirming the ambiguity of the previous quote. Indeed, this is a possibility that his use of "at least" leaves open, and this raises questions about what exactly his position is about the relationship between Islam, and not simply its theocratic strands, and democracy.

Investigating further Derrida's discussion of these issues in *Rogues*, as well as his reflections on autoimmunity, might help clarifying things. Derrida affirms that the hypothesis he puts forward calls for a double task.

> One of the two tasks would be of the order of theoretical or hermeneutic knowledge and would consist in an enormous,

> urgent, and thorough historical study of everything that does and does not authorize, in different readings of the Koranic heritage, and in its own language, the translation of a properly democratic paradigm. But it would be also essential to study and take seriously into account (something for which I have neither the time nor the competence), beginning with the Greece of Plato and Aristotle, with the political history and discourses of Athens but also of Sparta, of Hellenism and Neoplatonism, what gets passed on, transferred, translated from Europe *by* pre- and *post*-Koranic Arabic, as well as by Rome. (31/55)

Pointing to the political dimension of the production of knowledge, Derrida calls for a historically sensible study of what and who authorizes today, as in the past, the translation of a "democratic paradigm" in the Islamic tradition(s), whether such a paradigm is seen as an internal possibility or a result of external import, as it were. Declaring his limited knowledge on this topic, he, nevertheless, relies on a controversial reading of a specific moment in the history of Islamic philosophy.

> I don't know how much weight to give in this whole story to the rather troubling fact that Aristotle's *Politics,* by a curious exception, was absent in the Islamic importation, reception, translation, and mediation of Greek philosophy, particularly in Ibn Ruchd (Averroes), who incorporated into his Islamic political discourse only the *Nicomachean Ethics* or, like Al-Farabi, only the theme of the philosopher king from Plato's *Republic.* This latter theme seems to have been, from the point of view of what can be called Islamic "political philosophy," a locus classicus. From what I have been able to understand, certain historians and interpreters of Islam today regard the absence of Aristotle's *Politics* in the Arab philosophical corpus as having a symptomatic, if not determining, significance, just like the privilege granted by this Muslim theologico-political philosophy to the Platonic theme of the philosopher king or absolute monarch, a privilege that goes hand in hand with the severe judgment brought against democracy. (32/56)

Although Derrida mentions the opinions of "certain historians and interpreters of Islam," who consider as "symptomatic" the "absence of Aristotle's

Politics," and the paradigm of democracy, in the Greek philosophical heritage translated into Arabic, he considers this to be a "fact," when things are far from self-evident.[39] Further, he warns that his type of study "is not so obvious" and encounters limits "for the language of the Koran or for any non-European culture and language" of translating an originally Greek term into another idiom." Yet these limits, which concern any "linguistic or political translation" pertains to the instability of meaning—in this case the absence of a fix referent for democracy whether in Greek or European languages. The political conditioning affecting linguistic context and inheritance "should not destroy the possibility and necessity of a serious and systematic study of the *references* to democracy, of the democratic *legacy* and claim or *allegation*," whether such references occur "under this name or under another assumed to be its equivalent, in the ancient, and especially recent history of Arab-nation states, and more generally in societies of Islamic culture" (32/56).

The second task, more distinctively political, concerns "whoever, by hypothesis, considers him or herself a friend of democracy in the world" and consists in "doing everything possible to join forces with all those who, and first of all in the Islamic world, fight for secularization of the political (however ambiguous this secularization remains)" but also for the "emergence of a laic subjectivity" as well as for "an interpretation of the Koranic heritage that privileges, form the inside, as it were, the democratic virtualities" that are not apparent at first sight (33/57).

Two important considerations follow from this double task. First, investigating the relationship between Islam, and "a certain Islam," and democracy, requires paying attention to historical questions of inheritance and translation, which are significantly affected by linguistic contexts and politics, as well as selections and increased critical responsibility on the part of interpreters and translators. On this issue, Derrida is both uncritical and critical. On the one hand, by relying, however hesitantly, on received interpretations, and by leaving unaddressed the political and material context in which the Graeco-Arab translation occurred, he displays an uncritical attitude toward the inheritance of the Islamic philosophical tradition.[40] Indeed, although he reveals his limited competence and underscores his reliance on the opinion of others, he too quickly names as a fact what lacks historical support. He neither discloses nor questions an intellectual orientation that would seem to generate out of the *simple* "absence of Aristotle's *Politics* in the Arab Philosophical corpus" and "the privilege granted by this Muslim theologico-political philosophy to the Platonic theme of the philosopher

King," a "symptomatic, if not determining significance" of a position against democracy (32/57). On the other hand, by calling for a study of what, in the ancient and more recent history of Muslim societies, would have referred to democracy, thereby opening to the possibility that "facts" might have been otherwise, Derrida displays a critical attitude toward the process and forces involved in what does and does not get transmitted and translated, an attitude that more generally characterizes the logic of deconstruction. If we take this critical attitude and approach to interpretation, language, and translation as paradigmatic to the investigation of Islam's relation to democracy, as he suggests, it would seem difficult to hold onto it while also maintaining that there is in some sense something inherent to the Koranic heritage that sets mutually exclusive boundaries between Islam and democracy. Actually, the opposite would seem to be the case, as Derrida has maintained on other occasions by dismissing rigid cultural separations between East and West (*N*, 116; *IW*, 38–39/65–66).

Second, such an investigation calls for a political responsibility to join forces in the Islamic world that *already* resist subsuming the political under religious rule and that seek to open up the democratic potential of the Koranic heritage from *within* it. Framed this way, Derrida's view would seem to differ significantly from the modern framework of European secularization. Not only does he refrain from imposing heteronomous demands onto the Koranic heritage and Muslim societies, but he also seeks to work from within them to address questions that are recognizable and articulable under terms, conceptualizations, and experiences associated with Islamic history and thought. Indeed, Derrida does not advocate for the import of secularization seen as a universally valid historical process of human development, nor for the secular translation of the theological into the political, as in dominant modern narratives. As seen, these are versions of secularization that his thought has greatly contributed to challenge and that constitute the specific target ("European secularization") of the type of Islamism he criticizes. What he advocates for is joining all those who, especially in the Islamic world, support two things: first, the "secularization of the political" seen as the separation between political and religious authority, as he has explicitly mentioned in other occasions with specific reference to Islam or Muslim societies (*IW*, 53/85; TSA, 306), second, fighting for an interpretation of the Koranic heritage that, starting from its sources, is open to and favors its democratic potential. Thus, while apparently constraining Islam within "old" secular schemas, Derrida unites instead with forces and developments *already* at work within Islamic history and discourses. This is attested by long-lasting debates and practices supporting the separation between religious and political authority in Islamic societies,[41] as well as by modern Islamic discourses invested in opening up hermeneutics sources and approaches to the understanding of Islam in its time.[42]

Derrida's reflections on autoimmunity contribute to further clarify the relationship between Islam and democracy, especially when autoimmunity is appreciated as a mode of "thinking life otherwise" (33/57). As democracy survives at the price of compromising its identity, so do Islam and "Islamism" by embracing modern aspects that would appear to transform authentic religious features. Addressing the life of living systems, including political and religious ones, the notion of autoimmunity thus brings to light the irreducibility of the theological-political relationship to public *life*. Indeed, the discussion of chapter 4 has shown that Derrida's notion of autoimmunity illuminates the unsustainability of traditional theological understandings of sovereignty informing secular democracy, which continues, however, to be in need of foundations from which religious sources cannot be excluded. The reflections on Islam and globalizations through the same notion have highlighted the nonpurely religious features of Islam as well as of "Islamism," but also the critical potential Islamic sources share with radical democratic criticism against the hegemony of Western secular models.

But the discussion of the Algerian event has so far illuminated only one aspect of autoimmunity as applied to public life: the suicidal character of democracy. Yet, autoimmunity potentially highlights that when the solution of the theological-political nexus is sought, as in the case of "a certain Islam" aiming to subsume the political under the theocratic, what is at risk is not simply democracy, but (the life of) Islam itself. As Derrida says in "Taking a Stand for Algeria," a 1994 intervention in support of civil peace: "our idea of democracy implies the separation between state and religious powers" which "protects the practices of faith and, in this instance, the freedom of discussion and interpretation within each religion. For example, and here first of all, in Islam whose different readings, both exegetical and political, must develop freely, and not only in Algeria. This is in fact the best response to the racist anti-Islamic movement born of violence deemed Islamic or that would dare still affiliate themselves with Islam" (TSA, 306).

At stake, in the takeover of political authority by a theocratic Islamism is also the survival of Islam as a tradition that has since its early period historically been characterized by heterogeneity and contestation. Read in conjunction with Derrida's discussion of Islam and "religion," interpretation, and inheritance, the Algerian event would thus appear not so much symptomatic of a binary between Islam and democracy, though Derrida's language and formulations somehow equivocally point in that direction. Instead, it provides an occasion to illuminate some convergences between what these names evoke that have remained less visible, and perhaps intolerable, under traditional schemas of the political, but that the logic of deconstruction exposes and renders available to critical thought. Concurrently, such an example helps shed further light on the theological-political as an irreducible nexus to public *life* that contributes to keep it safe from closures, political or religious. Although Derrida advances an ambivalent view as to whether it opposes, at some level, Islam to democracy, and that is affected by historical inaccuracy and occasional reductionisms, the logic of his approach leans toward a different direction. Indeed, by opposing forces that would block both the life of democracy and of Islam, and by joining forces internal to Islamic traditions that engage in ongoing hermeneutic and sociopolitical processes of transformation, his view opens up the future of the political and of democracy to Islamicate perspectives and contexts, without nevertheless fixing a determinate political form. More broadly, Derrida's exposure of the critical potential of Islam to question the racialized character of modern political models and to resist assimilationist forms of secular translation contributes to decolonize the separatist logic of modern secular discourse, pointing to the possibility of alternative configurations of communal life beyond the secular. These are configurations that while not being solely political are not simply religious either. If these alternatives are involved in his suggestion that discussions about religion occurs "just at the moment when it is towards Islam, perhaps, that we ought to begin by turning our attention" (FK, 45/13), then Islam constitutes, in his thought, *a* significant and tangible example of these possibilities.

With these reflections, I do not intend to emphasize that Derrida offers a better understanding of Islam, also because he had limited access to it for a variety of reasons mentioned above and in earlier chapters. Clearly, Islamic discourses do not need Derrida to illuminate Islam as a tradition that, by drawing from distinct understandings and values, partly survived and resisted colonialism and the colonization of knowledge forms. Indeed, many scholars within the Islamic tradition(s) have done and continue to do this work more competently, connecting debates on secularism, Islam and decolonization, which, in many cases, are taken up together.[43] What I suggest is that Derrida joins in part these discourses and that some of his positions intersect with them. The potential contribution of Derrida's perspective on Islam developed here stems from his focus on translation and the resources that this offers, especially to Islamic discourses that take seriously: first, translation in the history and experience of Islam; second, the epistemic and political significance of translation for the impact Orientalism had on Islam in modern times, and on the responses to it; and third, the deconstruction of racial constructs based on the grasp of pure meaning (for example, "religion" as capturing the essence of all religion phenomena) in the task of decolonizing knowledge, its production and circulation. While some authors from various disciplines have mentioned, but not engaged, Derrida in the context of translation and religion such as Asad, but also on metaphysical binaries and language as in the work of Sayyid, substantial work on these however recognized connections has not been yet produced, but the potential seems there. This is unlike the reception of his insights on textual interpretation, which some prominent contemporary Muslim thinkers such as Mohammed Arkoun have developed from within Islam. Thus, besides pointing to the significance of Islam in Derrida's later works, the ambition of the book, in this respect, has been two-fold: first, to challenge those who quickly exclude the relevance of Derrida's thought to Islam, or uncritically buy into the dominant representation of him being a Judeo-Christian *European* thinker who has little to contribute to issues that are central to both Islam and decolonization; second, to call for a more critical, experimental, and open-ended approach that appreciates aspects of his philosophy that intersects with, perhaps are indebted to, the Islamic tradition, more than what many commentators or critics are willing to concede.

Notes

Introduction

1. In recent years, the concept of "religion" has been at the center of such attentive analysis and thorough criticism that have disallowed its uncritical use. See for example, Talal Asad, *Genealogies of Religion: Discipline and Reasons of Power in Christianity* (Baltimore: John Hopkins University Press, 1993); Tomoko Masuzawa, *The Invention of World Religions: Or, How European Universalism Was Preserved in the Language of Pluralism* (Chicago: Chicago University Press, 2005); and Brent Nongbri, *Before Religion: A History of a Modern Concept* (New Haven/London: Yale University Press, 2013). For more cross-disciplinary explorations of the concept of religion, see Hent de Vries, ed., *Religion: Beyond a Concept* (New York: Fordham University Press, 2008). It is with reference to this critical problematization that I use "religion" in this book.

2. While acknowledging its contested meaning, I use the term "secular" as referring to a space that is, semantically and politically, "free of religion," as it has been commonly used in modern discourse. I do so in order to identify the conceptualization my reflections seek to question. For recent studies on the "secular," see especially Talal Asad, *Formations of the Secular: Christianity, Islam, Modernity* (Stanford: Stanford University Press, 2003) and Charles Taylor *A Secular Age* (Cambridge, MA: Belknap Press of Harvard University Press, 2007).

3. See Asad's intervention in Jacques Derrida, *AANJ*. It is important to distinguish here secularization from secularism. While I recognize that both are contested concepts, whose normative and explanatory values have been thoroughly criticized in recent years, I will generally use them according to their traditional understandings in order to further problematize them: that is, secularism as referring to a normative doctrine prescribing the relationship between religion and politics, and secularization as designating the historical, sociological, and institutional modern process of differentiation between the religious and such other spheres as the economic, political, and scientific.

4. See Asad, *Formations of the Secular*, 1, 25, 31–36. In this work, I will use the notion of "West" as developed by Stuart Hall as pointing to an historico-political construct roughly going back to the sixteenth century and referring to a type of society characterized by capitalism, secularism, and modern science and whose material conditions are rooted in the experience of colonialism. See Stuart Hall, "The West and the Rest: Discourse and Power," in *The Formation of Modernity*, ed. Stuart Hall and Braem Gieben (Cambridge: Polity, 1992), 185 ff.

5. See especially Wilfred Cantwell Smith, *The Meaning and End of Religion* (San Francisco, CA: Harper & Row, 1978); Asad, *Genealogies of Religion*; Masuzawa, *The Invention of World Religions*; Timothy Fitzgerald, ed., *Religion and the Secular: Historical and Colonial Formations* (London Equinox, 2009); Marcus Dressler and Arvin Mandair, eds., *Secularism and Religion-Making* (Oxford/ New York: Oxford University Press, 2011).

6. For a historical investigation on knowledge production about religion within the framework of Orientalism, see Tomoko Masuzawa, *The Invention of World Religions*. For the connection between secularism and Orientalism, see Gil Anidjar, "Secularism," *Critical Inquiry* 33, no. 1 (2006): 52–77. Finally, for works that situate the beginning of "Orientalism" and its colonial and racist undercurrents in the fifteenth century and extending to the Americas, see respectively Ella Shohat, "The Sephardi-Moorish Atlantic: Between Orientalism and Occidentalism," in *Between the Middle East and the Americas: The Cultural Politics of the Middle East in the Americas,* ed. Evelyn Alsultany and Ella Shohat (University of Michigan Press 2013), pp. 42–63; Sylvia Wynter, "1492: A New World View," in *Race Discourse, and the Origin of the Americas,* ed. Vera Lawrence Hyatt and Rex Nettleford (Washington: Smithsonian Institution Press, 1995).

7. See Hent De Vries, "Introduction: Before, around, and beyond the Theologico-Political," in *Political Theologies: Public Religions in a Post-Secular World*, ed. Hent de Vries and Lawrence Sullivan (New York: Fordham University Press, 2006) 4, 8.

8. See Baruch Spinoza, *Theologico-Political Treatise*, trans. Samuel Shirley (London: Hackett, 2001); Jacques Derrida, unpublished manuscript "Théologico-Politique," UCI Libraries, University of California Irvine.

For an insightful discussion of the hyphenation in Spinoza and its connection to Derrida see, respectively, Willi Goetschel, *Spinoza's Modernity: Mendelssohn, Lessing, and Heine* (Madison: University of Wisconsin Press, 2004); and "The Hyphen in the Theological-Political: Spinoza to Mendelssohn, Heine, and Derrida," *Religions* 10.1 (2019): 1–13.

9. I borrow the formulation "theological-political complex" from Will Goetschel, adding important nuances to the use he makes of it. See Willi Goetschel "Derrida and Spinoza: Rethinking the Theologico-Political Problem," *Bamidbar: Journal for Jewish Thought and Philosophy*, Passagen Verlag, 1, no. 2 (2011): 9–25; *The Discipline of Philosophy and the Invention of Modern Jewish Thought* (New York: Fordham University Press, 2013), 163–66; and *Spinoza's Modernity: Mendelssohn,*

Lessing, and Heine (Madison: University of Wisconsin Press, 2004), 10, 185. For Goetschel, the term "theologico-political complex," which he traces back to Spinoza's understanding of the "theologico-political" occurring in the *Theologico-Political Treatise*, refers to an irreducible entanglement between the theological and the political, which are seen as mutually constituted and advancing claims to universality that require a continued, critical contextual examination ("Derrida and Spinoza: Rethinking the Theologico-Political Problem," 20). Like Goetschel, I employ the term "theological-political complex" to highlight the local character and irreducible interconnection between the theological and the political, as well as the problem of how to rethink universality. However, my use of it does not simply seek to distinguish itself linguistically by using "theological-political" instead of "theologico-political" in order to maintain the conceptual distinctiveness of the two terms and domains, "theological" and "political." It also seeks to amplify the recognition of the colonial and legacy and racialized schema undergirding the "theologico-political" nexus in modern discourse, with a view to increase the visibility of the stakes and implications involved in it.

10. Distinctive of Derrida's approach, the link between language and epistemology on the one hand, and the theological-political relation on the other, represents also an important and yet largely understudied point of intersection between Derrida and Spinoza, whom the former turned to in the 1980s, to reflect on these matters. As exceptions to this trend stand, Dana Hollander's *Exemplarity and Chosenness. Rosenzweig and Derrida on the Nation of Philosophy* (Stanford: Stanford University Press, 2008) and Goetschel, ed., "Rethinking the Theologico-Political Complex: Derrida's Spinoza," *Bamidbar: Journal for Jewish Thought and Philosophy*, Passagen Verlag, 1, no. 2 (2011).

11. See, for example, Nancy Holland, ed., *Feminist Interpretations of Jacques Derrida* (University Park: The Pennsylvania State University Press, 1997); Haddad, *The Inheritance of Democracy*; and Penelope Deutscher "Derrida's Impossible Genealogies" *Theory and Event* 8, no. 1 (2005); "Women and so On: Rogues and the Autoimmunity of Feminism" *Symposium: Canadian Journal of Continental Philosophy* 11, no. 1 (2007): 101–19.

12. See, for example, his asymmetric treatment of South Africa and Israel on issues of settler colonialism and race—made more explicit in the first case—as well as his only oblique treatment of the nexus between race and religion in his discussions of Judaism, Zionism, and secularization. For a discussion of some of these issues, see, respectively, Jospeh Massad, "Forget Semitism!" in *Living Together: Jacques Derrida's Communities of Violence and Peace*, ed. Elizabeth Weber (New York. Fordham University Press, 2013), 59–79; Gil Anidjar "Mal de Sionism," in *Living Together: Jacques Derrida's Communities of Violence and Peace*, ed. Elizabeth Weber (New York. Fordham University Press, 2013), 45–58. In their "No Names Apart: The Separation of Word and History in Derrida's 'Le Dernier Mot du Racism'" *Critical Inquiry* 13 (1986): 140–54, Anne McClintock and Rob Nixon point to

another dimension of race that Derrida does not really engage with—the connection between race and capitalism.

13. This is arguably the underlying common view of race emerging from a variety of ground-breaking works including: W. E. B. Dubois, "The Conservation of Races," in *Race*, ed. Robert Bernasconi (Oxford: Blackwell, 2001); *The Souls of Black Folk* (New York: Dover, 1994); Aimé Cesaire, *Discourse on Colonialism*, trans. Joan Pinkham (New York: Monthly Review: 2000); Frantz Fanon, *The Wretched of The Earth*, trans. Richard Philcox (New York: Grove, 2004); *Black Skin, White Masks*, trans. by Richard Philcox (New York: Grove, 2008); Edward Said, *Orientalism* (New York: Pantheon, 1978).

14. For a seminal work illustrating racialized forms of assimilatory translations, see Frantz Fanon, "The 'North African Syndrome,'" in *Toward the African Revolution* (New York: Grove, 1964).

15. I borrow the notion of lived experience from the use Frantz Fanon makes of it in his *Black Skin, White Masks*, adopting it from Maurice Merleau-Ponty, to refer to what Derrida *recalls* of the experience he lived in French Algeria. The idea, experience and philosophical practice of the margin is distinctive of Derrida's entire *oeuvre* and is also specific to one of his works, *MP*.

16. See also Jürgen Habermas and Jacques Derrida, "February 15, or What Binds Europeans Together: A Plea for a Common Foreign Policy, Beginning in the Core of Europe" *Constellations* 10 (2003): 291–97.

17. See, respectively, Ian Almond, *Sufism and Deconstruction*; Mustapha Marrouchi, "Decolonizing the Terrain of Western Theoretical Productions" *College Literature* 24, no. 2 (1997): 1–34.

18. For a criticism of Derrida's long "silence" on Algeria, which he eventually broke, see Mustapha Marrouchi, "Decolonizing the Terrain of Western Theoretical Productions," *College Literature* 24, no. 2 (1997): 1–34. For an account of the possible reasons why Derrida remained silent on the question of Algeria for a long time, see Baring, "Liberalism and the Algerian War: The Case of Jacques Derrida" *Critical Inquiry* 36 (2010): 239–61.

19. To highlight the figure of the Arab Jew, Gil Anidjar refers to Fethi Benslama's emphasis on the Judeo-Arabic cultural matrix in which and through which Derrida first accessed the so-called Abrahamic religions. See Anidjar, "Introduction: 'Once more, Once More': Derrida, the Arab, the Jew," in *Acts of Religion*, ed. Gil Anidjar (New York: Routledge, 2002), 10. Echoing Freud's Moses, Geoffrey Bennington suggests that Derrida is "neither Jew nor Greek, but 'Egyptian'" to point to the mixed and not simply or solely European origins of Derrida's identity. See his "Mosaic Fragment: If Derrida were an Egyptian . . . ," in *Legislations: The Politics of Deconstruction* (London: Verso, 1994), 209. Christopher Wise draws attention to the link between Derrida's use of conjuration and its cultural salience in the Sahel region in Africa. He calls Derrida an "African thinker" and points to the pre-Platonic and non-European sources that influenced Africa and the Middle East, sources from

which he sees deconstruction drawing. See his *Derrida, Africa and the Middle East* (New York: Palgrave, 2009), x, 1; and "The Figure of Jerusalem: Derrida's *Specters of Marx*," *Christianity and Literature* 54, no. 1 (2004): 73–91, note 1. Finally, Ian Almond calls attention to the relationship between Derrida and Islam, particularly on the intersection of some of his theoretical tropes and the work of Ibn Arabi. See his *Sufism and Deconstruction: A Comparative Study of Derrida and Ibn Arabi* (London: Routledge, 2004). While not developed, Derrida's Jewishness is not ignored here. Indeed, his Jewish identity in Algeria is taken as key to appreciate particularly the traumatic experience he underwent in French Algeria, and thus as decisively contributing—experientially, epistemically, and politically—to his personal and intellectual formation as a whole. His emphasis on the Arab Jew, and not simply the signifier Jew, and his proclaimed fidelity to more than one identity underscored above, has grounded the choice not to single out his Jewishness—an aspect that has been explored already in the literature. See, for example, *Judeities: Questions for Jacques Derrida*, ed. Bettina Bergo et al. (New York: Fordham University Press, 2007).

20. An exception to Derrida's lack of explicit treatment of race is his intervention to the "tRACEs: Race, Deconstruction and Critical Theory" Conference held at the University of California Humanities Research Institute in April 2003 (see https://www.youtube.com/watch?v=LfXdYefgKjw).

21. For discussions about the role of Derrida's empirical identity, see respectively Chantal Zabus's "Encre Blanche et Afrique orginelle: Derrida et la Postcolonialité" and Bennington's "Mosaic Fragment: If Derrida were an Egyptian . . ." discussed by Anidjar, who also recalls Derrida's leaning toward identity as a question in his *The Jew, the Arab: A History of the Enemy* (Stanford, CA: Stanford University Press, 2003), 42 ff. For perspectives on the genesis of Derrida's thought in relation to French Algeria, see Robert Young, "Deconstruction and the postcolonial," in *Deconstructions: A User's Guide*, ed. Nicholas Royle (London: Palgrave Macmillan, 2000), 187–21; and Michael Syrotinski, *Deconstruction and the Postcolonial: At the Limits of Theory* (Liverpool: Liverpool University Press, 2007). For a discussion of the French intellectual context in which Derrida's philosophy developed, see Edward Baring, *The Young Derrida and French Philosophy, 1945–1968* (New York: Cambridge University Press, 2011).

22. For a discussion of the idea that the colonial experience played a key role in fostering a "critical sensibility" in colonized thinkers, see Walter Mignolo, "Epistemic Disobedience, Independent Thought and De-Colonial Freedom," *Theory, Culture & Society* 26 (7–8): 1–23.

23. See Enrique Dussel, "World-System and 'Trans'-Modernity," *Nepantla: Views from South* 3, no. 2 (2002): 22–244, 233–34.

24. Walter Mignolo, "Delinking. The Rhetoric of Modernity, the Logic of Coloniality and the Grammar of Decoloniality," *Cultural Studies* 21 (2007): 449–514.

25. Mudimbe emphasizes the relationality Derrida talks about through his notion of the "colonial library," a metaphor representing the epistemological order

that has both repressed indigenous knowledge in Africa and imposed the framework through which African knowledge and imaginaries have been articulated by African thinkers. See Valentine Mudimbe, *The Invention of Africa. Gnosis, Philosophy and the Order of Knowledge* (Bloomington: Indiana University Press, 1988) and *Parables and Fables: Exegesis, Textuality and Politics in Central Africa* (Madison: University of Wisconsin Press, 1991). Similarly, Said underlines the epistemic and institutional limitations and constraints, especially in vocabulary and imaginary, imposed by Orientalism. See Edward Said, *Orientalism* (London: Vintage Books, 1978).

26. See Gayatri C. Spivak, *A Critique of Postcolonial Reason: Toward a History of the Vanishing Present* (Cambridge, MA: Harvard University Press, 1999); Robert J. C. Young, *Postcolonialism: An Historical Introduction* (Oxford: Blackwell, 2001).

27. For recent perspectives on Derrida's work on politics, see Geoffrey Bennington, *Legislations: The Politics of Deconstruction* (London: Verso, 1994); *Scatter 1: The Politics of Politics in Foucault, Heidegger, and Derrida* (New York: Fordham University Press, 2016); *Scatter 2: Politics in Deconstruction* (New York: Fordham University Press, 2021); Richard Beardsworth, *Derrida and the Political* (New York: Routledge, 1996); Jonathan Culler, ed., "Derrida and Democracy," in *Diacritics* 38 (2008): 1–2; Mathias Fritsch, "Derrida's Democracy to Come," *Constellations* 9, no. 4 (2002): 574–97; *The Promise of Memory: History and Politics in Marx, Benjamin and Derrida* (Albany: State University of New York Press, 2005); and *Taking Turns with the Earth: Phenomenology, Deconstruction, and Intergenerational Justice* (Stanford: Stanford University Press, 2018); Stella Gaon, *The Lucid Vigil: Deconstruction, Desire and the Politics of Critique* (New York/London: Routledge, 2020); Samir Haddad, *Derrida and the Inheritance of Democracy*; Catherine Kellogg, *Law's Trace: From Hegel to Derrida* (New York: Routledge, 2010); Michael Naas, *Derrida from Now On* (New York: Fordham University Press, 2008); Pheng Cheah and Suzanne Guerlac, eds., *Derrida and the Time of the Political* (Durham and London: Duke University Press, 2009); and Alex Thomson, *Deconstruction and Democracy* (London: Continuum, 2005). For Derrida on religion, see especially John Caputo, *The Prayers and Tears of Jacques Derrida: Religion without Religion* (Bloomington: Indiana University Press, 1997); *God, the Gift, and Postmodernism*, ed. John Caputo and Michael J. Scanlon (Bloomington: Indiana University Press, 1999); Hent de Vries, *Philosophy and the Turn to Religion* (Baltimore: Johns Hopkins University Press, 1999); *Religion and Violence: Philosophical Perspectives from Kant to Derrida* (Baltimore: Johns Hopkins University Press, 2002); Martin Hägglund, *Radical Atheism: Derrida and the Time of Life* (Stanford, CA: Stanford University Press, 2008); Kevin Hart, *The Trespass of the Sign: Deconstruction, Theology, Philosophy* (New York: Fordham University Press, 2000); Michael Naas, *Miracle and Machine: Jacques Derrida and the Two Sources of Religion, Science and the Media* (New York: Fordham University Press, 2012); Yvonne Sherwood and Kevin Hart, eds., *Derrida on Religion: Other Testaments* (New York: Routledge, 2005); and Edward Baring and Peter E. Gordon, eds., *The Trace of God: Derrida and Religion* (New York: Fordham University Press, 2014). For specific works

on Derrida's view of the secular, see Michael Naas, "Derrida's Laïcité" in *Derrida from Now On* (New York: Fordham University Press, 2008); Mark Cauchi, "The Secular to Come. Interrogating the Derridean "Secular," *Journal for Cultural and Religious Theory* 10, no. 1 (2009): 18.

28. See Asad, *Formations of the Secular*; Akeel Bilgrami, "Secularism: Its Content and Context," http://blogs.ssrc.org/tif/wp-content/uploads/2013/08/Secularism_Its_Content_and_Context.pdf; José Casanova, *Public Religions in the Modern World* (Chicago: University of Chicago Press, 1994); William Connolly, *Why I Am Not a Secularist?*; Jürgen Habermas, *Between Naturalism and Religion: Philosophical Essays* (Cambridge: Polity, 2008); *An Awareness of What Is Missing: Faith and Reason in a Post-Secular Age* (Cambridge: Polity, 2010); Masuzawa, *The Invention of World Religions*; and Jean-Luc Nancy, *Dis-Enclosure. The Deconstruction of Christianity* (New York: Fordham University Press, 2008); Taylor, *A Secular Age*.

29. See John Caputo, *The Prayers and Tears of Jacques Derrida: Religion without Religion* (Bloomington: Indiana University Press, 1997); Martin Hägglund, *Radical Atheism: Derrida and the Time of Life* (Stanford, CA: Stanford University Press, 2008); Naas, *Miracle and Machine*.

30. With the exception of Gil Anidjar, *The Jew, the Arab: A History of the Enemy* (Stanford: Stanford University Press, 2003), see the following for example: E. Baring and P. E. Gordon, eds., *The Trace of God: Derrida and Religion* (New York: Fordham University Press, 2014); Harold Coward and Toby Foshay, eds., *Derrida and Negative Theology* (Albany: State University of New York Press, 1992); Hent de Vries, *Philosophy and the Turn to Religion* (Baltimore: John Hopkins University Press, 2008); Noah Horwitz "Derrida and the Aporia of the Political, or The Theologico-Political dimension of Deconstruction," *Research in Phenomenology* 32 (2002), 156–77; Naas, *Derrida from Now On*, especially chapters 3 and 7; Kas Saghafi (ed.) "Special Issue: Spindel Supplement: Derrida and the Theologico-Political: From Sovereignty to the Death Penalty," *The Southern Journal of Philosophy* 50, no. 1 (2012): iv–iv, 1–174.

31. Carl Schmitt, *Political Theology: Four Chapters on the Concept of Sovereignty*, trans. George Schwab (Chicago: University of Chicago Press), 32.

32. See especially Walter Benjamin, "Critique of Violence," in *Reflections: Essays, Aphorisms, Autobiographical Writings*, ed. Peter Demetz (New York: Schocken Books, 1986); "The Task of the Translator," in *Illuminations*, trans. Harry Zohn, ed. and intro. Hannah Arendt (New York: Harcourt Brace Jovanovich, 1968). This point applies to Giorgio Agamben's development of Bejnamin's perspective as well. See his *State of Exception*, trans. Kevin Attell (Chicago: University of Chicago Press, 2005), 63–64.

33. Jürgen Habermas, "Religion in the Public Sphere," *European Journal of Philosophy* 14, no. 1 (2006): 1–25; John Rawls, "The Idea of Public Reason Revisited," *The University of Chicago Law Review* 64, no. 3 (1997):765–807.

34. See Rodolphe Gasché, *The Tain of the Mirror* (Cambridge, MA: Harvard University Press, 1986) and Geoffrey Bennington, "Derridabase" in Geoffrey Ben-

nington and Jacques Derrida, *Jacques Derrida*, trans. Geoffrey Bennington (Chicago: University of Chicago Press, 1999).

35. John D. Caputo, "On Not Circumventing the Quasi-Transcendental: The Case of Rorty and Derrida," in Gary Brent Madison, ed., *Working through Derrida* (Evanston, IL: Northwestern University Press, 1993), 147–69; de Vries, *Philosophy and the Turn to Religion*, especially chapter 3; Mathias Fritsch, *The Promise of Memory*, especially chapter 2; and Hägglund, *Radical Atheism*, especially chapter 2.

36. These include revisitations of liberal secularism such as that of Jürgen Habermas; decisionist political theologies à la Carl Schmitt; deconstructive inquiries privileging transcendental concerns as in the work of Jean-Luc Nancy; phenomenological approaches seemingly neutralizing the theological side of the theological-political relation such as that of Claude Lefort; critical political theologies that ambiguously privilege theological sources, as that of Walter Benjamin; those that embrace a secularized messianism as in the *oeuvre* of Giorgio Agamben and, finally, religious and nonreligious forms of fundamentalism that affirm the primacy of the theological or the political.

37. See, respectively, Naas, *Miracle and Machine*, 191; "Derrida's *Laïcité*," 63; Hägglund, *Radical Atheism*,1; and Caputo, *The Prayers and Tears of Jacques Derrida*, xxi.

38. See Bennington's *Scatter 1* and *Scatter 2*; Gaon's *Lucid Vigil*.

39. In adopting this expansive approach to the inheritance of Derrida's work, I join other commentators. See for example, Bennington's *Scatter 1* and *Scatter 2*; Fritsch's *The Promise of Memory*; Gaon's *The Lucid Vigil*; Hägglund's *Radical Atheism*; and Haddad's *Derrida and the Inheritance of Democracy*.

40. For an exploration of the political dimension of Derrida's philosophy that centers the question of critical vigilance, see Gaon's *Lucid Vigil*. While Gaon roots Derrida's vigilance within the European Enlightenment after postmodern critique, my argument shows that it exceeds such geopolitical and cultural context and reaches the racial and colonial undercurrents that undergirds it.

41. Cauchi, "The Secular to Come. Interrogating the Derridean "Secular"; Naas, "Derrida's *Laïcité*."

42. For the original articulation of the notion of "Islamicate" as designating social and cultural dimensions in majority Muslim contexts and thus referring only indirectly to Islam as a so-called religion, see Marshall G. S. Hodgson, *The Venture of Islam: Conscience and History in a World Civilization. Vol. 1. The Classical Age of Islam* (Chicago: University of Chicago Press, 1974).

Chapter 1

1. For a sustained discussion of these seminars in relation to issues of language and translation, but also secularization, see Dana Hollander, *Exemplarity and Chosenness*, especially chapters 4 and 5.

2. Usually translated as "without passage," the term "aporia" refers, in Derrida's lexicon, to a constitutive and irreducible situation of impasse that cannot be resolved through logical determination and that is best thought of as an experience characterized by a double bind: the conditions of possibility are also conditions of impossibility; that is, what makes something possible does also impede its full realization (*AP*, 12/20 ff.). In the case of philosophy and idiom, the linguistic conditions of possibility of a universal philosophy (it being spoken in a particular idiom) impede philosophy from being universal.

3. Though translated as "blood" here, the semantics of *Geschlecth*, which Derrida leaves untranslated, has, as he mentions elsewhere, a much more open-ended range of designations depending on its contextual usage. These designations include, among others, sex, race, species, genus, family, genealogy, and community (GES II, 28/36). It is also worth noting that the privileging of German as *the* language *of* spirit—obscure and ambiguous as this term remains—is also central to his critique of Heidegger's philosophical nationalism and its complex connections to German National Socialism (see specially *OS*).

4. Derrida also addresses the question of race in a recently published manuscript on Heidegger. See *Geschlecht III: Sex, Race Nation, Humanité*.

5. In this context, Derrida affirms: "I do not mean to criticize this humanist teleology. It is not doubt more urgent to recall that, in spite of all the denegations or all the avoidances one could wish, it has remained up till now (in Heidegger's time and situation, but this has not radically changed today) the price to be paid in the ethico-political denunciation of biologism, racism, naturalism etc. . . . Is this unavoidable? Can one escape this program? No sign would suggest it, at least neither in 'Heideggerrian' discourses nor in 'anti-Heidegerrian' discourses. Can one transform this program? I do not know. In any case, it will not be avoided all at once and without reconnoitering it right down to its most tortious ruses and most subtle resources" (56/87). Here it appears that although for Derrida this teleology has clear philosophical limits and serious political implications, it might not be avoided and it is not clear that alternatives exist. Yet, as I am arguing throughout, Derrida's thought can be read as an attempt to think according to a different, non-teleological schema that takes clearer shape in his later writings.

6. By making a reference to his "Declaration of Independence," where he takes up the issue of political founding, Derrida says explicitly that what is at work in the fixing of rules and the context of utterances is the structure of performativity that characterizes political founding (*LI*, 134–35).

7. See Habermas, "Excursus on Leveling the Genre Distinction between Philosophy and Literature" in *The Philosophical Discourse of Modernity: Twelve Lectures*, trans. Frederick Lawrence (Cambridge, MA: MIT Press, 1987).

8. For a broader discussion of context and unconditionality in relation to South African apartheid, see Noah Horwitz's "Derrida and the Aporia of the Political, or The Theologico-Political Dimension of Deconstruction."

9. The place in which "truth" and "reality" are most explicitly connected in Derrida's writings is his 1986 intervention in a discussion on South African apartheid in *Critical Inquiry*. It is there that he speaks of the need to reflect on the word and reality of apartheid in those terms (BB, 160–63; as referred to in *LI*, 150).

10. See Anne McClintock and Rob Nixon, "No Names Apart: The Separation of Word and History in Derrida's "Le Dernier Mot du Racism" *Critical Inquiry* 13 (1986): 140–54.

11. See for example Thomas McCarthy, "The Politics of the Ineffable" in *Ideals and Illusions* (Cambridge, MA: MIT Press, 1991), 111.

12. Habermas, "Religion in the Public Sphere"; Rawls, "The Idea of Public Reason Revisited."

13. For a critique of this predicament, see Ngugi, wa Thiongo. *Decolonising the Mind: The Politics of Language in African Literature* (London: James Currey, 1986).

14. See especially Derrida, AI, *BS 1*, *DIS;* EL, *EO*, *LI*, *MO*, *POS*, TB.

15. Habermas, "Excursus on Leveling the Genre Distinction between Philosophy and Literature."

16. Derrida affirms the following: "I therefore venture to present myself to you here, *ecce homo*, in parody as the exemplary Franco-Maghrebian" and adds, "as regards so enigmatic a value that of attestation or even of exemplarity in testimony here is a first question that, the most general one, without shadow of a doubt. What happens when someone resorts to describing an allegedly uncommon 'situation,' mine, for example, by testifying to it in terms that go beyond it in a language whose generality takes on a value that is on some way structural, universal, transcendental, or ontological?" (*MO*, 19–20/39–40).

17. In this respect there is a striking parallel between Derrida's witnessing approach and Frantz Fanon's idea that the colonized do not claim to represent the truth, but their being (colonized) is (in) the truth. See Fanon, *The Wretched of the Earth*, 13.

18. Emphasizing the colonial aspect of Derrida and more generally of the experience of Jews in North-Africa, however, is not to overlook, as mentioned in the introduction, that so-called indigenous Jews in these areas were not simply colonized subjects but also temporally benefited from privileges, such as temporary citizenship status, from which Arabs and Berbers where excluded. For a historical exploration of this issue, see Ethan B. Katz and Linda Moses Leff, eds., *Colonialism and the Jews* (Bloomington: Indiana University Press, 2017). An awareness of these shifting positions, between colonized and colonizer, does not "diminish" the critical positionality I refer to, but it actually underscores how colonial powers, in these areas, politicized ethnic and religious minority for their own purposes.

19. For an illuminating critique of Eurocentric accounts of modernity as a false universalism "unmasked" by the reality and continuing effects of colonialism, see Enrique Dussel, "Modernity, Eurocentrism, and Tras-Modernity," in *The Underside of Modernity: Apel, Ricoeur, Rorty, Taylor and the Philosophy of Liberation*, ed. and trans. Eduardo Mendieta (New Jersey: Humanity Press, 1996), 129–59.

20. For powerful development of this idea of critical positionality of colonized subjects, especially with reference to thinkers such as Aimé Cesaire and Frantz Fanon, see Nelson Maldonado Torres, "Cesaire's Gift and the Decolonial Turn" *Radical Philosophy Review* 9, no. 2 (2006): 111–38, and Lewis R. Gordon, "Through the Zone of Nonbeing: A Reading of Black Skin, White Masks in Celebration of Fanon's Eightieth Birthday," *The C. L. R James Journal* 11 no. 1 (2005) 1–43. For an illuminating connection between Derrida's use of exemplarity and Spinoza's critical universalism, see Goetschel, "Derrida and Spinoza: Rethinking the Theologico-Political Problem."

21. For a lucid analysis of this predicament, see Geoffrey Bennington "Double Tonguing: Derrida's Monolingualism," in *Other Analyses: Reading Philosophy* (Electronic Book, 2008), 152–82.

22. Derrida describes this as "one of the earth shattering Algerian experiences of my existence" (*IW*, 29/54).

23. In one of his last public interventions, Derrida affirms that "one could go forever—some have already begun to do so here and there—In recounting what we were told, indeed, about the history of France, meaning by that what was taught in school under the name of the history of France, an unbelievable discipline, a fable and a bible, but a semi-permanent indoctrination for the children of my generation: not a word about Algeria, not a single word about its history and geography" (*IW*, 34/59).

24. For a discussion of Derrida's "multiple identities" as resisting biographical identification and pointing to identity as a question, see Anidjar, "Introduction," 32 ff.

25. See Bennington "Double Tonguing."

26. Of course, one can conceive of metalanguage in a weaker sense, namely, as a "formal language," characterized by some kind of logico-formal relationships between signs. In this sense, one can still talk of *meta*language since this "formal language" could be seen as transcending natural languages without for this reason being also transcendent. Clearly, this is the view held by many thinkers in the tradition of "analytic philosophy" including Habermas, who thinks that a formal-pragmatic analysis of language does not lead to transcendent instances but merely reconstructs something that is necessarily inherent in language (see Habermas "What Is Universal Pragmatics," *On the Pragmatics of Communication,* ed. Maeve Cooke (Cambridge, MA: MIT Press, 2000)]. I owe this point to Adrian Atanasescu. Granted this, however, two outstanding questions remain that emphasize Derrida's point on metalanguage: Which language does one use to reconstruct a "formal language" and affirm its presence across natural languages? How and to what extent, if at all, can such a language be severed from the idiom and context in which is articulated?

27. In focusing on this short piece, I follow other commentators that have explored the relevance of translation as a feature of language in Derrida's thought. See for example, Catherine Kellogg, "Translating Deconstruction," *Cultural Values* 5, no. 3 (2001): 325–48; Jonathan Roffe, "Translation" in *Understanding Derrida,* ed. Jack Reynolds and Jonathan Roffe (New York: Continuum: 2004), 103–12.

28. See Roffe, "Translation," 105.

29. See Walter Benjamin, "The Task of the Translator," in *Selected Writings, Vol. 1*, ed. Markus Bullock and Michael W. Jennings (Cambridge, MA: Harvard University Press, 1996), 257–58, 257.

30. "The name is that through which, and in which, language itself communicate itself absolutely" in Walter Benjamin, "On the Language as Such and on the Language of Man" in *Selected Writings Vol. 1*, ed. Markus Bullock and Michael W. Jennings (Cambridge, MA: Harvard University Press, 1996), 65.

31. See Benjamin, "The Task of the Translator," 257, 262.

32. See Benjamin, "The Task of the Translator," 256. While a single footnote cannot render justice to this key point in Derrida's thought, it is, nevertheless, important to mention that for him, the longing for origins is both philosophically problematic and politically dangerous. Overall, his philosophical intervention shows that origins are elusive and their recovery is premised on a questionable metaphysical type of thinking, which, if put to the service of practical applications, excludes difference. Specifically, his analysis of the sign, as seen above, rules out the possibility that the chain of signification and process of dissemination could at any time stop and "find" an original reference, being this God, "Nature," "Being" and so forth. For an illuminating discussion on Derrida and Benjamin on translation addressing the issue of origins, see Kellogg, "Translating Deconstruction."

33. See Martin Heidegger, *Being and Time. A Translation of Sein und Zeit*, trans. J. Stambaugh (Chicago: University of Chicago Press, 1996), section 26.

34. Although before making this statement, Derrida refers to his "Plato's Pharmacy," where the word *pharmakon* was shown to be caught by undecidability between two possible translations (as "remedy" and "poison"), the word "Babel" fits this structure too (RT, 120/159–60).

35. On the philosophical and political significance of translation, see also Kellogg, "Translating Deconstruction." Here she goes so far as to suggest that what is at stake in translation is how we think about the nexus between philosophy and politics (327).

36. See B. Arfi, "Habermas and the Aporia of Translating Religion in Democracy" *European Journal of Social Theory* (2015): 489–506.

37. See Talal Asad, *Secular Translations: Nation-State, Modern Self, and Calculative Reason* (New York: Columbia University Press, 2018).

38. See also Lawrence Venuti, "Translating Derrida on Translation: Relevance and Disciplinary Resistance," *The Yale Journal of Criticism* 16, no. 2 (2003): 237–62, 240.

39. See for example, E. Nida, *Towards a Science of Translating, with Special Reference to Principles and Procedures Involved in the Bible Translating* (Leiden: Brill 2003); D. Sperber and D. Wilson, *Relevance: Communication and Cognition* (Cambridge, MA: Blackwell, 1986), and E. Gutt, *Translation and Relevance: Cognition and Context* (London and New York: Routledge, 2000) all mentioned in Venuti

"Translating Derrida on Translation: Relevance and Disciplinary Resistance," *The Yale Journal of Criticism* 16, no. 2 (2003): 237–62, 251. See also Tejaswini Niranjana, *Siting Translation History, Post-Structuralism, and the Colonial Context* (Berkeley: University of California Press, 1992); Padma Rangarajan, *Imperial Babel: Translation, Exoticism, and the Long Nineteenth Century* (New York: Fordham University Press, 2014). I thank Ruth Marshall for signaling these two sources.

40. See Geraldine Heng, *The Invention of Race in the European Middle Ages* (New York: Cambridge University Press, 2018).

41. This view of language, which Derrida attributes to John Searle, is arguably presupposed by dominant modern (especially liberal) political theory, and it informs the discourse of international law and politics (*LI*, 79).

42. For thoughtful commentaries on these passages, and more generally on Scholem's and Derrida's positions on the secularization of Judaism, see also Anidjar's "*Mal de Sionisme* (Zionist Fever)," 56 ff.

43. To my knowledge, Derrida refers to the semantics of colonialism on this issue twice. He speaks of "colonial settlements" with reference to the Occupied Palestinian Territories when discussing the unrealized "political invention" and peace called for by Levinas with regard to Judaism and the State of Israel (*AL*, 81/148). In a 1998 conference in Rabat with Muslim intellectuals when he speaks of "colonialist violence," he refers in a footnote again to his work on Levinas (FAPU, 259). So I say "explicitly" since Derrida can be taken as having spoken indirectly and yet not less decisively about questions of colonialism and the state of Israel, as Anidjar suggests in his *Mal de Sionisme* (Zionist Fever)." In the context of discussions involving Judaism, Zionism, and the state of Israel in *Adieu to Emmanuel Levinas* and *Archive Fever*, Derrida, for Anidjar, does two things. First, while commenting on the hospitality associated to Judaism and cherished by Levinas, Derrida exposes the host, Anidjar says, as a "colonizer" by remarking that the host of "hospitality" can be both "guest" and "host," one who receives but is also received in what "he takes to be his own home, or indeed his own land" (Anidjar, "*Mal de Sionisme* (Zionist Fever)," 52; *AL*, 42/79). Second, by interrogating the steps that would justify the passage from biblical claims to land to the formation of a state instituting an exclusive and hegemonic archive, Derrida highlights the evil of Zionism and its destructive and expropriatory drives (Anidjar, "*Mal de Sionisme* [Zionist Fever]" 52; *AF*, 77/101; 94/148).

44. While not explicitly connected, questions about the secularization of European discourses of law and race, and about settler colonialism appear in Derrida's texts on South Africa (LR, 66, 82; RLW, 290–99/385–94). In one of these texts, in which Derrida raises issues of settler colonialism and race through his reference to "white colonization," "the violent irruption of the white man" as well as the ruling of the white community while being "*too* much in the minority," he also associates South Africa uniquely to Israel to talk about "spaces" or "stakes" of "extreme concentration of all human history" (LR, 68, 71, 83), but he does not explore the

comparison further. While the settler colonial and racist features of South Africa under apartheid appear in his reflections, the same does not apply to his position on Israel *vis-à-vis* Palestinians. Indeed, to his clear opposition to the Israeli occupation of the West Bank and Gaza (IW, 138) does not follow explicit considerations on the nature of the State of Israel, both in relations to massive displacements in such state's formation—what Palestinians call the *Nakba* or catastrophe—and the legally sanctioned discriminations suffered by its Palestinian citizens since 1948 (see *Adalah*—The Legal Center for Arab and Minority Rights in Israel, https://www.adalah.org/en/law/index). Overall, when discussing the state of Israel, whose institution he tends to inscribe in the history, logics, and predicament of violence of "all state" founding (AWI, 29–30/39–40; *AL*, 77/140; *N*, 115; IPJD, 27), Derrida urges that its existence "must henceforth be recognized by all and definitively guaranteed" together with a continuous interrogation of "its prehistory, the conditions of its recent founding, and the constitutional, legal, political foundations of its present functioning, the forms and limits of its *self-interpretation*" (IW, 138). These considerations include attention for "the violence of the Shoah" also because it "had been one of the justifications of the formation of the State of Israel" as well as for the "violence towards the Palestinians, also internal violence" (IPJD, 27). While expressing "solidarity with all those, and in this land, who advocate for the end of violence, condemn the crimes of terrorism and of military police repression, and advocate a the withdrawal of Israeli troops from the occupied territories as well as the recognition of the Palestinians' right to choose their own representatives," Derrida also expresses "a certain respect for a certain image of Israel" and "hope for its future" (IW, 138) but still awaits a "political invention" aligned with ethical hospitality that the advancement of "colonial 'settlements' " and other "initiatives" still "suspend, derail, or interrupt" (*AL* 81–82/147–48). And these are phenomena connected to the fact the "the formation of the state of Israel is an event that has somehow not come to an end, and which is also very violent" (IPJD, 26–27). Concurrently, he repeatedly cautions about the disastrous implications of "realizing" Judaism politically in a specific place, following a theologically sanctioned "election" (*WD*, 80/101; *AF*, 77/110), and of collapsing it into political Zionism (*AL*, 79–81/143–47; AWI, 29/39), while pointing also to the effects these issues provoked in him in terms of insomniatic questioning (AWI, 29/39), infinite guilt (CP 263/259), and trembling (*AF*, 77/110). Perhaps, Derrida's view on this issue is best and clearly summarized, as Martin McQuillan suggests, in an interview in *For What Tomorrow*, where Derrida affirms that he has "great many reasons to believe that it is *for the best*, all things considered, and in the interests of the greatest number of people, including the Palestinians, including the other states in the region, to consider this foundation, despite its originary violence, as henceforth irreversible—on the condition that neighbourly relations be established either with a Palestinian state endowed with *all* its rights, in the fullest sense of the term, 'state' (at least insofar as anything remains of this full sense and of sovereignty in general; another very serious question I must leave aside for now while briefly relating, in an interview, a telephone interview), or, at the centre of the same 'sovereign' and binational 'state,' with a Palestinian people freed from all oppression or from all intolerable segregation. I have no particular hostility in principle toward the state of Israel, but I have almost always judged quite harshly the policies of the Israeli governments in relation to the Palestinians" (*FWT*, 118–19 [See Martin McQuillan, "Clarity and doubt: Derrida among the Palestinians" *Paragraph* 39, no. 2 (2016): 220–37, 224–25]. Several commentators have debated these issues, bringing to the fore different aspects of Derrida's view See, for example, Gil Anidjar, "*Mal de Sionisme* (Zionist Fever)" and Jospeh Massad, "Forget Semitism!"; Kadhim Jihad Hassan, "Les Palestiniens dans la pensée de Jacques Derrida," *Rue Descartes* 2 (2016): 218–30; Martin McQuillan, "Clarity and Doubt: Derrida among e Palestinians."

What interests me here is not so much reflecting on what Derrida said or did not say in specific instances, though this remains of scholarly and political relevance, and that is why I have schematically, and hopefully comprehensively, presented his saying, and not saying, on the matter. Rather I am interested in what the logic of deconstruction offers in terms of critical sources to deal with these issues, and here specifically, the link between secularization as translation, colonialism, and race. By the end of the chapter, I hope to have shown that Derrida's reflections on translation and secularization, indeed on secularization as assimilatory translation, expose the larger hierarchical schema and colonial mentalities undergirding traditional modern frameworks, together with their destructive political consequences.

45. See Schmitt, *Political Theology*, 36.

46. I do not intend to suggest that this is the only meaning of secularization at play in Habermas's work but the one with which I take issue.

47. Habermas's proposal about translation is similar in nature but not in scope to John Rawls's idea of proviso (See Rawls, "The Idea of Public Reason Revisited"). For Habermas, translation applies primarily to the formal public sphere of institutions and not also to the informal one of public deliberation as in Rawls.

48. For a similar point, see also Cauchi, "The Secular to Come," 11.

49. See Jacques Derrida, "Open Discussion," in *Jacques Derrida: Deconstruction Engaged: The Sydney Seminars*, ed. Paul Patton and Terry Smith (Sydney: Power, 2006), 241.

50. For a comprehensive and illuminating discussion of Derrida's position on religion, and to which my exposition is generally indebted, see Michael Naas, *Miracle and Machine*. I also owe a debt to my understanding of Derrida on religion to a seminar on Derrida and Kant offered by Rodolphe Gasche that I had the opportunity to attend in 2008 at the University of Buffalo.

51. As Derrida clarifies in the essay, "we" refers to "we Europeans," the participants of the conference in which the first part of this essay was presented. Yet

the "we" can be extended to the West and the way the modern discourse of religion has used this category to refer to an essential human phenomenon (FK, 70/53).

52. For an insightful discussion of Derrida's view of globalatinization, see Gil Anidjar, "Of Globalatinology," *Derrida Today* 6, no. 1 (2013): 11–22; Naas, *Miracle and Machine*, especially chapter 2.

53. Derrida (FK, 76/62). Samuel Weber, the translator of Derrida's essay, emphasizes the problem of translating *mondialiatinisation* as globalatinization. The problem lies in substituting "world (*monde*)" with "globe." Not only are these two terms not coextensive, but Derrida emphasizes that since the concept of "world" has a Christian formation, it helps to better emphasize the role Christianity plays in the process of globalization in a way that the more "neutral" term "globe" does not. For a discussion of the significance of Derrida's reflections on "world" for understanding globalization, see Naas, *Miracle and Machine*, 58 ff.

54. Although Derrida does not mention that for a so-called religion to present itself as "religion" in the modern period means, as Asad has shown in *Formations of The Secular*, to present itself as a privatized religion, this is what his argument implicitly assumes.

55. Derrida's relation with Islam and Judaism is complex. For remarks on his own "Islamic" background, see *IW* and FAPU. For focused remarks on his references to Judaism, see Derrida "Abraham, the Other," in *Judeities: Questions for Jacques Derrida.*, ed. Bettina Bergo et al.

56. See Arvin-Pal Mandair, *Religion and the Specter of the West: Sikhism, India, Postcoloniality and the Politics of Translation* (New York: Columbia University Press, 2009). Worthy of mention, even if not focusing specifically on Derrida's view of translation but on deconstruction more generally in non-Christian contexts, is also Abeysekara Ananda, *The Politics of Postsecular Religion. Mourning Secular Features* (New York: Columbia University Press, 2008). I thank Ruth Marshall for having called my attention to these texts.

57. Like Derrida, who seems to do it deliberately, I use here the masculine to underscore the patriarchal features of traditional conceptualizations of the master.

58. This point emerges also in his "Force of Law," where Derrida notes that "as is well known, in many countries, in the past and in the present, one of the founding violences of the law [*loi*] or of the imposition of state law has consisted in imposing a language on national or ethnic minorities regrouped by the state" (FL, 249/47).

59. Derrida refers to the power of naming as early as in *Of Grammatology*. Here he investigates, among other things, naming as central to the nature of language. Naming refers to the power of fixing reference and thus stabilizing the relationships between word, meaning, and object. In particular, Derrida emphasizes that this power is characterized by an original founding violence or "arche-violence" that is needed in view of fixing reference in as univocal a way as possible (*OG*, 112/165).

60. See Vincente L. Rafael, "Translation, American English, and the Insecurities of Empire," in *The Translation Studies Reader*, ed. Laurence Venuti, 2nd ed. (New York: Routledge, 2012), 451–68, 455.

61. This is what Derrida affirms in commenting on his *Monolingualism* and on the inappropriability of language. See his interview on "Language Is Never Owned," in *SQ*, 101.

62. On questions of religious symbols and protection of religious minorities, see respectively, Christian Jopkke, "State Neutrality and Islamic Headscarf Laws in France and Germany," *Theory and Society* 36, no. 4 (2007): 313–42; Saba Mahmood, "Religious Reason and Secular Affect: An Incommensurable Divide?" *Critical Inquiry* 35, no. 4 (2000): 836–62, and *Religious Difference in a Secular Age. A Minority Report* (Princeton: Princeton University Press, 2016).

63. This is arguably the view of language of deliberative democratic theories inspired by the work of Rawls and Habermas. See for example, Amy Gutmann and Dennis Thompson, *Democracy and Disagreement* (Cambridge, MA: Harvard University Press, 1996); James Fishkin, *Democracy and Deliberation* (New Heaven: Yale University Press, 1971); John Dryzek, *Discursive Democracy* (Cambridge: Cambridge University Press, 1990); *Deliberative Democracy and Beyond: Liberals, Critics, Contestations* (Oxford: Oxford University Press, 2000). Simone Chambers, *Reasonable Democracy: Jürgen Habermas and the Politics of Discourse* (Ithaca: Cornell University Press, 1996).

64. The reference to Heidegger, here, is not accidental but is made by Derrida in the context of his reflections on the *yes* that occurs also in other places. For example, in *OS*, while discussing, in a long footnote, the essence of language and its relation to the promissory faith, Derrida affirms that Heidegger's *Zusage*—referring to the accord or consent given in the promise—can be read as the *yes* at issue here, that is, as an implicit assent to language, a sort of "pre-originary pledge [*gage*] which precedes any other engagement in language" but that always "engages *in* language." See Derrida, *OS*, 130/148. Similarly, in FK, Derrida affirms that Heidegger's *Zusage* ("accord, acquiescing, trust or confidence") is not alien to an elemental faith that belongs to a "common experience of a language and a 'we,' " a faith that "would constitute the condition of *Mitsein*," the being-with typical of *Being and Time*. See Derrida, FK, 96, 98/93,96.

65. I borrow "critical intimacy" from Spivak, who uses it to distinguish Derrida's style from the "critical distance" typical of Enlightenment thinkers. See Spivak, *A Critique of Postcolonial Reason*, 425.

66. For insightful discussions of Derrida's relationship to Nietzsche and interpretation, see Ernst Behler, *Confrontations: Derrida, Heidegger, Nietzsche*, trans. Steven Taubeneck (Stanford: Stanford University Press, 1991); Alan Schrift, *Nietzsche and the Question of Interpretation: Between Hermeneutics and Deconstruction* (New York: Routledge, 1990).

67. "One might wonder why the only institution that ever succeeded in taking as its model the teaching of Nietzsche on teaching will have been a Nazi one" [*sic*]; "There is 'nothing absolutely contingent about the fact that the only political regimen to have effectively brandished his [Nietzsche] name as a major and official banner was Nazi" (OB, 24/39, 31/46).

68. "I do not say this in order to suggest that this kind of 'Nietzschean' politics is the only one conceivable for all eternity, nor that it corresponds to the best reading of the legacy, nor even that those who have not picked up this reference have produced a better reading of it. No. The future of the Nietzsche text is not closed. But if, within the still open contours of an era, the only politics calling itself—proclaiming itself—Nietzschean will have been a Nazi one, then this is necessarily significant and must be questioned in all of its consequences" (OB, 31/46–47).

69. For a recent discussion of interpretation as a political practice of inheritance so conceived and that is key to democracy, see Haddad's *Derrida and the Inheritance of Democracy*.

Chapter 2

1. Throughout the chapter, I will use quotations marks to refer to Derrida's "messianic" as a temporal structure of experience that is different from "messianism" conceived as a historical narrative typical of so called-religions.

2. For a sustained analysis of Derrida's treatment of time in this essay, especially in relation to Aristotle and Heidegger, see John Protevi, *Time and Exteriority: Aristotle, Heidegger, Derrida* (London and Toronto: Associated Presses, 1994), particularly chapter 3.

3. Barnor Hesse picks up on Derrida's awareness of questions of race in his "Racialized Modernity: An Analytics of White Mythologies," *Ethnic and Racial Studies* 30, no. 4 (2007): 643–63.

4. An exception to Derrida's limited attention to race is his intervention to the "tRACEs: Race, Deconstruction and Critical Theory" Conference held at the University of California Humanities Research Institute in April 2003. See https://www.youtube.com/watch?v=LfXdYefgKjw.

5. The focus on Western forms of racism does not obviously indicate that racism is not a phenomenon affecting other traditions.

6. It is worth mentioning that Derrida also addresses the question of race in a recently published manuscript on Heidegger. See Geoffrey Bennignton, Katie Chenoweth et Rodrigo Therezo, eds., *Geschlecht III: Sex, Race Nation, Humanité* (Paris: Seuil, 2018).

7. Here I follow Martin Hägglund's analysis of the trace as spacing in his *Radical Atheism*, especially chapter 2.

8. See Hägglund, *Radical Atheism*, 18.

9. It should be noted that Derrida does not seek to break *tout court* with metaphysics. In his "Structure, Sign and Play in the Discourse of Human Sciences," he questions any simple exit from metaphysics (*WD*, 280/412; see also *POS*, 19/29). For a brief, incisive account of Derrida's position on metaphysics, see Christopher Norris "Metaphysics," in *Understanding Derrida*, ed. Jack Reynolds and Jonathan Roffe, 14–25.

10. See Hägglund, *Radical Atheism*, 20, 14.

11. For an exploration of sovereignty that addresses the nexus between metaphysics and politics seen as key to traditional Western philosophy, see Bennington, *Scatter 2*.

12. Derrida repeatedly refers to the masculine, theological (Hellenic and Christian) character of sovereignty (*R; BS 1*). He also refers to the problematic nexus between birth as origin and fraternity as key ideas of Western conceptions of political community informed by a theological understanding of sovereignty, as well as to the theological-political nature of discourses about race (*PF; RLW*).

13. For a recent discussion of the relationship between time and political thinking in Derrida, see Cheah and Guerlac, *Derrida and the Time of the Political*.

14. Heidegger's epochal thinking is also mentioned as part of the teleologies Derrida criticizes (*SM*, 93/125).

15. Derrida claims that Marx's *German Ideology* is focused on the question of the idea, on the "proper" delineation of what an idea or concept is, and it displays the traditional philosophical attempt since Plato to establish a clear-cut distinction between idea and non-idea, between *Geist* (idea) and *Gespenst* (spectre). Yet, as Derrida remarks, since "Geist can also signify 'specter,'" the "semantics of *Gespenst* themselves haunt the semantics of *Geist*" (*SM*, 134/175). This haunting indicates that establishing concepts demands the suppression of spectral excess through means that exceed the philosophical domain.

16. This is one of the double binds Derrida sees at play in Marx's gesture, the other being very close to, if not foregrounding, deconstruction.

17. See especially Karl Marx, "Contribution to the Critique of Hegel's *Philosophy of Right*: Introduction" and "The German Ideology" in *The Marx-Engels Reader*, ed. Richard Tuck (New York: Norton, 1978): 16–25, 146–200.

18. See Karl Marx, "Contribution to the Critique of Hegel's," 53. In "Faith and Knowledge" Derrida even hazards the hypothesis that Marx started deconstructing religion when he affirmed "the critique of religion to be the premise of all-ideology critique" (FK, 52–53/24–25).

19. In the *Critique of Pure Reason*, Kant presents regulative ideas (the soul, world, and God) as something that can be thought but not known or experienced. Conceived as "given" to human beings, these ideas organize judgments about experience in order to guide further investigation. See Immanuel Kant, *Critique of Pure Reason*, ed. Paul Guyer and Allen Wood (Cambridge: Cambridge University Press, 1999).

20. In the case of Rawls, the ideas of a well-ordered society and of citizens as free and equal in the liberal sense constitute, together, the *telos* performing the regulative function. See John Rawls, *Political Liberalism* (New York: Columbia University Press, 1993). In Habermas, that function is carried out by the idea of understanding as the *telos* of communicative rationality, which is intimately connected to constitutional liberal democracy as the "model" political community. See Jürgen Habermas, *Between Facts and Norms: Contribution to a Discourse Theory of Law and Democracy*, trans. William Rehg (Cambridge: MIT Press, 1998).

21. Habermas, *Between Facts and Norms*, 82; "Religion in the Public Sphere," 14.

22. Rawls, *Political Liberalism*, xxvi.

23. For a development of this criticism, especially against Habermas, see Hesse, "Racialized Modernity: An Analytics of White Mythologies."

24. The forgotten contingency at issue here is what Walter Mignolo calls the "underside of modernity." See his *The Darker Side of Western Modernity: Global Futures, Decolonial Options* (Durham: Duke University Press, 2011).

25. For a recent work that exposes these debts and material entanglements of the liberal tradition, to which both Rawls and Habermas belong, see Domenico Losurdo, *Liberalism: A Counter-History*, trans. Gregory Elliott (London: Verso, 2014).

26. For a recent, powerful discussion of this view, see Asad, *Formations of the Secular*.

27. Habermas, "Religion in the Public Sphere"; Rawls, "The Idea of Public Reason Revisited."

28. For discussions on Derrida's "messianic" in *SM*, see Caputo, *The Prayers and Tears of Jacques Derrida*, especially chapter 3; Simon Critchley, "Derrida's Specters of Marx," *Philosophy & Social Criticism* 21 (1995): 1–30; Mathias Fritsch, *The Promise of Memory*, especially chapter 2; Ernesto Laclau "The Time Is out of Joint" *Diacritics* 25 (1995): 86–97; Gayatri Chakravorty Spivak, "Ghostwriting," *Diacritics* 25 (1995): 65–85.

29. On the necessary feature of such a possibility, see Kellogg, *Law's Trace*, 89; and Hägglund, *Radical Atheism*, 126. Both Kellogg and Hägglund highlight that the "must" (*il faut*) Derrida emphasizes in connection to the openness of the future (*avenir*) is not a normative but a logical requirement of temporal experience. For there to be future, the future "must be possible," namely, open to the unforeseeable, otherwise it would be something like a replica of the present or the past.

30. As indicated in note 9, Derrida does not seek to break entirely with metaphysics. Further, as he clarifies in "*BS 1*," his does not seek to overcome the synchronic understanding of time by opposing to it a diachronic one (*BS 1*, 333). For to do so would reinstitute the oppositions typical of the metaphysical thinking he questions.

31. Not irrelevant to the question of "others" and the disastrous implications of the schema of separation, hierarchization, and subjection at issue here is also Derrida's reflections on the "animal." Specifically, his challenge to how the Western

philosophical tradition from Plato to Heidegger has, despite its internal differences, conceptualized the human as superior to, and neatly separate and separable from what goes under the generic term "animal" (as the name that designates what in fact includes a multiplicity of nonhuman living animals that are not sexually undifferentiated) points to a complicity and participation, especially under modern conditions, in a "war of the species," a crime against animals (*ATTIA*, 31).

32. This where Derrida's debts to Levinas's understanding of justice appear. While Derrida mentions these debts in several places, he offers a clear and concise statement in the Villanova Roundtable, where he affirms: "Levinas says somewhere that the definition of justice—which is very minimal but which I love, which I think is really rigorous—is that justice is the relation to the other. That is all. Once you relate to the other as the other then something incalculable comes to the scene" (VR, 17).

33. Note here that Derrida's discussion of the honor of reason and unconditionality refers to both Kant and Husserl. Derrida connects in fact his analysis of Kant to Husserl's *The Crisis of European Sciences and Transcendental Phenomenology*, where Husserl called for a rehabilitation (*Ehrenrettung*) of reason in his attempt to "endure a heroism of reason" and save somehow its honor (*R*,130/182).

34. In *Archive Fever*, Derrida affirms that "the condition on which the future remains to come is not only that it not be known, but that it not be *knownable as such*" (*AF*, 72/96).

35. Before turning to biology, Derrida traces, in a long footnote, the notion of immunity as exemption as it was understood in political (i.e., diplomatic immunity) and religious contexts i.e., exemption to pay taxes for religious institution or inviolability of temples as places of asylum (FK, 80/67).

36. Hägglund, *Radical Atheism*, 232.

37. For an earlier articulation of this view, see Andrea Cassatella, "Normativity without Telos: The Messianic in the Thought of Jacques Derrida," *Bamidbar: Journal of Jewish Thought and Philosophy*, Passagen Verlag, 4 no. 2 (2012): 24–43.

38. See Gaon, *The Lucid Vigil*, 249.

39. Gaon, 11.

40. Gaon, 5, 8.

41. Gaon, 5.

42. Gaon, 247, 250.

43. Jacques Derrida, "Jacques Derrida, penseur de l' événement," interview in *L'Humanité*, January 28 2004, www.humanite.fr, quoted in Cheah and Guerlac, *Derrida and the Time of the Political*, 5.

44. See also Samir Haddad, "A Genealogy of Violence, from Light to the Autoimmune," *Diacritics* 38 (2009): 121–42.

45. See Beardsworth, *Derrida and the Political*; Caputo, *The Prayers and Tears of Jacques Derrida*; Critchley, *The Ethics of Deconstruction: Derrida and Levinas* (New York: Blackwell, 1992). Drucilla Cornell, *The Philosophy of the Limit* (New York:

Routledge, 1992); Leonard Lawlor, *This Is Not Sufficient: An Essay on Animality and Human Nature* (New York: Columbia University Press, 2007) and Matthias Fritsch, "Derrida's Democracy to Come" and *Taking Turns with the Earth*. For a critical discussion of these views, and more generally of the normative dimension of deconstruction, see Hägglund, *Radical Atheism*, Haddad's *Derrida and the Inheritance of Democracy*, and Gaon's, *The Lucid Vigil*.

46. Derrida, *PF*; *R*; AI. For an analysis and discussion of Derrida's preferences towards a particular understanding of democracy, see Fritsch, "Derrida's Democracy to Come."

47. See, Haddad, *Derrida and the Inheritance of Democracy*, especially chapter 4.

48. The only place I am aware of in which Derrida *seems* instead to predetermine the normative support to decision and action and to deny the possibility that there will be future occurs in an interview on terrorism where he declares that the actions and discourse of fundamentalisms "*open onto no future and, in my view, have no future.* . . . That is why, in this unleashing of violence without name, if I had to take one of the two sides and choose in a binary situation, well, I would" (AI, 113). The question, of course, is how to read this affirmation and whether it constitutes evidence of Derrida's predetermined normative commitments and a contradiction to his view of time. I would resist reading here a predetermined commitment for the reasons explained so far and also because Derrida's point seems to refer to a specific situation, "*this* unleashing of violence (my emphasis)" related to Al Queda. I would also resist identifying here a contradiction with his view of time. As Derrida clarifies in an interview published in *Paper Machine*, his statements refer to the future of "foundamentalisms as such" and thus to the possibility of fundamentalism to last as fundamentalism without being subject to the disruption brought by the logic of autoimmunity I mention below (*PM*, 116–17).

49. In a roundtable at the University of Villanova, Derrida clarifies that he uses a religiously derived term ("messianic") to talk about messianicity "in order to let people understand" what he does when he speaks about the latter, and in spite of the awareness that such a term maintains a direct link to the Messiah of Jewish or Christian culture (VR, 24).

50. On this point, see also Fritsch, *The Promise of Memory*, 62ff.

51. See Bennington, "Transcendental Questions," in "Derridabase"; Caputo, *The Prayers and Tears of Jacques Derrida*, chapter 10; De Vries's *Philosophy and the Turn to Religion*, chapter 5; Gasché, *The Tain of the Mirror*, especially chapter 9; Fritsch, *The Promise of Memory*, especially chapter 2; Naas's *Miracle and Machine*, chapter 6.

52. For a particularly insightful discussion of this nexus, see especially Fritsch's *The Promise of Memory*, chapter 2.

53. See for example, Caputo's *The Prayers and Tears*, chapter 10; De Vries's *Philosophy and the Turn to Religion*, chapter 5; Fritsch's *The Promise of Memory*, chapter 2; and Naas's *Miracle and Machine*, chapter 6.

54. See Naas, *Miracle and Machine,* 363ff.
55. Naas, 363.
56. See also Enrique Dussel, "World-System and 'Trans'-Modernity," *Neplanta: Views from South* 3, no. 2 (2002): 222–44, 233–34.
57. See Hent de Vries, *Philosophy and the Turn to Religion* (Baltimore: John Hopkins University Press, 2008), 331, 311.
58. See Fritsch, *The Promise of Memory,* 66ff.
59 Fritsch, 66.
60. For an exploration of Derrida's critical philosophy through the notion of vigilance that does not however capture the depth and scope of this vigilance as extending to issues of colonialism and race, see Stella Gaon's *The Lucid Vigil.*
61. Hägglund, *Radical Atheism,* 48.
62. Hägglund, 30.
63. Hägglund, 166.
64. See Naas, *Miracle and Machine,* 93. For a comprehensive discussion of Derrida's notion of elementary faith, see Naas, *Miracle and Machine,* 92ff.
65. Naas, 95.
66. See, respectively, Schmitt, *The Concept of the Political*; Habermas, *On the Pragmatics of Communication*; and Charles Taylor, "The Politics of Recognition," in *Multiculturalism: Examining the Politics of Recognition,* ed. Amy Gutmann (Princeton: Princeton University Press, 1992). For insights about the racialized features of these approaches, see, respectively, Derrida's *PF* and my discussions in chapters 3 and 4; Hesse, "Racialized Modernity: An Analytics of White Mythologies"; and Glen Coulthard, *Red Skin, White Masks: Rejecting the Colonial Politics of Recognition* (Minneapolis: University of Minnesota Press, 2014).
67. See Derrida, tRACEs: Race, Deconstruction and Critical Theory."

Chapter 3

1. For Derrida, Schmitt's separatist approach is evident not simply in his endeavors to provide an only "apparently secular thought of the political" by isolating the political from all other domains, but also in his attempt to ensure that the friend/enemy distinction, especially in the case of Islam, remains purely political (*PF,* 87–89/ 106–9).

2. See Anidjar, "Introduction," 4, 22. Derrida's "Abrahamic" has been the object of discussion. Massad, for example, has severely criticized Derrida's use of it for being only apparently inclusive of Jews, Muslims, and Christians while surreptitiously reinforcing a false levelling between Semites that eventually "consolidates and maintains the exclusion of the Semite" reduced to Muslims only, as detailed in Edward Said's *Orientalism.* See Massad, "Forget Semitism!" 68ff. Closer to Anidjar's,

my position underscores Derrida's awareness of the political stakes of ordering religious phenomena and people through "religion" and the juridico-political arrangements that come with it, an awareness that is partly indebted to the "Abrahamic" as referring to the complex relationships between Judaism, Christianity, and Islam. While Massad's emphasis on the Orientalist genealogy and possible function of the "Abrahamic" is helpful to maintain critical vigilance, his criticism does not fully account for the nature and implications of Derrida's critical approach to "religion," which is in fact a larger critique of an ahistorical and racializing modality of thinking based on naturalizations, hierachizations, and separations that remains entangled with, and in part continues in novel forms, the legacy of colonialism. In the specific case of so-called Abrahamic religions, Derrida exposes, as Anidjar also emphasizes, the hierarchy inbuilt in the modern discourse of religion—with Judaism and Islam being, respectively the internal and external excluded other of Christianity—thereby pointing to exclusions, rather than its opposite.

3. In the very opening of FK, Derrida uses the term "perhaps" twice in the space of few lines in order to signal his tentative and careful approach to the question of religion. The motive of the "perhaps," which he explores in relation to Nietzsche in *PF*, is complemented by a systematic questioning of any pre-comprehension of being *à la* Heidegger (i.e., what the "is" stands for in any formulation of the sort "religion *is*. . . ."), by the insistence on abstraction as a form of epoché as in the tradition of phenomenology, and finally by scruples and hesitation (FK, 42/9, 44/11, 68/50).

4. For a comprehensive exploration of the relationship between miracle and machine in Derrida, see Naas, *Miracle and Machine*.

5. See Schmitt, *Political Theology*, 36.

6. Naas, "Derrida's *Laïcité*."

7. See Goetschel, "Derrida and Spinoza: Rethinking the Theologico-Political Problem," 9–25. See also his *Spinoza's Modernity*.

8. For a discussion of the aporetic dimension of the law in Derrida, see Beardsworth, *Derrida and the Political*.

9. See Alexander Hamilton, James Madison and John Jay, *The Federalist: With Letters of Brutus* (Cambridge: Cambridge University Press, 2003), 6.

10. I owe suggestions about this clarification to comments from John R. Pottenger and Edward Andrew.

11. On the question of legitimacy, see also Horwitz's "Derrida and the Aporia of the Political, or The Theologico-Political Dimension of Deconstruction."

12. See Anidjar, "*Mal de Sionisme* (Zionist Fever)," 52.

13. See Mark Lilla, "The Politics of Jacques Derrida," *The New York Review of Books* 45, no. 11 (June 25, 1998); 36–41; Richard Wolin, "Derrida on Marx, or The Perils of Left Heideggerianism" in *Labyrinths: Explorations in the Critical History of Ideas*, ed. Richard Wolin (Amherst: University of Massachusetts Press, 1995),

231–40. Although not specifically addressed by Derrida, the connection between "decisionism" and totalitarianism is suggested by Giorgio Agamben as well. In his discussion of sovereignty and the law, Agamben emphasizes the latent totalitarianism of any politico-legal order, including democracy, since legal validity ultimately relies on a decision. See Giorgio Agamben, *State of Exception*. For a discussion of the difference between Schmitt and Derrida on this issue see, John P. McCormick, "Derrida on Law; Or, Poststructuralism Gets Serious" *Political Theory* 29 (2001): 395–423; "Schmittian Positions on Law and Politics? CLS and Derrida," *Cardozo Law Review* 21 (2000): 1693–2119. For a critical response to this view, see Gayatri Chakravorty Spivak, "Schmitt and Poststructuralism: A Response," *Cardozo Law Review* 21 (2000): 1723–37.

14. Carl Schmitt, *Political Theology*, 10.

15. Schmitt, 13, 66.

16. Schmitt, *The Concept of the Political*, 26, 28.

17. Schmitt, 38, 46.

18. For Derrida's most sustained criticism of Schmitt, see his *Politics of Friendship*.

19. Note here that Derrida contests only Schmitt's belief in effecting clear cut-distinctions and his desire to close the political space, but not the *actual* closure of such a space, which cannot be effected given Schmitt's recognition of a normative void underlying the political.

20. For Derrida's denunciation of the erasure of sexual difference in the Western tradition, especially in the work of Schmitt, Heidegger, and Levinas, see respectively *PF*, *GES I* and *GES III*, and *ATT*. His position on the same with regard to Nietzsche is more complex and is explored in *SP*. Derrida's position on the matter is perhaps best captured by a 1982 interview, in which he speaks of a "desire" and a "dream" of sexual difference that is "beyond the binary difference that governs the decorum of all codes, beyond the opposition feminine/masculine, beyond bisexuality as well, beyond homosexuality and heterosexuality" (CO, 76, 78). While Derrida's exposure of the erasure of sexual difference in connection to the theological-political is to be welcome, it is hardly sufficient as a treatment of such an important issue marking the modern secular paradigm and its institutional embodiments. Nor does this straightforwardly make Derrida into a "feminist" thinker. For a criticism of Derrida's own "exclusion" of women, see *Feminist Interpretations of Jacques Derrida*, ed. Nancy Holland; Haddad, *The Inheritance of Democracy*; and Penelope Deutscher, "Derrida's Impossible Genealogies"; "Women and so On": *Rogues* and the Autoimmunity of Feminism."

21. In *Rogues*, Derrida clarifies that it is precisely the politicization of common genealogy that raises questions on the link between fraternity, friendship, and citizenship (*R*, 61/92).

22. See also Anidjar's illuminating analysis of this point in his *The Jew, the Arab: A History of the Enemy*, especially chapter 2.

23. See also Bonnie Honig, "Declaration of Independence: Arendt and Derrida on the Problem of Founding a Republic," *The American Political Science Review* 85 (1991): 97–113.

24. For discussions on Derrida and the law, including his "Force of Law," see Beardsworth, *Derrida and the Political*; Alan Brudner, "The Ideality of Difference: Toward Objectivity in Legal Interpretation," *Cardozo Law Review* 11 (1990): 1133–1210; Roberto Buonamano, "The Economy of Violence: Derrida on Law and Justice," *Ratio Juris* 11 (1998):168–79; Drucilla Cornell, "The Thinker of the Future—Introduction to the Violence of the Masquerade: Law Dressed Up as Justice." *German Law Journal* 6, no. 1 (2005): 125–48; Margaret Davies, "Derrida and Law: Legitimate Fictions," in *Jacques Derrida and the Humanities: A Critical Reader*, ed. Tom Cohen (Cambridge: Cambridge University Press, 2001), 213–37; Nancy Fraser, "The Force of Law: Metaphysical or Political?"; Kellogg, *Law's Trace*; Petra Gehring, "Force and 'Mystical Foundation' of Law: How Jacques Derrida Addresses Legal Discourse," *German Law Journal* 6 (2005): 151–69; Dominick La Capra, "Violence, Justice, and the Force of Law" in *Cardozo Law Review* 11 (1990): 1065–78; and John P. McCormick, "Derrida on Law; Or, Poststructuralism Gets Serious."

25. "Laws are now maintained in credit, not because they are just, but because they are law. It is the mystical foundation of their authority; they have no other" (FL, 239/30).

26. In "Critique of Violence" Benjamin argues for the undecidability affecting the law when he affirms the "ultimate insolubility of all legal problems." See Walter Benjamin, "Critique of Violence," 247. Schmitt, as we have seen, sees such problems solvable through the sovereign's decision.

27. See also Drucilla Cornell, "The Thinker of the Future—Introduction to the Violence of the Masquerade: Law Dressed Up as Justice." *German Law Journal* 6, no. 1 (2005): 125–48.

28. For an insightful discussion of iterability, see Rodolphe Gasché, "More than a Difference in Style," in *The Honor of Thinking: Critique, Theory, Philosophy* (Stanford: Stanford University Press, 2007); see also his *The Tain of the Mirror: Derrida and the Philosophy of Reflection* (Harvard, MA: Harvard University Press, 1986).

29. For rich accounts and discussions of iterability as differential repetition affecting the law, see Beardsworth, *Derrida and the Political* and Matthias Fritsch, *The Promise of Memory*.

30. Benjamin, "Critique of Violence," 237–38.
31. Benjamin, 247.
32. Benjamin, 248.
33. Benjamin, 251.
34. Benjamin, 249.
35. Benjamin, 236, 251.
36. Benjamin, 249.

37. Benjamin, 252. For a thorough exploration of the notion of "deposing" in Benjamin's "Critique of Violence," see Werner Hamacher, "Afformative, Strike," *Cardozo Law Review* 13 (1991): 1133–57.

38. Benjamin, 252. To exemplify divine violence, Benjamin mentions the biblical story of Korah and the general strike. In the case of Korah, he refers to how God's judgment striking the Levites effected a manifestation of divine violence by annihilating them without spilling blood. In the second case, he argues that the violence of the general strike—which, unlike the political strike, does not replace those in power while maintaining the state but seeks to abolish the state altogether—can be taken as an example of the possible manifestation of divine violence in human affairs. See Benjamin, 246, 250.

39. With reference to the mixture of law-making and law-preserving violence in the police, Benjamin talks about an "unnatural combination" (242) rendering the police an institution in which one "encounters nothing essential at all" (243). Similarly, when differentiating a political from a general strike, he says that the two are "essentially different" (245). The theme of decay appears especially in Benjamin's discussion of parliamentary democracy (244) and the history of law as a history of law's decay (251). See Benjamin, "Critique of Violence."

40. Rodolphe Gasché, "Critique, Hypercriticism, Deconstruction," *The Honor of Thinking. Critique, Theory, Philosophy* (Stanford: Stanford University Press, 2007), 35–36.

41. See Benjamin, "Critique of Violence," 242–43.

42. Most notably his "Theses on the Philosophy of History." For a discussion of Derrida's "unfair" reading of Benjamin see John P. McCormick, "Derrida on Law; Or, Poststructuralism Gets Serious"; and Mathias Fritsch, *The Promise of Memory: History and Politics in Marx, Benjamin and Derrida*.

43. Gillian Rose, *Judaism and Modernity: Philosophical Essays* (Oxford: Oxford University Press, 1993), 81–86.

44. John P. McCormick, "Derrida on Law; Or, Poststructuralism Gets Serious," 407.

45. See Richard, J. Bernstein, *Violence: Thinking without Banisters* (Cambridge: Polity, 2013).

46. In addition to Fritsch, Bernstein, Gasché, McCormick, and Rose mentioned in the preceding footnotes, see De Vries, Hent, *Religion and Violence*; James Martel *Divine Violence: Walter Benjamin and the Eschatology of Sovereignty* (Routledge/GlassHouse, 2011).

47. Ben Corson, "Transcending Violence in Derrida. A Reply to John McCormick" in *Political Theory* 29, no. 6 (2001): 855–75. For interpretations on the relationship between iterability and violence in Derrida, see also Beardsworth, *Derrida and the Political*; and Samir Haddad, "A Genealogy of Violence, from Light to the Autoimmune."

48. Cauchi, "The Secular to Come: Interrogating the Derridean 'Secular,'" 13.

49. The charge of dangerous equalization is put forward by Dominick La Capra in his "Violence, Justice, and the Force of Law" and critically discussed in Drucilla Cornell's "The Thinker of the Future."

50. See Paul Patton and Terry Smith, eds., "Justice, Colonization, Translation," in *Jacques Derrida: Deconstruction Engaged: The Sydney Seminars*, 82.

51. Patton calls this a "partial" deconstruction since the High Court formulated the decision through the language of the colonizing power and in the name of the colonizer, thereby perpetuating, in some sense, historical injustice.

52. This is the source of disagreement between Derrida and Agamben with regard to the interpretation of Kafka's story. While, for Derrida, the story shows the impossibility of surpassing the abyssal character of the law, for Agamben it suggests that the patient waiting of the man of the country led to a closure of the law's gate, the deposition of the law, and thus the opening up of a new politics without law that is closer to justice by standing at the gate leading to it [Agamben, *Homo Sacer*, 49–62; *State of Exception*, 64]. Yet this disagreement cuts deeper. While Derrida resists any form of messianism capable of seeing which gate leads to justice and thus where justice lies, or that severs the nexus between justice and law, Agamben envisages a new politics without law, a historical epoch that is "closer" to justice, since it stands at the gate "that leads to it." In this way, Agamben's messianism retains a thin yet substantive character that allows for seeing from the present where the future of justice lies. For a thorough discussion of the relationship between Derrida and Agamben, see Adam Thurschwell, "Specters of Nietzsche: Potential Futures for the Concept of the Political in Agamben and Derrida," *Cardozo Law Review* 24 (2003): 1193–1231.

53. Commenting on this topic in *The Beast and the Sovereign*, Derrida says, in a Kantian fashion, that the "*thought* of exception," the Schmittian exception exemplified here by the "pure performative," is "necessary" but "impossible qua *philosophical theory*" (BS 1, 49/80).

54. C. E. Evink "Jacques Derrida and the Faith in Philosophy," *The Southern Journal of Philosophy* 42 (2004): 313–31. See Mark Cauchi, "The Secular to Come: Interrogating the Derridean 'Secular.'" It should be noted that Cauchi directs his charge at Derrida's view of the secular by referring specifically to the latter's view of identity and culture. Yet he also addresses the question of "faith" as central to this charge.

55. See C. E. Evink "Jacques Derrida and the Faith in Philosophy," 319–20.

56. Cauchi, "The Secular to Come: Interrogating the Derridean "Secular,'" 19.

57. This point marks the proximity and difference between Derrida and Lefort. While both thinkers consider the foundation of the political—where "political" refers specifically to modern democracy for Lefort—to be always provisional, Derrida resists row categorical exclusion of religious sources from the event of political institution. Lefort, in contrast, assigns to them an "imaginary" character that requires

that higher point of view his phenomenological perspective on democracy would seem to disallow. See Lefort, "The Permanence of the Theologico-Political?," 187.

58. Samuel Weber, "Taking Exception to Decision: Walter Benjamin and Carl Schmitt," 11.

59. On this reading, it is the reference to some form of the theological and not simply the philosophical (quasitranscendental), as Chantal Mouffe and Ernesto Laclau have argued, that offers resources for interrogating the political in terms of its possibilities and limits. See Chantal Mouffe and Ernesto Laclau, *Hegemony and Socialist Strategy*. The same reference calls into question Hagglund's characterization of Derrida's philosophy as a "radicalial atheism." See his *Radical Atheism*.

60. For perspectives that associate Derrida's thought to religion and theological discourse, see especially Caputo, *The Prayers and Tears of Jacques Derrida*; de Vries, *Philosophy and the Turn to Religion*; and Kearney, "Desire of God."

61. Derrida, "Authorship, Sovereignty and the Axiomatics of the Interview: Derrida 'Live,'" in James Smith *Jacques Derrida: Live Theory* (London: Continuum, 2005): 104–17. As such, Derrida's resistance to the antireligious impulse of the Enlightenment calls into question Hagglund's characterization of Derrida's philosophy as a "radical atheism." See Hagglund, *Radical Atheism*.

62. Cauchi, "The Secular to Come: Interrogating the Derridean 'Secular'"; Naas, "Derrida's *Laïcité*."

63. Naas, "Derrida's *Laïcité*," 63.

64. Naas, 64.

65. Cauchi, "The Secular to Come," 11. Specifically, Cauchi shows how, for Derrida, the impossibility of self-identity of secular Europe equally applies to religious Christianity.

66. Cauchi, 13.

67. In his explication of the "secular" as a concept, Cauchi does mention that it refers to a field of sociopolitical relationships but never relates it to questions of force, violence, law, and authority that appear central to the investigation of the secular so conceived. See Cauchi, "The Secular to Come," 3.

68. For Habermas, see "Faith and knowledge," in *The Future of Human Nature*, ed. J. Habermas (Cambridge: Polity, 2003); "Religion in the Public Sphere," *European Journal of Philosophy* 14, no. 1 (2006): 1–25; "What Is Meant by a Post-Secular Society?," in *Europe: The Faltering Project*, trans. C. Cronin (Cambridge: Polity, 2009); "An Awareness of What Is Missing: Faith and Reason in a Post-secular Age" (Cambridge: Polity, 2010). For Taylor, see "Why We Need a Radical Redefinition of Secularism," in *The Power of Religion in the Public Sphere*, ed. E. Mendieta and J. VanAntwerpen (New York: Columbia University Press, 2011); *A Secular Age*; "Modes of secularism," in *Secularism and Its Critics*, ed. Rajeev Bhargava (Delhi: Oxford University Press, 1998).

69. The emphasis on fundamentalism as primarily a problem of religion(s) has been recently advanced by Habermas and Nancy. See Habermas, "Fundamentalism

and Terror. A Dialogue with Jürgen Habermas," in *Philosophy in a Time of Terror*, ed. Giovanna Borradori, 31–32; Nancy, *Dis-Enclsoure*, 5.

70. For the notion of "epistemic privilege" as a culturally and geopolitically specific site of enunciation producing knowledge claimed as universal, see Mignolo, "Epistemic Disobedience, Independent Thought and De-Colonial Freedom."

71. For example, on this issue, Salman Sayyid notes that Hinduism, Islam, and Judaism are examples of valuable traditions that do not articulate views about political subjectivity along the division religious/nonreligious. See Sayyid, *Recalling the Caliphate*, 41.

Chapter 4

1. For an earlier and less-focused treatment of democracy, see especially Derrida, *WAP*, FL, *PF*, and *OH*.

2. See Derrida, *FWT*, 144/233, 147/239. Derrida specifies that by "proper to man," he refers to what, in the philosophical tradition, has been considered the ability to elevate oneself above life, to be worth "something more and other than his [of man] life." In this regard, he mentions Plato's view of philosophy as a discipline preparing for death (*epimeleia tou thanatou*); Kant's view of the person whose dignity transcends his/her condition as a living being; Hegel's struggle for recognition that passes through the putting at risk of one's own life; and Heidegger's being-towards-death of *Dasein* as the only being that can experience his own death.

3. Speaking of the history of Western philosophy Derrida affirms: "Never, *to my knowledge*, has any philosopher *as a philosopher, in his or her strictly and systematically philosophical discourse*, never has any philosophy *as such* contested the legitimacy of the death penalty. From Plato to Hegel, from Rousseau to Kant (who was undoubtedly most rigorous of them all), they expressly, each in his own way, and sometimes without much hand-wringing (Rousseau), took a stand *for* the death penalty" (*FWT*, 146–48/235–40).

4. While Wendy Brown makes this choice a point of weakness, for the purposes of this study, it represents a point of strength since it allows us to emphasize how the theological-political nexus relates to the foundation of political community. See her "Sovereign Hesitations," in *Derrida and the Time of the Political*.

5. For an insightful discussion of these figures in relation to Derrida's political thought, see Bennington, *Scatter 2*.

6. Derrida refers here to that passage in the *Politics* in which Aristotle affirms that "for man of pre-eminent excellence there is no law—they are themselves the law" (1284a.13–14).

7. Of course, one could argue that the kingship of an excellent man is not the model constitution of Aristotle. However, allowing room for interpretation here does not change Derrida's point that Aristotle conceives of the representation of

sovereign power as unitary and indivisible, if certain conditions apply. Bennington picks up on the point of plurality in Aristotle and criticizes Derrida for reducing the distance between Plato and Aristotle, which are both seen, without due distinctions, as exemplar thinkers of unity. See his *Scatter 2*, 69ff.

8. As Derrida notes, Hobbes concedes that a "mediated" contract with God is possible "by mediation of some body that representeth God's person, which none doth but God's Lieutenant, who hath sovereignty under God" (*BS 1*, 50/82). This logic of lieutenancy, Derrida remarks "leaves open the possibility of a Christian foundation of politics" and also "clearly marks the fact the *proper place*" of human sovereignty is "that of an authority that is subject, subjected and submitted to, and underlying divine sovereignty. Be it Moses, Christ, the monarch king as Christian king or an assembly of men elected and instituted as sovereign, their place always stands for the place of God [*tient lieu de Dieu*]" (52–54/84–86). This is what is missed by recent interpretations of Hobbes as a theorist of civil religion providing a political foundation of (Christian) religion. See Ronald Beiner's *Civil Religion. A Dialogue in the History of Political Philosophy* (Cambridge, MA: Cambridge University Press, 2011).

9. Wendy Brown, "Sovereign Hesitations," 118.

10. Besides Pascal, whom we discussed in the previous chapter, and Machiavelli and Hobbes, considered above, Derrida mentions explicitly Plato's discussion of Thrasymachus in the *Republic*; Rousseau's reflections on the right of the strongest in *The Social Contract*; and especially Kant's doctrine of strict right in the *Metaphysics of Morals*, a doctrine that implies in the concept of right the possibility of reciprocal constraint and "thus the possibility of a reason of the strongest in accordance with universal laws and consistent with the freedom of all" (*R*, 93/134).

11. Although mentioning it only in passing at this point in the text, Derrida crucially refers to Plato's Idea of the Good in the *Republic*. In *Rogues*, he observes that the Idea of the Good is the cause of the human capacity and power (*dynamis*) to know. He recalls a famous passage in which Plato, after using the words "power (*dynamis*)," "king (*basileus*)," and "sovereign (*kurion*)" to qualify respectively reason, the Sun and the Good, articulates the Idea of the Good as a "surpassing power (*dunamei huperkhontos*)" that is "beyond being" (*epekeina tēs ousias*) and that generates knowledge without being itself subjected to genesis. For Derrida, this characterization opens an understanding of knowledge as sovereign since it ascribes to the Idea of the Good an "ultimate sovereign power" that "gives reason or proves reason right [*donne raison*], that wins over [*a raison de*] everything" (*R*, 138/192ff.).

12. Derrida notes that Heidegger, in his *Introduction to Metaphysics*, calls Aristotle's definition of man as *rational animal* (*zōon logon ekhon*) "zoological" because it links *logos* to *zoon* and because he associates the essence of man to logos as reason, as well as to the "animal" as a "living being." For Heidegger, Aristotle's definition is problematic both because it grounds his definition on an unexamined basis, namely, the unexplored ontological essence of what "being alive" or "life"

might mean; and also because it takes logos as reason, understanding, and logic, thereby ignoring a more originary sense of *logos* as gathering (*Versammlung*) (*BS 1*, 263–64/354, 314–19/418–25).

13. Here Derrida expands the scope of his reflection to criticize Agamben's theory of modern politics as "biopolitics," a theory grounded on a distinction between *zōē* (bare life) and *bios* (qualified life, or group life) seemingly advanced by Aristotle. Drawing attention to Aristotle's relevant passages in the *Politics* and *Metaphysics* and to Heidegger's reflections in *The Introductions of Metaphysics* and *Letter on Humanism*, Derrida emphasizes several points. First, that the distinction at issue is never as clear and secure in Aristotle as Agamben makes it appear and the association of *zōē* to political life is not pre-eminently modern. Derrida mentions passages (that Agamben acknowledges as exceptions) in which Aristotle uses *zōē* to designate a life that is not bare when he associates *zōē* to God. He also shows that since for Aristotle man is immediately zoo-political, his (Aristotle's) view contains already, though perhaps not intentionally, the possibility of thinking about "biopolitics." Furthermore, Agamben's silence with regard to Heidegger's critique of the biologism informing the understanding of modern life and to Aristotle's zoologism is perplexing. It is so because Heidegger's critique moved already in the direction of biopolitics and Agamben is well-versed in Heideggerian scholarship (*BS 1*, 319/425ff.).

14. For the first articulation of this thought, see Derrida, "University without Condition," in *WA*.

15. Derrida makes this point even clearer when he affirms that the fate of "democracy to come" depends to a large extent on the future of the UN Security Council, which is run by the most powerful nation-states according to the principle of indivisible sovereignty (98/141).

16. For a first articulation of the inventive character of deconstruction, see Derrida, "Psyche: The Invention of the Other" (*PSY 1*, 1–47/11–62).

17. In *The Concept of the Political*, Schmitt opposes the use of concepts such as humanity and humanitarianism to wage war in the interests of man. For him, this represents a hypocritical attempt to achieve particular interests through a falsifying rhetoric of universalism. As he claims, "the 'concept of humanity' is an especially useful ideological instrument of imperialist expansion, and in its ethical-humanitarian form it is a specific vehicle of economic imperialism." See Schmitt, *The Concept of the Political*, 54. Emphasizing this point, though, does not in any way validate Schmitt's judgment with regard to the imperialism and antisemitism that his overall theory of politics advances and that Derrida criticizes especially in *PF*.

18. Note that Derrida tends to prefer "liberty" to "freedom" but, arguably, is referring to the same thing. In an interview, he explains his caution in using "freedom" since such a term is loaded with metaphysical presuppositions that ascribe to the subject a sovereign independence over what, among other things escapes consciousness (*FWT*, 48/85).

19. Derrida's formulation here is significantly similar to how Claude Lefort in "The Permanence of the Theologico-Political" considers as distinctive of modern democracy that the place of power is an empty one, impeding the final configuration of modern democracy. Like Lefort, Derrida appeals to the figure of an empty place at the core of democracy. Unlike him, though, Derrida refers to the concept of democracy itself and not simply to modern democracy.

20. "The syntagma "democracy to come"—where "to come" refers, among other things, to the indeterminacy and nonunivocal meaning of democracy—"belongs to at least one of the lines of thought coming out of the Platonic tradition" (*R*, 25/47).

21. The emphasis on life is here central since autoimmunity is a process affecting life. For Derrida, only by "thinking life otherwise" can democracy be thought of differently (*R*, 33/57). On the emphasis Derrida puts on life when discussing autoimmunity, see also Naas, *Miracle and Machine*, 86.

22. Paul Patton has argued that had Derrida engaged with theorists of liberal democracy such as Mill and Rawls he would have confronted a more complex understanding of the relationship between freedom and equality and would have probably been in a position to offer a more "helpful" account of the logic of autoimmunity. Patton emphasizes that for all such thinkers, the value of individual freedom puts a limit to equality of numbers since no majority would be allowed to breach that freedom. Assigning to this limit an immunizing function against violations of the freedom of others, Patton also recognizes the logic of autoimmunity lurking behind the limits to the permissible exceptions granted to the respect of the freedom of each. See Patton, "Derrida, Politics and Democracy to Come" *Philosophy Compass* 2, no. 6 (2007): 766–80, 776.

23. For a criticism of Derrida on this issue, see especially Anne Norton, "Called to Bear Witness. Derrida, Muslims, and Islam," in E. Baring and E. P. Gordon, *The Trace of God: Derrida and Religion* (New York: Fordham University Press, 2014), 88–109.

24. See Alex Thomson, "What's to Become of 'Democracy to Come'?" *Postmodern Culture* 15, no. 3 (2005), 20.

25. Although the evidence for this claim is limited, it can, nevertheless, be taken to contrast with a recent criticism made by Wendy Brown of Derrida's underestimation of shared government due to his emphasis on sovereign freedom. In a puncturing analysis of Derrida's view of sovereignty, Brown argues that by considering individual freedom as "essential" to democracy, Derrida construes freedom as a "freedom from one another, including our freedom from ruling together or taking responsibility for the whole," thereby locking the semantic scope of democracy and freedom to their liberal understandings (see her "Sovereign Hesitations," 124–25). Yet, the claim we have highlighted refers to a wide spectrum of classical representations of freedom and thus one might suppose, with an interpretative stretch, that these include also republican understandings of freedom, at least those of Rousseau

and Kant. As such, his claim would speak to the concern of Brown, who actually notes that had Derrida stretched his view to comprise freedom as understood also in the republican tradition, it would have been "less contentious." My point is that Derrida's claim about the dominant politico-philosophical discourse about democracy and freedom in Western political philosophy allows for that stretch. His call for more power sharing against indivisible democratic sovereignty would seem to speak to Brown's other worry (the underestimation of shared government) by extending, though, the scope of sharing beyond the boundaries of the nation-state.

26. Derrida, "Remarks on Deconstruction and Pragmatism," in Mouffe, *Deconstruction and Pragmatism*, 85.

27. Derrida, "Performative Powerlessness: A Response to Simon Critchley," in *Constellations* 7, no. 4 (2000): 466–68.

28. For an analysis and discussion of Derrida's preference for modern democracy, see Matthias Fritsch, "Derrida's Democracy to Come."

29. See also Bennington, *Scatter 1*, 246–49.

30. In "Democracy to Come," Fritsch argues that secularization is the condition of possibility of democracy to come without problematizing the former as Derrida does in several places. See Fritsch, "Democracy to Come," 575.

31. Derrida "Open Discussion," 241.

32. Samir Haddad identifies another risk connected to viewing democracy as autoimmune. This appears particularly in Derrida's inconsistent use of autoimmunity in a strict sense (as a defense against one's own defense) as opposed to a broader one (as a defense against any part of the self), both of which he uses to talk about religion. For Haddad, using autoimmunity in the first sense when applied to "democracy to come" implies an understanding of democracy as "a political regime structured around the notion of defense." This understanding is rather questionable. For not only in democracy, unlike in religion, "there is nothing" that "necessitate the unscathed as one of its sources," but also because it differs from the type of "democracy to come" Derrida advocates for (40). See Haddad, "Derrida and Democracy at Risk."

33. For some powerful positions that speak to this point, see Mohammed Abed al-Jabri, *Democracy, Human Rights and Law in Islamic Thought* (London: I. B. Tauris, 2009); Enrique Dussel, *Politics of Liberation: A Critical Global History*, trans. Thia Cooper (London: SCM, 2011); Ziba Mir-Hosseini, *Islam and Gender, the Religious Debate in Contemporary Iran* (Princeton, NJ: Princeton University Press, 1999); Saba Mahmood, *Politics of Piety: The Islamic Revival and the Feminist Subject*; Walter Mignolo, *Local Histories/Global Designs: Coloniality, Subaltern Knowledges, and Border Thinking* (New Jersey: Princeton University Press, 2000); Ashis Nandy and D. L. Sheth, eds., *The Multiverse of Democracy: Essays in Honour of Rajni Kothari* (New Dehli: Sage 1996); Abdulaziz Sachedina, *The Islamic Roots of Democratic Pluralism* (Oxford: Oxford University Press, 2000); Salman Sayyid, *Recalling the*

Caliphate: Decolonization and World Order (London: Hurst & Company, 2014).; Leanne Simpson, *Dancing on Our Turtle's Back: Stories of Nishnaabeg Re-Creation, Resurgence, and a New Emergence* (Winnipeg: Arp 2011).

34. See Mill, *On Liberty* (Oxford: Oxford University Press, 1991); Rawls, *Political Liberalism*; Habermas, *Between Facts and Norms*. See also Fritsch, "Derrida's Democracy to Come," 578–80.

35. The notion of *khora*, Derrida notes, is introduced by Plato in the *Timeus*. Plato understands it as a "receptacle," a figurative site that is neither being nor nonbeing but an interval, a "between" in which the forms were originally held and made possible. Because *khora* is "other than being," it escapes philosophical categories and conceptualization and yet is not nonbeing. By associating democracy to *khora*, Derrida underscores that democracy is both a reality we cannot exhaust conceptually as it always exceeds semantic fixation as well as a sort of space that allows for a provisional meaning of living together to be determined in the first place by providing an opening that does not prescribe any particular type of politics. For an excellent discussion of Derrida's understanding of *khora* as a way through which he rethinks the political, see Naas, "Jewgreek is greekjew," in *Miracle and Machine*, 152–96. Here Naas argues for something similar to what I have proposed in this chapter, namely, that "democracy to come" would take distance from the traditional understanding of secularism, without however addressing issues of race and the colonial legacy associated with it that I have tried to emphasize throughout (187). While he reaches this conclusion primarily through a discussion of *khora* as a spatial dimension, I do so through a discussion of "democracy to come" in relation to its political and temporal dimension (sovereignty, freedom, and the "messianic") and the way they help break with the colonial afterlife of "White mythology."

36. For a discussion that supports and expands this point, see Thomson "What's to Become of 'Democracy to Come' "?

37. On this point, see also Paul Patton, "Derrida, Politics and Democracy to Come," 774.

38. "Deconstruction, I have insisted, is not *neutral*. It *intervenes*" (*P*, 93; see also *PF*, 105/128).

49. It should be noted, though, that Derrida's view of hospitality presents strong ethical connotations and that his view about the relationship between ethics and politics remains somewhat underdeveloped. See Peng Cheah and Suzanne Guerlac, "Introduction," in *Derrida and the Time of the Political*, 25.

40. Note, however, that although Derrida emphasizes in *Rogues* and other writings the importance of both calculability and incalculability, in *FWT* he affirms that "deconstruction is on the side of unconditionality, even when it seems impossible, and not sovereignty, even when it seems possible" (*FWT*, 92/153).

41. See Bennington, *Scatter* 2, 28.

42. Bennington, 38.

43. Bennington, 208.

44. Bennington's exploration of Al-Farabi's thought can hardly constitute enough evidence to weaken my point.

Chapter 5

1. Commentators have also focused on *The Gift of Death*, where Derrida mistakenly attributes to Islam a reading of the story of Abraham based on Genesis, and thus pertinent to Judaism and Christianity, while neglecting the version of it based on the Qu'ran. For critical remarks on this mistaken reading, see Ian Almond, *The New Orientalists. Representations of Islam from Foucault to Baudrillard* (New York: I. B. Tauris, 2007); Anne Norton, "Called to Bear Witness. Derrida's error is in line with some other problematic accounts he offers in "Faith and Knowledge" and *Rogues* and bespeaks a certain uncritical attitude that is at odds with the critical thrust of deconstruction that I try to develop here in relation to Islam.

2. In a discussion about negative theology, focusing especially on the Greek and Christian traditions, Derrida affirms the following: "I thus decided *not to speak* of negativity or of apophatic movements in, for example, the Jewish or Islamic traditions. To leave this immense place empty, and above all that which can connect such a name of God with the name of the Place, to remain thus on the threshold—was this not the most consistent possible apophasis? Concerning that about which one cannot speak, isn't best to remain silent?" (HAS, 79). For a criticism of Derrida's inability to speak about Islam seen as both consistent with his limited engagement with it and typical of negative theology, see Ian Almond, *The New Orientalists* 43ff. For an illuminating discussion of "not speaking" that is not so easily reducible to a form of avoidance as in negative theology, see Anidjar, "Introduction," 24ff.

3. For classic and still indispensable treatments to understand the psychological, religious, and political dimensions of colonial and postcolonial violence in Algeria, and more generally in (formerly) colonized spaces, see Frantz Fanon, *L'An V de la révolution algérienne* (Paris: La Découverte, [1959] 2011); *Les Damnés de la Terre* (Paris: La Découverte, [1961] 2002); *Pour la révolution africaine. Écrits politiques* (Paris: La Découverte (1964) 2006). I thank Abdulkader Tayob for drawing my attention to the importance of recalling the broader context in which Islamism in Algeria developed, lying in the background of Derrida's reflections.

4. For a position opposing this view, see Ian Almond, *The New Orientalists*, 42.

5. Anidjar makes this point in his discussion of the figure of the Arab Jew also with reference to the work of Fethi Benslama. See, Anidjar, "Introduction,"10.

6. For a discussion of this point, see Anidjar, *The Jew, the Arab: A History of the Enemy*, 49ff.

7. For a seminal articulation of this processes *vis-à-vis* Islam, see Said, *Orientalism*.

8. For a discussion of the becoming-religion of Islam, see especially Masuzawa, *The Invention of World Religions*; Brent Nongbri, *Before Religion*. For a groundbreaking work that considers Islam as exceeding "religion," see Cantwell Smith, *The Meaning and End of Religion*.

9. Massad has further criticized Derrida's association of "Abrahamic" with "religions" that finds no textual support in Islamic texts. See Massad, "Forget Semitism!" 71.

10. See also Massad, "Forget Semitism!" 78. Wise criticizes Derrida for the same reason with regard to the way in which he addresses the city of Jerusalem in *Specters of Marx*, 72. Wise sees Derrida's formula "war of appropriation of Jerusalem" as obscuring the lived reality of Palestinian people with the historical city of Al Quds, whose Arabic rendering is etymologically linked to the Aramaic "Qaddosh" preceding both the Arabic "Gaddos" and Hebrew "Gaddosh," and thus referring to a city older than "Jerusalem." See his "The Figure of Jerusalem: Derrida's *Specters of Marx*," 76. Commenting on the same passage, Massad claims that Derrida's formula equates the anticolonial struggle of Palestinians who defend the city they have lived in for generations to "Zionist colonial settler thefts." See his "Forget Semitism!," 75. In response to Wise, Martin McQuillan argues that Derrida's formula "war of appropriation of Jerusalem," which Derrida puts in quotation marks, is not literal and refers to a critique of election and of appropriation of a place as he advanced especially in *Archive Fever*. See Martin McQuillan, "Clarity and Doubt: Derrida among the Palestinians," *Paragraph* 39, no. 2 (2016): 220–37, 229. There are reasons to agree with McQuillan. Derrida's use of quotation marks in *Specters of Marx*—which do not however appear in the same formulation in "Faith and Knowledge"—is hardly accidental, and it inscribes such an expression in a problematics that, much larger than "religion," regards modern understandings and forms, including the nation-state, international law, and capitalism (*SM*, 72/101). Yet, it is also difficult to disagree with Massad's reference to the recurrence of a somehow symmetrical framing in Derrida's treatments of Israel/Palestine, which connects to Derrida's only indirect treatment of questions of race and settler colonialism in such contexts, as indicated in chapter 1, note 44.

11. For a recent discussion of the epistemic opportunities, but also difficulties, associated with the use of the Arabic *dīn*, see Ahmet T. Karamustafa, "Islamic *Dīn* as an Alternative to Western Models of 'Religion' " in *Religion, Theory, Critique: Classic and Contemporary Approaches and Methodologies*, ed. Richard King (New York: Columbia University Press, 2017).

12. Susan Bock-Morss offers a useful, yet not exhaustive, list of such diverse projects, which include the works of Akbar Ahmed, Leila Ahmed, Mohammed Arkoun, Talal Asad, Ahmet Davutoglu, Saba Mahmood, Ziba Mir-Hosseini, Abdel-

wahab El-Messiri, Ali Mirsepassi, Ali Moussalli, Salman Sayyid, Hisham Sharabi, Azzam Tamimi, and Bassam Tibi. See "Critical Theory and Islamism," in *Thinking Past Terror: Islamism and Critical Theory on the Left* (New York: Verso 2003). Other thinkers worth mentioning who are engaged in critical scholarship drawing from and/or focusing on the Islamic tradition are Fatima Mernissi, Amina Wadud, Kecia Ali, Shahed Ahmed, Mohammed Abdel al-Jabri, Tariq Ramadan, Abdullahi Ahmed An-naim, and Abdulkader Tayob.

13. Salman Sayyid too develops an understanding of Islam through the question of the name. While displaying a similar line of reasoning as the one proposed here, Sayyid's perspective is not linked to the question of translation that is instead central to Derrida's thought. See Sayyid, *Recalling the Caliphate*, especially chapter 1.

14. I owe the development of this point to conversations with Abdulkader Tayob and the research group connected to the "Islam, African Publics and Religious Values" Research Project at the University of Cape Town, South Africa, I participated in 2020.

15. See Asad, *Secular Translations*, 58.

16. See Almond, *The New Orientalists*, 55.

17. On this point, there is a certain proximity between Derrida and Asad. Appealing to Ludwig Wittgeinstein, Asad draws a parallel between the idea of language game and religious language emphasizing that while the Islamic traditions "aspire to coherence" the "historical conditions" under which discursive traditions are produced and maintained involve also "their transformations." See "The Idea of Anthropology of Islam," 17; *Secular Translations*, 96.

18. See An-Naim, *Islam and the Secular State*, 270.

19. For a discussion of modern developments in Islamic discourse, see, for example, Abdulkhader Tayob, *Religion in Modern Islamic Discourse* (London: C. Hurst; New York: Columbia University Press, 2009). For contemporary examples of Islam in Europe, see the work of Tariq Ramadan, *To Be a European Muslim: A Study of Islamic Sources in the European Context* (Leicester: Islamic Foundation, 1999) and BassanTibi, "Les conditions d'un 'Euro-Islam'" in *Islams d'Europe : Intégrationou insertion communautaire?*, ed. Robert Bistolfi et Francis Zabbal (Paris: Editions de l'Aube, 1995); for development of Islam discourse from the United Sates, see Abdullahi Ahmed An-naim *Islam and the Secular State: Negotiating the Future of Shari'a* (Cambridge, MA: Harvard University Press, 2008).

20. Referring to Talal Asad, "Muslims and European Identity: Can Europe Represent Islam?" in *Cultural Encounters: Representing Otherness*, ed. Elizabeth Hallam and Bran Street (New York: Routledge, 2000), 11–28, 17. Almond levels this charge against Derrida for his use of Islam in the plural. See his *The New Orientalists*, 60. While Derrida occasionally uses the term "Islams," he oddly goes against the logic that informs his own understanding of language (IW, 39/66; *CF*, 28), as presented here. Yet, it would seem a significant stretch to use these occasions as evidence of

an Orientalist logic which his entire oeuvre has sought, and greatly contributed, to dismantle.

21. Anidjar poses this possibility as a question. See his "Introduction," 28.

22. See Sayyid, *Recalling the Caliphate*, 1.

23. For a classic treatment of the separation between religion and political authority starting from the development of early and Islamic societies, see Ira Lapidus, "State and Religion in Islamic Societies," *Past and Present* 151 (1996): 3–27. "The Separation of State and Religion in the Development of Early Islamic Society," *International Journal for Middle East Studies* 6 (1975): 363–85. For a criticism of this view, which however recognizes a general consensus in modern scholarship about the separation between religious and political authority rooted in early Islamic societies, see Muhammad Quasim Zaman, "The Caliphs, the 'Ulamā', and the Law: Defining the Role and Function of the Caliph in the Early Aabbāsid Period," *Islamic Law and Society* 4, no. 1 (1997): 1–36. For developments about various configurations and political implications ensuing from the distinction between religion and politics, in modern and contemporary Islamic thought respectively, see Hamid Enayat, *Modern Islamic Political Thought* (Austin: University of Texas Press, 1982), and Tayob, *Religion in Modern Islamic Discourse*, especially chapter 5. I thank Abdulkader Tayob for pointing me to these sources.

24. See Markus Dressler, Armando Salvatore, and Monika Wohlrab-Sahr, eds., "Islamicate Secularities: New Perspective on a Contested Concepts," *Historical Social Research / Historische Sozialforschung* 44, no. 3 (2019): 7–34, 14.

25. For a discussion of an influential individualistic model of Islam, see Abdulkader Tayob, "Divergent Approaches to Religion in Modern Islamic Discourses," *Religion Compass* 3/2 (2009): 155–67.

26. See Enayat, *Modern Islamic Political Thought*, 1.

27. For important works addressing questions of women and gender, see Laila Ahmed, *Women and Gender in Islam: Historical Roots of a Modern Debates Women and Gender in Islam: Historical Roots of a Modern Debates* (New Haven: Yale University Press, 1992); Asma Barlas, *Believing Women in Islam: Unreading Patriarchal Interpretations of the Qur'an* (Austin: University of Texas Press, 2002); Amina Wadud, *The Qur'an and Women: Rereading the Sacred Text from a Woman's Perspective* (New York: Oxford University Press, 1996); Kecia Ali, *Sexual Ethics and Islam: Feminist Reflections on Qur'an, Hadith, and Jurisprudence* (Oxford, UK: Oneworld, 2006); Ziba Mir-Hosseini, *Islam and Gender, the Religious Debate in Contemporary Iran* (Princeton, NJ: Princeton University Press, 1999). On pluralism, see Farid Esack, *Qur'an, Liberation and Pluralism: An Islamic Perspective of Interreligious Solidarity against Oppression* (Oxford: Oneworld, 1997); Sachedina, *The Islamic Roots of Democratic Pluralism*; "Advancing Religious Pluralism in Islam For discussions about Islamic ethics, and specifically ethics of piety and of giving, see Saba Mahmood, *Politics of Piety*, and Amira Mittermaier, *Giving to God: Islamic*

Charity in Revolutionary Times (Oakland: University of California Press, 2019). For interventions in question of religion and politics in modern Islamic thought, see Enayat, *Modern Islamic Political Thought*, and Tayob, *Religion in Modern Islamic Discourse,* especially chapter 5.

28. Derrida's carefulness is also visible in his discussion of Algeria, in *Rogues,* as a type ("an Islamism") of phenomena that is antidemocratic (*R*, 31/55).

29. I owe the development of this point to conversations with Abdulkader Tayob.

30. See Anidjar, "Introduction," 27.

31. Arguably, this predicament has marked the development of Islamic discourses since the encounter with European colonialism, with various degree of critical and self-critical acceptance, refusal or creative repurposing of modern models. For recent critical scholarship that speak to this issue, see Shahab Ahmed, *What Is Islam? The Importance of Being Islamic* (Princeton University Press, 2016); al-Jabri, *Democracy, Human Rights and Law in Islamic Thought*; *The Formation of Arab Reason: Text, Tradition and the Construction of Modernity in the Arab World* (London: I. B. Tauris, 2011); Mohammed Arkoun, *Pour une critique de la Raison Islamique* (Paris: Editions Maisonneuve et Larose, 1984); *Rethinking Islam: Common Questions, Uncommon Answers* (Oxford University Press, 1994); Asad, *The Idea of an Anthropology of Islam* (Washington, DC: Center for Contemporary Arab Studies, 1986): 1–22, and *Formations of the Secular*; Mahmood, *Politics of Piety*; Armando Salvatore, *Islam and the Political Discourse of Modernity* (Ithaca, NY: Ithaca Press, 2000); *The Sociology of Islam: Knowledge, Power, and Civility* (Hoboken: Wiley, 2016); Sayyid, *Recalling the Caliphate*; Samuli Schielke, "Hegemonic Encounters: Criticism of Saints day Festivals and the Formations of Modern Islam in Late 19th Century and Early 20th Century Egypt," *Die Welt des Islams* 47, nos. 3–4 (2010) 320-55; Tayob, *Religion in Modern Islamic Discourse*.

32. See An-Naim, *Islam and the Secular State*, 270; David Robinson, *Muslim Societies in African History* (Cambridge: Cambridge University Press, 2012).

33. See Dimitri Gutas, *Greek Thought, Arab Culture: The Graeco-Arabic Translation Movement in Baghdad and Early Abbasid Society* (New York: Routledge, 1988).

34. See Tayob, *Religion in Modern Islamic Discourse*.

35. A recent and, to my knowledge, isolated work connecting explicitly the question of translation to Islam is Asad's *Secular Translations*.

36. See Norton, "Called to Bear Witness. Derrida, Muslims, and Islam," 88–109, 89.

37. See Norton, "Called to Bear Witness. Derrida, Muslims, and Islam," 92.

38. See Arthur Bradley, "The Theocracy to Come: Deconstruction, Autoimmunity, Islam," in *The Politics to Come: Power, Modernity and the Messianic*, ed. Arthur Bradley and Paul Fletcher (London: Bloomsbury, 2011), 178.

39. While the translation of Aristotle's *Politics* into Arabic is a contentious matter, to talk about its absence is not confirmed by historians. Yet it remains unclear

whether the translation of the first two books of the *Politics* that circulated in the Arab world was from the original or recensions of it, and why only the parts in which democracy is not substantively discussed were available. For a discussion of Aristotle's *Politics* in Arabic thought and its availability, see Shlomo Pines, "Aristotle's *Politics* in Arabic Philosophy," in *The Collected Works of Shlomo Pines* (Jerusalem: Hebrew University Magnes Press, 1989), 146–56.

40. On this issue, see also Saneem Ahmed, "The Genesis of Secular Politics in Medieval Philosophy: The King of Averroes and the Emperor of Dante," in *Labyrinth: An International Journal of Philosophy, Value Theory and Socio-Cultural Hermeneutics* 18 (2016): 209–30. For a discussion of the complexity of the Graeco-Arab translation movement that highlights the historical, political, and economic background conditioning it, see Dimitri Gutas, *Greek Thought, Arab Culture: The Graeco-Arabic Translation Movement in Baghdad and Early Abbasid Society*.

41. See note 25.
42. See note 33.
43. See note 32.

Bibliography

Abeysekara, Ananda. *The Politics of Postsecular Religion: Mourning Secular Futures.* New York: Columbia University Press, 2008.
Afsaruddin, Asma. *Contemporary Issues in Islam.* Edinburgh: Edinburgh University Press, 2015.
Agamben, Giorgio. *Homo Sacer: Sovereign Power and Bare Life.* Translated by Daniel Heller-Roazen. Stanford: Stanford University Press, 1998.
———. *State of Exception.* Translated by Kevin Attell. Chicago: University of Chicago Press, 2005.
Ahmed, Laila. *Women and Gender in Islam: Historical Roots of a Modern Debates.* New Heaven & London: Yale University Press, 1992.
Ahmed, Sabeen. "The Genesis of Secular Politics in Medieval Philosophy: The King of Averroes and the Emperor of Dante." *Labyrinth: An International Journal of Philosophy, Value Theory and Socio-Cultural Hermeneutics* 18 (2016): 209–30.
Ahmed, Shahab. *What Is Islam? The Importance of Being Islamic.* Princeton, NJ: Princeton University Press, 2016.
Al-Jabri, Mohammed Abed. *Democracy, Human Rights and Law in Islamic Thought.* London: I. B. Tauris, 2009.
———. *The Formation of Arab Reason: Text, Tradition and the Construction of Modernity in the Arab World.* London: I. B. Tauris, 2011.
Ali, Kecia. *Sexual Ethics and Islam: Feminist Reflections on Qur'an, Hadith, and Jurisprudence.* Oxford: Oneworld, 2006.
Almond, Ian. *The New Orientalists: Postmodern Perspectives of Islam from Foucault to Baudrillard.* London: I. B. Tauris, 2007.
———. *Sufism and Deconstruction: A Comparative Study of Derrida and Ibn Arabi.* London: Routledge, 2004.
An-naim, Abdullahi Ahmed. *Islam and the Secular State: Negotiating the Future of Shari'a.* Cambridge, MA: Harvard University Press, 2008.
Anidjar, Gil. "Introduction: "Once More, Once More": Derrida, the Arab, the Jew." In *Acts of Religion*, edited by Gil Anidjar. New York: Routledge, 2002.

———. *The Jew, the Arab: A History of the Enemy*. Stanford: Stanford University Press, 2003.

———. "Of Globalatinology." *Derrida Today* 6.1 (2013): 11–22.

Arfi, Badredine. "Habermas and the Aporia of Translating Religion in Democracy." *European Journal of Social Theory* (2015): 489–506.

———. "Secularism," *Critical Inquiry* 33, no. 1 (2006): 52–77.

Arkoun, Mohammed. *Pour une critique de la Raison Islamique*. Paris: Editions Maisonneuve et Larose, 1984.

———. *Rethinking Islam: Common Questions, Uncommon Answers*. Oxford: Oxford University Press, 1994.

Asad, Talal. *Formations of the Secular: Christianity, Islam, Modernity*. Stanford: Stanford University Press, 2003.

———. *Genealogies of Religion: Discipline and Reasons of Power in Christianity*. Baltimore: Johns Hopkins University Press, 1993.

———. *The Idea of an Anthropology of Islam*. Washington, DC: Center for Contemporary Arab Studies, 1986.

———. "Muslims and European Identity: Can Europe represent Islam?" In *Cultural Encounters: Representing Otherness*, edited by Elizabeth Hallam and Bran Street. New York: Routledge, 2000.

———. *Secular Translations. Nation-State, Modern Self, and Calculative Reason*. New York: Columbia University Press, 2018.

Baring, Edward. "Liberalism and the Algerian War: The Case of Jacques Derrida." *Critical Inquiry* 36 (2010): 239–261.

———. *The Trace of God: Derrida and Religion*. Edited by P. E. Gordon. New York: Fordham University Press, 2014.

———. *The Young Derrida and French Philosophy, 1945–1968*. New York: Cambridge University Press, 2011.

Barlas, Asma. *Believing Women in Islam: Unreading Patriarchal Interpretations of the Qur'an*. Austin: University of Texas Press, 2002.

Beardsworth, Richard. *Derrida and the Political*. New York: Routledge, 1996.

Behler, Ernest. *Confrontations. Derrida, Heidegger, Nietzsche*. Translated by Steven Taubeneck. Stanford: Stanford University Press, 1991.

Beiner, Ronald. *Civil Religion: A Dialogue in the History of Political Philosophy*. Cambridge, MA: Cambridge University Press, 2011.

Benjamin, Walter. "Critique of Violence." In *Reflections: Essays, Aphorisms, Autobiographical Writings*, edited by Peter Demetz. New York: Schocken Books, 1986.

———. "The Task of the Translator." In *Selected Writings*, vol. 1, edited by Markus Bullock and Michael W. Jennings. Cambridge, MA: Harvard University Press, 1996.

———. "Theses on the Philosophy of History." In *Illuminations: Essays and Reflections*, edited by Hannah Arendt and translated by Harry Zhon. New York: Schocken Books, 2007.

Bennington, Geoffrey. "Derridabase." In *Jacques Derrida*, translated by Geoffrey Bennington. Chicago: University of Chicago Press, 1993.
———. "Double Tonguing: Derrida's Monolingualism." In *Other Analyses: Reading Philosophy* (Electronic Book, 2008).
———. *Legislations: The Politics of Deconstruction*. London: Verso, 1994.
———. "Mosaic Fragment: If Derrida Were an Egyptian . . ." In *Legislations: The Politics of Deconstruction*. London: Verso, 1994.
———. *Scatter 1: The Politics of Politics in Foucault, Heidegger, and Derrida*. New York: Fordham University Press, 2016.
———. *Scatter Scatter 2: Politics in Deconstruction*. New York: Fordham University Press, 2021.
Bennington, Geoffrey, and Jacques Derrida. *Jacques Derrida*. Translated by Geoffrey Bennington. Chicago: University of Chicago Press, 1993.
Bergo, Bettina, Cohen Joseph, Raphel Zagury-Orly, and Michael B. Smith. *Judeities: Questions for Jacques Derrida*. New York: Fordham University Press, 2007.
Bernstein, Richard. *Violence: Thinking without Banisters*. Cambridge: Polity, 2013.
Bilgrami, Akeel. "Secularism: Its Content and Context." http://blogs.ssrc.org/tif/wp-content/uploads/2013/08/Secularism_Its_Content_and_Context.pdf.
Bock-Morss, Susan. *Thinking Past Terror. Islamism and Critical Theory on the Left*. New York: Verso, 2003.
Bonner, Michael. "Poverty and Economics in the Qur'an." *Journal of Interdisciplinary History* 35, no. 3 (2005): 391–406.
Bradley, Arthur. "The Theocracy to Come: Deconstruction, Autoimmunity, Islam." In *The Politics to Come: Power, Modernity and the Messianic*, edited by Arthur Bradley and Paul Fletcher. London: Bloomsbury, 2011.
Brown, Wendy. "Sovereign Hesitations." In *Derrida and the Time of The Political*, edited by Pheng Cheah and Suzanne Guerlac. Durham and London: Duke University Press, 2009.
Brudner, Alan. "The Ideality of Difference: Toward Objectivity in Legal Interpretation." *Cardozo Law Review* 11 (1990): 1133–1210.
Buonamano, Roberto. "The Economy of Violence: Derrida on Law and Justice." *Ratio Juris* 11 (1998): 168–79.
Butler, Judith. *Excitable Speech: A Politics of the Performative*. New York: Routledge, 1997.
Caputo, John. *Deconstruction in a Nutshell. A Conversation with Jacques Derrida*. New York: Fordham University Press, 1997.
———. "On Not Circumventing the Quasi-Transcendental: The Case of Rorty and Derrida." In *Working through Derrida*, edited by Gary Brent Madison. Northwestern University Press, 1993.
———. *The Prayers and Tears of Jacques Derrida: Religion without Religion*. Bloomington: Indiana University Press, 1997.

Caputo, John, and Michael J. Scanlon, eds. *God, the Gift, and Postmodernism.* Bloomington: Indiana University Press, 1999.
Casanova, José. *Public Religions in the Modern World.* Chicago: University of Chicago Press, 1994.
——. "A Secular Age: Dawn or Twilight." In *Varieties of Secularism in a Secular Age*, edited by Michael Warner et al. Cambridge, MA: Harvard University Press, 2010.
Cassatella, Andrea. "Normativity without Telos: The Messianic in the Thought of Jacques Derrida." *Bamidbar: Journal of Jewish Thought and Philosophy* 4, no. 2 (2012): 24–43.
Cauchi, Mark. "The Secular to Come: Interrogating the Derridean 'Secular.'" *Journal for Cultural and Religious Theory* 10, no. 1 (2009): 1–18.
Cesaire, Aimé. *Discourse on Colonialism.* Translated by Joan Pinkham. New York: Monthly Review Press, 2000.
Chambers, Simone. *Reasonable Democracy: Jürgen Habermas and the Politics of Discourse.* Itacha: Cornell University Press, 1996.
Cheah, Pheng, and Suzanne Guerlac, eds. *Derrida and the Time of the Political.* Durham: Duke University Press, 2009.
Chérif, Mustapha. *Islam and the West: A Conversation with Jacques Derrida.* Translated by Teresa Lavender Fagan. Chicago: University of Chicago Press, 2008.
Connolly, William. *Why I Am Not a Secularist?* Minneapolis: University of Minnesota Press, 1999.
Cornell, Drucilla. *The Philosophy of the Limit.* New York: Routledge, 1992.
——. "The Thinker of the Future—Introduction to The Violence of the Masquerade: Law Dressed Up as Justice." *German Law Journal* 6, no. 1 (2005): 125–48.
Corson, Ben. "Transcending Violence in Derrida: A Reply to John McCormick." *Political Theory* 29, no. 6 (2001): 855–75.
Coulthard, Glen. *Red Skin, White Masks: Rejecting the Colonial Politics of Recognition.* Minneapolis: University of Minnesota Press, 2014.
Coward, Harold, and Toby Foshay, eds. *Derrida and Negative Theology.* Albany: State University of New York Press, 1992.
Critchley, Simon. "Derrida's Specters of Marx." *Philosophy & Social Criticism* 21 (1995): 1–30.
Culler, Jonathan, ed. "Derrida and Democracy." *Diacritics* 38 (2008): 1–2.
——. *The Ethics of Deconstruction: Derrida and Levinas.* Oxford: Blackwell, 1992.
Czajka, Agnes, ed. *Europe After Derrida: Crisis and Potentiality.* Edinburgh: Edinburgh University Press, 2014.
Davies, Margaret. "Derrida and Law: Legitimate Fictions." In *Jacques Derrida and the Humanities: A Critical Reader*, edited by Tom Cohen. Cambridge: Cambridge University Press, 2001.
Derrida, Jacques. "Above All, No Journalists!" In *Religion and Media*, edited by Hent de Vries and Samuel Weber. Stanford CA: Stanford University Press. 2001.

———. "Abraham, the Other." In *Judeities: Questions for Jacques Derrida*, edited by Bettina Bergo, et al., translated by Bettina Bergo and Michael B. Smith. New York: Fordham University Press, 2007.

———. *Adieu to Emmanuel Levinas*. Translated by Pascale Ann-Brault and Michael Naas. Stanford, CA: Stanford University Press, 1999. Translation of *Adieu à Emmanuel Levinas*, Paris: Galilée, 1997.

———. *The Animal That Therefore I Am*. Edited by Marie-Luise Mallet, and translated by David Wills. New York: Fordham University Press, 2008. Translation of *L'animal que donc je suis*. Paris: Galilée, 2006.

———. *Aporias: Dying—Awaiting (One Another at) The "Limits of Truth."* Translated by Thomas Dutoit. Stanford, CA: Stanford University Press, 1993. Translation of *Apories*, Paris: Galilée, 1996.

———. *Archive Fever: A Freudian Impression*, translated by Eric Prenowitz. Chicago: University of Chicago Press, 1996. Translation of *Mal d'archive*. Paris: Galilée, 1995.

———. "As If It Were Possible 'Within Such Limits.' " In *Paper Machine*, translated by Rachel Bowlby. Stanford, CA: Stanford University Press. 2005. Translation of "Commes si c'était possible, 'within such limits.' " In *Papier machine*. Paris: Galilée, 2001.

———. "Authorship, Sovereignty and the Axiomatics of the Interview: Derrida 'Live.' " In James Smith, *Jacques Derrida: Live Theory* (London: Continuum, 2005): 104–17.

———. "Avowing—The Impossible: 'Returns,' Repentance, and Reconciliation A Lesson." In *Living Together: Jacques Derrida's Communities of Violence and Peace*, edited by Elizabeth Weber. New York: Fordham University Press, 2013.

———. "Autoimmunity: Real and Symbolic Suicides—A Dialogue with Jacques Derrida." In *Philosophy in a Time of Terror: Dialogues with Jürgen Habermas and Jacques Derrida*, edited by Giovanna Borradori. Chicago: University of Chicago Press, 2003.

———. *The Beast and The Sovereign Vol. I*. Edited by Michael Lisse, Marie-Luise Mallet, and Ginette Michaud, translated by Geoffrey Bennington. Chicago: University of Chicago Press, 2008. Translation of *Séminaire. Le bête et le souverain. Volume I (2001–2002)* Paris: Galilée, 2008.

———. "But, beyond . . . (Open Letter to Anne McClintock and Rob Nixon)." Translated by Peggy Kamuf. *Critical Inquiry* 13, no. 1 (1986): 155–70.

———. "Before the Law." In *Acts of Literature*, edited by Derek Attridge. New York: Routledge, 1992. Translation of "Devant la loi. Préjugés." In *La Faculté de juger*. Paris: Minuit, 1985.

———. "Circumfession." In *Jacques Derrida*, translated by Geoffrey Bennington. Chicago: University of Chicago Press, 1993. Translation of *Jacques Derrida*. Paris: Editions du Seuil, 1991.

———. "Choreography: Interview." In *Feminist Interpretations of Jacques Derrida*, edited by Nancy Holland. University Park: Pennsylvania State University Press, 1997.

———. "Declarations of Independence." *New Political Science* 7, no. 1 (1986): 7–15.

———. "Différance." In *Margins of Philosophy*, translated by Alan Bass. Chicago: University of Chicago Press, 1982. Translation of "Différance." In *Marges de la philosophie*. Paris: Minuit, 1972.

———. *Dissemination*. Translated by Barbara Johnson. Chicago: University of Chicago Press, 1981. Translation of *La dissemination*. Paris: Seuil, 1972.

———. "Ethics and Politics Today." In *Negotiations: Interventions and Interviews 1971–2001*, translated by Elizabeth Rottenberg. Stanford: Stanford University Press, 2002.

———. "Epoché and Faith: An Interview with Jacques Derrida." In *Derrida on Religion: Other Testaments*, edited by Yvonne Sherwood and Kevin Hart. New York: Routledge, 2005.

———. "The Eyes of Language: The Abyss and the Volcano." In *Acts of Religion*, edited by Gil Anidjar. New York: Routledge, 2002.

———. *The Ear of the Other*. Translated by Peggy Kamuf. New York: Schocken Books, 1985. Translation of *L'Oreille de l'autre: otobiographies, transferts, traductions. Textes et débats avec Jacques Derrida*. Montreal: VLB, 1982.

———. "Fidélité à plus d'un." In *Idiomes, nationalités, déconstructions: rencontre de Rabat avec Jacques Derrida*, en collaboration avec Jean-Jacques Forté. Casablanca: Les Editions Toubkal, 1998.

———. "Faith and Knowledge. Two Sources of 'Religion' at the Limits of Reason Alone." In *Acts of Religion*, edited by Gil Anidjar. New York: Routledge, 2002. Translation of "Foi et savoir." In *Foi et savoir: Suivi de le siècle et le pardon*. Paris: Seuil, 2001.

———. "Force of Law: The Mystical Foundation of Authority." In *Acts of Religion*, edited by Gil Anidjar. New York: Routledge, 2002. Translation of *Force de loi: Le "Fondement mystique de l'autorité."* Paris: Galilée, 1994.

———. *For What Tomorrow*. Translated by J. Fort. Stanford, CA: Stanford University Press, 2004. Translation of *De quoi demain*. Paris: Fayard and Galilée, 2001.

———. "*Geschlecht*: Sexual Difference, Ontological Difference." In *Psyche: Invention of the Other Volume II*, edited by Peggy Kamuf and Elizabeth Rottenberg. Stanford, CA: Stanford University Press, 2008. Translation of *Psyche: Inventions de l'autre*, Paris: Galilée, 1987.

———. "*Geschlecht* II: Heidegger's Hand." In *Deconstruction and Philosophy. The Texts of Jacques Derrida*, edited by John Sallis. Chicago: University of Chicago Press, 1989.

———. *Geschlecht III: Sex, Race Nation, Humanité*. edited by Geoffrey Bennignton, Katie Chenoweth, and Rodrigo Therezo. Paris: Seuil, 2018.

———. *The Gift of Death*. Translated by David Wills. Chicago: University of Chicago Press, 1995. Translation of "Donner la mort." In *L'éthique du don*, edited by J.-M. Rabaté and M. Wetzel. Paris: Transition, 1992.

———. *Given Time: 1. Counterfeit Money*. Translated by Peggy Kamuf. Chicago: University of Chicago Press, 1992. Translation of *Donner le temps I. La fausse monnaie*. Paris: Galilée, 1991.

———. "How to Avoid Speaking: Denials." In *Derrida and Negative Theology*, edited by Harold Coward and Toby Foshay. Albany: State University of New York Press, 1992. Translation of "Comment ne pas parler: Denegations." In *Psyché: Inventions de l'autre*. Paris: Galilée, 1987.

———. "An interview with Professor Jacques Derrida." Michal Ben-Naftali, translated by Moshe Ron. Yad Vashem, Shoah Research Center, 1998.

———. "Interpretations at War: Kant, the Jew, the German." Translated by Moshe Ron. In *Acts of Religion*, edited by Gil Anidjar. New York: Routledge, 2002. Translation of "*Interpretations at War: Kant, le Juif, l'Allemand.*" In *Psyche: Inventions de l'autre*, Paris: Galilée, 1987.

———. *Islam and the West: A Conversation with Jacques Derrida*. Translated by Teresa Lavender Fagan. Chicago: University of Chicago Press, 2008.

———. "Language Is Never Owned." In *Sovereignties in Question: The Poetics of Paul Celan*, edited by Thomas Dutoit and Outi Pasanen. New York: Fordham University Press, 2005.

———. *Limited Inc*. Evanston, IL: Northwestern University Press, 1988.

———. "The Laws of Reflections: Nelson Mandela, in Admiration." In *Psyche: Invention of the Other Volume II*, edited by Peggy Kamuf and Elizabeth Rottenberg. Stanford, CA: Stanford University Press, 2008. Translation of Admiration de Nelson Mandela, ou Les lois de la réflexion." In *Psyche: Inventions de l'autre II*, Paris: Galilée, 1987.

———. *Margins of Philosophy*. Translated by Allan Bass. Chicago: University of Chicago Press, 1982. Translation of *Marges de la philosophie*. Paris: Minuit, 1972.

———. "Marx & Sons." In *Ghostly Demarcation: A Symposium on Jacques Derrida's Specters of Marx,* edited by Michael Sprinker. London: Verso, 1999.

———. "Me-Psychoanalysis." In *Psyche: Invention of the Other Volume 1*, edited by Peggy Kamuf and Elizabeth Rottenberg. Stanford, CA: Stanford University Press, 2007. Translation of "Moi—la psychoanalyse." In *Psyche: Inventions de l'autre*, Paris: Galilée, 1987.

———. *Monolingualism of the Other, or The Prosthesis of Origin*. Translated by Patrick Mensah Stanford, CA: Stanford University Press 1996. Translation of *Le monolinguisme de l'autre: Ou la prothèse d'origine*. Paris: Galilée, 1996.

———. *Negotiations: Interventions and Interviews 1971–2001*. Edited and translated by Elizabeth Rottenberg. Stanford, CA: Stanford University Press, 2002.

———. "Nietzsche and the Machine. In *Negotiations: Interventions and Interviews 1971–2001*, edited and translated by Elizabeth Rottenberg. Stanford, CA: Stanford University Press, 2002.

———. "A Number of Yes." In *Psyche: Invention of the Other Volume II*, edited by Peggy Kamuf and Elizabeth Rottenberg. Stanford, CA: Stanford University Press, 2008. Translation of "Nombre de oui." *Psyche: Inventions de l'autre*, Paris: Galilée, 1987.

———. *Of Grammatology*. Translated by Gayatri Chakravorty Spivak. Baltimore: Johns Hopkins University Press, 1974. Translation of *De la grammatologie*. Paris: Minuit, 1967.

———. *Of Hospitality*. Translated by Rachel Bowlby. Stanford, CA: Stanford University Press, 2000. Translation of *De l'hospitalité*. Paris: Calmann-Lévy, 1997.

———. *Of Spirit: Heidegger and the Question*. Translated by Geoffrey Bennington and Rachel Bowlby. Chicago: University of Chicago Press, 1989. Translation of *De l'esprit*, Paris: Galilée, 1987.

———. *On Cosmopolitanism and Forgiveness*. Translated by Mark Dooly and Michael Hughes. London/New York: Routledge. 2001. Translation of Cosmopolites de tous les pays encore un effort! Paris: Galilée, 1997; "Le siècle et le pardon." In Le Monde des Débats. 1999.

———. "The Onto-Theology of National Humanism (Prolegomena to a Hypothesis)." *Oxford Literary Review* 14, nos. 1–2 (1992): 3–23.

———. "Open Discussion." In *Jacques Derrida: Deconstruction Engaged: The Sydney Seminars*, edited by Paul Patton and Terry Smith. Sydney: Power, 2006.

———. *The Other Heading: Reflections on Today's Europe*. Translated by Pascale-Anne Brault and Michael Naas. Bloomington: Indiana University Press, 1992. Translation of *L'autre cap*. Paris: Minuit, 1991.

———. "Otobiographies: The Teaching of Nietzsche and the Politics of the Proper Name." In *The Ear of the Other*, translated by Peggy Kamuf. New York: Schocken Books, 1985. Translation of *L'Oreille de l'autre: otobiographies, transferts, traductions. Texteset débats avec Jacques Derrida*. Montreal: VLB, 1982.

———. "*Ousia* and *Grammē*: Note on a Note from *Being and Time*." In *Margins of Philosophy*, translated by Alan Bass. Chicago: University of Chicago Press, 1982. Translation of "*Ousia* and *Grammē*: note sur un note de Sein un Zeit." In *Marges de la philosophie*. Paris: Minuit, 1972.

———. *Paper Machine*. Translated by Rachel Bowlby. Stanford, CA: Stanford University Press. 2005. Translation of *Papier Machine*, Paris: Galilée, 2001.

———. "Performative Powerlessness: A Response to Simon Critchley." In *Constellations* 7, no. 4 (2000): 466–68.

———. *Politics of Friendship*. Translated by George Collins. London: Verso, 1997. Translation of *Politiques de l'amitié*. Paris: Galilée, 1994.

———. *Positions*. Translated by Alan Bass. Chicago: University of Chicago Press, 1981. Translation of *Positions*. Paris: Minuit, 1972.

———. *Psyche: Invention of the Other Volume 1*. Edited by Peggy Kamuf and Elizabeth Rottenberg. Stanford, CA: Stanford University Press, 2007. Translation of *Psyche: Inventions de l'autre*, Paris: Galilée, 1987.

———. *Psyche: Invention of the Other Volume II*. Edited by Peggy Kamuf and Elizabeth Rottenberg. Stanford, CA: Stanford University Press, 2008. Translation of *Psyche: Inventions de l'autre*, Paris: Galilée, 1987.

———. "Racism's Last Word." Translated by Peggy Kamuf. *Critical Inquiry* 12 (1985): 290–99.

———. "Remarks on Deconstruction and Pragmatism." In *Deconstruction and Pragmatism*, edited by Chantal Mouffe. New York: Routledge, 1996.

———. *Rogues: Two Essays on Reason*. Translated by Pascale-Anne Brault and Michael Naas. Stanford, CA: Stanford University Press, 2005. Translation of *Voyous: Deux essais sur la raison*. Paris: Galilée, 2003.

———. "Roundtable on Translation." In *The Ear of the Other*, translated by Peggy Kamuf. New York: Schocken Books, 1985. Translation of *L'Oreille de l'autre: otobiographies, transferts, traductions. Textes et débats avec Jacques Derrida*. Montreal: VLB, 1982.

———. *A Taste for the Secret*. With Maurizio Ferraris, translated by Giacomo Donis. Cambridge: Polity, 2001.

———. "Théologico-Politique." UCI Libraries, University of California Irvine.

———. "Signature Event Context." In *Margins of Philosophy*, translated by Alan Bass. Chicago: University of Chicago Press, 1982. Translation of "Signature Événement Contexte." In *Marges de la philosophie*. Paris: Minuit, 1972.

———. "Semiology and Grammatology." In *Positions*, translated by Alan Bass. Chicago: University of Chicago Press, 1981. Translation of "Sémiologie et grammatologie: entretien avec Julia Kristeva." In *Positions*. Paris: Minuit, 1972.

———. *Specters of Marx: The State of the Debt, the Work of Mourning and the New International*, translated by Peggy Kamuf, New York: Routledge, 1994. Translation of *Spectres de Marx*. Paris: Galilée, 1993.

———. *Spurs: Nietzsche's Styles*. Translated by Barbara Harlow. Chicago: University of Chicago Press, 1978.

———. *Sovereignties in Question: The Poetics of Paul Celan*. Edited by Thomas Dutoit and Outi Pasanen. New York: Fordham University Press, 2005.

———. "Des Tours de Babel." In *Acts of Religion*, edited by Gil Anidjar. New York: Routledge, 2002.

———. "Taking a Stand for Algeria." In *Acts of Religion*, edited by Gil Anidjar. New York: Routledge, 2002.

———. "The Villanova Roundtable: A Conversation with Jacques Derrida." In John Caputo, *Deconstruction in a Nutshell. A Conversation with Jacques Derrida*. New York: Fordham University Press, 1997.

———. *Without Alibi*. Ed., translation and introduction by Peggy Kamuf. Stanford, CA: Stanford University Press, 2002.

———. *Who Is Afraid of Philosophy: Right to Philosophy I.* Translated by Jan Plug. Stanford, CA: Stanford University Press, 2002. Translation of *Du droit à la philosophie.* Paris: Galilée, 1990.

———. *Writing and Difference.* Translated by Alan Bass. Chicago: University of Chicago Press, 1978. Translation of *L'écriture et la différence.* Paris: Seuil, 1967.

———. "White Mythology: Metaphor in the Text of Philosophy." In *Margins of Philosophy*, translated by Alan Bass. Chicago: University of Chicago Press, 1982. Translation of "La Mythlogie blanche: La Metaphore dans le texte philosophique." In *Marges de la philosophie.* Paris: Minuit, 1972.

———. "What Is a 'Relevant' Translation?" *Critical Inquiry* 27 (2001): 174–200.

———, with Bernard Stielger. *Echographies of Television: Filmed Interviews.* Cambridge: Polity, 2002. Translation of *Échographie de la television.* Paris: Galilée, 1996.

———, with Catherine Malabou and David Wills. *Counterpath.* Stanford, CA: Stanford University Press, 2004.

Deutscher, Penelope. "Derrida's Impossible Genealogies" *Theory and Event* 8, no. 1 (2005).

———. "'Women and so On': *Rogues* and the Autoimmunity of Feminism" *Symposium: Canadian Journal of Continental Philosophy* 11, no. 1 (2007): 101–19.

deVries, Hent. *Philosophy and the Turn to Religion.* Baltimore: John Hopkins University Press, 1999.

———, ed. *Religion: Beyond a Concept.* New York: Fordham University Press, 2008.

deVries, Hent, and Lawrence Sullivan, eds. *Political Theologies: Public Religions in a Post-Secular World.* New York: Fordham University Press. 2006.

deVries, Hent, and Samuel Weber, eds. *Religion and Media.* Stanford: Stanford University Press. 2001.

———. *Religion and Violence: Philosophical Perspectives from Kant to Derrida.* Baltimore: Johns Hopkins University Press, 2002.

Dressler, Marcus, and Mandair, Arvin, eds. *Secularism and Religion-Making.* Oxford/New York: Oxford University Press, 2011.

Dressler, Markus, Armando Salvatore, and Monika Wohlrab-Sahr, eds. "Islamicate Secularities: New Perspective on a Contested Concepts." *Historical Social Research / Historische Sozialforschung* 44, no. 3 (2019): 7–34.

Dryzek, John. *Deliberative Democracy and Beyond. Liberals, Critics, Contestations.* Oxford: Oxford University Press, 2000.

———. *Discursive Democracy.* Cambridge: Cambridge University Press, 1990.

Dubois, William Edward Burghardt. "The Conservation of Races," In *Race*, edited by Robert Bernasconi. Oxford: Blackwell, 2001.

———. *The Souls of Black Folk.* New York: Dover, 1994.

Dussel, Enrique. *Politics of Liberation: A Critical Global History.* Translated by Thia Cooper. London: SCM, 2011.

———. *The Underside of Modernity: Apel, Ricoeur, Rorty, Taylor and the Philosophy of Liberation*. Edited and translated by Eduardo Mendieta. New Jersey: Humanity, 1996.

———. "World-System and 'Trans'-Modernity." *Nepantla: Views from South* 3, no. 2 (2002): 222–44.

Enayat, Hamid. *Modern Islamic Political Thought*. Austin: University of Texas Press, 1982.

Esack, Farid. *Qur'an, Liberation and Pluralism: An Islamic Perspective of Interreligious Solidarity against Oppression*. Oxford: Oneworld, 1997.

Esposito, John L., and Azzam Tamimi. *Islam and Secularism in the Middle East*. London: Hurst, 2000.

Evink, Eddo C. "Jacques Derrida and the Faith in Philosophy." *The Southern Journal of Philosophy* 42 (2004): 313–31.

Fanon, Frantz. *Black Skin, White Masks*. Translated by Richard Philcox. New York: Grove, 2008.

———. *L'An V de la révolution algérienne*. Paris: La Découverte, 2011.

———. *Toward the African Revolution*. New York: Grove, 1964. Translation of *Pour la révolution africaine. Écrits politiques*. Paris: La Découverte, 2006.

———. *The Wretched of the Earth*. Translated by Richard Philcox. New York: Grove, 2004. Translation of *Les Damnés de la Terre*. Paris: La Découverte, 2002.

Fishkin, James. *Democracy and Deliberation*. New Heaven: Yale University Press, 1971.

Fitzgerald, Timothy, ed. *Religion and the Secular: Historical and Colonial Formations*. London: Equinox, 2009.

Fraser, Nancy. "The Force of Law: Metaphysical or Political?" In *Cardozo Law Review* 13 (1991): 1325–31.

Fritsch, Mathias. "Derrida's Democracy to Come." *Constellations* 9.4 (2002): 574–97.

———. *The Promise of Memory: History and Politics in Marx, Benjamin and Derrida*. Albany: State University of New York Press, 2005.

———. *Taking Turns with the Earth: Phenomenology, Deconstruction, and Intergenerational Justice*. Stanford: Stanford University Press, 2018.

Gaon, Stella. *The Lucid Vigil: Deconstruction, Desire and the Politics of Critique*. New York: Routledge, 2020.

Gasché, Rodolphe. "Critique, Hypercriticism, Deconstruction." In *The Honor of Thinking: Critique, Theory, Philosophy*. Stanford: Stanford University Press, 2006.

———. "More Than a Difference in Style." In *The Honor of Thinking: Critique, Theory, Philosophy*. Stanford: Stanford University Press, 2006.

———. *The Tain of the Mirror*. Cambridge, MA: Harvard University Press, 1986.

Gehring, Petra. "Force and 'Mystical Foundation' of Law: How Derrida Addresses Legal Discourse." *German Law Journal* 6 (2005): 151–69.

Goetschel, Willi. "Derrida and Spinoza: Rethinking the Theologico-Political Problem." *Bamidbar: Journal for Jewish Thought and Philosophy* 1, no. 2 (2011): 9–25.

———. *The Discipline of Philosophy and the Invention of Modern Jewish Thought.* New York: Fordham University Press, 2013.

———. "The Hyphen in the Theological-Political: Spinoza to Mendelssohn, Heine, and Derrida." *Religions* 10.1 (2019): 1–13.

———. *Spinoza's Modernity: Mendelssohn, Lessing, and Heine.* Madison: University of Wisconsin Press, 2004.

Gordon, R. Lewis. "Through the Zone of Nonbeing: A Reading of Black Skin, White Masks in Celebration of Fanon's Eightieth Birthday" *The C. L. R James Journal* 11, no. 1 (2005): 1–43.

Gutas, Dimitri. *Greek Thought, Arab Culture. The Graeco-Arabic Translation Movement in Baghdad and Early Abbasid Society.* New York/London: Routledge, 1988.

Gutmann, Amy and Thompson, Dennis. *Democracy and Disagreement.* Cambridge, MA: Harvard University Press, 1996.

Habermas, Jürgen. *An Awareness of What Is Missing: Faith and Reason in a Post-secular Age.* Cambridge: Polity, 2010.

———. *Between Facts and Norms: Contribution to a Discourse Theory of Law and Democracy.* Translated by William Rehg. Cambridge: MIT Press, 1998.

———. *Between Naturalism and Religion: Philosophical Essays.* Cambridge: Polity, 2008.

———. "Excursus on Leveling the Genre Distinction between Philosophy and Literature." In *The Philosophical Discourse of Modernity: Twelve Lectures,* translated by Frederick Lawrence. Cambridge, MA: MIT Press, 1987.

———. "Faith and knowledge." In *The Future of Human Nature,* edited by J. Habermas. Cambridge: Polity, 2003.

———. "Fundamentalism and Terror. A Dialogues with Jürgen Habermas." In *Philosophy in a Time of Terror. Dialogues with Jürgen Habermas and Jacques Derrida,* edited by Giovanna Borradori. Chicago: University of Chicago Press, 2003.

———. *On the Pragmatics of Communication.* Edited by Maeve Cooke. Cambridge, MA: MIT Press, 1998.

———. "Religion in the Public Sphere." *European Journal of Philosophy* 14, no. 1 (2006): 1–25.

———. "What Is Meant by a Post-Secular Society? A Discussion on Islam in Europe." In *Europe: The Faltering Project.* Translated by C. Cronin. Malden, MA: Polity, 2009.

———, and Jacques Derrida. "February 15, or What Binds Europeans Together: A Plea for a Common Foreign Policy, Beginning in the Core of Europe" *Constellations* 10 (2003): 291–97.

Haddad, Samir. "Derrida and Democracy at Risk." *Contretemps* 4 (2004): 29–44.

———. *Derrida and the Inheritance of Democracy.* Bloomington: Indiana University Press, 2013.

———. "A Genealogy of Violence, from Light to the Autoimmune." *Diacritics* 38 (2009), 121–42.

———. "Inheriting Democracy to Come." *Theory & Event* 8, no. 1, 2005.
Hägglund, Martin. *Radical Atheism: Derrida and the Time of Life*. Stanford, CA: Stanford University Press, 2008.
Hall, Stuart. "The West and the Rest: Discourse and Power." In *Formations of Modernity*, edited by Stuart Hall and Bram Gieben. Cambridge: Polity, 1992.
Hamacher, Werner. "Afformative Strike." *Cardozo Law Review* 13 (1991): 1133–57.
Hamilton, Alexander, James Madison, and John Jay. *The Federalist: With Letters of Brutus*. Edited by Terence Ball. Cambridge: Cambridge University Press, 2003.
Hart, Kevin. *The Trespass of the Sign: Deconstruction, Theology, Philosophy*. New York: Fordham University Press, 2000.
Hassan, Kadhim Jihad. "Les Palestiniens dans la pensée de Jacques Derrida." *Rue Descartes* 2 (2016): 218–30.
Holland, Nancy, eds. *Feminist Interpretations of Jacques Derrida*. University Park: Pennsylvania State University Press, 1997.
Heidegger, Martin. *Being and Time*. Translated by Joan Stambaugh. Chicago: University of Chicago Press, 1996.
Heng, Geraldine. *The Invention of Race in the European Middle Ages*. New York: Cambridge University Press, 2018.
Hesse, Barnor. "Racialized Modernity: An Analytics of White Mythologies." *Ethnic and Racial Studies* 30, no. 4 (2007): 643–63.
Hodgson, Marshall G. S. *The Venture of Islam, Conscience and History in a World Civilization. Vol. 1. The Classical Age of Islam*. Chicago: University of Chicago Press, 1974.
Hollander, Dana. *Exemplarity and Chosenness: Rosenzweig and Derrida on the Nation of Philosophy*. Stanford: Stanford University Press, 2008.
Honig, Bonnie. "Declaration of Independence. Arendt and Derrida on the Problem of Founding a Republic." *The American Political Science Review* 85 (1991): 97–113.
Horwitz, Noah. "Derrida and the Aporia of the Political, or The Theologico-Political Dimension of Deconstruction." *Research in Phenomenology* 32 (2002): 156–77.
Jopkke, Christian. "State Neutrality and Islamic Headscarf Laws in France and Germany." *Theory and Society* 36, no. 4 (2007): 313–42.
Kant, Immanuel. *Critique of Pure Reason*. Edited by Paul Guyer and Allen Wood. Cambridge: Cambridge University Press, 1999.
Karamustafa, Ahmet T. "Islamic *Din* as an Alternative to Western Models of 'Religion.'" In *Religion, Theory, Critique: Classic and Contemporary Approaches and Methodologies*, ed. Richard King. New York: Columbia University Press, 2017.
Katz, Ethan B., and Linda Moses Leff, eds. *Colonialism and the Jews*. Bloomington: Indiana University Press, 2017.
Kearney, Richard. "Desire of God." In *God, the Gift, and Postmodernism*, ed.by John Caputo and Michael J. Scanlon. Bloomington: Indiana University Press, 1999.

Kellogg, Catherine. *Law's Trace. From Hegel to Derrida*. New York: Routledge, 2010.
———. "Translating Deconstruction." *Cultural Values* 5, no. 3 (2001): 325–48.
La Capra, Dominick. "Violence, Justice, and the Force of Law." *Cardozo Law Review* 11 (1990): 1065–78.
Laclau, Ernesto. "Deconstruction, Pragmatism, Hegemony." In *Deconstruction and Pragmatism*, edited by Chantal Mouffe. London/New York: Routledge, 1996.
———. "The Time Is out of Joint." *Diacritics* 25 (1995): 86–97.
Lapidus, Ira. "The Separation of State and Religion in the Development of Early Islamic Society." *International Journal of Middle East Studies* (1975): 363–85.
Lawlor, Leonard. *This Is Not Sufficient: An Essay on Animality and Human Nature*. New York: Columbia University Press, 2007.
Lefort, Claude. "The Permanence of the Theologico-Political." In *Political Theologies: Public Religions in a Post-Secular World*, edited by Hent de Vries and Lawrence Sullivan. New York: Fordham University Press. 2006.
Lilla, Mark. "The Politics of Jacques Derrida." *The New York Review of Books* 45, 11 (25 June 1998): 36–41.
Losurdo, Domenico. *Liberalism: A Counter-History*. Translated by Gregory Elliott. London: Verso, 2014.
Mahmood, Saba. *Politics of Piety: The Islamic Revival and the Feminist Subject*. Princeton: Princeton University Press, 2011.
———. *Religious Difference in a Secular Age: A Minority Report*. Princeton: Princeton University Press. 2016.
———. "Religious Reason and Secular Affect: An Incommensurable Divide?" *Critical Inquiry* 35, no. 4 (2000): 836–62.
Maldonado-Torres, Nelson. "Cesaire's Gift and the Decolonial Turn." *Radical Philosophy Review* 9, no. 2 (2006): 111–38.
Mandair, Arvind-Pal. *Religion and the Specter of the West: Sikhism, India, Postcoloniality and the Politics of Translation*. New York: Columbia University Press, 2009.
Marrouchi, Mustapha. "Decolonizing the Terrain of Western Theoretical Productions." *College Literature* 24, no. 2 (1997): 1–34.
Martel, James. *Divine Violence: Walter Benjamin and the Eschatology of Sovereignty*. New York: Routledge/GlassHouse, 2011.
Marx, Karl. "Contribution to the Critique of Hegel's *Philosophy of Right*: Introduction." In *The Marx-Engels Reader*, edited by Richard Tuck. New York: Norton, 1978.
———. "The German Ideology." In *The Marx-Engels Reader*, edited by Richard Tuck. New York: Norton, 1978.
Massad, Joseph. "Forget Semitism!" In *Living Together: Jacques Derrida's Communities of Violence and Peace*, edited by Elizabeth Weber. New York: Fordham University Press, 2013.

Masuzawa, Tomoko. *The Invention of World Religions: Or, How European Universalism Was Preserved in the Language of Pluralism*. Chicago: University of Chicago Press, 2005.
McCarthy, Thomas. "The Politics of the Ineffable." In *Ideals and Illusions*. Cambridge, MA: MIT Press, 1991.
McClintock, Anne, and Rob Nixon. "No Names Apart: The Separation of Word and History in Derrida's 'Le Dernier Mot du Racism.'" *Critical Inquiry* 13 (1986): 140–54.
McCormick, John P. "Derrida on Law; Or, Poststructuralism Gets Serious." *Political Theory* 29 (2001): 395–423.
———. "Schmittian Positions on Law and Politics? CLS and Derrida." *Cardozo Law Review* 21 (2000): 1693–2119.McQuillan, Martin. "Clarity and Doubt: Derrida among the Palestinians." *Paragraph* 39, no. 2 (2016): 220–37.
Mignolo, Walter. *The Darker Side of Western Modernity: Global Futures, Decolonial Options*. Dhuram: Duke University Press, 2011.
———. "Delinking: The Rhetoric of Modernity, the Logic of Coloniality and the Grammar of Decoloniality." *Cultural Studies* 21 (2007): 449–514.
———. "Epistemic Disobedience, Independent Thought and De-Colonial Freedom." *Theory, Culture & Society* 26 (2010): 1–23.
———. *Local Histories/Global Designs: Coloniality, Subaltern Knowledges, and Border Thinking*. Princeton, N.J.: Princeton University Press, 2000.
Mill, John Stuart. *On Liberty*. Edited by John Gray. Oxford: Oxford University Press, 1991.
Mir-Hosseini, Ziba. *Islam and Gender: The Religious Debate in Contemporary Iran*. Princeton: Princeton University Press, 1999.
Mittermaier, Amira. *Giving to God: Islamic Charity in Revolutionary Times*. Oakland, CA: University of California Press, 2019.
Mouffe, Chantal, and Ernesto Laclau. *Hegemony and Socialist Strategy: Towards a Radical Democratic Politics*. London: Verso, 1985.
Mudimbe, Valentine. *The Invention of Africa: Gnosis, Philosophy and the Order of Knowledge*. Bloomington: Indiana University Press, 1988.
———. *Parables and Fables: Exegesis, Textuality and Politics in Central Africa*. Madison: University of Wisconsin Press, 1991.
Naas, Michael. "Derrida's Laïcité." In *Derrida from Now On*. New York: Fordham University Press, 2008.
———. *Miracle and Machine: Jacques Derrida and the Two Sources of Religion, Science and the Media*. New York: Fordham University Press, 2012.
Nancy, Jean-Luc. *Dis-Enclosure: The Deconstruction of Christianity*. Translated by Bettina Bergo, Gabriel Malenfant, and Michael, B. Smith. New York: Fordham University Press, 2008.
Nandy, Ashis, and D. L. Sheth, eds. *The Multiverse of Democracy: Essays in Honor of Rajni Kothari*. New Dehli: Sage 1996.

Ngugi, wa Thiongo. *Decolonising the Mind: The Politics of Language in African Literature*. London: James Currey, 1986.
Niranjana, Tejaswini. *Siting Translation History, Post-Structuralism, and the Colonial Context*. Berkeley: University of California Press, 1992.
Nongbri, Brent. *Before Religion: A History of a Modern Concept*. New Haven: Yale University Press, 2013.
Norris, Cristopher. "Metaphysics." In *Understanding Derrida*, edited by Jack Reynolds and Jonathan Roffe. New York/London: Continuum, 2004.
Norton, Anne. "Called to Bear Witness. Derrida, Muslims, and Islam." In *The Trace of God. Derrida and Religion*, edited by E. Baring and E. P. Gordon. New York: Fordham University Press, 2014.
Patton, Paul. "Derrida, Politics and Democracy to Come." *Philosophy Compass* 2, no. 6 (2007): 766–80.
———. "Justice, Colonization, Translation." In *Jacques Derrida: Deconstruction Engaged: The Sydney Seminars*, edited by Paul Patton and Terry Smith. Sydney: Power, 2006.
Pheng, Cheah, and Suzanne Guerlac, eds. *Derrida and the Time of the Political*. Durham: Duke University Press, 2009.
Pines, Shlomo. "Aristotle's *Politics* in Arabic Philosophy." In *The Collected Works of Shlomo Pines*. Jerusalem: Hebrew University Magnes Press, 1989.
Protevi, John. *Time and Exteriority: Aristotle, Heidegger, Derrida*. London and Toronto: Associated Presses, 1994.
Rafael, Vincente L. "Translation, American English, and the Insecurities of Empire." In *The Translation Studies Reader*, edited by Laurence Venuti, 2nd Edition. New York: Routledge, 2012, 451–68.
Ramadan, Tariq. *To Be a European Muslim: A Study of Islamic Sources in the European Context*. Leicester: Islamic Foundation, 1999.
Rangarajan, Padma. *Imperial Babel: Translation, Exoticism, and the Long Nineteenth Century*. New York: Fordham University Press, 2014.
Rawls, John. "The Idea of Public Reason Revisited." *The University of Chicago Law Review* 64, no. 3 (1997): 765–807.
———. *Political Liberalism*. New York: Columbia University Press, 1993.
Reynolds, Jack, and Jonathan Roffe, ed. *Understanding Derrida*. New York: Continuum, 2004.
Robinson, David. *Muslim Societies in African History*. Cambridge: Cambridge University Press, 2012.
Roffe, Jonathan. "Translation." In *Understanding Derrida*, edited by Jack Reynolds and Jonathan Roffe. New York: Continuum, 2004.
Rose, Gillian. *Judaism and Modernity: Philosophical Essays*. Oxford: Oxford University Press, 1993.
Sachedina, Abdulaziz. "Advancing Religious Pluralism in Islam." *Religion Compass* 4, no. 4 (2010): 221–33.

———. *The Islamic Roots of Democratic Pluralism*. Oxford: Oxford University Press, 2000.
Saghafi, Kased. "Special Issue: Spindel Supplement: Derrida and the Theologico-Political: From Sovereignty to the Death Penalty." *The Southern Journal of Philosophy* 50 (2012).
Said, Edward. *Orientalism*. New York: Pantheon Books, 1978.
Salvatore, Armando. *Islam and the Political Discourse of Modernity*. Ithaca, NY: Ithaca Press, 2000.
———. *The Sociology of Islam: Knowledge, Power, and Civility*. Hoboken: Wiley, 2016.
Sayyid, Salman. *Recalling the Caliphate. Decolonization and World Order*. London: Hurst, 2014.
Schielke, Samuli. "Hegemonic Encounters: Criticism of Saints Day Festivals and the Formations of Modern Islam in Late 19th Century and Early 20th Century Egypt." *Die Welt des Islams* 47, nos. 3–4 (2010): 320–55.
Schmitt, Carl. *The Concept of the Political*. Translated by George Schwab. Chicago: University of Chicago Press, 2007.
———. *Political Theology: Four Chapters on the Concept of Sovereignty*. Translated by George Schwab. Chicago: University of Chicago Press, 2005.
Schrift, Alan. *Nietzsche and the Question of Interpretation: Between Hermeneutics and Deconstruction*. New York: Routledge, 1990.
Sherwood, Yvonne, and Hart, Kevin, eds. *Derrida on Religion: Other Testaments*. New York: Routledge, 2005.
Shohat, Ella. "The Sephardi-Moorish Atlantic: Between Orientalism and Occidentalism." In *Between the Middle East and the Americas: The Cultural Politics of the Middle East in the Americas*, edited by Evelyn Alsultany and Ella Shohat. Ann Arbor: University of Michigan Press, 2013.
Simpson, Leanne. *Dancing on Our Turtle's Back: Stories of Nishnaabeg Re-Creation, Resurgence, and a New Emergence*. Winnipeg: Arp, 2011.
Smith, James. "Authorship, Sovereignty and the Axiomatics of the Interview: Derrida 'Live.'" In *Jacques Derrida: Live Theory*. London: Continuum, 2005.
Smith, Wilfred Cantwell. *The Meaning and End of Religion*. San Francisco: Harper & Row, 1978.
Spinoza, Baruch. *Theologico-Political Treatise*. Translated by Samuel Shirley. Indianapolis: Hackett, 2001.
Spivak, Gayatri Chakravorty. *A Critique of Postcolonial Reason: Toward a History of the Vanishing Present*. Cambridge, MA: Harvard University Press, 1999.
———. "Ghostwriting." *Diacritics* 25 (1995): 65–85.
———. "Schmitt and Poststructuralism: A Response." *Cardozo Law Review* 21 (2000): 1723–37.
Sprinker, Michael, ed. *Ghostly Demarcation: A Symposium on Jacques Derrida's Specters of Marx*. London: Verso, 1999.

Syrotinski, Michael. *Deconstruction and the Postcolonial: At the Limits of Theory.* Liverpool: Liverpool University Press, 2007.

Taylor, Charles. "Modes of Secularism." In *Secularism and Its Critics,* edited by Rajeev Bhargava. Delhi: Oxford University Press, 1998.

———. "The Politics of Recognition." In *Multiculturalism: Examining the Politics of Recognition,* edited by Amy Gutmann. Princeton: Princeton University Press, 1992.

———. *Religion in Modern Islamic Discourse.* London: C. Hurst; New York: Columbia University Press, 2009.

———. *A Secular Age.* Cambridge, MA: Belknap Press of Harvard University Press, 2007.

———. "Why We Need a Radical Redefinition of Secularism." In *The Power of Religion in the Public Sphere,* edited by E. Mendieta and J. VanAntwerpen. New York: Columbia University Press, 2011.Tayob, Abdulkhader. "Divergent Approaches to Religion in Modern Islamic Discourses." *Religion Compass* 3, no. 2 (2009): 155–67.

Thomson, Alex. *Deconstruction and Democracy.* London: Continuum, 2005.

———. "What's to Become of 'Democracy to Come'?" *Postmodern Culture* 15, no. 3 (2005).

Tibi, Bassan. "Les conditions d'un 'Euro-Islam.'" In *Isams d'Europe: Intégration ou insertion communautaire?,* edited by Robert Bistolfi et Francis Zabbal. Paris: Editions de l'Aube, 1995.

Thurschwell, Adam. "Specters of Nietzsche: Potential Futures for the Concept of the Political in Agamben and Derrida." *Cardozo Law Review* 24 (2003): 1193–1231.

Venuti, Lawrence. "Translating Derrida on Translation: Relevance and Disciplinary Resistance." *The Yale Journal of Criticism* 16 (2): 237–62.

Wadud, Amina. *The Qur'an and Women: Rereading the Sacred Text from a Woman's Perspective.* Oxford: Oxford University Press, 1999.

Weber, Elizabeth, ed. *Living Together: Jacques Derrida's Communities of Violence and Peace.* New York: Fordham University Press, 2013.

Weber, Samuel. "Rogue Democracy." *Diacritics* 38 (2002): 104–20.

———. "Taking Exception to Decision: Walter Benjamin and Carl Schmitt." *Diacritics* 22 (1992): 5–18.

Wise, Christopher. *Derrida, Africa, and the Middle East.* New York: Palgrave, 2009.

———. "The Figure of Jerusalem: Derrida's *Specters of Marx,*" *Christianity and Literature* 54, no. 1 (2004): 73–91.

Wynter, Sylvia. "1492: A New World View." In *Race, Discourse, and the Origin of the Americas,* edited by Vera Lawrence Hyatt and Rex Nettleford. Washington: Smithsonian Institution Press, 1995.

Wolin, Richard. "Derrida on Marx, Or the Perils of Left Heideggerianism." In *Labyrinths: Explorations in the Critical History of Ideas.* Amherst: University of Massachusetts Press, 1995.

Young, Robert. "Deconstruction and the Postcolonial." In *Deconstructions: A User's Guide*, edited by Nicholas Royle. London: Palgrave Macmillan, 2000.
———. *Postcolonialism: An Historical Introduction*. Oxford: Blackwell, 2001.
Zaman, Muhammad Quasim. "The Caliphs, the 'Ulamā', and the Law: Defining the Role and Function of the Caliph in the Early Aabbāsid Period." *Islamic Law and Society* 4, no. 1 (1997): 1–36.

Index

Abrahamic: messianism, 94, 95; Religions, 6, 192–194; traditions, 114, 191
Absolute commencement, 81, 121
African Bantu, 9
Algerian culture, 7, 192
Algerian Jews, 6
Anidjar, Gil, xi, 114, 122, 203
Annihilation of the law, 130
Anti-Semitic legislation, 7
Anti-Semitic, 23, 64, 65, 69, 157
Anti-Semitism, 23, 64, 65
Antiracist: drive, 12; force, 189; form, 14; thrust, 83, 92
Arab Jew, 6, 9, 31, 114, 192
Arab spring, 1
Arab-Jewish, 6
Arab-Muslim, 6
Archive fever, 72, 81, 82, 96, 121, 122
Aristotle, 62, 67, 153, 154, 247
Artificial insemination, 117
Asad, Talal, 2, 196
Assimilation forced, 120
Assimilative translation, 6, 126
Assimilatory translation, 18, 65, 150
Austin, John, 24
Autoimmune: character, 86, 168, 175; logic, 170, 208

Autoimmunitary character, 179, 181, 183, 188
Autoimmunity: of democracy, 169, 170; integrity of 172; logic of, 121; notion of, 116, 157, 164, 171, 172, 189, 200, 213

Babel, Confusion, 35
Babelian story, 36, 37
Beardsworth, Richard, 92
Benjamin, Walter, 11, 35, 126
Beast and the Sovereign, The, 144, 154, 155, 160, 162, 172
Bennington, Geoffrey, 12, 13, 31, 138
Biblical traditions, 161
Buddhism, 2, 47

Canonical understanding, 15, 68
Capitalism, 64, 74, 102, 218
Capitalist Imperialism, 70, 80
Caputo, John, 10, 12, 13, 92, 98
Cauchi, Mark, 135, 147, 148, 149
Christian history, 2, 46
Christian: enlightenment, 143, 144, 200; hegemony, 114; history, 2, 46; incarnation, 39; juridico-political culture, 65, 192; religion, 40, 46, 102; secular world, 75; sources, 144

Colonial: expansion, 2; implications, 14, 122; legacy, 10; library, 10; logic(s), 53, 90, 202; mentalities, 13, 18, 183; oppression, 200; policies, 31; schemas, 204; violence, 36, 37

Colonialism, 1, 2, 4, 5, 9, 12, 13, 31, 43, 45, 46, 53, 54, 64, 65, 74, 75, 99

Colonialism: European, 45, 46, 52–54, 64, 65, 204; language of, 43; legacy of, 12, 13, 75; resisted, 214; settler, 1, 43, 121, 192; Western, 9

Communal, 176

Communal: bond(s), 116; ethical orientation of, 2; identities, 105; life, 2, 15, 28, 37, 105, 106, 150, 185, 186, 199, 214

Communism, 71, 84

Communitarian: bond(s), 3; nexus, 17

Confucianism, 2

Contamination, 24, 41, 57, 59, 123, 126, 129, 132, 157

Contamination: differential, 128, 131, 132, 133, 146; structure of, 118

Contemporary Liberalism, 73

Cornell, Drucilla, 92

Critchley, Simon, 92

Critical: awareness, 3, 5, 30, 79, 96; idea, 94; intimacy, 57; messianism, 15; potential of, 9, 60, 62; practice, 58; reason, 91; sources, 13, 104, 107, 190; spirit, ix, 113, 143; thinking, 11, 99, 203; vigilance, 13, 20, 28, 133, 143, 186, 199

Cultural: assumptions, 4; complexity, 192; debt, 6; difference(s), 36, 91; diversity, 5; expressions, 64; hegemony, 50; heritage, 7; hierarchies, 4, 65, 164; identification, 22, 50, 52; meaning(s), 9; moments, 9; pluralism 4, 188; representations, 164; sources, ix, 203, 204; tradition(s), 4, 39, 41, 91, 184, 204; usurpation, 50; values, 4, 97; wealth, 7, 192

Cybertechnology religions, 116

De Vries, Hent, 3, 12, 98, 99
Death penalty, 132, 152
Decolonizing thrust, 7, 10
Deconstructive gesture, 13
Democracy: agenda of, 177; autoimmune logic of, 170; character of, 183, 213; to come, 15, 151, 152, 163, 167, 168, 176–189; conceptualization of, 164; constitutive idea of, 177; discourse, 186; elements of, 179; enemy of, 206; essential features of, 152; future of, 72, 184, 205; liberal, 72, 73, 75; life of, 214; modern thinkers of, 168; modern, 60, 159, 177, 180, 184, 191, 209; origin of, 174; paradigm of, 211; practice of, 167, 172; root of, 176; secular, 15, 73, 184, 188, 208, 213; self-limitation of, 175; as sovereignty, 15, 68, 159; spirit of, 184; thinking of 176; truth of, 185; universal, 188

Democratic: discourse, 186; elections, 169; equality, 168, 175, 208; freedom, 167, 168–169, 171–172, 176, 177, 208; institution, 158; legacy, 211; life, 112, 163, 171, 205; paradigm, 210; regimes, 135, 159, 170, 208; rhetoric, 201; societies, 188; sovereignty, 153–155, 158–162, 163, 165, 166, 179, 180, 197; spirit, 177, 181, 184; thinking, 73, 151

Derrida, Jacques, 4–10, 11–30, 70–90, 110–140, 100–180, 181–210
Différance, 14, 33, 61, 62, 66, 67, 88, 89, 169
Differential contamination, 128, 131–133, 146
Divided sovereignty, 159
Divine: justice, 130, 131; language, 35; origin, 35; power, 39; violence, 130–133, 146
Dogmatic: faith, 101, 102; slumber, 100, 137
Dussel, Enrique, 9

Earth-and-blood, 23
Economic: environmental degradation, 186; forces, 27, 74; oppression, 73; recessions, 186
Elementary faith, 12, 54, 103–108, 111, 112, 115, 116, 136, 140–150, 173, 185, 187, 189, 190
Enlightenment, 101, 106, 108, 111, 113–115, 117, 136, 142, 143, 144, 147, 207. *See also* Christian
Enlightenment: amnesia, 136; of reason, 86, 90; secularism, 150
Epistemic: hierarchizations, 13; island, 9; orders, 12, 146, 203; potency, 8; resistance, 9; resources, 10, 149; salience, 5
Eschatological content, 55
Ethical, 2, 4, 113
Ethical: political stakes, 26; political values, 163; priority, 92; responsibility(ies), 68; values, 63, 203
Ethno-religious nationalism, 1
Event(s), founding, 96, 97, 112, 118, 119, 120, 121, 122, 126
Expression: cultural, 64; forceful, 176; freedom of, 170, 184

Faith and Knowledge, 17, 41, 44, 62, 65, 98, 101, 102, 103, 113, 140, 141, 144, 191, 193
Faith: elementary, 103–108, 115, 116, 136, 140–147, 173, 190; founding, 137; promissory, 115; reflective, 102; and violence, 120
False neutrality, 18
Fichte, 19, 21, 22, 24, 29, 98
Force of law, 89, 112, 126, 129, 139, 141, 142, 152
Forced: assimilation, 120; hegemony, 52, 162; translations, 51, 52, 64, 162, 173
Founding: act, 146, 120, 127, 128, 136, 145, 146; faith, 137; law, 127; moment, 25, 80, 85, 99, 120, 127, 134, 136, 137, 144; political, 15, 80, 81, 96, 99, 111, 118–121, 123, 134, 140–143, 146–148, 163; violence, 121, 131, 132. *See also* events
Franco-Maghrebian Jew, 31
Fraternization: symbolic, 124, 155
Freedom: expression of, 170; individual, 168, 208; to play, 167; principles of, 164. *See also* Democratic
French Algeria, 9, 192
French culture, 6, 31
Fritsch, Mathias, 12, 92, 98, 99
Fukuyama, Francis, 70, 72, 73
Fundamentalism, 15, 113, 114, 150, 191, 194–197, 201

Gaon, Stella, 13, 90
Gasché, Rodolphe, xi, 12, 132
Genealogies of colonialism, 4
Genealogical investigation, 12, 135
Genetic manipulation, 117
Global: demography, 201; hegemony, 2, 10, 18; inequalities, 10;

Global *(continued)*
  migration, 186; secularization, 47, 114, 143, 193
Globalization, 3, 8, 10, 44–46, 64, 102, 116, 126, 148, 191, 198, 199, 200, 213
Greek logos, 161
Greek mythology, 117, 153

Habermas, Jürgen, 11, 14, 28, 43, 149
Haddad, Samir, 93
Hägglund, Martin, 10, 12, 13, 66, 67, 88, 100, 101
Hamlet's phrase, 78, 79
Hani, Chris, 69
Hegel, 69, 97, 113
Hegemony, 2, 4, 10, 20–22, 31, 47, 54, 57, 156, 191, 201, 206, 213
Heidegger, 23, 24, 62, 82, 97, 98, 113, 130, 144, 161, 162
Hinduism, 2
Historical injustice, 74, 84, 99, 101
Homo-hegemony, 53, 55, 56
Homogenization, 13, 20
Hospitality, 51, 60, 95, 185, 186
Human: agency, 100; community, 36; condition(s), 32, 36, 41, 44, 48, 49, 91, 96, 131, 188; consciousness, 32, 71, 125, 128; culture, 22; destruction, 81; experience, 64, 82; finitude, 62, 100, 130; freedom, 2; groups, 46, 63, 64, 157, 187; interaction, 141; languages, 35; life, 2, 46; nature, 69; predicament, 29, 30, 48, 132, 157, 166, 186; realities, 64, 203; rights, 53, 77, 165, 181; sovereignty, 156; understanding, 67
Humanitarian wars, 186
Humanitarian, 113, 165, 186, 197, 201, 202

Ideal orientation, 73, 74
Idealized regulative schema, 178
Imperatives, 113, 197
Indigenous: groups, 73; languages, 29; law, 137; people, 80, 120; values, 53
Indo-European mythology, 63
Inherited tradition, 137
Injustice: historical, 74, 84, 99, 101
Institutional apparatuses, 42, 137
International: affairs, 164; corporations, 166; institutions, 53, 74, 164; law, 45, 47, 64, 65, 102, 152, 158, 159, 165, 166, 186, 194, 197; peace, 158; relations, 166
Interpretation transformative, 60
Interpretation(s), 100, 111, 126, 170, 176, 196. *See also* secular
Interpretative: constraints, 101; force, 127; grid, 96; order, 127; practices, 58, 59; schemas, 47; system, 135
Investigation: genealogical, 12, 135; philosophical, 31, 58
Islam: articulations of, 198; and democracy, 205, 206, 207, 208, 209, 211, 212, 213, 214; experience of, 215; intellectual construct of, 193; invocation of, 194; as a religion, 194, 196, 201, 202; religious feature of, 213; treatment of, 15
Islamic: contexts, 193; culture, 211; discourse(s), 191, 196, 198, 204; ethics, 199; form of life, 202; history, 204, 212; importation, 210; philosophy, 210; political discourse, 198, 204, 210, 215; reformism, 198; scholarship, 199; sources, 213; states, 199; thought, 204; traditions, 12, 13, 191, 192, 199, 210; world, 212

Islamism, 192, 195, 201, 202, 212, 213
Islamist groups, 1, 198
Islamophobic: legislation, 1; undercurrents, 8

Jay, John, 52, 119
Jew Shylock, 38
Jewish identity, 31
Judaism, 6, 43, 47, 81, 114, 122, 200
Judeo-Christian: ideology, 8; tradition, 98, 141
Judeo franco-maghrebian, 7
Juridico-political: culture, 65, 192 (*see also* Christian); institutions, 96; norms, 46; power, 136; revolutions, 137; space, 53, 165; sphere, 177

Kant, 12, 26, 67, 69, 72, 85, 86, 89, 101, 102, 108, 113, 127, 171, 178
Knowledge: and community, 2, 11, 53, 203; and faith, 17, 14, 44, 62, 65, 98, 101–103, 113, 140, 141, 144, 191, 193; colonization of, 214; decolonizing, 215; forms of, 10, 14; foundations of, 72; modern, 10; of tele-mediatization, 116, 201; and thinking, 62; politics and, 2, 12, 142, 150; production of, 10, 100, 149, 204, 206, 210; racialization of, 121
Koranic heritage, 170, 210, 211, 212

Land expropriation, 8, 10, 186
Language: of Christianity, 46; conceptions of, 14; divine, 35; essentialist, 131, 133; evil of, 42; human, 35; of Koran, 207, 210, 211, 215 (*see also* heritage); minority, 52; national, 25; natural, 48, 96; neutral, 14, 21, 41, 44,
53; official, 52; politics of, 48, 50, 51, 52, 53; of promise, 54, 55, 56, 59, 60, 141; of Quranic, 196; of religion, 193; sacred, 41, 42, 54; secular, 20, 29, 43, 44, 54; of secularism, 14; universal, 36, 54, 162; univocal, 162
Latin Christian, 10, 65, 124, 143, 193
Law: divine, 156; force of, 112, 126, 129, 141, 142; international, 45, 47, 64, 65, 73, 102, 113, 152, 158, 159, 166, 186, 194, 197; of iterability 132; language of, 52; national, 155; natural, 135; preserving violence, 129, 131, 132, 133, 146; of property, 56; rule of, 53, 170; state, 156
Lawlor, Leonard, 92
Legal: equality, 174; evolution, 119; identity, 175; institutions, 81; structures, 135, 136
Liberal: constitutionalism, 122, 135; democracy, 72, 73, 75, 169, 172; freedom, 171; humanitarianism, 165; ideologies, 186; modernity, 74; tradition, 53, 84, 159
Linguistic: context, 14, 18, 21, 24, 25, 27, 29, 33, 40, 48, 50, 51, 52, 53, 127, 211; differences, 20, 37; foundations, 25, 48, 53, 56, 156; hegemony, 20; nationalism, 53, 56; understandings, 57
Lived experience, 6, 7, 8, 9, 30, 31, 84, 90, 195, 204
Living tongue, 21

Machiavelli, 120, 160
Market-driven science, 201, 202
Marx, Karl, 14, 70, 71, 72, 77, 83, 94
Mental representations, 67, 71

Messianic: politics, 89; thinking, 62, 92, 93, 96, 97
Messianicity, 12, 54, 98, 103, 140, 189
Messianism, 11, 12, 15, 54, 77, 78, 82, 93, 94, 95, 97, 98, 99, 101, 140
Metalanguage, 32, 43, 44, 48, 49, 96, 98, 128, 134, 137, 197
Metaphysical: assumptions, 68, 151; binaries, 10, 67, 215; discourse, 63, 145; language, 66; reductionism, 190; thinking, 14, 52, 63, 64, 70, 71, 91, 128, 145, 146, 165, 180, 183, 188, 189; traditions, 22, 65, 76, 95, 130, 146
Metaphysics, 7, 23, 63, 67, 68, 70, 71, 76, 79, 87, 89, 92, 105, 123, 124, 153, 154, 157, 188, 189, 190, 248
Mignolo, Walter, 9
Mixed origins, 65, 158
Modernization, 3, 199, 200
Modern: knowledge, 10; secular discourse, 2, 4, 5, 9, 12, 46, 54, 64, 112, 141, 149, 150, 183, 187, 200, 202, 214
Monolingualism of the other, 18, 30, 33, 48, 50, 51, 52, 55
Montaigne de Michel, 126, 127, 141
Montesquieu, 159
Moral principles, 83
Moslem, religion, 196
Mudimbe, Valentine, 10
Muslim: faith, 207; government, 207; scholars, 198; societies, 199, 204, 212; theologians, 196; theologico-political, 210, 211; traditions, 124, 192, 210 (*see also* Islamic traditions)
Mythic violence, 131, 133
Mystical foundation, 112, 127, 134, 135, 141, 145

Naas, Michael, 10, 98, 104, 147, 148
Name, question of, 45, 195, 198, 199
Nation state(s), 2, 4, 10, 15, 42, 43, 102, 152, 164, 165, 175, 176, 177, 179, 180, 187, 210
National: humanism, 17, 18; idiom, 18, 19, 21; law, 155
Nationalism, 1, 3, 10, 18, 19, 20, 22, 23, 53, 56, 124
Natural property, 25, 56
Naturalization, 8, 13, 15, 23, 53, 60, 63–65, 68, 74, 83, 92, 98, 102, 106, 121, 135, 150, 159, 162, 176, 183–190, 203
Naturalized representation, 112
Neo-Kantian: political thought, 82; theories, 11, 72

Onto-Theology, 17, 18
Orientalist Islamophobia, 16, 198
Other Heading, The, 22, 65, 164, 165, 179

Pascal, Blaise, 126
Performative force, 127
Philosophical nationalism, 3, 19, 20
Political: alternatives, 120, 137; analogy, 154; arrangements, 4, 53, 69, 74, 165, 186; authority, 2, 53, 68, 126, 135, 136, 145, 150, 180, 187, 199, 206, 213; boundaries, 163; character, 126; closures, 13; commitments, 12; community(ies), 15, 69, 96, 112, 120, 121, 123, 135, 151, 157, 159, 168, 169, 170, 176, 177, 179, 180, 185, 186; concepts, 118, 146, 180, 184; critique, 181; cultures, 45; determinants, 51, 157; dimensions, 13, 14, 18, 25, 56, 92; enemy, 125; enforcements, 100; exclusionary

hierarchies, 6; formations, 12, 125, 126, 149, 199, 204; foundations, 79, 83, 96, 99, 112, 118, 122, 126, 136, 145, 147, 149, 187; history, 210; identity, 52, 84, 122, 163, 166, 168, 189; imaginary(ies), 13, 105, 159, 177, 188, 199; implications, 4, 113; institutions, 118, 165; interests, 25; issues, 205; legal system, 136; life, 65, 92, 124, 147, 155, 163, 167, 169, 180, 193, 199, 200; models, 10, 100, 191, 202, 214; need, 75; orders, 3, 5, 9, 13, 68, 109, 145, 165, 204; philosophy, 82, 100, 105, 160, 171, 188, 210, 211; responsibility, 58, 59, 212; significance, 3, 11, 36, 112, 114, 173, 215; space, 61, 71, 76, 79, 123; theology, 65, 117, 145, 150–157, 163, 165–167, 172, 179, 180, 182, 183, 186, 187, 209; thinking, 68, 89, 153, 177, 182, 184; thought, 4, 14, 16, 54, 61, 68, 69, 76, 82, 120, 151, 155, 160, 161, 188, 192, 199; value(s), 162, 203, 204

Politico-legal: authority, 127; order 118, 121, 123, 127, 134, 135, 179; space, 46

Politics of Friendship, 65, 123, 175, 182, 209

Politics: contemporary, 3; foundation of, 147, 150, 156; of language, 17, 18, 24, 25, 48, 50–53; of surveillance, 106

Power: abuse, 156, 159; sharing, 165, 166

Power-making violence, 129, 130

Preserving violence, 131, 132, 133, 146

Promissory: affirmation, 12, 54, 77, 140; faith, 115

Public: debates, 193; disputes, 28, 29, 44, 75; domain, 150; institutions, 25, 29; knowledge, 159; life, 2, 6, 29, 40, 44, 46, 47, 63, 65, 75, 100, 113, 149, 150, 163, 180, 200, 203, 204, 213, 214; religions, 3, 4; sphere, 2, 8, 14, 53, 117

Pure thinking, 6

Quasitranscendental: aspect, 99; concept 95; condition, 103, 77; figure, 99, 103, 141; offers, 99; point, 99; trope, 56

Quasitranscendentalism, 12, 99

Question of religion, 17, 45, 192

Racial: connotations, 150, 158; constructs, 215; dimensions, 91; features, 13, 18, 40, 102, 112, 114, 165; formations, 3, 10, 15, 40; hierarches, 89; implication, 134, 187; logics, 7, 109; models, 13, 46, 189; ordering, 150; thinking, 6; traits, 177; undercurrents, 146

Racialized: discourse(s), 98, 118, 149; features, 5, 62, 67, 68, 76, 79, 97, 102, 114, 165; hierarchies, 92; logics, 13, 62, 76, 130; mythology, 157; naturalization, 74; schemas, 11, 14, 40, 61, 79, 100, 104, 105, 176, 187; thinking, 12, 63, 64, 65, 68, 72, 81, 106, 124, 149, 155, 165, 187; traits, 108, 121

Racism: deconstruction of, 64; logic of, 157; modern, 64; structural, 186

Racist: discourse(s), 69, 106; foundations of, 123; ideologies, 106, 203; orientations, 123; views, 64

Radical: atheism, 13, 67, 100; criticism, 15, 113, 136, 182, 213; secularity, 13, 148

Rational judgments, 73, 135
Rawls, John, 11, 14, 28, 72–75, 184, 208
Reason alone, 101, 111, 134, 144, 190
Reason of sovereignty, 162
Relational thinking, 150
Religion, 1–6, 10–13, 15, 17, 18, 25, 28, 37, 40, 41, 44–48, 52, 53, 60, 61, 65, 68, 70–72, 75, 76, 77, 79, 81, 91, 94, 101–104, 106, 107, 109, 111–117, 121, 126, 140, 141, 142, 144–150, 157, 170, 180, 181, 183, 186, 187, 188, 190–203, 209, 213, 214, 215
Religious: affiliations, 117, 147; authority, 107, 112, 183, 212; beliefs, 17, 71; character, 5; consciousness, 71; cults, 116; cultures, 183, 207, 209; difference, 75, 114; diversity, 5; experience, 37, 103, 115, 148; faith, 101, 103, 107, 120, 143, 144; foundation, 147, 199; freedom, 53, 183, 187, 206; fundamentalism, 15, 150; groups, 99, 116; hierarchies, 164; language, 44, 94, 99; messages, 116; milieu of the, 104, 106, 141; movements, 2, 3; orthodoxies, 203; passion, 13, 17; phenomena, 3, 41, 44–46, 102, 109, 114, 192, 193, 203; pluralism, 4, 188; presuppositions, 5; sources, 5, 101, 118, 143, 145, 147, 148, 187, 189, 213; studies, 10; symbols, 53; traditions, 2, 114, 193
Return of religion, 2, 3, 11, 17, 150, 195
Rogue state, 158, 159
Rogues, 62, 65, 85, 92, 108, 151, 152, 155, 158, 163, 164, 165, 167, 169, 172, 177, 179, 191, 205, 206, 207, 209
Rosenzweig, Franz, 41

Rousseau, 120, 160, 163, 168, 171, 178, 208

Sacred idioms, 44, 113
Said, Edward, 10
Schema of concealment, 21, 29
Schmitt, Carl, 11, 15, 43, 44, 65, 113, 117, 122, 125, 127, 130, 145, 146, 156, 157, 165, 166, 202
Scholem, Gershom, 41, 42, 43
Searle, John, 18, 24
Secular: democracy, 1, 15, 184, 208, 213; discourse, 2, 4, 5, 9, 12, 18, 54, 62, 141, 149, 150, 183, 187, 188, 200, 202, 214; domain, 2, 115, 118, 135, 136, 142, 145, 146, 151, 185; imaginaries, 150; modern, 149, 150, 157, 176, 202; paradigm, 5, 149, 150; schemas, 212; separation, 114; teleologies, 82; understanding, 15, 45, 113, 151, 167, 179, 181, 186, 187, 203; world order, 12, 46
Secularism, 14, 15, 31, 54, 60, 93, 102, 114, 117, 118, 143, 145, 147, 150, 170, 177, 179, 180, 191, 193, 200, 201, 206, 207, 209, 211, 212
Secularism: deconstructed version of, 147; enlightenment, 86, 90, 101, 103, 106, 111, 113–116, 136, 142, 143, 144, 146, 150, 200, 207; global spread of, 3, 14, 75; language of, 14, 18; modern theories, 2, 101, 159, 166; and nationalism, 10; neutral, 29; and religion, 112, 44; theories of, 11, 72, 101; traditional, 187
Secularization, 2, 3, 8, 10, 11, 14, 18, 39, 41–44, 47–48, 53, 101, 102, 112–114, 117, 118, 126, 143, 145, 147, 150, 170, 177–180, 191, 193, 200, 201, 206, 207, 209, 211, 212

Self-hood: political theology of sovereignty, 172, 186; sovereign, 154, 165, 176, 180
Self: affirmation, 23; assertion, 23; consciousness, 19; criticism, 87, 136; criticizability, 181; critique, 90, 182, 184; defenses, 200; destruction, 157, 168, 169, 183; determination, 122, 153, 162, 163, 164; evident, 211; exclusion, 157; hood, 180; identical, 33, 148; identity, 189; interpretations, 51; legislation, 153; legitimation, 127; limitation, 175; preserving, 131; protection, 87, 116, 157, 167, 168, 183, 200; reflexivity, 54, 74; sacrifice, 168; sufficient, 153, 154, 187; vigilant, 100
Semantics of faith, 103
Separatist logic, 12, 124, 143, 157, 183, 214
Sexual: biases, 155; connotations, 124; differences, 15, 124, 155; hierarchies, 4, 69; minorities, 84, 163, 183; revenge, 196
Social contract, 160
Social: bond, 103–108, 116, 175, 203; forms, 108; hierarches, 40, 122; institutions, 25; interactions, 25; justice, 199; nexus, 17; realities, x, 3; relations, 103; relationship, 104
Sociopolitical: divisions, 82; forms, 99; hierarchy, 176; life, 5, 13, 106; phenomena, 198, 199; processes, 214
Separations, 65, 69
Sovereign: agency, 155; freedom, 173, 177; power, 39, 52, 152, 161, 163, 171, 173; state, 104
Sovereignty: authority, 152; auto immunity of, 157; conceptions of, 189; constitution of, 156; definition of, 152; democratic, 153, 154, 158–160, 162, 163, 166, 187; divided, 159; divisions of, 165; foundation thinking of, 164; human, 156; indivisible, 60, 154, 163–165, 182, 186; language, 156; legitimate, 152, 158, 159; monarchic, 154; mythology of, 154; nation-state, 160; notion of, 146, 157, 177; paradox of, 152; political, 39, 145, 160, 164; political theology of, 172; pure, 156; rethinking, 164; state, 39, 40, 160; traditional discourses about, 165
Specters of Marx, 62, 65, 69, 70, 77, 78, 85, 88, 95, 97, 100, 137, 165
Spinoza, Baruch, 3, 41, 118
Spirits of Marxism, 71
Spiritual: heading, 22; hierarchies, 4, 65, 69; legitimacy, 24
Stalinism, 97
State power, 112, 151, 166, 170, 183, 184

Taylor, Charles, 149
Teleological: conceptions, 10; scheme, 62, 86, 186; thinking, 69, 71, 72, 76, 108
Televisual diplomacy, 116
Temporal, 11, 33, 62, 66, 68, 69, 76–82, 88, 89, 93, 96–101, 109, 118, 120, 123, 127, 128, 135, 138, 169, 170
Temporal: dimension, 3, 10–14, 18, 22, 24, 25, 38, 43, 51, 52, 54, 56, 57, 68, 77, 88, 91, 92, 100, 103, 106, 112, 119, 126, 138, 139, 141, 142, 145–147, 179, 193, 199, 210; disjuncture, 78, 79, 81, 83, 88–99, 120, 128
Terrorism, 1, 169, 201
Terrorist organizations, 158
Testimonial faith, 104, 105

Theological origin, 148
Theological-political: complex, 3–6, 11, 13, 15, 17, 18, 28, 41, 43, 53, 60, 61, 64, 68, 75, 76, 83, 91, 94, 108, 109, 111, 158, 185, 188, 191, 199; dimension(s), 52, 53, 145, 146; features, 12, 38, 153, 155, 159, 163; imaginaries, 199; issues, 11; natures, 65; nexus, 11–14, 48, 57, 62, 72, 76, 101, 150, 180, 186, 200, 213; phantasy, 174; predicament, 4, 129; relationship, 12–15, 28, 33, 60, 72, 111, 145, 147, 149, 150, 213, 230
Theological: dimension, 12, 139, 145, 146, 147, 179; discourse, 65, 146; foundation of politics, 156; heritage, 43, 117; idioms, 11, 43, 118
Time, ix, 7, 10–14, 17, 22, 24, 33, 34, 36, 37, 38, 39, 52, 54, 55, 61–64, 66–69, 71, 72, 74–80, 83, 84, 85, 88, 90, 91, 92, 95, 96, 97, 100, 101, 103, 115, 119, 127, 128, 137, 138, 141, 152, 156, 157, 166, 169, 170, 172, 174, 178–182, 186, 197, 205, 210, 213, 215
Totalitarianism(s), 8, 70, 71, 80, 169
Totalizing character, 8
Tradition, inherited, 137
Traditional, 4, 7, 8, 12, 13, 15, 22, 23, 30, 38, 39, 61, 62, 64, 65, 67, 74, 79, 81, 89, 91, 92, 98, 100, 108, 111, 113, 122, 129, 140, 142, 145, 146, 147, 148, 155, 156, 161, 165, 186, 187, 189, 198, 213, 214
Traditional: opposition, 8; religion, 13
Transcendental: concepts, 95; conditions, 77, 95; Inquiry, 97; language, 66; perspectives, 82; philosophy, 95, 98; reflection, 130; schemas, 98; structures, 56; tradition, 12

Translation, 5, 6, 10, 11, 14, 18, 19, 22, 29, 30–60, 64, 65, 75, 92, 96–98, 113, 114, 118, 126, 140, 148–150, 162, 163, 165, 173, 176, 184, 186, 188, 193, 197, 198, 204–206, 210, 211, 212, 214, 215
Translation: forced, 162, 173; forceful, 187; law, 35; political, 211, 176; secular, 212, 214
Traumatic experience, 7

Unconditional, x, 85, 86, 87, 88, 92, 100, 153, 170, 173, 174, 179, 186
Unconditionality, 26, 159, 164, 167, 184, 185
Unitary: agent(s), 163; character, 153, 154; moments, 61
Universal: aspirations, 18, 163; bond, 147; Christianity, 125; concepts, 157; democracy, 188; discourse, 24, 29; emancipation, 81; essence, 8, 22; faith, 147; humanism, 51; language, 28, 29, 36; legitimacy, 120; nationality, 63; norms, 89; principle, 45; rationality, 141; representation(s), 26, 68, 79, 108; rule, 89; validity, 9, 30, 47, 54, 65, 68, 204; values, 55; vocation, 19, 47, 56
Universalism: enlightenment, 143; foundational, 143

Victims of: oppression, 80; war(s), 70, 80, 99
Violence: anti-Muslim, 1; archaic, 196, 197; capital punishment, 132; critique of, 129, 133, 134; cycle of, 133; divine, 130–132, 146; founding, 121, 131; fundamental, 131, 132; historical, 80, 83, 84; interpretative, 127; law-preserving, 131–133, 146; lethal, 201; physical,

194; power-making, 129, 130; reactionary, 201; structural, 80
Voltaire, 113

Weber, Samuel, 145
Western-centric traditions, 10
Western: Christian, 4, 5, 40, 47, 64, 102, 109, 124, 125, 126, 200; colonialism, 9; discourse, 8, 9, 65, 79, 143, 193; tradition, 6, 47, 52, 60, 67, 90, 91, 100, 120, 161, 188, 189, 190

White mythology, 7, 14, 22, 31, 47, 61, 63, 64, 67, 70, 91, 93, 95, 96, 98, 100, 102, 106, 108, 124, 126, 157, 162, 163, 182, 183, 186, 190, 193, 203
World civilization, 22

Xenophobia, 23

Yerushalmi, Yosef, 82

Zionism, 42, 43, 64, 219

www.ingramcontent.com/pod-product-compliance
Lightning Source LLC
Chambersburg PA
CBHW021652230426
43668CB00008B/593